Education as
history

Education as history

interpreting nineteenth- and
twentieth-century education

Harold Silver

Foreword by David B. Tyack

Methuen London & New York

First published in 1983 by
Methuen & Co. Ltd
11 New Fetter Lane, London EC4P 4EE

Published in the USA by
Methuen & Co.
in association with Methuen, Inc.
733 Third Avenue, New York, NY 10017

© 1983 Harold Silver

Printed in Great Britain
at the University Printing House, Cambridge

British Library Cataloguing in Publication Data

Silver, Harold
Education as history.
1. Education – England – History
I. Title
370'.942 LA631.7

ISBN 0-416-33310-9
ISBN 0-416-33320-6 Pbk

Library of Congress Cataloging in Publication Data

Silver, Harold.
Education as history.
Bibliography: p.
Includes index.
1. Education – Great Britain – History.
2. Education – United States – History. 3. Educational
sociology – Great Britain – History. 4. Educational
sociology – United States – History. I. Title.
LA631.7.S44 1983   370'.941   82-20853
ISBN 0-416-33310-9
ISBN 0-416-33320-6(pbk.)

Contents

Acknowledgements

The Introduction and Chapter 4 contain material originally used in an inaugural lecture entitled 'Nothing but the Present or Nothing but the Past?' (Chelsea College, 1977). Chapter 1 was originally published under this title in *Oxford Review of Education* (1977), here slightly amended. Chapter 2 was originally published in Phillip McCann (ed.), *Popular Education and Socialization in the Nineteenth Century* (Methuen, 1977), here slightly extended. Chapter 3 was originally published as 'Robert Owen's Reputation as an Educationist' in Sidney Pollard and John Salt (eds), *Robert Owen: Prophet of the Poor* (Macmillan, 1971), here with amendments. Part of Chapter 8 appeared under the title 'Institutional Differences: expectations and perceptions' in *Studies in Higher Education* (1982). Chapter 9 is a substantially expanded version of a review essay originally published in *British Journal of Sociology of Education* (1981). Chapter 10 is based on a paper published in Edgar Gumbert (ed.), *Poverty, Power and Authority in Education* (Georgia State University, 1981). Chapter 11 is an amended version of a contribution to John H. Best (ed.), *History of Education: A Research Agenda* (American Educational Research Association, 1982). My thanks are due to the publishers concerned for permission to use this material.

Some chapters are based on research supported by funding bodies. Chapters 5 and 6 originated in work on British and American social science movements in the nineteenth century supported by the Social Science Research Council (SSRC). Chapter 10 also originated in work funded by the SSRC – a project entitled 'British and American Educational Strategies against Poverty in the 1960s and 1970s'. Chapter 8 was originally written, in collaboration with Pamela Silver, as a report of a project funded by the Department of Education and Science, as a contribution to a project on 'Higher Education: Objectives, Expectations and Institutional Response', based at Brunel University. I am indebted to both bodies for their support.

Versions of some chapters were presented as papers as follows: Chapter 5 to the American History of Education Society (1979); Chapter 6 to a seminar on the history of academic disciplines held in London in 1980; Chapter 10 to the Center for Cross-Cultural Studies, Georgia State University, Atlanta; Chapter 12 to the British Educational Research Association (1980). These chapters have benefited greatly from the discussions held under those auspices.

I owe especial thanks to Pamela Silver. She worked as research associate on the project which produced 'Expectations of Higher Education', and at the time of writing is also research associate on the project of which 'Education against Poverty' is an early outcome. Without her collaboration this research could not have been done, and her help deserves much greater acknowledgement than this note is able to convey.

H.S.
Bulmershe College of Higher Education
Reading
1983

Foreword

In academia historians are the only people paid for looking backwards. That may seem odd, because administrators are supposed to be forward-looking. They also frequently become presidents or deans in higher education. Lawrence Cremin, a pre-eminent historian of American education, is also President of Teachers College, Columbia. Harold Silver, known on both sides of the Atlantic as one of the most penetrating and productive historians of education, is also Principal of Bulmershe College of Higher Education. It is perhaps not coincidental that the talents that mark Cremin and Silver as observers of the past also render them astute policy analysts, for as political scientist James Q. Wilson argues, wise decision-makers need to gauge the trajectory of events, assessing their momentum and density over historical time. Effective policy analysis, he says, 'involves statements about what has happened in the past, not speculations about what may happen in the future'.

Education as History should be of particular interest to two groups: to educational policy-makers who wish to take a longer view of alternative policies and their consequences; and historians who are open-minded enough to learn about the tunnel vision of, yes, even historians. Here is a book by a fine craftsman *and* a capable theorist who raises highly provocative questions about how people construct meaning. Indeed, the creation of opinion – and its more complex construct, ideology – is really the central theme that unites these essays. John Maynard Keynes's aphorism might well be the motto of the book: 'A study of the history of opinion is a necessary preliminary to the emancipation of the mind. I do not know which makes a man more conservative – to know nothing but the present, or nothing but the past.' Silver does not want his readers to be mindlessly conservative, but he is equally critical of present-minded Whig historians and declamatory radicals.

Silver writes of a number of policy issues of concern to decision-makers today – the liberal and the vocational, expectations engendered by higher education, the relation of education and poverty, the contesting versions of 'social science' in education – but his approach is not to gain 'relevance' for history by investigating whatever is the current absorption of policy-makers. In a sense what he is doing is *meta*-policy-analysis rather than looking for neat historical answers to current problems. What does this mean? He looks *beyond* the current list of policy issues to inquire about who is defining events as problems, 'what structures of power lie behind the question mark'. He points out, for example, that poverty has been a continuous human condition but that it has been 'discovered' (regarded as a problem to attack) only at certain times. The same might be said for youth, or the family, or the educational 'basics'. For the historian to ignore interpretations of the recent past is to leave the ground 'not just to social and political science, but to ahistorical social and political science, not just to political rhetoric but to fiction and romance'. By asking when and why issues have become defined as problems at certain times and in certain places, historians can call attention to underlying structural issues, which in turn helps to determine a more effective policy than accepting current terms of debate as controlling.

Silver shows that whatever the polite discourse may have been about liberal versus vocational higher education, at issue was a great status divide, a 'diverse pattern of snobberies, heresies, distinctions, and hierarchies which make "expectations" of higher education complicated'. He suggests that the stages of the educational war on poverty – hope in the 1960s, growing scepticism in the 1970s, neglect or worse in the 1980s – had more to do with fashionable opinion than it did with the actual lives of people who lived in Liverpool slums or Appalachian hollows. Some of his most interesting pages dissect the claims of social scientists, both the do-gooder variety of the late Victorian era and the would-be objective evaluators of the last generation. The paternalistic assumptions and aims of the Victorians embarrassed their successors, but Silver is quite telling in his criticisms of 'the sophisticated arrogance of a primitive science' exemplified in recent investigations. The social scientists examining the effects of compensatory education, for example, he sees as masters of the tinsel of technique but inferior detectives, looking in the wrong place for clues.

But they became influential shapers of opinion because their findings appealed both to those on the right and on the left who wanted to torpedo reform.

Silver believes that history can contribute to informed policy discussion by subjecting the timing and definition of 'problems' to close analysis and by trying to gauge the trajectory of events against a longer and richer background than is customarily the case in policy analysis. To do this effectively, he argues, historians themselves need to become more self-conscious, less blandly pragmatic and crude conceptually, and less prone to a top-down interpretation of developments (dictated too often by the fact that official documents are easier to find than sources that illustrate the underside of history). He asks precisely the questions that I think are crucial to the improvement of the craft: how to combine social history with the impact of ideas; how to use explanations from social science sensitively in history without losing the immediacy and power of dense description; and how to rephrase the questions that have been poorly posed.

First, consider the issue of how to treat ideas in the social history of education. The earliest phase in the history of education was the study of the social philosophies and pedagogical theories of the great educators from Plato to Herbart and Dewey. This remains a common approach, but all too often historians have assumed rather than documented the actual impact of these thinkers. As Silver shows in his essay on Robert Owen, there has been a curious myopia in selecting which great figures to publicize. By contrast, some social historians have relegated ideas to the attic of historiography while counting this or that variable and assembling tables to prove the obvious, in emulation of sociologists of empirical bent. Both versions of history suffer from ignoring the dialectic of idea and behavior. What Silver proposes and exemplifies is 'historical excursions into how people, groups of people, people in action, have interpreted and reinterpreted their world'. It is of course essential to realize that ideologies and opinions do not float in space; they arise from particular social strata, serve particular groups and interests, and change over time as the relations of people change. Silver's investigation of social science and changing conceptions of education and poverty illustrate two such topics that relate ideas to particular segments of the society.

Second, he illuminates the issue of how to use social science theory in history. Silver rejects three common approaches used by historians. One takes the 'commonsense' stance that all that is needed is to tell a story straight without the need to have or use theories. All this does is to bury the explanatory model in the narrative. Another approach is to adopt some broad and preferably ponderous term – 'modernization' will serve well, being suitably vague – borrowed from some social science (usually well after the concept's inadequacies have been detailed by scholars in the field of origin). A third is to adopt a cogent theory in a simplified form and find only evidence that supports it, producing a uni-dimensional and uni-directional form of history. An example of this is the cruder form of Marxist analysis in which the capitalist state produces such predictable and overwhelming effects that investigation of particulars seems hardly worth the effort.

The book *Unpopular Education*, a prime and interesting example he dissects, 'became a reminder to the 1980s', Silver asserts, 'that historical intention, when coupled with strong theory, remains an elusive ambition. It became a case study in theory attempting to use, or to be, history, and in the ease with which history, theory, and radical rhetoric can coexist without communicating.' What is needed, Silver asserts and demonstrates in his own substantive and historiographical chapters, is 'sensitive dialogue between the experience and the theory'. Theories are in essence elegant simplifications of complex transactions, useful in laying bare the connections between phenomena, but rarely useful if accepted whole without the nuance and sense of surprise which the particulars of the past constantly offer to the discerning scholar.

While there are exceptions on both sides of the Atlantic, English historians seem to have some advantage over their American brethren in dealing with Marx and with class analysis. The McCarthyite hysteria of the 1950s cast a long shadow on American scholarship in history and social science, while in England some of the most distinguished work since the Second World War has continued to explore class relationships in a sophisticated Marxian mode. English liberal or conservative scholars might have regarded their Marxist peers as foolish but not as subversive.

The promising work of American scholars like George Counts (in his brilliant studies of the 1920s), Horace Mann Bond, and Merle Curti found few successors in the frightened climate of the cold war. Even conservative scholars in England wrote openly about the significance of social and economic class, but American writers mostly shied away from the impact of class relationships. In the late 1960s, when American radical revisionists in education, inspired by the brilliant work of Michael B. Katz, turned to a darker vision of education as class oppression and social control, they largely ignored the more nuanced and culturally-sensitive versions of radical analysis that were represented by the best English and continental Marxists and even the native American tradition of left-liberal analysis represented by Curti and Bond.

One of the virtues of this book is that Silver does not have a double standard of criticism, one for the scholars who stand outside the general Marxist framework within which he works and another for those of contrary persuasion. He is as ready to criticize the stridency and Luddite policy consequences of much radical analysis as he is the top-down and atheoretical narratives of the traditional historians. By raising previously unasked questions in a kind of prospective historiography he has given scholars a new agenda. By stressing the value – indeed, the necessity – of examining the past in shaping wise decisions about the future of education he has challenged the faddishness of educational policy. He calls for a dialogue that uses an informed scepticism to realize the principles of social justice.

David B. Tyack
Stanford University

Introduction

There are few, if any, uncontroversial fields, themes, concepts and judgements in the writing of history. The history of education has often appeared uncontroversial until it has been brought into a relationship with other social phenomena, structures and processes, and the firm basis of its historical reconstruction has been made to look more fragile. In relation to the economy, for example, it has become increasingly uncertain what the history of education reveals about social mobility or status, and what in that history constitutes cause and effect. In relation to politics and political ideologies, it has become unclear how to represent the points of maximum connection in unambiguous terms: was the 1902 Education Act a step forwards or backwards, and what were the intentions and outcomes of payment by results? In relation to the histories of the church, the labour movement or pressures for reform or democratic improvements, there are alternative pictures and explanations. In relation to the classroom, the curriculum, the teaching profession, there are rival historical descriptions and claims.

Take, for example, the period 1790–1830, and the origins of mass or popular education. The period remains, in spite of the libraries of historical literature, a controversial field for political, economic and social historians, and for the history of education. When, if at all, in this period is the 'making of the English working class' to be located? How important and influential was the political radicalism of the 1790s? Was there a 'tradition' of radical, popular and working-class attitudes to and activity in education which carried ideas and practices through this period, into that of Chartism and beyond to the later labour movement? How are the activities and especially the motives of political and social reformers to be analysed and understood? In what ways are precise, detailed, complex social events to be situated in the broad sweep of capitalism and industrialism – or any other concept designed to describe and interpret fundamental social processes? Was mass schooling a function of the humanitarian, reforming instinct and purpose, or of the need for new forms of social order and control? These and a variety of similar and related questions are embedded in all attempts to describe and explain the strands of popular education as they emerged in this period. As firmly as any other period of educational history, this period of economic and social change, new popular and radical pressures and politics, reform and innovation, resistance and reaction, conservative self-defence and conservative innovation, makes the boundary between historical description and interpretation impossible to discover.

Description and narrative *are* emphasis, choice, interpretation. The organizing concepts and categories are interpretation. The concepts of social order and social control which are basic to David Rothman's *The Discovery of the Asylum* in the United States, and Michael Ignatieff's study of the penitentiary in the Industrial Revolution in England, *A Just Measure of Pain*, have been illuminating but controversial attempts at historical reconstruction and interpretation. The very starting-point is an act of interpretation. As Edward Thompson points out, 'too often, since every account must start somewhere, we see only the things which are new. We start at 1789, and English Jacobinism appears as a by-product of the French Revolution. Or we start in 1819 and with Peterloo, and English Radicalism appears to be a spontaneous generation of the Industrial Revolution'.[1] Historical revision has become concerned more and more not only with starting-points but also with the validity of the concepts associated with them. When did the Renaissance begin, and was there a Renaissance? When was the take-off of the Industrial Revolution, and was there *an* Industrial Revolution? When did reformers discover the specialized institution as a form of social control – and was it in fact a form of social control? How did educational developments relate to the formation of a working class, or to the expression of aspects of working-class culture – and was there a working class or a working-class culture? In examining education and its related processes (and which processes?) in this period, therefore, we are involved with judgements about beginnings, about processes, and about the concepts and categories in which they are organized and interpreted by historians.[2]

Data, concepts and judgements can and are being constantly renego-tiated and revised. Styles and structures of analysis change, are challenged, are replaced, co-exist. Things pass, in Albert Goodwin's phrase, into 'the limbo of frozen historiography'.[3] There is no longer, in history or elsewhere, a monolithic conservatism, or Marxism or liberalism. Escape into historical certainty is not difficult, but it is increasingly difficult to justify. Take, again, the period 1780–1830. Crucial though the industrial developments of the late eighteenth and early nineteenth centuries were to modern Britain, it is important to be cautious about how the whole range of social and educational changes are explained in relation to the concept of industrialization. Richard Johnson, in a discussion of E. P. Thompson's *The Making of the English Working Class*, asserts the need to analyse change without abandoning the analysis of economic relations. He detects 'a tendency to fall back on the categories of a non-Marxist economics; "process of industrialisation"; "problems of economic growth" '.[4] However, in a discussion of Johnson's own interpretation of the period 1780–1850, Malcolm Dick considers that Johnson's stress on the role of the emerging bourgeoisie 'in promoting the "hegemony" of industrial capitalism in the early nineteenth century . . . exaggerates the significance of industrialization for the development of education'.[5]

Thompson has elsewhere struggled with the difficulties of this and related concepts:

It has been a common complaint that the terms 'feudal', 'capitalist' or 'bourgeois' are too imprecise, and cover phenomena too vast and disparate, to be of serious analytic service. We now, however, find constantly in service a new set of terms, such as 'pre-industrial', 'traditional', 'paternalism', and 'modernization', which appear to be open to very much the same objections; and whose theoretical paternity is less certain.[6]

If 'industrial' and 'pre-industrial' are open not only to objection but also to theoretical debate, so, for example, are the vocabularies of corporate, urban, bureaucratic life which have become basic to the history of education. As historically usable categories they are as elusive and contentious as those which Thompson lists, but historians have a tendency to persist with them as common-sense, indisputable categories in which to package contiguous data. In the United States, C. F. Kaestle and M. A. Vinovskis have demonstrated the unreliability of a general view of educational development based on the concept of urbanization. They have shown that commonly held assumptions about the relationship of educational attitudes and actions to the process of urbanization are either crude or misleading, and that much more subtle and sensitive indicators and explanations need to be and can be arrived at. They demonstrate – as do some other American historians – how important it is to escape from 'obvious' explanations derived from coincident phenomena such as industrialization, urbanization and the expansion of schooling. They suggest, through a study of urban variations and the variables associated with the actors and decision-makers, that over-simplified connections have in the past been established by many historians, in their analyses of the relationship of education to, for example, industrial capitalism, 'human exploitation in our economic system', and urban growth and needs:

> educational participation as well as reform attitudes were indeed often related to the economic status of an individual, a town, or a region, but education itself is so complex that it cannot be treated as a single variable and then pegged to a single historical development, out of which all other concerns flowed.[7]

The American warning applies to the British situation also, precisely because too much reliance has been placed, however unconsciously, on assumption, at the expense of the analysis of practice and experience, and on analysis without attention to its conceptual and theoretical bases and difficulties.

The history of education is in fact multiple histories, because education is itself no simple and homogeneous concept or category, and because its history can be explored in relation to almost endless variables. Whether education is conceived as itself an indefinite cluster of experiences[8] or as a more narrowly definable process related to a variety of other processes, it has no meaning when presented in isolated and discretely institutional terms. Its history can be discussed in alternative forms, and the problems of interpretation can be illustrated by suggesting two different ways of approaching the history of the purposes of education – the history of education *for* and the history of education *against*. If this is an over-simplification of the alternatives, it at least indicates how history involves selection, emphasis and interpretation.

The first outline of the history of nineteenth- and twentieth-century education would rest on a number of personal qualities and socially desirable skills and categories for which education might be seen as preparation. Some of these might be compatible one with another; some might be mutually exclusive, depending on a variety of standpoints and current social priorities. Education might be seen as *for* obedience or happiness or creativity, or the fulfilment of human potential, or adulthood, employment and future citizenship. The history of education in the nineteenth and twentieth centuries abounds with pronouncements and movements which in one way or another have pursued such positively expressed aims, and have sought to reform the system or the classroom or the curriculum or the teacher and teacher training in order to achieve such aims. Their proponents might have been utilitarians or 'progressives', theosophists or industrialists, Christians or secularists, socialists or conservatives. Aims of such a kind have tended to assume some kind of consensus, actual or potential, either of society or of educationists, and have stated their target groups and ideals in terms of a relatively autonomous social context and the relative unimportance of the social relationships involved. In other words, they have argued less in terms of the school and the social and political world than of personality, human nature, intimate relationships, personal responsibility, dedication, creative skills, understanding and everything that points from the child's immediate present to the expanded personality or fulfilled human being or self-determining citizen he or she is to become. The concern, in this case, has been with the child as a child, and with the child as future adult. The focus of educational thought and practice has been seen in this version of educational history as embracing psychology and ethics, education-as-activity, the creative arts, and elements of vocational education. To varying degrees, the spokesmen for such movements have seen the school as a relatively enclosed institution.

The history of such an emphasis in the nineteenth and twentieth centuries would include aspects of the history of the definition of and attitudes towards childhood and adolescence; the emergence of the child study movement, Sloyd and eurhythmics; the language laboratory and Nuffield Science; the humanization of teaching, or teacher training and/or the teacher; the infant school, vertical grouping, the open classroom, classroom interaction and observation, and the tension between progressive methods and pressures for the teaching of basics. If there is a central nexus to the story as thus outlined it is the child and the teacher in the classroom, and psychology.

Obviously, any second version of this history will overlap with this first one, but it can have quite different emphases. Education *against* aspects of the educational and social system has given priority consideration to those educational and social obstacles which prevent the attainment of reforms which may have been specified positively, but in either more ambiguous or vaguer terms. Education has been seen in this case as against privilege and injustice, against exploitation and poverty, against racial prejudice and a variety of socially undesirable trends which have been given different priority ratings at different times – for example promiscuity and venereal disease, drug abuse and traffic accidents, and uncritical addiction to the media and to commercial advertising. The converse of such concepts can, of course, be presented in positive terms, and education can be seen as *for* justice, a better society, racial harmony and so on, but the argument has been most frequently presented in terms of the *against* rather than the *for* position, with relatively immediate targets for rectification. The aims have been presented as elements in a wider conflict or struggle, with obstacles to be overcome, barriers to be removed, distinctions to be erased. The assumptions in such cases have centred on the conflict of values in a democratic or liberal or pluralist or class-divided state; on the need for changed relationships between the school and the wider society, on those aspects of society which are carried into the classroom from family and social background, privilege and under-privilege; on inequalities in the system; on public and private education; on discrimination against racial and ethnic minorities, and against girls. The concern in this case is with the child as a participant in or victim of the social class structure, with the social and political determinants of the system, with access to parts of the system, to knowledge, to qualifications and credentials, to status, to employment, to power.

The history of such an emphasis in the nineteenth and twentieth centuries focuses on the sociology of class, the family and the school, on the politics of the education system, on the relationships between education and economic and social relations, on the attempted strategies to reform the system and the schools, and the socially and politically defined motives of the reformers. The history therefore considers the democratization of the structure in the nineteenth century and through secondary school reorganization in the second half of the twentieth century; the nature and purpose of government intervention, legislation, compulsory schooling; selection for the secondary school, the 'ladder' of promotion through the system, meritocracy; changing patterns of control and of dominant values as reflected in the system, its expansion and the balance of its component parts; education and welfare; disadvantage and deprivation, compensatory education and positive discrimination, government committees and commissions, educational priority areas and urban aid; education and occupational mobility; the discriminatory nature of curriculum content and school practices, sexism in textbooks, racism in schools. If there is an over-whelming nexus of explanation in this version of the history it is in terms of the child and the school in relation to social class and status within the system, the politics and sociology of education.

There are, of course, other ways of writing the history, and of combining the *for* and *against* analyses, but the writing provokes serious difficulty and debate about the focus and priority for attention and explanation. This is not just a question of Marxist and anti- or non-Marxist approaches, since the concept of social class is fundamental to almost all approaches to the history of education in Britain. The early historians of education – Adamson, Smith, Birchenough, and others – found themselves having to present the nineteenth- and twentieth-century picture in clear terms of social class. A kind of Fabian social, or sociological, or social class history became an essential ingredient in almost all approaches to the history of education or any part of it, even if the end-messages were liberal or conservative in emphasis. The role of Marxist historians, particularly of Brian Simon in the 1960s, was to introduce a more systematic version of such a history, elements of which were already far more visible in the existing historical work than was true of the United States, for example, when the radical revisionists came to review their educational history in the 1960s. Nevertheless, the history of the infant school or the mechanics' institute, of the 1870 Act or the Hadow Report on *The Education of the Adolescent* in 1926, presents problems of interpretation and emphasis. Brian Simon and Marjorie Cruickshank have debated alternative interpretations of the 1902 Education Act and the ending of the school board era.[9] There have been rival interpretations of the 1862 Revised Code and the introduction of payment by results.[10] The first sustained study of the Sunday schools has provoked controversy about their control and purpose.[11] The 'radical tradition' of the nineteenth century has been viewed in different ways. To the picture of a continuous tradition has been counterposed the suggestion of a major discontinuity around the early 1840s between an earlier 'popular' radicalism and a later 'working-class' radicalism, with implications for the interpretation of popular educational movements.[12]

The history of education has therefore increasingly become compli-cated by the recognition of relationships with other social phenomena. An older history of institutions and of ideas has become subject to an

awareness of the ambiguous or controversial nature of historical interpretations in other and related fields – including economic history, the
history of political institutions and ideologies, the history of class
formation, social welfare and reform. The interpretation of education
for and *against* therefore points not only towards rival views of the
educational process, but also towards rival views of the education-
society relationship, and of the definition of education itself.

The problem of the historical meaning or meanings of education and
the scope of the historical exercise has been particularly explored and
debated in the United States, mainly surrounding the work of Lawrence
Cremin and his pursuit of a historical definition which takes in a wide
range of processes beyond the traditionally accepted educational
institutions.[13] The attraction and importance of extending the history
into such fields as the history of the press and the modern media,
church activities and popular culture, are obvious. So are the dangers,
with the possibility of the emergence of an amorphous history which
fails to locate discrete educational institutions in a clear relationship
with other processes, and also fails to establish acceptable and understandable definitions of the wider educational territories.[14] The historiographic problem in relation to education can be approached from the
starting-point of exploring the relationship between education and
opinion.

Opinion, in the context of the history of education, suggests a
different set of emphases and preoccupations from the concept of
ideology. Ideology, in whichever of the forms it has been presented over
the past century or more, comprises a theory of society, in which the
actors are allocated more or less conscious roles in representing and
interpreting their world. The relationship between the material world
and human consciousness was presented in Marx's famous formulation
in the 1850s: 'The mode of production of material life conditions the
social, political and intellectual life process in general. It is not the
consciousness of men that determines their being, but, on the contrary,
their social being that determines their consciousness.'[15]

For Engels, in the 1890s, the human actor was – in existing social
conditions – imprisoned in forces controlling or circumscribing his
consciousness, and therefore a creature of ideology: the latter was a
process 'accomplished by the so-called thinker consciously, it is true,
but with a false consciousness. The real motive forces impelling him
remain unknown to him . . . Hence he imagines false or seeming motive
forces . . . He works with mere thought material.'[16] It is not important

for us here to pursue in detail the outcome of these formulations, critical though they are for any definition of the role of the historian and what he attempts to portray or uncover. The central point is the emphasis on the 'real' motive forces as against the 'imagined' ones of 'false consciousness', an emphasis which has been fundamental to Marxist historiography. In the history of education, its sharpest expression, in spite of its attempts to escape from the almost inevitable trap, has been Samuel Bowles and Herbert Gintis's *Schooling in Capitalist America*, the central aim of which was to reveal the 'real', underlying economic determinants of educational decisions and institutions.[17] Variants or alternatives to the classical Marxist formulations have been sought over the past century, increasingly within Marxism itself, in order to unravel the complex problems of the relationship between the 'real' and the represented and the perceived. The concept of ideology therefore has an extensive history.[18] Max Weber, for example, pursued the connection between ideas and their sources, seeing ideologies emerge as ideas became 'discredited in the face of history unless they point in the direction of conduct that various interests promote'.[19] Karl Mannheim developed a theory of ideology and utopia as distortions of reality for different purposes, and governed by different unconscious drives. Like Weber, he looked at the way 'antiquated and inapplicable norms, modes of thought, and theories are likely to degenerate into ideologies whose function it is to conceal the actual meaning of conduct rather than to reveal it'.[20] His analysis of this degeneration, however, took him away from Marx's position, into a relativist or 'relational' stance in which the Marxist position was seen as another ideology, as equally dependent on its circumstances as any that the Marxist described: 'those who think in socialist or communist terms discern the ideological element only in the thinking of their opponents'.[21]

All of these approaches to the concept of ideology focus, to one extent or another, on the unreal, degenerative, out-of-date, misrepresentative nature of the ideological versions of reality. The concept has, however, also acquired a meaning which possesses none of these attributes, emerging from an attempt to see how men picture their world, but without the element of control by underlying or decaying social and economic forces. Ideology in this sense is a philosophical tool, an approach to knowledge as the product of interactions differently conceived, and elevating the human actor to a more controlling position in the process. Theodore Brameld, for example, describes ideology as 'the complex of attitudes, beliefs, ideas, purposes, and customs that expresses more or less systematically and more or less accurately the program and practices of a culture or an important part of it'. He continues:

> It is the prosaic word-picture, fashioned on their own level of enlightenment by the people of any tribe or any country in any period, to serve as an ostensibly reliable description of the dominant patterns of practice and belief of their culture. Clearly, ideology should not be thought of invidiously; it may take the form of the sincere effort of an age to depict itself.[22]

Ideology, in Brameld's portrayal, is both more deliberate and more reliable, and although it remains rooted in time and place, it relates to a dominant culture, not to unknown and imprisoning forces. Some Marxist historians, of course, have also engaged with the nature of social experience in ways which attempt to release history from a sense of powerlessness in face of the hidden, 'unknown' forces impelling the socially conditioned, 'imagined' drives of the participants. Foster, for example, in his analysis of the radicalism of the Industrial Revolution, is concerned about changing *levels* of radical consciousness and the importance of language in the analysis, given what does not show up in statistics unless the historian is looking at the 'right' things, in the 'right' places, and for the 'right' clues.[23] Nevertheless, there is the common element in all pursuits of the concept of ideology that they seek to explain in generalized terms the relationship between consciousness and world representations on the one hand, and the economic, social or cultural shapes of society on the other.

The concept of opinion is a weaker version of ideology, but at the same time points to different assumptions about the operation of society. Opinion points towards the diverse elements amongst and within social movements, towards conflict and influence, rather than manipulation and control, towards the complexities of decision-making rather than the self-portrayal of tribes or nations or ages. It has less claim than ideology to a body of theory, and is closer to policy analysis than to theories of culture or class conflict. J. M. Keynes uses the concept in *The End of Laissez-Faire* when he suggests that 'A study of the history of opinion is a necessary preliminary to the emancipation of the mind. I do not know which makes a man more conservative – to know nothing but the present, or nothing but the past.'[24]

It is possible, from such a starting-point, to set on one side the important but often historically unenlightening debate around ideology, and to focus on social action at a different level. Keynes's common-sense division between the past and the present as people experience them is, of course, untenable, in that the messages of the past are in and around us. We incorporate them even in resisting them. Historians have long disputed about changing interpretations of history, about what one of the disputants calls this 'unending dialogue between the present and the past'.[25] The disputes revolve around the nature of historical analysis and historical facts. Is there, or is there not, as Sir George Clark told his inaugural lecture audience that there was, 'a hard core of facts, however much it may be concealed by the surrounding pulp of disputable interpretation'?[26] Or is all historical knowledge relative to the position and time of the historian? The interest in historical silence discussed in later chapters of this book is a long way from Clark's assumptions, and suggests that a relative view of history does not paralyse the historian, any more than relative views about the accuracy of committee minutes or the desirability of a committee decision paralyses a committee.

Opinion is an important concept in such an approach, and to what one might call a social history of policy. An opinion-related history is one in which significant moments of change are explored, counter-pressures for innovation and established practice are probed, the subtleties of social interaction and their public articulation investigated. The basis of such explorations lies not in theoretical models or quantifiable data but in historical interpretation of issues, of how they emerge, of their disappearance. One example of emergence discussed later in the book is the rapid combination in the United States of the early 1960s of an awareness of poverty, the civil rights movement and the activities of early childhood specialists into a new approach to education as a policy instrument. An example of disappearance is the reasons why, at different stages and for different reasons, Robert Owen, Lyon Playfair and Herbert Spencer disappeared from the historical record of education. Once policy is brought down from a traditional, elevated position in ministerial, parliamentary, bureaucratic and to some extent pressure group history, it relates to complex processes of social interaction and many levels of attempts at influence and intervention. The discussion in this book of attitudes to factory children, of the social science forums in which public assumptions about education and other processes were articulated, of the concepts of liberal and vocational education as interpreted in practice by students or consultative committees, are illustrations of territories in which a 'social history of policy' merges with an attempt to write a history of educational opinion. Reservations about accepted versions of the history of institutions or of the state, and about the reasons for certain kinds of historical silence in the field of education, point up the need to re-examine established bases on which historical accounts and interpretation have often been constructed. The chapters which follow are inevitably, therefore, concerned both with substantive historical themes, and historiographic and methodological issues.

What is attempted is a form of social history, and Keynes's view of the study of changing opinion is an important beginning in the search for that form. This is not, therefore, a history of ideas or intellectual history, but historical excursions into how people, groups of people, people in action, have interpreted and reinterpreted their world – and particularly those parts of it which they have called education. Social history has to some extent in recent years become identified with quantitative approaches to the history of population, the family, urban growth and similar areas, partly in an attempt to detach it from its old identity as an antiquarian concern with the history of costume and kitchen utensils. Whatever else social history may be, however, the many dimensions of ideology and the workings of crude opinion must remain cornerstones. James Mill, writing about economists at the beginning of the nineteenth century, proclaimed – at a point before the ideology/opinion division became possible or recognizable – that 'opinion, of one sort or another, governs the world. Even when it is but a prejudice, an error, there is no power in the moral world comparable to its power'. Mill, aware of the emphasis given by the economists to 'the publicity of evidence', spelled out the power of opinion as a source of good and evil, of will and action, of truth and falsehood, of 'the great man or the villain . . . at one time it founds empires, at another destroys them. Every man is therefore a little kingdom upon the earth, governed despotically by opinion'.[27] An awareness of these powers of opinion was for Mill, as for Keynes a century later, emancipatory. For Mill and for Keynes the despotism was removable, and in their search for the sources of emancipation they were pursuing a similar quest to that of the analysts of ideology, but different in the emphasis they place on the individual and the tussle of the market-place. The power of opinion, in their sense, is a crucial focus for the social historian. It adds complexity and dimension to the study of change, resistance to change and absence of change, to the discussion of historical clamour and historical silence.

Notes

1 E.P. Thompson, *The Making of the English Working Class* (London, 1963), p. 24.
2 For previous discussion of education and radicalism in the 1790s see Harold Silver, *The Concept of Popular Education: A Study of Ideas and Social Movements in the Early Nineteenth Century* (London, 1965), and Harold Silver, *English Education and the Radicals, 1780-1850* (London, 1975).
3 Albert Goodwin, *The Friends of Liberty: The English Democratic Movement in the age of the French Revolution* (London, 1979), p. 81.
4 Richard Johnson, 'Edward Thompson, Eugene Genovese, and Socialist-Humanist History', *History Workshop*, no. 6, 1978, p. 94.
5 Malcolm M. Dick, 'English Conservatives and Schools for the Poor *c*. 1780-1833: A Study of the Sunday School, School of Industry and the Philanthropic Society's School for Migrant and Criminal Children', Leicester University PhD, 1979, p. 3.
6 E. P. Thompson, 'Eighteenth-Century English Society: Class Struggle Without Class?', *Social History*, vol. 3, no. 2, 1978, p. 133.
7 Carl F. Kaestle and Maris A. Vinovskis, *Education and Social Change in Nineteenth-Century Massachusetts* (Cambridge, 1980), p. 233. For another analysis of the unsatisfactory nature of discussions of the effects of urbanization and industrialization on American schooling see John W. Meyer *et al.*, 'Public Education as Nation-Building in America: Enrolments and Bureaucratization in the American States, 1870-1930', *American Journal of Sociology*, vol. 85, no. 3, 1979, pp. 591-613.
8 The most persuasive proponent of this approach is Lawrence A. Cremin, who has defined education in such broad terms in a number of places as a basis for his own historical work on American education. See, for example, his *Public Education* (New York, 1976).
9 See Marjorie Cruickshank, 'A Defence of the 1902 Act', and Brian Simon, 'The 1902 Act - A Wrong Turning', in *History of Education Society Bulletin*, no. 19, spring 1977.
10 See, for example, A.J. Marcham, 'Recent Interpretations of the Revised Code, 1862', *History of Education*, vol. 8, no. 2, 1979, and subsequent contributions by Laaden Fletcher and Marcham in vol. 10, nos 1 and 2.
11 See Thomas Walter Laqueur, *Religion and Respectability: Sunday Schools and Working-class Culture 1780-1850* (New Haven, 1976). For attacks on Laqueur's thesis of the Sunday schools as an expression of working-class community, see Malcolm Dick, 'The Myth of the Working-Class Sunday School', *History of Education*, vol. 9, no. 1, 1980, and Michael Brian Frost, 'The Development of Provided Schooling for Working Class Children in Birmingham 1781-1851', University of Birmingham L1M thesis, 1978, pp. 118, 161, 163, 204, 205, 379.
12 For the theme of the radical tradition see Brian Simon, *The Two Nations and the Educational Structure 1780-1870* (first published as *Studies in the History of Education 1780-1870*, London, 1960), and Harold Silver, *The Concept of Popular Education* and *English Education and the Radicals*. For an alternative view see Richard Johnson, ' "Really Useful Knowledge": Radical Education

and Working-Class Culture, 1790–1848', in J. Clarke *et al.* (eds), *Working Class Culture* (London, 1979).

13 Two volumes of a projected three-volume history of American education by Cremin based on such a definition have so far appeared: *American Education: The Colonial Experience 1607–1783* (New York, 1970), and *American Education: the National Experience 1783–1876* (New York, 1980).

14 This danger is pointed out by R. Freeman Butts, who attempts to direct attention back towards a narrower definition of educational institutions and processes in *Public Education in the United States: From Revolution to Reform* (New York, 1978).

15 Karl Marx, Preface to *A Contribution to the Critique of Political Economy* (1859), in Karl Marx and Friedrich Engels, *Selected Works* (Moscow, 1950), vol. I, p. 329.

16 Engels to F. Mehring, 14 July 1893, in ibid., vol. II, p. 451.

17 Samuel Bowles and Herbert Gintis, *Schooling in Capitalist America: Educational Reform and the Contradictions of Economic Life* (London, 1976).

18 See, for example, George Lichtheim, 'The Concept of Ideology', *History and Theory*, vol. 5, 1965.

19 See H.H. Gerth and C. Wright Mills, *From Max Weber: Essays in Sociology* (London, 1948), pp. 62–3.

20 Karl Mannheim, *Ideology and Utopia: an Introduction to the Sociology of knowledge* (London, 1936, edition of 1960), p. 85.

21 Ibid., p. 111.

22 Theodore Brameld, *Toward a Reconstructed Philosophy of Education* (New York, 1956, edition of 1962), p. 87.

23 John Foster, *Class Struggle and the Industrial Revolution: Early Industrial Capitalism in Three English Towns* (London, 1974), pp. 109, 123.

24 John Maynard Keynes, *The End of Laissez-Faire* (London, 1926), p. 16.

25 E.H. Carr, *What Is History?* (London, 1961, edition of 1964), p. 30.

26 G.N. Clark, *Historical Scholarship and Historical Thought* (Cambridge, 1944), p. 20.

27 James Mill, 'Economists', in *Encyclopaedia Britannica*, eighth supplement (London, 1818), vol. III, p. 715.

Part One
Nineteenth-century studies

1 Aspects of neglect: the strange case of Victorian popular education

More has been researched and written about education in Victorian England than in any other period, and the majority of it has been about popular education. Yet we have neglected it. Most of what has been written has in fact disguised our neglect and ignorance of it. This is not just a question of 'gaps' that need to be filled, of historical inattention. It is a more basic question of the kind of historical enterprise in which we have been engaged. Judgements about historical 'neglect', of course, depend on assumptions about what is, could be, or should be known. They entail definitions of the area, purpose and value of study. Such judgements and definitions are ideological statements.

The themes that have attracted the most attention in Victorian popular education have been those of policy formation and legislation, commissions and committees, the provision, control and administration of education, and the changing shape of different 'levels' of education – elementary and technical, infant and adult, and 'types' of education – board and voluntary. Some attention has been paid to the broader 'context' of educational decisions and functions – notably that of the churches and the radical and labour movements, and the nature and extent of literacy. Studies have been national and (especially in the case of theses and dissertations) local – with a vast amount of (mainly unpublished) work on local school boards and local institutions. The most researched and discussed areas can be summarized as: the school boards, the voluntary school system, and the development of a national system of administration (focusing on Kay-Shuttleworth and the Committee of Council, Robert Lowe and the Revised Code, Forster and the 1870 Education Act, the politics of the school board era and the events leading up to the 1902 Education Act). Attention has also been paid (again, often in unpublished work) to pressure groups, from the Central Society of Education in the 1830s to the bodies campaigning for public education in the late 1840s and 1850s, the National Education League of the late 1860s, and the socialist organizations of the last decades of the century.[1] It seems a well-surveyed field, and it has produced such publication peaks as Brian Simon's first two volumes of *Studies in the History of Education* which encompass the Victorian period (1960, 1965), John Harrison's *Learning and Living 1780–1960* (1961), Mabel Tylecote's *The Mechanics' Institutes of Lancashire and Yorkshire before 1851* (1957), David Rubinstein's *School Attendance in London 1870–1904* (1969), Richard Selleck's *The New Education 1870–1914* (1968), and above all – though only marginally concerned with the Victorian period – A.E. Dobbs's pioneering *Education and Social Movements 1700–1850* (1919). All of these successfully explored education in important relationships with social movements, social change, and related ideas and ideals. The period of major contributions stretches from the early wide-ranging histories by Charles Birchenough, J.W. Adamson and Frank Smith in the 1920s and 1930s, to such detailed studies since the 1950s as those of educational policy, politics and administration by Eric Eaglesham, Peter Gosden and Gillian Sutherland, of religion and education by Marjorie Cruickshank and James Murphy, and of school architecture by Malcolm Seaborne.[2] The bibliographies of work published and unpublished are substantial.[3]

My dissatisfaction with the mass of books, articles, theses and dissertations began to take shape during my co-authorship of *A Social History of Education in England*[4] but became explicit after the completion of another book of which I was co-author, *The Education of the Poor*, a history of a Church school for the children of the poor in Kennington, South London.[5] The work on this book eventually raised some awkward questions about this perhaps 'atypical' monitorial school – as it was when it was created in 1824. The school sources revealed a more imaginative and humane approach to children and to school affairs, and stronger school–community links than we had expected, or could explain. The school was as concerned in its early decades with the children's health as it was with their souls, and the school and its managers were the focal point for Lambeth's fight against cholera, bad sanitation and other environmental nuisances. The teachers were competent and the school efficient. From the 1880s boys were winning a stream of scholarships to London's grammar and other schools. A record of humanity, efficiency and - in a variety of ways - innovation seemed to stretch from the 1820s to the twentieth century. There could be reason for thinking that this school, in the 1820s and 1830s, or in the 1880s, was atypical, but if so what was typical? There was no answer to this question (and when the book was completed it became clear that we had ourselves shied away from it) because historians had surprisingly done no research on the monitorial system as it was operated in practice. Only one British historical thesis had been written at the time on monitorial schools (and we had not seen it when we wrote our *Education of the Poor*). J.R. Carr's thesis on certain Lancasterian schools in London, Middlesex and Surrey investigates some of the subtle differences between the financing, management and operation of these schools and concludes that judgements based on local schools are at variance with those derived from a study of the parent body or of its Borough Road school. Many of the schoolteachers (unlike the ones in Kennington) had no local support, but others did. There were differences between Lancaster's claims and the realities. The Lancasterian schools 'were not units of a nationally planned system of providing education for the poor'.[6] The possibilities of this kind of investigation - and the importance of its findings - have gone largely ignored. There have continued to be abundant statements about the intentions of the founders of the monitorial system, about its stated methods, about its defects, its critics and its demise - but nothing about the detailed operation of monitorial schools, no sustained attempts to match theory with reality. Yet the monitorial system dominated English popular education for half a century. It is arguable that it was the most influential innovation in the history of English education, but the books on the history of educational innovation have used definitions of the term which exclude any consideration of the monitorial system, refuse to handle it with more 'progressive' innovations.[7] The very terms, like 'innovation' and 'progressive' and 'reform', that historians have used have ensured certain kinds of neglect. The historians of nineteenth-century education have presented the monitorial system as a wraith, and discussed it as if it were flesh.

A project on which I had also been working for some time involved an investigation of the concept of 'social science' in the nineteenth century, and particularly the organizations created in Britain and the United States in the second half of the century for the 'promotion of social science'. The National Association for the Promotion of Social Science

(NAPSS) and its American counterparts had Education Departments which discussed a range of educational issues and campaigned on some of them. No serious attention has been paid to the educational content of these bodies, either in the published or in the thesis literature.[8] The point of central interest that emerged from this and related studies was that little historical attention had been paid to precisely those themes that were of most interest to the NAPSS and people active in it – including, from the mid-1850s to the mid-1880s, the education of factory and workhouse children, ragged and reformatory schools.[9] During this period at least 50,000 children a year were being educated under the poor law. Between the creation of the ragged school movement in the 1840s and 1881, it was estimated, the London schools alone had 'rescued' some 300,000 children.[10] The number of factory children attending school part-time (in factory schools or elsewhere) was something of the order of 40,000 in 1851.[11] The numbers are not inconsiderable. The question is not, however, just one of quantities. When my collaborator and I began work on the history of one workhouse school, for example, we found beyond doubt that in 1838 it was educationally more 'progressive' than we had expected. It had a Glasgow-trained teacher who made it a condition of acceptance of the appointment that the Guardians should purchase various series of reading books, maps, slates, coloured pictures of animals, battledores and shuttlecocks, and gymnastic poles. For this and other reasons we found the standard stereotype of the workhouse school unhelpful. We were faced with questions about what was 'typical' similar to those raised by the monitorial study. Again, almost nothing in the published literature helped to disentangle statements of intention, motive and policy, on the one hand, from the reality on the other hand – though one unpublished thesis, by Alec Ross, had extremely skilfully handled questions of quality and variety in poor law schooling.[12]

Related questions, unanswered and unexplored, abounded – for example about major nineteenth-century controversies and about the work of crucial figures engaged in these neglected areas – for instance Edwin Chadwick *as educationist*, Leonard Horner and other factory inspectors prominent in educational discussions, Mary Carpenter, and others.[13] Vital areas of the history of educational ideas, it became clear, had been ignored – especially where such ideas could be understood only in relation to deeper currents of social thought – Darwinism, and Marx's views on education, for example. Historians of education have in general taken superficial account of the complexities of the history of social ideas of which education is a part, but it should be added that historians of sociology have been equally unable to recognize and assess the role of educational thought. Poor Herbert Spencer. From the standard histories of education it would be difficult to deduce the extent (or even the existence) of his impact on social thought, and from the books on Spencer's sociology it would be difficult to deduce that he wrote anything at all about education![14]

The conclusion, therefore, was that the great majority of what had been written about popular education in the Victorian period offered few or no real clues as to relationships in schools, their role in the community, or as to the social structures and processes, controversies and changing ideas and assumptions, in which education was intricately involved. The canon of published literature and the majority of unpublished research seemed (a) top heavy, in that it was concerned (and even then selectively) with the provision and administration of education; (b) empty, in that it made few serious attempts to look at the content of schooling or other educational processes; (c) one-dimensional, in that it made no attempt to consider the impact of schooling, and responses to it (or even the range of resistances to it); (d) isolated, in that it made no convincing attempt to explore links between school and family, school and work, school and recreation, school and politics, school and community (though some *formal* relationships, notably that between school and church, have, of course, been widely studied); (e) purblind, in that it recognized only limited areas of 'education' as being suitable for investigation.

The underlying pattern that begins to emerge from these judgements is one of neglect of questions relating to educational realities, to the impact of education, to its role in cultural and social processes. The easier route of describing the structure of educational systems, the motives of providers, the intricacies of policies, has been followed. Although it is an easier route, and one which describes changes and developments, it is not one that often arrives at rounded explanations of change – or even at a felt need to offer any. The 'bits' of neglect therefore fit together to form a picture of widespread historical ignorance, 'disguised', I have suggested, by the very bulk of what has been written. Some of these items of neglect can be clustered into groups, for example:

> *The impact and 'use' of schooling.* There is an absence of work on reactions to school experience, on the *use* of basic schooling by

largely self-educated working men, and on the important area of:
The relationship between schooling and literacy. Although useful
statistical work has been done in this area, there is little systematic
analysis (at least for the period after the 1830s) of literacy and
reading matter,[15] literacy and participation in social and political
movements (e.g. the co-operative movement), literacy and the commercial press from the mid-1840s.

The quality of educational experience. There are no published studies
of possible varieties of educational experience in monitorial schools,
workhouse schools, factory schools, dame schools[16] – indeed *all*
schools.

The role of the school in total social relationships. The half-time system
produced tensions between the child's role in the school, as
employee and as an important part of the family economy. Teachers
had varying roles and statuses in the community. Ragged schools
produced controversy about the undermining of the family.
Elementary schools often attracted former pupils and others to
evening classes (for example, organized science schools), and served
as a focus for other 'community' activities. These and other ways in
which schools, pupils, teachers, educational activities in general,
related to wider areas of social experience have been largely
ignored, and what little research has been done on these areas is
mainly unpublished.[17]

Educational ideologies. Preoccupation with the provision and administration of the educational system in the narrowest sense has led to a
high degree of selectivity in discussions of 'influential' nineteenth-
century educationists. Men and women considered central to
educational debates in their own time have been omitted from the
twentieth-century records partly because they have not left educational 'monuments' in the shape of recognizable twentieth-century
institutions. George Combe and James Simpson, important figures
in the controversies and campaigns of the middle decades of the
nineteenth century, have vanished with their phrenology or their
secularism; Edwin Chadwick, Mary Carpenter, Louisa Twining,
have vanished with their interest in other vanished objects like poor
law schools, workhouse schools and ragged schools; William Ellis
and William Ballantyne Hodgson have vanished with the Birkbeck
schools and the teaching of social science. The *Transactions* of the
NAPSS are occasionally raided for bits of data, but the relationships
between educational and social ideas and ideologies have been

ignored. (In this connection also it should be added that historians of ideas in Victorian England have tended to ignore education.)[18]

This is neither an exhaustive nor a sophisticated categorization. It is enough, however, to suggest a need to examine the prevalent directions of historical attention, and the assumptions they reveal.

In some respects this is a situation similar to that which obtained in American educational historiography at the end of the 1950s. The historians engaged in revising American educational history were concerned initially both with areas of neglect and with distorted perceptions of what has held the centre of the historical stage – the American public or common school. The radicalization of American politics and intellectual life in the 1960s did, of course, draw attention to areas of neglect – the education of the black, the female, the Catholic, and the under-privileged, for example – but the neglect was in some respects relative, as there was distinguished work in existence on the history of the education of minorities.[19] The questions to which Bernard Bailyn and Lawrence Cremin drew attention at the beginning of the 1960s, and which in various ways a generation of different kinds of revisionists then pursued, related most centrally to the way historians had presented the common school.[20] The history of American education, they suggested, had been distorted and truncated by focusing almost exclusively on the growth of the public school as a basic instrument of American liberal, progressive, industrial, democratic development – adjectives which all became focal points of debate in the political controversies of the 1960s. The old story was not adequate, in Bailyn's view, because it read 'present issues and definitions back into the past', and led – amongst other things – to a 'casual, inconsequential treatment of the colonial period'.[21] Narrowness of historical vision had produced falsified history. 'The moral of educational history', wrote Cremin, 'is the common school triumphant' – a triumph which had become not 'merely an article of popular or professional faith; it had become a canon of sound historical scholarship'.[22] The 'revisionist' nineteenth-century historians who followed – for example Michael Katz, Marvin Lazerson, David Tyack, Carl Kaestle and Diane Ravitch – to different extents and in different ways broadened the discussion from institutions to communities, to complex patterns of demographic and urban change, to the historical role of school and other educational enterprises in social and political dynamics.[23] Explorations of the familiar and of the neglected were being conducted, and new insights and judgements being arrived

at and debated. New concepts and definitions were involved, and as
Bailyn and Cremin in particular indicated, at the heart of the historical
problem was the definition of the educational historian's terms of
reference. What *was* education, and therefore what *was* the history of
education? Cremin has persistently argued that the history of popular
education cannot just be the history of schools, since the school is only
part of a configuration of education agencies: 'public schools are only
one among several important public institutions that educate the
public'. He has argued that education is about 'families, churches,
libraries, museums, publishers, benevolent societies, youth groups,
agricultural fairs, radio networks, military organizations, and research
institutes'.[24] How broad or how narrow educational history can and
should be has become part of the unending historiographical debate
that characterizes American educational history.

Although there are important differences between the questions asked
in the 1960s and 1970s about the history of education in the United
States, and those which I am trying to formulate here, there are some
important ideological similarities. The pre-1960s history of American
popular education, and the contemporary concerns of British historians
of popular education, stem from encapsulation in the present. American
historians found in the common school a necessary explanation of
twentieth-century industrial democracy. British historians have found
in the elementary school and its surrounding legislation and policies an
explanation of the development of twentieth-century welfare state
democracy. Both obsessive concerns have involved ideological commitments which have prevented important questions from being asked
about the past, or – if asked – from being followed through.

In British terms this seems to me to have entailed an acceptance by
historians of crude models of social structure and social change. It has
meant that at any moment of time only those phenomena which serve to
explain what has survived in institutional form have been seen as
worthy of attention. Only those structures, events, ideas, campaigns,
successes, failures, in Victorian education and society that have
meaning in twentieth-century terms have been admitted to the definition of the history of education. An understanding at any depth of the
work of George Combe or Edwin Chadwick, an appreciation of the
nature and impact of poor law or factory education, a sense of the
forgotten controversies which agitated public opinion, an indication of
the subtleties of educational and social experience, the relationships

between school and wider social and educative agencies, have not been seen as of major importance in justifying twentieth-century models of institutions implicit or explicit in historical research. Failure to pursue such aspects of Victorian education and society has therefore resulted in the imposition of narrow and inappropriate models of social structure, social interaction and social change on nineteenth-century experience. It has resulted in profound distortions of the history of education, of social and cultural realities. It has, incidentally, resulted in some of the best and most useful thesis literature (for example that of W. P. McCann, D. K. Jones, A. M. Ross, J. R. Carr and P. J. Rooke), remaining unpublished – as the references in this paper suggest.

Even when attempts have been made to widen the understanding of Victorian popular education, and to explore some of the conceptual difficulties in our existing historical analysis, they have been half-hearted. One well-known attempt was that of Richard Johnson in 1970 to apply the concept of 'social control' to the work of Kay-Shuttleworth in particular, in an effort to redeploy some familiar historical material. Johnson's article on 'Educational Policy and Social Control in Early Victorian England'[25] expressed an awareness of gaps in historical knowledge, including 'the founding and maintenance of schools for the poor in thousands of local communities, the critical subject of an educational history that still largely waits to be written'. It spoke of the 'rather familiar grooves' of educational research. Outlining various possible approaches to explaining the interests of those who helped to provide voluntary popular education, Johnson admitted to selecting the 'more accessible and more traditional' one – 'to scrutinize the social assumptions implicit in a particular measure; to study, in a critical way, declarations of intent in conjunction with an item of educational practice'. Such an attempt removed any value there might have been in using the concept of social control, and Johnson relapsed into an unenterprising analysis, concerned with 'intent', using social control as a uni-directional concept, failing to disentangle intent from practice, and practice from effect (and seemingly unaware of the sociologists' difficulties in establishing meanings for the concept). He remained involved in a discussion not, as he suggested, of authority and power, but of the *intentions* of those in authority in power – which is a starting-point for an analysis of real situations, but can ultimately mean – as it did in this case – an evasion of it. There is no point in approaching areas of ignorance with crude analytical concepts and a timid version of 'critical' study. But at least Johnson was making an attempt, and had the courage to admit what he was doing. Most historians who have reached the edges of difficult or embarrassing questions have turned away from them altogether, unwilling or unable to acknowledge and scrutinize their own ideological reluctance.

Embarrassment is perhaps as frequent an obstacle as conceptual crudity. Let me take two examples. The first is that of attitudes towards punishment in school, which of course suggest wider questions about social and human relationships. To know how far corporal punishment, for instance, was administered in Victorian elementary schools would seem to be at least a useful indication of aspects of the educational process, and of wider cultural questions. We do not know, and we have either pretended that we do, or have not thought it important enough to include among the aspects of education we wish to know. None of the published work on elementary schools confronts the material, asks questions, worries about the phenomenon. The Kennington school I was involved in investigating appears to have been without corporal punishment until probably the 1880s – over half a century after its foundation. Did other monitorial schools use corporal punishment? The National Society's records indicate that the society discouraged it from the outset. Why? How typical was the Kennington school in resisting it? That the answer is difficult and confusing is clear from the only research done on the subject – a very capable, unpublished thesis by P.J. Rooke in 1962.[26] It emphasizes the enlightened view of punishment held by the founders of the monitorial schools, the nature of the discipline sought in the schools, and the 'rarity' of corporal punishment at institutions like the National Society's school in Baldwin's Gardens. At the same time it shows that corporal punishment was in fact used in many, though by no means all, National schools in the 1840s, though with widely differing degrees of frequency. Rooke begins to raise some important questions – mainly about conflicts of attitude, and about the reasons for 'enlightened' views – but in the tradition of English research lets them drop. The point is that it could be embarrassing to pursue them, because what the standard works offer is a set of stereotypes of the monitorial or later elementary school, which might suffer damage if the realities of the punishment situation were pursued too far. Historians have *assumed* that physical punishment was the rule in the Victorian elementary school – because it was the rule in the grammar and public school. They have not thought it necessary to test, or have preferred not to test, this and many other such assumptions.[27] Some monitorial and other schools, schoolmasters, managers and patrons were more humane than the textbook summaries suggest. Most of the histories in any case summarize what Bell and Lancaster *said* about punishment, without attempting to match a stereotype of a discredited system against evidence that might exist of possible diversities in the schools. Too much attention to the realities of punishment raises the embarrassing spectre of having to ask questions about what we think we know of monitorial and indeed all popular education in the nineteenth century. Why the National Society resisted corporal punishment when the middle-class schools relied on it, is ultimately the same sort of question as whether the monitorial system was an innovation, and how much diversity was possible among schools, teachers, curricula and attitudes to children in Victorian England – all questions to which no answers exist.

The second example of silence which results from embarrassment is Marx. Marx's views on the combination of manual work and school have been highly influential in the twentieth century and are constantly quoted in Soviet, Chinese and other analyses of 'polytechnic' education. I would here like to make three points about Marx's theory and his use of the British half-time system to support his case.[28]

First, Marx's use of precedent involved reference to Robert Owen's experience and views – which Marx misrepresented, and to evidence in his favour from the factory inspectors – evidence which he misquoted and distorted (as well as ignoring comments hostile to the half-time system by some factory inspectors and their witnesses, and the solid opposition of the school inspectors). Second, his view of the half-time system was cold-shouldered by the socialist movement from the 1880s, which campaigned against the half-time system as a dehumanizing process. Third, Marx's views on education, their relationship to earlier educational ideas and experience, and their position in Marx's overall views about society have not been researched and analysed in any serious manner. There are implicit in these statements so many possible sources of intellectual discomfort that the reasons for the silence about Marx's educational opinions may not be far to seek. If Marx distorted the evidence on which he based his case for a combination of manual labour and school (which he did), his views on education become more difficult to treat sympathetically. If Marx's views on education do not fit easily into modern – or even nineteenth-century – socialist or progressive thinking on education (which they don't) his educational philosophy becomes difficult to handle. Marx's views on education and labour are pivotal to this theme. Historians have therefore either made assumptions about Marx and failed to test them, or they have fled from the embarrassment and omitted the central feature of Marx's educational position.[29]

Instead of serious historical analysis what the field of Victorian popular education seems to me to reveal is a pragmatism and a conceptual crudity that inhibit proper research and analysis. Historians of education are not, of course, the only historians who have avoided risks to their stereotypes from the controversies in sociology, philosophy and the social sciences generally that might challenge their foundations. Work on Victorian education rests on assumptions about society, social structure, social class, social change, economic and urban development, democracy, power and a host of other conceptual tools, rarely exposed to analysis by the historians using them, but subject to profound controversies amongst social scientists. The combination of pragmatism and unexamined concepts and models constitutes a historical ideology, and it is one that can be seen clearly in operation both in the areas of neglect and in the areas of apparently intensive research in the Victorian period. It is not possible here to discuss ideologies or the sociology of knowledge. The 'aspects of neglect' about which I have made judgements point towards such a discussion, however, and a number of summary points need to be made. First, this is not an illusory argument for raising history 'above ideology'. It is an argument for a greater commitment to exploring the assumptions on which historical research rests – a direction which historians of education have been particularly reluctant to take. Second, it is an argument for recognizing that 'gaps' in knowledge, difficulties in locating sources, shortage of evidence and data, may not be 'technical' explanations of silence and neglect – they may be indications of the historian's inbuilt reluctance to test the difficulties, or even the existence of such obstacles. (I cannot, for example, accept that the absence of research on monitorial schools, pupil teachers, factory children, reformatories, poor law schools, school-community relations, or – to take a different kind of example – the educational activities of the Chartist movement,[30] is purely a question of the lack of resources.) Third, it is certainly not an argument for replacing one ideology by another – setting out to prove something different. E.G. West's attempt to show how unnecessary has been state intervention in English education (in *Education and the Industrial Revolution* and elsewhere),[31] is such an exercise in substitution, a kind of protracted polemic based on little or none of the kind of research for which I am arguing. West uses insecure and selected nineteenth-century statistics, for example, without exploring the controversies to which they were subjected *at the time*, their nineteenth-century meanings. What he produces is an ideologically slanted analysis intended to support a thesis about the contemporary state. The trouble with alternative ideologies of this kind is that they touch upon important questions, but are inhibited from sustained or sensitive research or analysis by the ideological passion. A new 'version' of an old argument is produced, instead of basing an argument in and around new insights into historical reality. West's struggles to overturn accepted pictures of educational developments in the nineteenth century remind us that there are important questions to be asked (including about statistics), but by imposing misleading patterns on his sources, and even on his adversaries' 'accepted pictures', he makes it *more* difficult to answer the questions he raises. The intervening ideology prevents any clarification of the relationships of education and society (or economics or politics) in nineteenth-century England.

A fourth and final point is that the ideological framework in which historians establish their definitions dictates the whole nature of the enterprise. Discussions of English education in the middle of the twentieth century have been overwhelmingly about *the system*, about the structure of the system, about access to the system, about the organization of secondary education, about the organization of universities and teacher education and technical education and the binary system, about numbers and ages of transfer and sizes of school, about percentages and finances, about the policies of political parties, about the structure of examinations, about urban aid and priority areas. Involved in all of this are implications about and interests in the role of the state, the balance of national and local government, the roles of professional experts and the lay public, pressure groups and interest groups and decision-making, the power of the exchequer, manpower forecasting and economic efficiency. Also involved are concepts such as those of rights (of children or of parents), democracy and equality (in relation to educational and social mobility), and freedom (to buy private education). That there are widely differing views about all of these does not hide the fact that this kind of political and ideological discussion has been dominant in education, certainly since the 1930s. In looking for historical explanations of this system and all it entails historians have accepted a set of definitions or terms of reference that have produced most, though certainly not all, historical work on Victorian education. The interests of the twentieth century help to explain the silences about the nineteenth. There are, indeed, historians who have asked questions about the educational content or impact of social movements and the press, architecture and publishing, industry and towns. Overall, however, the historian's perspectives have tended to focus his attention on the growth of the system, people who have demonstrably made contributions to the system, processes which are still discernible in the system, social and economic changes easily (if mechanically) applicable to a discussion of the system.

The diversities and conflicts within our own system have not alerted historians enough to the dangers in the kind of pursuit to which they have been most committed. The dangers of seeing local studies purely as an extension or confirmation of national trends have not been detected (as the large number of local studies undertaken by BEd students, with their inevitable first 'background' and 'national' chapters testify).[32] Historians have not seen the school child as also a family child, a street child, a working child, an aspiring child, an encouraged child, a discouraged child, a bewildered child, a child whose social class, school, urban and other experiences are not necessarily identical to those of similar children elsewhere. The history of 'education' has, certainly in its nineteenth-century format, been of a certain kind of education, one that is divested of such complexities, in which children exist only in a set of conceptual stereotypes, are involved in no relationships, belong only to an 'emergent system', and can by and large be ignored by historians – preferring another discussion of Kay-Shuttleworth and the pupil teacher system or Lowe and the Revised Code (though not a discussion of pupil *teachers* or of the operation of the Revised Code in *practice*).

It is arguable how far historians should extend their definitions to encompass all of Lawrence Cremin's wide sweep of 'configurations'. It is necessary, however, to see education not just 'in context' (with all the lack of relationships that the phrase implies), but in society, as something of society, as forming and being formed by society. It is also necessary to identify educational institutions and processes ('education-bearing phenomena' might be a clumsy way of describing them), workhouses and barracks, churches and factories, pupils' families and community activities, for example, which extend our existing concerns. It is necessary to escape from untested, comfortable assumptions. It is necessary to take difficult paths in research, ones which lead to serious questions about real, complex societies – and which take account of difficulties encountered by social scientists in analysing those complexities. It is necessary to approach educational phenomena with sharper tools of analysis and insight, so as not just to open up questions, but also to be willing to pursue them, whatever the difficulty, the embarrassment, or the discomfort.

Notes

1 See D.K. Jones, 'The Lancashire Public School Association, Later the National Public School Association', Sheffield University MA thesis, 1965, and his *The Making of the Education System 1851-81* (London, 1977), particularly chs 2 and 5; V.G. Toms, 'Secular Education in England 1800-1870', London University PhD thesis, 1972; W.P. McCann, 'Trade Unionist, Co-operative and Socialist Organisations in Relation to Popular Education 1870-1902', Manchester University PhD thesis, 1960.

2 Charles Birchenough, *History of Elementary Education in England and Wales* (London, 1927); J.W. Adamson, *English Education 1789 to 1902* (Cambridge, 1930); Frank Smith, *A History of English Elementary Education 1760-1902* (London, 1931); E. Eaglesham, *From School Board to Local Authority* (London, 1956); P.H.J.H. Gosden, *The Development of English Administration in England and Wales* (Oxford, 1966); Gillian Sutherland, *Policy-Making in Elementary Education, 1870-1895* (London, 1973); Marjorie Cruikshank, *Church and State in English Education 1870 to the Present Day* (London, 1964); James Murphy, *The Religious Problem in English Education* (Liverpool, 1959).

3 See, for example, J.S. Hurt, 'Education and the Working Classes', Society for the Study of Labour History, *Bulletin*, nos 30, 31 and 43; chapter and general bibliographies in John Lawson and Harold Silver, *A Social History of Education in England* (London, 1973).

4 Lawson and Silver, *Social History of Education*.

5 Pamela and Harold Silver, *The Educational of the Poor: The History of a National School 1824-1974* (London, 1974).

6 John Ralph Carr, 'The Origin, Development and Organization of Certain Lancasterian Schools in London, Middlesex and Surrey: A Comparative Study', London University MA thesis, 1963, pp. 41, 423 and *passim*. A recent, valuable contribution to this area of research is Beryl Madoc-Jones. 'Social Implications of Elementary Education 1800-1850, with Particular Reference to the Work of the Monitorial Schools', Exeter University PhD thesis, 1977. Two relevant American theses, using manuscript sources in the United States, are Edward Flavin Wall, 'Joseph Lancaster and the Origins of the British and Foreign School Society', Columbia University PhD thesis, 1966, and Ray C. Rost, 'The Influence of Joseph Lancaster and the Monitorial System on Selected Educational Institutions, 1800-1850', Rutgers University DEd thesis. None of the standard British histories refer to anything other than the publications of the main protagonists and (after 1839) to the *Minutes* of the Committee of Council.

7 W.A.C. Stewart and W.P. McCann, *The Educational Innovators 1750–1880* (London, 1967), for example, does not include the monitorial system as an 'innovation'.

8 L.L. and Jessie Bernard, *Origins of American Sociology: The Social Science Movement in the United States* (New York, 1943) contains a monumental study of the American Social Studies Association and related movements, but does not discuss the Education Department of the ASSA. There are references, but no serious discussion, in Lawrence Ritt, 'The Victorian Conscience in Action: the National Association for the Promotion of Social Science', Columbia University PhD thesis, 1959, and Robert Pemble, 'The National Association for the Promotion of Social Science, 1857–1886: Some Sociological Aspects', Nottingham University MA thesis, 1968. For further discussion, see ch. 5 below.

9 Also secular education, adult education, the teaching of social science and physiology, and many aspects of elementary and grammar school education. For reformatory schools see Eleanor Parkinson, 'The Origins and Development of the Reformatory and Industrial Schools Movement to 1874', Leicester University MA dissertation, 1976.

10 R.G. Bloomer, 'The Ragged School Movement before 1870', Manchester University MEd thesis, 1967, p. 103. The main existing work on ragged schools is unpublished. See, for example, D.H. Webster, 'The Ragged School Movement and the Education of the Poor in the Nineteenth Century', Leicester University PhD thesis, 1971, and E.A.G. Clark, 'The Ragged School Union and the Education of the London Poor in the Nineteenth Century', London University MA thesis, 1967.

11 Census of Great Britain, 1851, *Education in Great Britain* (London, 1854), pp. lxiv–lxvi.

12 A.M. Ross, 'The Care and Education of Pauper Children in England and Wales, 1834 to 1896', London University PhD thesis, 1955. See also J.E. Woods, 'The Development of the Education of Pauper Children in Workhouse Schools (1834–1870)', Leicester University MEd dissertation, 1975. The only relevant published works are: Ray Pallister, 'Workhouse Education in County Durham: 1834–1870', *British Journal of Educational Studies*, vol. XVI, 1968, and Francis Duke, 'Pauper Education', in Derek Fraser (ed.), *The New Poor Law in the Nineteenth Century* (London, 1976) – both only marginally concerned with the content and quality of pauper education.

13 Jo Manton, *Mary Carpenter and the Children of the Streets* (London, 1976) is an excellent study which elucidates her work, but there is much room for wider explorations of her ideas, relationships and areas of concern.

14 Adamson, *English Education 1789 to 1902*, gives a typical summary of Spencer's *Education* without mentioning that he wrote anything else. Stanislav Andreski, *Herbert Spencer: Structure, Function and Evolution* (London, 1971), is a sociologist's account which manages to avoid mentioning Spencer's view of education. For an American example of a fuller awareness of Spencer's social impact see Clarence J. Karier, *Man, Society, and Education* (Glenview, Illinois, 1967).

15 There are two valuable studies of the 1830s: Patricia Hollis, *The Pauper Press: A Study in Working-Class Radicalism of the 1830s* (Oxford, 1970), and Joel H. Wiener, *The War of the Unstamped: The Movement to Repeal the British Newspaper Tax, 1830-1836* (New York, 1969). Two earlier studies made useful beginnings in mapping some of the territory: R.K. Webb, *The British Working Class Reader 1790-1848* (London, 1955), and Richard D. Altick, *The English Common Reader: A Social History of the Mass Reading public 1800-1900* (Chicago, 1957).

16 An important piece of pioneering in this connection was J.H. Higginson, 'The Dame Schools of Great Britain', Leeds University MA thesis, 1939, a slim but valuable pointer in a direction others have not followed.

17 Cheryl Parsons, 'Elementary Education in the Local Community: A Study of Relationships in the Attercliffe Area of Sheffield 1870-1940', Leicester University MEd dissertation, 1975, is a perceptive study of school and community in late nineteenth and twentieth-century Sheffield. The published version is *Schools in an Urban Community: A Study of Carbrook 1870-1965* (London, 1978).

18 For example, Walter E. Houghton, *The Victorian Frame of Mind 1830-1870* (New Haven, 1957), barely acknowledges the existence of ideas about popular education. Historians of ideas as social processes, for example Élie Halévy and Raymond Williams, have not made this mistake.

19 Notably Merle Curti, *The Social Ideas of American Educators* (New York, 1935).

20 The two classic statements are Bernard Bailyn, *Education in the Forming of American Society* (Chapel Hill, 1960), and Lawrence Cremin, *The Wonderful World of Ellwood Patterson Cubberley* (New York, 1965). An excellent outline and discussion of 'revisionist' historiography is R. Freeman Butts, 'Public Education and Political Community', *History of Education Quarterly*, vol. XIV, no. 2. The American historiography of the 1960s and 1970s is the subject of the chapter on 'Public Control, Choice and the State' in Harold Silver, *Education and the Social Condition* (London, 1980).

21 Bailyn, *Education in the Forming of American Society*, pp. 8-13.

22 Cremin, *The Wonderful World of Ellwood Patterson Cubberley*, pp. 17-26.

23 For example, Michael B. Katz, *The Irony of Early School Reform* (Cambridge, Mass., 1968); Marvin Lazerson, *Origins of the Urban School* (Cambridge, Mass., 1971); David Tyack, *The One Best System* (Cambridge, Mass., 1974); Carl F. Kaestle, *The Evolution of an Urban School System* (Cambridge, Mass., 1973); Diane Ravitch, *The Great School Wars* (New York, 1974). Ravitch's later work - notably her *The Revisionists Revised: Studies in the Historiography of American education* (New York, 1977) - has been critical of the radical revisionists, but *The Great School Wars* was an exercise in reinterpretation.

24 Lawrence A. Cremin, *Public Education* (New York, 1976), p. 58; Cremin, *American Education: The Colonial Experience*, p. 11.

25 Richard Johnson, 'Educational Policy and Social Control in early Victorian England', *Past and Present*, no. 49, 1970.

26 P. J. Rooke, 'A Study of Rewards and Punishments in the Elementary

Schools of England and Wales, 1800–1893', London University MA thesis, 1962.

27 An example is Manton, *Mary Carpenter and the Children of the Streets*, which stresses the dominance of punishment in Victorian schools, but draws its examples from *middle*-class schools, and suggests that 'very few people questioned that it was right, proper, and for the child's own good' (p. 3). When Mary Carpenter at mid-century rejects the use of corporal punishment (p. 87), the author does not see the discrepancy and the question that need to be investigated.

28 See ch. 2.

29 Two studies that have approached these issues have evaded them: Brian Simon, 'Karl Marx and Education', in *Intelligence, Psychology and Education: A Marxist Critique* (London, 1971), and Edmund and Ruth Frow, *A Survey of the Half-Time System in Education* (Manchester, 1970). See below, pp. 48–51.

30 No serious, extended work on Chartism and education has been done since R. A. Jones, 'Knowledge Chartism', Birmingham University MA thesis, 1938. There is almost nothing on education in the contributions on local history to Asa Briggs (ed.), *Chartist Studies* (London, 1959). Although there is a section on Chartism and education in David Jones, *Chartism and the Chartists* (London, 1975), it serves to underline the paucity of research on the considerable educational activities and impact of the Chartist movement. How such studies might develop is suggested by a chapter on Chartism in Maureen Greenwood, 'Education and Politics in Leicester 1828–1850', Leicester University MEd dissertation, 1973.

31 E.G. West, *Education and the Industrial Revolution* (London, 1975).

32 Norman Morris, 'The Contribution of Local Investigations to Historical Knowledge', in History of Education Society, *Local Studies and the History of Education* (London, 1972), argues that local studies, as carried out mainly by students, have no value. Morris also sees local as mainly an extension of national educational analysis – seeing the question purely as one of policy. J.R. Carr's thesis on monitorial schools shows how important local studies, differently conceived, can be (see note 6 above).

2 Ideology and the factory child: attitudes to half-time education

The half-time system offers a particularly sharp illustration of the ideological imprints made on education by the nineteenth-century protagonists, and therefore the difficulties and discomforts of later analysis. It also suggests some further reflections on questions of historical silence and neglect. As a phenomenon on the borderline between education and industrial development, on the battleground of social reform, individual initiative and competition, and the intervention of the state, it presents particular dangers and difficulties of interpretation. It stands, as we have suggested, outside what has often been taken to be the legitimate sphere of interest of the historian of education – the antecedents of the state system of education which became triumphant in the late nineteenth century. The half-time system was at the centre of debate from the 1850s about the desirability and possible forms of compulsory schooling. It related to the development both of legislation and of inspection. It impinged directly on the concerns of the labour movement in the late nineteenth century, and it produced divergent and contradictory responses, based in the main on different sectional interests. It fed into Marxist and therefore into international debate. It has, like the reformatory and the workhouse school, been for the most part lost from sight in the concerns of historians of education.

The half-time system, foreshadowed in the early Factory Acts and effective from 1845, began as a strategy for combating excessive child labour and became, in the 1850s and 1860s, an educational theory. Its basis was described by one of the first factory inspectors as 'combining school education with an industrial education in a wages-yielding employment'.[1] It began as an instrument of the state for the protection of children in certain kinds of employment. The half-time system was attacked as an industrial measure when, especially in the last quarter of the century, opinion turned in favour of achieving compulsory education for all by other means. Discussion of the half-time system has been previously concerned primarily with the tactics of its early introduction and with the politics of its later decline and defeat.[2] Between the two, however, considerable interest was shown in the educational implications of the half-time process: evidence was accumulated, educational theories were elaborated, ideological positions were adopted. It is with these, and with the effects of the system on the children, that we are mainly concerned.

The principle of education for factory children was introduced in the 1802 Health and Morals of Apprentices Act, and that of a minimum age for factory employment was enacted in 1819: the first 'protected children, being apprentices, against their masters. The second protected all children against their parents.'[3] Neither was in any important sense successful. Under the Factories Act of 1833 children between the ages of nine and eleven (rising to thirteen over a two-year period) employed in the main textile industries were to receive two hours' schooling on six days a week. The factory inspectors appointed under the Act soon complained of the difficulties of implementing the law.[4]

The Factories Act of 1844 crystallized the half-time system emerging under the previous legislation. It lowered the age of employment to eight, but provided for half a day's (normally three hours) education, five days a week, for children employed in textiles, up to the age of thirteen (eleven in the case of silk mills). Firms could, if they preferred, provide five hours' education on alternate days. The early inspectors tried to enforce what one of them, Leonard Horner, more than once described as 'attendance within four walls of a room called a school', over the quality of which they had no control.[5] The Factory Acts were extended to cover children in other sectors – printworks in 1845 (children having to attend school for at least thirty days each half year), mining, bleaching and dyeing in 1860 and lace in 1861. In 1864 the potteries children were 'brought under discipline'.[6] In 1867 foundries, metal, tobacco and other industries were covered, as were workshops employing fifty or more workers. In 1870 printworks, dyeing and bleaching were assimilated into the Factory Acts. In 1874 the minimum age of employment was raised to ten, and children covered by the Factory Acts who had not attained a given standard of education by the age of thirteen were required to stay at school another year. The disparities and confusions produced by the mid-1870s were summarized by an inspector of schools, pointing out that industrial legislation required

> the attendance of children up to 13, the Mines Act, for some unaccountable reason, releasing them from all obligation to attend school at 12 years of age. The Workshops' Act, again, requires five hours a week less school attendance than the Factory Act; and they all differ from the requirements of school boards acting under the Education Act.[7]

The factory and workshops legislation was consolidated in 1878. The 1870 Education Act and the principle of compulsory attendance enacted in 1876 and 1880 resulted in stronger pressures to raise the minimum age of employment, and to ensure full-time schooling for all children, but the half-time system was to continue until 1918.

The provision of education for factory children was rare before the 1833 Act. Some mills did provide schooling for the children they employed or provided pre-employment education.[8] After 1833 some employers were anxious to comply with the Act. Horner, for example, met with a willing response among many cotton mill-owners, notably Henry McConnel, Manchester's largest cotton spinner, who established what Horner described as an 'excellent school', attending three hours a day to the children's 'religious and moral training and habits of order, good breeding, and cleanliness and attention to neatness in dress'.[9] Before 1833 the Strutts tried to employ only children who had received education in the firm's day school. Factory education often included a requirement to attend Sunday school and religious worship: in 1839 it was reported that young persons under sixteen at Strutts' had for several years been 'required to attend the Sunday school'.[10] Even after 1833 progress was slow and sporadic. A visitor to Wood and Walker's school for their mill children at Bradford in 1841 reported on the generous school provisions which the schoolmaster 'evidently took a pleasure in showing me',[11] but such reports were rare. Horner's report on his district in 1839 contained both McConnel's 'excellent school', one where children were taught by the fireman, 'and there are many intermediate grades'.[12] Evidence of apathy and inefficiency was abundant in the early 1840s. From the 1844 Act employers were also faced with the question of whether to send the children to local schools or provide their own. Only gradually did the educational content of the half-time system become a matter of widespread interest. In the 1840s discussion about the half-time system was primarily concerned with its role in limiting and therefore humanizing child labour.

Discussion of the educational value of the system was a feature of the late 1850s and 1860s. It was discussed, for example, at an educational conference in London in 1857.[13] Between 1859 and 1865 its educational significance was analysed at the National Association for the Promotion of Social Science (NAPSS) by such well-known figures as Nassau and Edward Senior, Mary Carpenter, Edward Wilks – Secretary of the British and Foreign School Society – and former HMI Seymour Tremenheere. The Newcastle Commission asked for opinions about the system in a questionnaire in 1860. Edwin Chadwick compiled some 75,000 words of evidence on the system which he submitted together with a commentary to Nassau Senior, a member of the Commission. Chadwick's interest had stemmed from an address he intended to give to the NAPSS in 1859.[14] In 1861 Senior published the documents he had drafted for the Commission in *Suggestions on Popular Education*, in which the half-time system featured prominently. The ideas of this quasi-pressure group, together with reports by the factory inspectors, were used by Marx in drafting a document for the First International in 1864, and in the first volume of *Capital*, published in German in 1867. The same sources were used by J.M. Ludlow and Lloyd Jones in their book on the *Progress of the Working Class 1832–67*, published in the same year. The discussion of the half-time system across these ten or so years is the centre-piece of any analysis of the process of half-time education.

The half-time system was intended, in Chadwick's words, 'as a primary security against overwork; inasmuch as if we secured their presence in school for three hours, we prevented their presence for that time in the workshop'.[15] The system was rooted in the controversies and campaigns of the 1830s and 1840s over the factory system, and especially over working hours and child labour. Our concern here is with the range of arguments used in support of half-time education.

The early reports of the factory inspectors describe attempts to provide factory schools, and their conviction that the half-time system represented major progress. Even in the late 1850s and 1860s the view was being constantly expressed that half-time education was better than none. In 1861, for example, factory inspector Robert Baker stressed that in Lancashire and Cheshire 'but for the provisions of the Factory Act, the numbers of uneducated children . . . must be greatly increased'. Three years later he declared that 'the half-time Act is a godsend to the Potteries, it being the only opportunity whereby the poor children can gain any education'.[16] A correspondent told Chadwick that schoolmasters and other witnesses in Rochdale agreed 'that the half-time system has given to the children of these districts an education which they most certainly would not have obtained if long school hours had been required'. HMI Tufnell told him that 'the question with the parents frequently is, education on the half-time plan, or no education at all'.[17]

A second, increasingly explicit set of arguments related to the system's likely moral and social utility. Mill-owners were discovering what others had discovered before them – that education could be a useful, socially manipulative instrument. 'Many of the mill-owners', reported one of the factory inspectors in 1839, 'who now approve of education, were among those who formerly deemed the application of it almost impossible, and not likely to be in the least degree beneficial'.[18] Once its utility was realized the important questions became how much education, and of what kind? When the factory inspectors reported on the effects of the 1833 education clauses they offered evidence that the prevailing answers to these questions were as little as necessary, and of a kind to instil right moral attitudes. An extreme version was that expressed by a firm of cotton manufacturers in Derbyshire: 'We are of opinion that it is more conducive to the welfare of our people to endeavour to make them enlightened Christians than wise in wordly knowledge; we do not want statesmen in our factories, but orderly subjects.' At a flax spinners in Westmorland education was said to have improved 'the conduct and habits of subordination of the factory hands generally, which is very observable in the disuse of bad language, their orderly behaviour, neat and cleanly appearance, and increased diligence in the attendance of places of worship'. Education counteracted bad home influences, inculcated desirable moral attitudes, and led to a 'thorough knowledge of the nature and sins of lying, stealing, swearing and the like'. At least one school was also seen as an instrument of punishment for behaviour *in the factory*: at a cotton spinners near Bury the conduct of the children in the factory was reported to the school, where necessary punishment was inflicted, and 'general conduct is improved thereby, and ... the school discipline is acknowledged beyond the precincts of the school'.[19]

The importance of this second set of arguments lies in its precise and confident assertion of the long-standing effects of half-time education – in terms, for example, of punctuality, obedience and other virtues. Education would *make* enlightened Christians and orderly subjects, thereby protecting the industrial system, society itself. Edward Wilks offered such a perspective when he saw the need for the half-time principle to 'be defended on the grounds of common humanity, social progress, and public security'.[20] Such arguments were not, of course, confined to the half-time system. Social discipline and 'public security' were familiar touchstones in debates about industry and education. At the end of the 1860s even a prominent voice in the National Education League could talk about children at work 'learning lessons of order, obedience, and industry in a factory, shop, or office'.[21] Most nineteenth-century English educationists saw a continuum between questions of popular education and those of social order.

A third cluster of arguments in favour of the half-time system concerned its contribution to the future well-being of the workers. This was often a subsidiary to other arguments, but occasionally the welfare and even the social mobility of the factory child became a focus of discussion. Mobility related, for example, to opportunities that were mentioned for children to become pupil teachers. The basic argument, however, was the future role of the working-class child in industry, and incidentally the prosperity of the economy. Employers and school-masters testified to Chadwick, for example, that boys who began work early 'begat a greater aptitude and readiness in any employment they may be called to'. Farmers found that boys who had combined education with out-of-doors work were 'much better servants than the mere school-boy'. Mary Carpenter thought one of the chief problems was 'how best to prepare the young person for the future work of life', and Edward Senior explained that he and his fellow Poor Law Commissioners believed it to be of the greatest importance that 'children who have to live by their labour should be trained to labour early ... boys should be accustomed to work at the earliest practicable age'.[22] Some factory children did graduate from half-time education to higher-status occupations: a Rochdale teacher reported, for instance that of his half-timers 'one is an Independent minister at Barlow-on-Humber, one a Baptist minister in America, another in the same country as an Independent; three clerks in one establishment, and several others in different country houses in the town'.[23] The numbers making such a transition must have been minute, but any such educational development in the nineteenth century caused unease somewhere that working-class children were being educated 'above their station'. The head of a half-time school in Manchester thought that a child's education 'must be adapted, as far as possible, to his probable future position in society', which meant that 'it should not be so extended as to make him vain and conceited'. HMI Tufnell recorded that many people objected that children were being over-educated at half-time schools, 'but my reply has always been, that I never wished them to receive more education than is necessary to ensure that they shall never become paupers again'. Mary Carpenter, discussing working-class children, thought 'the study of languages and other branches of knowledge which require great length of time, is not necessary for this class'.[24] She told the NAPSS in 1861 that in the education of such children 'there must be nothing to pamper self-indulgence, to raise the child in his own estimation above his natural position in society'.[25] Even the most eager supporters of the half-time system had a clear notion of the limits beyond which education should not go, limits related to the 'natural' structures of society.

Other declared reasons for support for the half-time system included important claims – to which we shall return – for combined manual and intellectual effort. Reasons for support were not always, however, clear or unambiguous. Few respondents to the Newcastle Commission's questionnaire were able to explain their attitude to the system. Of the fifty-nine published replies from educationists, headmasters, clergymen and others, only twenty-one can be construed as positively supporting the half-time system: thirty either failed to answer the question about it or declared their inability to do so. Those who expressed support did so generally with vague expressions of its being 'very valuable' or suited to manufacturing districts or worthy of trial.

Support for the system went together with a defence of its efficiency or effectiveness. Examples of efficient half-time schools, or of schools which effectively combined half-time and full-time education, were publicized by HMIs, interested manufacturers and others in the 1850s.[26] The reputation of such schools, and of those which had operated since before 1844, began to increase confidence in the system. Fresh claims began to be made for it, particularly as, by the late 1850s and 1860s, it was widely held that the quality of available schools was improving.

Edward Wilks summarized the optimistic view in 1859 by declaring that results had 'proved the principle sound in theory, wise in legislation, and practical in working': schools were now more widespread and more efficient.[27] The Newcastle Commission commented that 'the difficulties of providing efficient education are not so great now as they were in 1833'.[28] Nassau Senior, as a member of the Newcastle Commission, criticized the quality of the education of most half-timers, but in the mid-1860s Tremenheere pointed to 'a very great improvement' in the schools since Senior's comments.[29] Chadwick's documents for the Newcastle Commission were designed to show that the half-time system was working efficiently. HMIs and factory inspectors occasionally reported broadly to the same effect. In 1861 the secretary of the NAPSS wrote that the half-time system would soon 'be established over the whole country. This is one of the subjects on which the quiet influence of the Association . . . had been productive of great benefit'.[30] A group within the NAPSS had convinced it, mainly on the basis of Chadwick's evidence, that the system was being increasingly successful. Charles Kingsley, like others connected with the Association, considered the matter proven: the half-time system had been 'proved to work so well . . . by so many able judges, and especially by my friend . . . Mr Chadwick, in his letter to Mr Senior, of 1861'.[31]

Triumphant claims made for the half-time system and the evidence on which they rested concealed uncertainties. They also produced counter-claims. Although later in the century criticism of the system was to be directed primarily against its role in perpetuating child labour, in the 1850s and 1860s the most frequently expressed concern was about the system's inefficiency or failure. The main complaints were directed against the effect of the system on National and British schools. HMIs reported that the attendance of factory children disrupted the work of the schools.[32] There was some support for the idea of isolating half-timers in separate schools, though there were practical difficulties.[33] Some schools refused to admit half-timers or made them unwelcome.[34] Evidence to the Cross Commission confirmed the complaint that 'the admixture of half-timers with the whole-time scholars injures the organization and working of the school'.[35]

Reservations about the system's effectiveness sometimes led to stronger statements. Wilks, in 1859, thought that 'the educational results have not been as satisfactory as might be desired'. Baker was frank about the system's deficiencies, whilst defending it against 'any who may speak . . . of education in combination with labour as a failure'.[36] Voluntaryists who had since the 1843 bill opposed state involvement in education naturally attacked the half-time system. In 1856 the chairman of a voluntaryist meeting criticized laudatory comments by Lord John Russell about the system, on the grounds that half-timers 'were very indifferent to teaching, and came to school half asleep after their half-day's work, whilst they disregarded the institution also, because it was forced on them by law'.[37] Whatever welcome school inspectors gave to the educational clauses of the Factory Acts they were aware of the often crippling effects of the system on schools attended by half-time children, but also of its inadequacy for the half-timers themselves. In 1851 Morell found 'the most conflicting reports among schoolmasters' as to the possibility of communicating a 'satisfactory amount of mental culture to the children' once they had begun work in the factories: the results were 'very discouraging'. Education for factory children, he found, was 'far from what education ought to be, and far from giving any cause of congratulation as to the future history of the scholars now under instruction'. The tiredness of the children (especially when attending in the afternoons) was, said another HMI, one of the main 'hindrances to the progress of education'. A third felt 'unable to speak with the unhesitating confidence of some better authorities' and thought 'experience thus far affords little ground for an expectation that the half-time system will produce a working population fairly educated'.[38]

Such reservations about the adequacy and effectiveness of half-time education were being expressed from the 1850s. Factory inspector Redgrave concluded in 1857 that it possessed 'in the abstract, all the elements of success; but in practice it has entirely failed'. Neither employers nor parents had understood its purpose: 'it is not looked upon as a system of education, but as an adjunct to employment'.[39] Horner in 1857 was defending the system against those who had 'confidently stated on various occasions that the long-tried experiment in the factories has proved a failure',[40] and many of the respondents to the Newcastle Commission's enquiry thought the system of doubtful value. In the absence of legislation to improve the quality of schools, Chadwick himself was bound to admit that half-time education had by the end of the 1850s been 'extensively nominal and illusory, and often fraudulent. From officers who have seen only the failures, the majority of cases, you will get testimony that the half-school time is an utter failure.'[41] The campaign in support of half-time education had to reckon with its known drawbacks and with sustained doubts and criticisms.[42]

At the centre of discussion emerged a comparison of the relative effectiveness of full-time and half-time education. This involved a comparison not only of the standards reached, but also of such factors as attendance, since the enforced regular attendance of many half-timers could compensate for their lack of previous education. Given the problems of securing regular attendance at elementary schools generally, factory children may have had a better attendance record than full-timers. The discussion came to pivot, however, round the possibility that half-time education not only might be better than nothing, but might actually be more effective than full-time education. Attitudes to the education and culture to be transmitted to factory children were implied, and sometimes made explicit, in the discussions about the merits of half-time and full-time education.

From the beginning claims were made that half-timers fared educationally as well as, or even better than, full-timers. In 1839 factory inspector Saunders reported testimonies from two mills that half-time children often made 'as great progress' or 'very frequently as much progress as the others'.[43] The Newcastle Commission heard that schoolmasters thought 'half-time teaching is far more nearly equal to full-time than would be supposed. Some go so far as to assert that it is "very nearly as good"'.[44] Chadwick's 'Communications' to the Commission contain repeated claims as to the 'relative superiority of the short-time school children', who were 'quite equal' to the full-timers, 'nearly equal' or 'fully equal in attainments', 'not quite up to the full-timers, but there is really very little difference', or made 'greater progress than the full-timers'. Half-timers are described as giving 'more fixed attention'. They 'come fresh from work to school, and they go fresh from school to work'. One witness calculates the ratio of attainment as 'about five to seven of the full-day scholars'.[45] Similar claims are echoed in the reports of the factory and school inspectors.[46] Chadwick himself believed that half-timers made greater progress than full-timers and developed a 'superior habit of mental activity'. He thought the evidence 'of all the best teachers . . . clear and decisive' on this score.[47]

These claims were contradicted – often in the same places as the ones we have quoted – though not as part of a coherent counter-campaign. While factory inspector Saunders was quoting positive evidence in 1839 his colleague T.J. Howell was reporting that 'in schools admitting Factory children together with other pupils, the latter, so far as my inquiries have extended, invariably outstrip the former'. One (though only one) of Chadwick's witnesses confessed that in his school the full-time scholars were 'certainly in advance of the half-time scholars, and get on faster' – and he accounted for this by reference to differences in the social backgrounds of the children.[48] The master of the Birkbeck secular school at Peckham told the Newcastle Commission that 'after you have done all that the half-time system will enable you to do, children are turned out much less efficient in school matters than they would be if they had the whole time' – a view which Nassau Senior rejected on the 'remarkably full and complete' evidence as to the equality of half-timers and full-timers in good schools.[49] The Newcastle Assistant Commissioner who reported positive views also attacked the extravagance of some claims for the system: teachers admitted universally, he stated, that 'under similar conditions of attendance, half-time teaching cannot, as some enthusiasts have said, produce as great a result as full-time'.[50] Inspector Baker quoted a witness whose views he thought deserved respect, and who talked of the opinion 'gaining ground that "half-timers are almost as proficient in their studies as day scholars"; in this opinion I cannot concur'. The opinion had, in the witness's view, 'taken possession of the minds of certain learned but not very practical men'. Baker quoted views on the factors which affected differences of attainment between full-timers and half-timers – different intellectual, moral and other powers among the two groups, their family backgrounds, visual and verbal abilities and memories.[51]

The school inspectors also provided evidence as to the relative backwardness of half-time children. J.G. Fitch, for example, in 1864 made a forthright ' protest against the extravagant claims which are sometimes made for the half-time system'. Factory children might often learn relatively more than full-timers, but 'that they learn absolutely more, or nearly as much, is, I think, a mischievous fallacy'.[52]

The Code regulations sharpened hostility to the half-time system among teachers from the early 1860s, because the same grant-earning standards were required of the half-time children.[53] The HMIs' reports, particularly in the 1860s, and evidence later to the Cross Commission and in the pages of *The Schoolmaster*, show that teachers, resentful of payment by results, found the Code regulations for half-timers particularly unfair.[54]

The critics of exaggerated claims for the half-time system produced not a comprehensive explanation of the relative success of some half-timers, but occasional insights. Baker's reports show an awareness that half-timers from better homes performed better. Half-timers also had an advantage over full-timers in being older.[55] Since factory children tended to start school from a lower educational base line, they might be seen to be making comparatively rapid progress.[56] Their regular attendance was seen to be a factor. An argument pressed by *The Schoolmaster* from the 1880s was that half-timers only did comparatively well because full-timers did comparatively badly. Full-timers in Bradford, for instance, had 'no further advantage over half-timers than of getting the same lesson twice over. They are not carried forward to any new educational ground.' Full-timers in Oldham, similarly, were 'merely double half-timers', having 'no educational advantages beyond the iteration of the work which the others get at intervals'.[57] When a commentator in 1907 talked of the repetition of lessons and of day scholars having to 'mark time' for the half-timers,[58] he was describing what had always been true. Only the most perceptive witness would have seen the force of 'double half-timer' much before the 1880s.

Nevertheless, evidence accumulated to defend the half-time system was received relatively uncritically in earlier decades, when the Factory Acts needed to be shown to be working. Contrary evidence and critical views were, as we have seen, available.

Some of these considerations explain the appearance at the end of the 1850s of the group of half-time enthusiasts whom we have seen described as 'learned but not very practical men'.

Chadwick was the crucial figure. In 1861 Lord Brougham described Chadwick's collection of 'Communications' on the subject as 'an event in the history of education'.[59] Chadwick compiled this collection of interviews and statements to show, among other things, the number of hours he and his witnesses thought children could sustain attention, and to justify a preference for half-time over full-time education. Others joined him as campaigners, and Chadwick's 'Communications' was their campaign guide.

The witnesses questioned by Chadwick tended to agree that three hours a day was the maximum period for what a British schoolmaster called 'bright voluntary attention' on the part of the children. Most witnesses thought three hours was the number that would 'suffice', would secure 'concentrated and willing attention', and would not exhaust the children's 'capacity of attention'. Some witnesses suggested how the three hours might best be divided up or discussed the different spans of attention of children of different ages.[60] A factory schoolmaster spoke of the 'common opinion of school teachers that school time in such (full-time) schools is much wasted in the afternoons'.[61] Chadwick's own commentary underlined that full-time schooling was mentally and physically injurious.

Mary Carpenter, one of Victorian England's authorities on the education of the poor, made the social class basis of her psychology explicit: she told Chadwick that 'in the higher or more cultivated classes, where the organization is more adapted to mental exercise, and the culture of the intellectual powers is essential to after life, I do not think eight hours per diem too much to be employed in direct instruction'. On the other hand, she believed 'three hours per diem of good scholastic instruction would be amply sufficient for the children of the working classes, and of the neglected classes, if I may so call that class below them'. She told the NAPSS that it had been 'proved that three hours daily of direct intellectual instruction is quite as profitable as a longer period, and even more so' - calling the witnesses of the Newcastle Commission to her support.[62] At the same meeting Edward Senior quoted the Chadwick evidence - and Mary Carpenter's - with especial enthusiasm, commenting that 'of the six hours' school, nearly two or three hours are real literary labour, and three or four enforced sedentary idleness'.[63] Leonard Horner thought that lengthening the school day for factory children would be 'an entire mistake' since the effect would be 'that their prolonged confinement and wearisome activity would render the school still more hateful to them'.[64] Nassau Senior told the NAPSS in 1863 that - in full-time schools, for all social classes - 'we are employing labour on the part of our masters, and time, health and energy on the part of our children not only fruitlessly but absolutely mischievously'. Repeated assertions were often referred to as proof.[65]

The three-hour philosophy was not without its critics. Inspector Baker reported in full the critic who argued against the 'very able men' who favoured a maximum of three hours' mental effort. Children's minds were already taxed for only a small proportion of the day - in fact by scriptural knowledge and arithmetic, not by less demanding reading and writing. HMI Fitch considered 'the opinion of some philanthropists that five hours at school per day, for five days a week, is too much for a healthy child' to be a 'wholly imaginary' evil.[66] The educational theory born of the half-time system drew, of course, on the pervasive opinion that popular education should reach out for only limited objectives. The question for Chadwick was not how long 'the children of the labouring classes may be kept in school', but 'in how short a time they may receive elementary instruction, and be freed from it'.[67] This is a profoundly important concept. Even more than was common in discussion of elementary education Chadwick was here postulating an educational optimum for working-class children: once it was attained, they could be 'freed' from education.

The argument for a 'sufficient' education was an interpretation of the class function of education. This was also expressed clearly in related support for drill as a school activity, particularly by Chadwick. Half-time began to be interpreted as any combination of mental and manual work (including, in some cases, needlework), or even of book learning and drill. Drawing especially on the experience of naval and military schools, Chadwick saw the half-time system as including a major component of drill.[68] The cultural and social intentions of the advocacy of drill were precise, typified by the witness who told Chadwick that it was an important way to 'maintain the attention, and insure decorum and promptitude'. Drilled boys were 'prompt, obedient, and punctual', and less inclined to mischief and insubordination. One vivid description of the effects of drill contrasted 'the loutish bearing of the Lancashire lad and the firm, erect, respectful, and self-respecting carriage and behaviour of the same person after he had been thoroughly disciplined and polished by the military drill'.[69] Nassau Senior thought the effect of drill 'a remarkable educational phenomenon', and it began to be seen even as an alternative to industrial experience, and as a contribution to national defence.[70]

From the outset Horner and others had hinted at the educational soundness of combining mental and industrial activity. Much subsequent discussion underpinned such a theory, which was elaborated by factory inspectors, in contributions to the NAPSS, in evidence to the Newcastle Commission, by Chadwick, Mary Carpenter and Nassau Senior, and by Marx and Engels.

Marx and Engels's use of this theory was based partly on the evidence and views we have discussed, and partly on educational views given particular emphasis in early nineteenth-century Britain by Robert Owen. In his *Condition of the Working Class* (published in German in 1845) Engels criticized the failure adequately to implement the educational provisions of the 1844 Act: 'the attempt to introduce compulsory education for factory children has failed, since the Government did not provide good schools'.[71] This was almost exactly the standpoint that Horner had adopted after 1833. In *The Communist Manifesto* in 1848 Marx and Engels went further and called for 'public and free education for all children. Abolition of factory work for children in its present form. Education and material production to be combined'.[72] They had seen in the Factory Acts the herald of a future pattern of education. Marx was receptive to ideas and experience in this field, and in 1866 expressed the theory more firmly, considering 'the tendency of modern industry to make children and juvenile persons of both sexes co-operate in the great work of social production, as a progressive, sound and legitimate tendency'. This tendency had been 'distorted into an abomination' by capitalism, but in a rational state of society every child from the age of nine 'ought to become a productive labourer', though protected against excessive hours of labour. For Marx education now contained three elements – mental education, bodily education ('such as is given in schools of gymnastics, and by military exercise') and technological training ('which imparts the general principles of all processes of production'). Marx had adopted a great deal from the discussions of the half-time system in the early 1860s, and turned it into a conviction that 'the combination of paid productive labour, mental education, bodily exercise and polytechnic training, will raise the working class far above the level of the higher and middle classes'.[73]

Capital, published in German the following year, contained a similar discussion, quoting from Inspector Baker and Nassau Senior. The 'paltry' education clauses of the Factory Act, said Marx, 'provided for the first time the possibility of combining education and gymnastics with manual labour'. The factory inspectors had discovered that 'the factory children, although receiving only one half the education of the regular day scholars, yet learnt quite as much and often more'. Senior had shown the monotony and uselessness of long school hours; Robert Owen had shown the factory system to contain 'the germ of an education that will, in the case of every child over a given age, combine productive labour with instruction and gymnastics, not only as one of the methods of adding to the efficiency of production, but as the only method of producing fully developed human beings'.[74] In 1875 Marx wrote that

> A general prohibition of child labour is incompatible with the existence of large-scale industry . . . Its realization – if it were possible – would be reactionary, since, with a strict regulation of the working time according to the different age groups and other safety measures for the protection of children, an early combination of productive labour with education is one of the most potent means for the transformation of present day society.[75]

The objective no longer lay in the future. Ten years later Engels defended Marx's view, rejecting technical education in schools, opposing a view that it should replace gymnastics, and quoting *Capital* against what he considered a weaker programme of educational reform.[76]

A full discussion of the use that Marx in particular made of the theory of 'combined' education would require detailed discussion of the educational views of Owen and other early nineteenth-century radical educators, and of how far Marx, intepreting Owen, diverged from him. It would need to show that Owen was not concerned with – and in fact resisted – early paid employment, but with education as a preliminary to occupying a place in a changed society. It would need to show that Marx's 'early combination of productive labour with education' does not derive from the tradition he claimed for it.[77]

More important, Marx selected only positive statements from Senior and Baker, and used them uncritically. Marx claimed, quoting from Baker's 1865 report, that

> The factory inspectors soon found out by questioning the school-masters, that the factory children, although receiving only one half the education of the regular day scholars, yet learnt quite as much and often more. 'This can be accounted for by the simple fact that, with only being at school for one half of the day, they are always fresh . . . The system on which they work, half manual labour, and half school, renders each employment a rest and a relief to the other.'[78]

The quotation in this passage is not, in fact, from Baker, but from one witness quoted by Baker, in a report which contained opposite testimony from other teachers. Marx's view of what the factory inspectors had found out is also misleading, since – as we have seen – they reported conflicting evidence, and Baker himself had in other reports quoted critical attacks on the half-time system. Marx ignored the criticism and the critics, and gave the impression of impregnable support by the factory inspectors (which was certainly not true of Redgrave, for example), and he completely ignored the evidence of the school inspectors. It is true, as Baker points out, that in the early 1860s opinion was 'very strong in the direction, that wherever children are employed at all, education shall be combined with labour'.[79] Marx's use of Senior and Baker reflected this trend in public opinion, but his assertions that half-timers were 'always fresh' and experienced 'a rest and a relief' through the system did not reflect the disquiet that already existed about such evidence even while Chadwick was collecting it. HMI Stokes reflected the basically contradictory and inconclusive nature of the kind of evidence Marx accepted when he concluded in 1868 that 'the time seems opportune for some inquiry into the effects of the half-time system upon the children themselves as well as upon the schools which they frequent'.[80] Marx clung to the most optimistic reading of his sources, as no doubt did the secretary of the Catholic Poor School Committee, who justified the half-time system by reference to the combination of agricultural labour and mental cultivation in the Benedictine and Cistercian monasteries.[81]

By the 1880s the 'half manual labour, and half school' system was being widely condemned, as having 'no intellectual advantage',[82] at the Cross Commission, by socialist organizations,[83] and in *The Schoolmaster*. In 1891, when the half-time system was presented as a combination of school and technical education which 'sharpens the children's wits' - an argument used from Horner in the 1830s to Marx in the 1860s - A.J. Mundella called the theory 'one of the most preposterous fallacies ever trotted out by an interested class to hoodwink the community'.[84]

Margaret McMillan described the half-timers' school in 1906 as, at best, 'a place where Hope becomes so very moderate that Ambition dies'.[85] The following year the half-timer was described as 'practically condemned (unless unusually intelligent) to unskilled and low-paid labour for life'.[86] Both of these were true for the whole period during which the system operated. Half-timers were often said to be from the lowest, poorest strata of the working class. As early as 1846 an HMI mentions that full-timers' parents sometimes removed their children from school, 'afraid of contact and contamination from their poorer school-fellows' who came as half-timers. The Newcastle Commission heard from Rochdale and Bradford that half-timers 'spring from a lower grade of society than the day scholars'. Factory inspectors reported teachers' comments that half-timers who had not previously attended school were 'generally of an inferior class, frequently depraved', or were 'the children of negligent or improvident parents, or orphans, and otherwise destitute'.[87] Mary Carpenter, as we have seen, distinguished between 'the children of the working classes, and of the neglected classes, if I may so call that class below them'. The reality for these children was summed up by the Bradford teacher who commented in 1884 - though it could have been said at any time during this period - on the meagre amount of learning acquired by the half-timer: he was 'inclined to think it will be sufficient to meet the wants of their case. It must not be forgotten what they are likely to remain, and the stations they will fill in life'.[88] The half-time system was an important means of cementing the hierarchy of stations of life.

Given the extreme poverty of most half-timers' parents, the half-timer acquired an early status as wage-earner, and developed a characteristic behaviour resulting from this sense of independence. In the 1860s there were references to the fact that early half-time employment induced insubordination not found among full-time pupils: half-timers 'bring into school rude manners and clothes; they are less amenable to discipline than others, as in fact they pay for themselves'.[89] The children were learning adult roles and behaviour in the factory, whilst at school – in many cases being attended for the first time – they were children. In necessitous families their wage-earning capacity resulted in prematurely adult behaviour. Fullest evidence is available from the 1880s, but again it is equally applicable to earlier decades.

The Schoolmaster quoted a report on the behaviour patterns of half-timers in Bradford:

> I have watched children enter the mill for the first time, come to this school bright, happy, obedient, and with every desire to win the approbation of their teachers. This gradually gives place to feelings of indifference and carelessness, which rapidly degenerate into obstinacy and a disposition to resist any authority.[90]

Half-timers, the Cross Commission heard from one witness, 'already make their money, and they are inclined to insubordination'. Their factory-acquired 'sharpness', said another witness, made them 'more ambitious to baffle and defy the teacher than to make educational progress'. Mixing with older boys in the mill weakened 'their willingness to subject themselves to anything like school discipline'. The witness had seen parents cry 'because of the change in conduct of their children', resulting in 'heartless impudence', because children could remind their parents 'that they are earning their own living and ought to be their own masters'. The children became 'too worldly for their age'.[91] All of these must have been true of earlier decades, as was the comment in 1907 that half-timers 'become clever at repartee and in the use of "mannish" phrases . . . They lose their childish habits.'[92]

For these and other reasons the schools themselves aimed at rigidly defined patterns of social and cultural behaviour. The adequacy of three hours' education a day was expressed in terms of a very low cultural level at which schools for half-timers should aim. Good half-time teaching from nine to thirteen was 'abundantly sufficient to furnish a child of average capacity with a sound elementary education', said a

Newcastle Assistant Commissioner. Half-time education should not concern itself with matters of 'taste', said a Bradford mill-owner. The problem was how quickly children 'may receive elementary education, and be freed from it', said Chadwick (adding that 'the convenience of the school teacher and of the school should at every stage be made subordinate to the fair demands of labour').[93]

All such arguments were aimed at securing an efficient education which would 'free' children as rapidly as possible, but which would in the process inculcate a necessary social discipline – something made particularly explicit in the case of factory children. One HMI described the effects of the Factory Acts as being to make the children of the poor 'more accessible to Christian, literary, and all other ennobling influences'. Another thought its effects would reform 'the discipline of our humbler homes'.[94] All discussion of the half-time system was ultimately concerned with its social purposes, expressed primarily in terms of conduct and order. The factory inspectors were always anxious to demonstrate that education made the children more 'civil in their manners'. But learning to read and write was by itself unimportant, because

> unless the result of such training was to have the effect of correctly instructing a child in its relative duties, and inducing him to conduct himself in accordance with those instructions, it might in reality prove to be injurious, rather than beneficial.[95]

The permanent habits induced by half-time education would make a youth 'more likely to look to the Mechanics' Institute or the local night school for the employment of his leisure hours'.[96] Instruction in moral duties was fundamental. A works library was said to promote 'habits of sobriety and order'.[97] Drill produced habits of decorum and promptitude.[98] The half-time system helped to spread moral virtues and adherence to the Christian faith.[99]

Decency and cleanliness were commonly expressed objectives. 'The moral condition of the lower classes cannot be ameliorated', wrote a factory inspector, 'until their social habits are changed, until decency is introduced into their dwellings, until cleanliness is a system and no longer an exception.' Arguing for swimming and plunge baths, Mary Carpenter commented that 'the free application of cold water to the person of children is very important, both physically and morally'.[100] Schools were also seen as combating bad language, and promoting the right use of leisure. The latter, in the opinion of one commentator, would encourage the singing of 'something that would be worth hearing, instead of those filthy and obscene songs, so much in use in our factories at present', and the reading of 'publications which would do them good, instead of the infidel productions of Paine, Volney, &c.'[101] The half-time system was in general, said Wilks, 'a union between the classes of society', and 'that mutual interest which really exists between the employed and the employer'.[102]

Education would, therefore, contribute to the future well-being – defined in specific terms – of the half-timer. He would be adapted 'to his probable future position in society'.[103] At the heart of this perception of the half-timer was the knowledge of his low social status, and prevailing social difficulties and tensions. As one of Inspector Baker's witnesses commented in 1865: 'besides being rough and seldom using "thank you", many scarcely knew there were such words as "Sir", or "Ma'am"'.[104]

We have been concerned with features of the half-time system and with the interpretation of its purposes. Ideological positions are discernible in the discussion of its educational details from the middle of the nineteenth century. In the last quarter of the century teachers, socialists and others were concerned to show not only that half-time education was inefficient, but that the continued employment of young children was evil. In the conditions of the 1850s and 1860s those who, like the early factory inspectors, saw flaws in the existing system looked forward to improved schools, an educational test before admission to employment, and a higher age of exemption from education.[105] Some, like Nassau Senior, looked towards compulsory education.[106] Some, including HMIs and factory-owners, wished at least to extend the Factory Acts to agricultural and other employments.[107] In 1870 Lyon Playfair looked forward ambitiously to the conversion – under a system of compulsory education for all children – of half-time factory schools 'into useful secondary schools to teach the principles of science and art relating to the actual industries of the half-timers'.[108] By the 1860s there were demands for a wider system of national education and for further restrictions on child labour. Higher levels and ideals of education for working-class education were being canvassed than were embodied in the half-time system. Doubts, opposition, proposals for improvements were being voiced. Ideological capital was being made out of enthusiastic interpretations of what was possible and desirable in an industrial society. Those involved must be judged not by our ideologies but by close scrutiny of what they made of their own.

Notes

1 Quoted in PP 1861 XXI (I), Report of the Commissioners Appointed to Inquire into the State of Popular Education in England (Newcastle), p. 205.
2 For the early period see Sanderson, 'Education and the Factory in
Industrial Lancashire, 1780-1840', *Economic History Review*, 2nd ser.,
Vol. XX, 1967, and Gertrude Ward, 'The Education of Factory Child
Workers, 1833-1850', *Economic Journal Supplement*, February 1935. For a
general account see A.H. Robson, *The Education of Children Engaged in
Industry in England 1833-1876* (London, 1931), and for the political
discussions of the later period see Edmund and Ruth Frow, *A Survey of the
Half-time System in Education* (Manchester, 1970).
3 Newcastle Commission, I, p. 202.
4 Cf. e.g. PP 1839 XLII, Reports by the Four Factory Inspectors on the
Effects of the Educational Provisions of the Factories Act, p. 26.
5 PP 1852-3 XXIV, Report from the Select Committee on Education
(Manchester and Salford, etc.), p. 193; see also Nassau W. Senior,
Suggestions on Popular Education (London, 1861), p. 179.
6 PP 1866 XXIV, Reports of the Inspectors of Factories for the Half Year
ending 31 October 1865 (Baker), p. 115.
7 Report of the Committee of Council on Education 1876-7 (Sandford)
(London, 1877), p. 553.
8 Cf. e.g. Frances Collier, *Family Economy of the Working Classes in the
Cotton Industry 1784-1839* (Manchester, 1965), p. 45, for education at the
Gregs' Styal mill.
9 K.M. Lyell (ed.), *Memoir of Leonard Horner* (London, 1890), vol. I, p. 329;
Reports by the Four Factory Inspectors (1839), pp. 5-6. For McConnel's
see also W.C.R. Hicks, 'The Education of the Half-Timer: As Shown
Particularly in the case of Messrs McConnel and Co. Of Manchester',
Economic History, February 1939.
10 Reports by the Four Factory Inspectors (1839), pp. 38-9.
11 W. Dodd, *The Factory System Illustrated in a Series of Letters to the Right
Hon. Lord Ashley* (London, 1842; edition of 1968), p. 41.
12 Reports by the Four Factory Inspectors (1839), p. 6.
13 Cf. A. Hill (ed.), *Essays upon Educational Subjects Read at the Educational
Conference of June 1857* (London, 1857; edition of 1971), particularly
contributions by E. Akroyd, C.H. Bromby and A. Redgrave.
14 PP 1862 XLIII, E. Chadwick, Letter to N.W. Senior, Esq . . . . explanatory of
Communications and of Evidence on Half School Time Teaching . . . ,
p. 2. The evidence was submitted under the title, Communications from
Edwin Chadwick, Esq., C.B., respecting Half-Time and Military and
Naval Drill, and on the Time and Cost of Popular Education on a Large
and on a Small Scale.
15 Chadwick, Letter to Senior, p. 4; see also R. Bray, *Boy Labour and
Apprenticeship* (London, 1911), p. 78.
16 PP 1862 XXII, Reports of the Inspectors of Factories for the Half Year
ending 31 October 1861 (Baker), p. 37, Reports . . . 1865, p. 124.
17 Chadwick, Communications, pp. 12, 74.
18 Reports by the Four Factory Inspectors (1839), p. 29.

19 Ibid., pp. 11, 15, 28, 41, 47.
20 E.D.J. Wilks, 'On the Educational Clauses of the Factory Acts, Their Practical Working and the Possible Extension of Their Principle', *Transactions of the National Association for the Promotion of Social Science, 1859* (London, 1860), p. 363.
21 G. Melly, *The Children of Liverpool, and the Rival Schemes of National Education* (Liverpool, 1869), p. 11.
22 Chadwick, Communications, pp. 9–10, 41; E. Senior, 'The Half-time System and Agricultural Schools', *Transactions of the NAPSS, 1861* (London, 1862), pp. 326–7.
23 Chadwick, Communications, p. 9.
24 Ibid., pp. 28, 45, 74.
25 M. Carpenter, 'The Application of the Principles of Education to Schools for the Lower Classes of Society', *Transactions of the NAPSS, 1861* (London, 1862), p. 348.
26 Cf. e.g. Minutes of the Committee of Council on Education 1855-6 (Morell), pp. 465–9; Matthew Arnold's report for 1856 in F. Sandford (ed.), *Reports on Elementary Schools 1852-1882* (London, 1889), pp. 58–9; Akroyd, in Hill, *Essays upon Educational Subjects*, pp. 266–73, and in *Transactions of the NAPSS, 1864*, pp. 479–80.
27 Wilks, *Transactions of the NAPSS, 1859*, pp. 363–4.
28 Newcastle Commission, vol. I, p. 208.
29 H.S. Tremenheere, 'The Extension of the Factory Acts', *Transactions of the NAPSS, 1865* (London, 1866), p. 291.
30 [G.W. Hastings] Introduction, *Transactions of the NAPSS, 1861*, p. xxxi.
31 C. Kingsley, *The Address on Education Read before the National Association for the Promotion of Social Science ... 1869* (London, 1869), p. 3.
32 Cf. e.g. Minutes of the Committee of Council, 1846, vol. I, p. 439; Minutes of the Committee of Council, 1848-49-50, vol. II, p. 190.
33 Some such schools were created, for example by Leicester School Board. See Report of the Committee of Council, 1878-9, p. 470.
34 Cf. Reports of the Inspectors of Factories ... 1861 (Baker), p. 34; Newcastle Commission, vol. II, p. 231; Report of the Committee of Council, 1868-9 (Stokes), p. 317.
35 PP 1888 XXXV, Royal Commission Appointed to Inquire into the Working of the Elementary Education Acts, England and Wales (Cross Commission), Final Report, p. 161. The Commission heard many witnesses attacking and urging the abolition of the system; see, for example, Second Report (1887), pp. 18, 26, 34, 41, 196, 208.
36 Wilks, *Transactions of the NAPSS, 1859*, p. 364; Reports of the Inspectors of Factories, 1865 (Baker), p. 127.
37 *Illustrated London News*, vol. XXVIII, no. 792, 5 April 1856, p. 343.
38 Minutes of the Committee of Council, 1851-2 (Morell), pp. 565, 569; Report of the Committee of Council, 1868-9 (Pickard), p. 159, (Stokes) p. 318. For similar comments see Report of the Committee of Council 1876-7 (Stokes), pp. 580–1; Report of the Committee of Council 1879-80 (Pennethorne), p. 360.

39 Hill, *Essays upon Educational Subjects*, p. 219.
40 Newcastle Commission, vol. I, p. 204.
41 Chadwick, Letter to Senior, p. 4.
42 The most detailed commentaries, applicable to the earlier period also, were in *The Schoolmaster*. See especially a series of articles entitled 'In Clog-Land: The Troubles of the Half-Timer', 20 December 1884, 27 December 1884, 3 January 1885, and a special supplement on 'The Half-Timer', 9 February 1895.
43 Reports by the Four Factory Inspectors (1839), pp. 45, 51.
44 Newcastle Commission, vol. II, p. 232; see also Bromby, in Hill, *Essays upon Educational Subjects*, pp. 260-1, and Senior, *Transactions of the NAPSS, 1861*, p. 327.
45 Chadwick, Communications, pp. 8-12, 14, 26, 32, 38, 41.
46 Cf. e.g. Reports of the Inspectors of Factories . . . 1865 (Baker), p. 119; Report of the Committee of Council, 1868-69 (Steele), p. 221.
47 Chadwick, Letter to Senior, pp. 11, 33, 35; for similar later claims see Swire Smith, *Night Schools and Technical Education* (Leeds, 1886), p. 14, dubiously using Keighley statistics; A.J. Evans, 'A History of Education in Bradford During the Period of the Bradford School Board (1870-1904)', Leeds university MA thesis, 1947, p. 146, quoting Bradford employers, 1891.
48 Reports by the Four Factory Inspectors (1839), p. 20; Chadwick, Communications, p. 11.
49 Senior, *Suggestions*, pp. 267-8, 289.
50 Newcastle Commission, vol. II, p. 232.
51 Reports of the Inspectors of Factories . . . 1861 (Baker), pp. 31-3; Reports of the Inspectors of Factories . . . 1865, pp. 117-23.
52 Report of the Committee of Council, 1864-65 (Fitch), p. 179; cf. also Minutes of the Committee of Council, 1851-52, vol. II (Morell), pp. 565-9.
53 For comments cf. Report of the Committee of Council, 1866-67 (Routledge), pp. 175-7; Report of the Committee of Council 1868-69 (Capel), p. 60.
54 Cf. e.g. *The Schoolmaster*, 8 January 1881, p. 41, and 1 June 1889, p. 763. Cf. also Cross Commission, Second Report, pp. 18, 20, for examples of evidence; Final Report, p. 160 for managers' hostility.
55 Cf. Reports of the Inspectors of Factories . . . 1861 (Baker), p. 35; Chadwick, Letter to Senior, p. 33.
56 Cf. discussion by Alexander Redgrave quoted in Robson, *The Education of Children Engaged in Industry*, pp. 91-3.
57 *The Schoolmaster*, 20 December 1884, p. 924; 27 December 1884, p. 956.
58 Peter Sandiford, 'The Half-Time System in the Textile Trades', in M.E. Sadler (ed.), *Continuation Schools in England and Elsewhere* (Manchester, 1907), pp. 334-5.
59 Quoted by Nassau Senior in 'Address on Education', *Transactions of the NAPSS, 1863* (London, 1864), p. 68.
60 Chadwick, Communications, 3-5, 7, 10-12, 34.

61 Ibid., p. 8; see also pp. 19, 39.

62 Ibid., pp. 44–5; Carpenter, *Transactions of the NAPSS, 1861*, p. 348. She made similar comments in answer to the Newcastle Commission's enquiry; see Newcastle Commission, vol. V, p. 111.

63 E. Senior, *Transactions of the NAPSS, 1861*, pp. 326, 330–1.

64 Newcastle Commission, vol. I, p. 205.

65 N. Senior, *Transactions of the NAPSS, 1863*, p. 71. See also a later contribution to the NAPSS, by Chadwick: report of a paper 'On the Rise and Progress of the Half-School-Time System of Mixed Physical and Mental Training', *Transactions of the NAPSS, 1880*, p. 501.

66 Reports of the Inspectors of Factories . . . 1861 (Baker), p. 32; Report of the Committee of Council, 1864–65 (Fitch), p. 179.

67 Chadwick, Letter to Senior, p. 39.

68 By 1880, drill had for Chadwick replaced the role of factory employment (see note 65 above).

69 Chadwick, Communications, pp. 8, 10, 13, 16, 19, 25, 33, 75.

70 N. Senior, *Transactions of the NAPSS, 1863*, p. 68. For a comment on the national implications see Report of the Committee of Council, 1868–9 (Sandford), p. 210. Chadwick interested Matthew Arnold in the subject: see Sandford, *Reports . . . by Matthew Arnold*, p. 242. Cf. also Chapter 7.

71 F. Engels, *The Condition of the Working Class in England* (1845, first published in English 1887; 1958 Oxford edition), p. 195.

72 D. Ryazanoff (ed.), *The Communist Manifesto of Karl Marx and Friedrich Engels* (London, 1930), p. 10. The *Manifesto* was published in German in 1848 and in English in 1850.

73 *Documents of the First International, 1864–1866*, vol. I (Moscow, n.d.), pp. 343–6. The document is Marx's 'Instructions for the Delegates of the Provisional General Council'.

74 K. Marx, *Capital* (1867, first published in English 1887; 1954 Moscow edition), pp. 299n., 482–4, 488.

75 K. Marx, 'Critique of the Gotha Program', in K. Marx and F. Engels, *Selected Works* (Moscow, 1949), vol. II, pp. 33–4.

76 F. Engels, *Anti-Dühring* (1878, first published in English 1934; London edition, n.d.), pp. 352–3.

77 Cf. e.g. Owen's 'Report to the County of Lanark' (1820), in H. Silver (ed.) *Robert Owen on Education* (Cambridge, 1969), pp. 183–6; Owen's 'Six Lectures Delivered in Manchester' (1837), in ibid., pp. 205–8.

78 Marx, *Capital*, p. 483; see Reports of the Inspectors of Factories . . . 1865 (Baker), pp. 118–20.

79 Reports of the Inspectors of Factories . . . 1861, pp. 31–3, 36.

80 Report of the Committee of Council, 1868–69, p. 317.

81 Newcastle Commission, vol. V, pp. 28–9.

82 Cross Commission, Second Report, p. 29.

83 See Frow, *A Survey of the Half-Time System*, chs III–V.

84 Quoted in *The Schoolmaster*, 9 February 1895, p. 255; see also F. Keeling, *Child Labour in the United Kingdom* (London, 1914), pp. xxiv–xxv.

85 M. McMillan, *Child Labour and the Half-Time System* (London, 1896), p. 3.

86 Sandiford, in Sadler, *Continuation Schools*, p. 337.
87 Minutes of the Committee of Council, 1846, vol. I, p. 440; Newcastle Commission, vol. II, p. 231; Reports of the Inspectors of Factories ... 1861 (Baker), pp. 33-7. See also Baker's 1865 report, pp. 119, 123, and Report of the Committee of Council, 1868-9 (Steele), p. 221.
88 *The Schoolmaster*, 20 December 1884, p. 925.
89 Report of the Committee of Council, 1868-9 (Stokes), pp. 317-18.
90 *The Schoolmaster*, 20 December 1884, p. 925.
91 Cross Commission, Second Report, pp. 18, 21, 26, 29, 379.
92 Quoted by Sandiford, in Sadler, *Continuation Schools*, p. 334.
93 Newcastle Commission, vol. V, pp. 446-7; Chadwick, Letter to Senior, p. 39.
94 Report of the Committee of Council, 1864-5 (Fitch), p. 179; Report of the Committee of Council, 1876-7 (Steele), p. 578.
95 Reports by the Four Factory Inspectors (1839), p. 21.
96 Bromby, in Hill, *Essays upon Educational Subjects*, pp. 250-1, 263-4.
97 T. Tooke *et al.*, *The Physical and Moral Condition of the Children and Young Persons Employed in Mines and Manufactures* (London, 1843), p. 235.
98 Chadwick, Communications, pp. 8, 16, 25, 75; see also Chadwick, *Transactions of the NAPSS, 1880*, p. 503.
99 See Bromby, in Hill, *Essays upon Educational Subjects*, pp. 263-4, and Akroyd, in ibid., p. 269; also Horner in Reports by the Four Factory Inspectors (1839), p. 195.
100 Redgrave, in Hill, *Essays upon Educational Subjects*, p. 220; Chadwick, Communications, p. 45. See also, Carpenter, *Transactions of the NAPSS, 1861*, p. 348.
101 Dodd, *The Factory System*, pp. 55-6, 118, 156.
102 Wilks, *Transactions of the NAPSS, 1859*, p. 364.
103 Chadwick, Communications, p. 16.
104 Reports of the Inspectors of Factories ... 1865 (Baker), p. 121.
105 Cf. e.g. Reports by the Four Factory Inspectors (1839), pp. 15, 30, 49-50.
106 Cf. Senior, *Suggestions*, p. 241.
107 Cf. Kingsley, *Address on Education*, p. 3; Report of the Committee of Council, 1868-9, pp. 69, 96, 184; Akroyd's reported comments in *Transactions of the NAPSS, 1864*, p. 479.
108 L. Playfair, 'Address on Education', *Transactions of the NAPSS, 1870* (London, 1871), p. 59.

3 Reputation and the educational system: the case of Robert Owen

If a 'system' raises complex questions about ideologies and the interplay of currents of opinion, so does the fate of an idea or of a reputation. Robert Owen's reputation as an educationist is an outstanding nineteenth-century example. The details of Owen's educational activities at New Lanark and elsewhere have been extensively investigated and debated in recent years,[1] but it is revealing to consider what happened to his ideas and reputation after the most visible period of his influence as an educator and educationist in the 1820s and 1830s. The case of Owen offers sharp – though by no means unique – insights into how historians learn their points of interest, of emphasis and of silence.

In this chapter, therefore, we are concerned more with how people have seen Robert Owen in relation to education than with his ideas and efforts in themselves. In very general terms it can be said that his reputation in this field, after the early interest generated by his work, suffered a hiatus from the mid-1820s until (among socialists) the 1880s and (among educationists) the twentieth century. Certainly, at the height of his fame at New Lanark, Owen's work could win enormous acclaim as a system 'both in point of theory and practice, new, and unrivalled'. His system at that time was considered to be 'adequate to the great purposes of forming the character of individuals and collective bodies, civil, moral and religious, of nations and empires'.[2] Yet, at the beginning of the twentieth century, Owen's most important biographer was to regret that 'the name of Robert Owen is little known to the present generation as an educational reformer'.[3]

It is, of course, easiest to follow through influences and reputations when they have been upheld by such obvious end-products as legislation, administrative apparatus or collected works. The value and relevance of the work of Lord Brougham and Kay-Shuttleworth, for instance, has been consistently upheld. Owen's reputation, however, has needed rescue operations, and on this point it is perhaps important to bear in mind that the national reputation which Owen established whilst at New Lanark, based on both the success of the mills and the authority which this success lent to Owen's views, was being eroded even before his actual connection with New Lanark ended in the period 1824-9. Central to this process of erosion was, of course, Owen's attack, in keeping with a social philosophy of which 'educational' ideas were an integral part, on established religion. But the process itself was of a complex nature.

The first New Lanark mill had been completed by David Dale, in association with Richard Arkwright, in 1785. A description written before Owen came from Manchester to assume full managerial control in 1800 explained that 'the spinning of cotton yarn is carried on to a greater extent, than at any other place in Scotland, or probably in Britain'. Over 400 children were employed, and were not 'neglected with regard to their health, education, or morals, every exertion being used for the accomplishment of these purposes, which, as yet, have been attended with a degree of success hitherto unprecedented at any other public works in this kingdom'.[4] Owen (who acknowledged in his *New View of Society* the foundations Dale had laid) improved vastly on the conditions and facilities, but it was his educational arrangements in particular which were enthusiastically and internationally praised. Dr Macnab, investigating New Lanark on behalf of the Duke of Kent, 'was at once thrown into an ecstasy of admiration; his unpractised pen was sorely taxed to depict the feelings with which he was inspired . . . . The Duke at once professed himself a disciple.'[5] For Macnab, the Duke, deputations, visitors and the onlooking world Owen had 'proved he is an extraordinary man'.[6] Macnab, it should be remembered, was extolling this 'proof' some two years after Owen had publicly denounced religion and set out along the road that was to bring upon him widespread abuse for his infidelity and socialism.

The New Lanark schools were too overwhelming a piece of evidence for Owen's standing as an educationist to be undermined at once. George Combe, phrenologist and secularist educator, unsympathetic to Owen's views generally, visited New Lanark in November 1820 and described the Institution for the Formation of Character, opened some four years earlier. The children were admitted at the age of two, 'three women watch them until they are four years old; they then go to school . . . We saw them romping and playing in great spirits. The noise was prodigious, but it was the full chorus of mirth and kindliness.' He describes the children dancing and 'singing three or four songs of the sweetest melody and merriest measure'. Owen had ordered £500 worth of 'transparent pictures representing objects interesting to the youthful mind' so that children could 'form ideas at the same time that they learn words'. The greatest lessons Owen wished the children to learn were 'that life may be enjoyed, and that each may make his own happiness consistent with that of all the others'. Combe's most revealing comment, in this period of monitorial education, was that 'the teachers had studied the dispositions and faculties of the children more than any teachers I had met with'.[7]

Combe's testimony is important in showing the close working relationship and sympathy of aims of Owen, who built and shaped the schools, and his teachers. There is clear evidence from this period of the amount of time Owen spent in the schools, and of the children's affection for him. One of them, writing to Owen at the age of twenty-one, referred to 'the very condescending politeness with which you are pleased to regard those in an humble sphere of life and the amiable disposition you have always preserved towards, such: especially those who are more imediately under your charge'. Owen was 'the cause from which I learned to think and act'.[8] A deputation from the Leeds Poor Law Guardians in 1819 considered that the most remarkable thing about the education of the children was 'the general spirit of kindness and affection which is shown towards them'.[9] Owen's reputation, based on the evidence of such humanity, and on the educational programme of *A New View* into which it could be seen to fit, remained unshaken in the early 1820s. A meeting held in 1822 of a society to promote community settlements as advocated by Owen since 1817 had as imposing a list of vice-presidents and members as had the committee set up in 1819 to investigate his plan. The Earl of Blessington, as ecstatic as Macnab, referred to Owen's 'humane and enlightened mind' and his plans which had 'been brought into successful practice'. The public were indebted to him 'for the most valuable collection of facts and successful experiments that have ever been attended to in the cause of suffering humanity'. Sir Walter de Crespigny, MP, had at New Lanark seen little children playing 'with a degree of harmlessness, of fondness, and of attention to each other, which we do not often witness in this country'.

The chairman, Lord Torrington, declared that 'no language can do justice to the excellence of the arrangements in that establishment'.[10]

Nevertheless, Owen's reputation *was* being undermined. He was not at this or any other point concerned about his own social standing. 'In after life,' commented G.J. Holyoake, 'Mr Owen was really reckless of his own fame. No leader ever took so little care in guarding his own reputation'.[11] After the public meetings in London in 1817 opposition began to mount, though most of it at first combined criticism with sympathy. Major Torrens, for all his recognition of Owen's 'disinterested labours and perfect benevolence', was attacking his views in the *Edinburgh Review* in 1819,[12] echoing the general resistance of the political economists to Owen's community plans. *Blackwood's*, in 1821, was insisting that it was necessary to discriminate between Owen the New Lanark philanthropist and Owen the system-builder. New Lanark was 'a pattern for manufacturing establishments' and Owen disseminated 'contented cheerfulness among the grown population under his charge, and application and study among the fine children, whose education, almost step by step, he superintends'. Everyone who had been to New Lanark, the writer continued, knew that Owen's life was passed at his mills, and that in superintending their details, displaying these to visitors, and caressing the children at his school, scarcely all the hours of the day are sufficient for him'. Owen's notion that character was formed by circumstances was 'opposed both to reason and to revelation', and the practice at New Lanark was quite unrelated to Owen's theories.[13]

In view of the essentially unitary nature of Owen's thought, it was perhaps inevitable that attempts to distinguish between what was 'educational' and what was 'social' could only pave the way for a more general opposition. A.J. Booth in the 1860s saw the position clearly: Owen's 'claims to our gratitude as an educational reformer are now almost forgotten. His fame as a philanthropist is obliterated by the notoriety he subsequently acquired as the exponent of Socialism, a system of society not generally regarded with favour.'[14] The truth was that, in so many fundamental ways, Owen's message was regarded as unacceptable or even irrelevant in the rapidly advancing, achievement-orientated industrial society of the mid-nineteenth century. Apart from the fact that Owen was never again associated with an educational enterprise that appeared to offer the same degree of positive 'proof' that New Lanark had done, the breadth of Owen's optimism was unacceptable in an age of deep-seated uncertainty and confusion. 'Man has walked by the light of conflagrations', pronounced Carlyle in 1831, 'and amid the sound of falling cities; and now there is darkness, and long watching till it be morning'.[15] Owen was one of those who had been imbued with a sense of moving through the long watch towards brighter things. There were others, like Thomas Pole, a Quaker and early infant education enthusiast, whose language could be as visionary at that of Owen himself: 'Man is now emerging from the deep shades of ignorance, and the light of a celestial morning is breaking forth with unprecedented splendour since the commencement of the nineteenth century'.[16] The people who made and preserved reputations in high Victorian England were attempting to move away from the state of mind in which such enthusiams and visions were perpetrated.

One element in the memory of Owen, therefore, was a sense of indignation at the vastness of his projects. At its most tolerant, this opinion of Owen was as a 'sanguine old projector, who, through an almost innumerable succession of baffled projects, hopes on as fervently as ever'[17] – a tone of voice met frequently in mid-century comments on Owen. To be a man of panaceas in the Victorian 'Golden Age' was to be irrelevant. To be a man of 'one idea' was even more intolerable to the Victorians than it had been to Hazlitt,[18] and only a small number of prominent non-Owenites managed to combine irritation at this aspect of Owen with a certain sympathy: they included Harriet Martineau and Charles Bradlaugh (who described Owen as 'a good, pure, one-idead man').[19] The one idea was, of course, consistently defended by Owen's supporters. William Pare, for example, on the centenary of Owen's birth, recalled that 'it has been said that Owen was a man of one idea. If so, the idea was at once grand, catholic, and comprehensive'.[20] Lloyd Jones compared Owen's one idea with St John's constant cry of 'Little children, love one another'. Owen had spent fifty years, Jones pointed out, being concerned about the importance of a sound education as a means of securing justice and humanity, and it was 'natural, therefore, that his persistence in urging this view upon the attention of others, should be irksome to those who differed from him'.[21]

Another point is that, after his return from America in 1829, Owen became associated with working-class movements whose educational efforts were in general deprecated by those who were engaged from the 1830s in an attempt to strengthen the administrative process represented in the Committee of Council on Education or the voluntary efforts which were aimed at making that intervention unnecessary.

A crucial milestone was being passed. The Committee of Council symbolized the growing conviction that the battles to legitimize education (even if not to agree on its control) had been largely won. There were no longer, as Macnab had pointed out in 1819, men persecuted 'for advocating the right of the poor to education'.[22] The Dean of Durham, in 1848, told mechanics' institute members of 'an almost obsolete prejudice against institutions such as yours'.[23] But the 'legitimizing' of education involved the appearance of the 'legitimate educator', who, among other things, must not advocate the provision of too much education. As the historian of a later period of English education has pointed out, debates about the appropriate amount of education continued right through the century. Discussion of the Revised Code, for example, reflected the continuing belief 'that too much education was undesirable', and he quotes the opposition of *The Times* in 1880 to A.J. Mundella's attempt to revise the Code: the danger was, it was suggested, that 'education might turn the heads of ploughboys and make them look down on their destined walks in life'.[24]

It was clearly important to the legitimate educator that his work must not be considered socially subversive. Owen is not mentioned in the reports from 1840 in the minutes of the Committee of Council (his name is also absent from such contemporary journals as the *Quarterly Journal of Education*, the *Quarterly Educational Magazine* and the *London Scholastic Journal*), but a comment in one inspector's report for the year 1840-1 is revealing. The mechanical teaching of reading and writing with a little arithmetic, and the dogmatic inculcation of scripture, were, in his view, inadequate, because, 'if the legitimate educator does no more than this, there are those that will do more: the Chartist and Socialist educator – the publisher of exciting, obscure and irreligious works – he who can boldly assert, and readily declaim upon false and pernicious dogmas and principles'.[25] Ten years later the same inspector was horrified at the extent of the sales of 'Chartist and infidel' newspapers 'of an immoral nature, hostile to the existing state'.[26] Such a view, it must be emphasized, coloured educational history as well as policy. In 1845 another inspector explained in a report to the Committee of Council how 'desultory individual efforts' had been outstripped since the first infant schools were established, largely through the efforts of the Home and Colonial Infant School Society: 'previous and even subsequent to the date of its formation, some of the promoters of infant schools appear to have considered them merely as asylums for healthful amusement'.[27] Owen was expunged from the record partly because of the need to cleanse the newly emerging national educational machine of unacceptable influences. He could not now be safely accepted as a 'legitimate educator'.

Owen's reputation had not been based, then, on the combination of features which made that of, say, Lancaster and Bell, Brougham and Kay-Shuttleworth, Herbert Spencer and Matthew Arnold more secure. There were no schools, societies, parliamentary bills (the 1819 Factory Act has to be discounted in this connection) or administrative machineries to associate with him. His ideas were too entangled with vast schemes of social reorganization for them to continue to feature for long in educational debate, as did – in a later generation – those of Spencer on the curriculum or Arnold's on payment by results. The very problems Owen was trying to solve were unacceptable, in the form he approached them, to 'legitimate' opinion from the 1830s onwards. Even Owen's earlier writings did not appeal, for these reasons, to Victorian England. His *New View of Society*, a document of considerable stature in the 1810s and 1820s, is scarcely mentioned in educational and social debate afterwards, and has only very recently become part of the canon of educational texts.[28] The nature of the requirements for a firm reputation in Victorian Britain, and the way in which any form of radical or secularist ingredient distorted the educational record, are confirmed in the case of George Combe, who was by the 1840s one of the most important, and subsequently one of the least remembered, figures in British education. There are many parallels between the careers of Owen and Combe (both of whom, it was suggested in 1842, had 'the same type of mind').[29] Combe was not in any sense a socialist or radical of the Owenite stamp, but his phrenological panaceas and educational secularism played a similar part in the decline of his reputation to the ones we have traced in the case of Owen. Combe's reputation as a pioneer of the teaching of social studies, health education and science did not survive, when that of, for instance, Spencer and Huxley did. One of the few attempts to revive interest in Combe (since Jolly's massive edition of Combe's writings in 1879) laments the lack of reference, or scant reference, to Combe in twentieth-century histories of education, a neglect traced back to the fact that 'as a leader of the "Secularists" he was subjected to much misrepresentation and obloquy.'[30]

It is not difficult, then, to see why Owen's reputation wilted, and that of, for example, Samuel Wilderspin and the Mayos did not. Owen was only the founder of the first infant school, which had an important relationship to a wide set of ideas; Wilderspin was the founder of the first infant school movement, and he and the Mayos brought infant education into an unambiguous relationship with the existing educational order.

Considerations such as these define not only the nature of reputation, but also the type of historical writing in which it is to some extent regulated. The Victorian history of education measured importance in terms of the permanency of institutions or the continuing utility of ideas (the most valiant, but largely isolated, attempt to approach popular education with wide terms of reference being George Bartley's *The Schools for the People*).[31] One of the first historical pamphlets in the field of popular education was, symbolically, a summary of 'the education question in Parliament'.[32] A review of R.H. Quick's *Essays on Educational Reformers*, when it appeared in 1868, emphasized the difficulty a teacher would have in gratifying a desire 'to know about the various educational experiments that have been now and then made, or about the men who have most influenced the methods and work of education. There is a lamentable deficiency in our literature of works that deal with the history of education or educationists'.[33] The tradition of 'institutional history', confirmed in books like Henry Craik's *The State in its Relation to Education* (1884), which does not mention Owen, was the dominant one until well into the twentieth century. Quick's book (published in a first edition of 500 copies and for twenty years out of print) did not mention Owen, and in a chapter on Froebel added for a later edition he refers to the early history of infant schools and the way in which this Continental idea was 'taken up by James Buchanan and Samuel Wilderspin'.[34] J. Gill's *Systems of Education* and J. Leitch's *Practical Educationists* were both published in 1876, both merely mention Owen in passing, and both devote their main attention in the field of English infant education to Wilderspin.[35] The president of the Education Department of the NAPSS in 1875 mentioned, among early contributors to popular education, Raikes, Bell and Lancaster, and believed that Wilderspin gave us 'our first Infant School in 1824'.[36] Wilderspin had in fact promoted the idea that he was the founder of infant schools, and the historians were glad to follow the lead he gave. Typical of the approach was Holman's *English National Education* (1898), which mentioned Owen in parenthesis to both Wilderspin and Buchanan – 'another hero of popular education was Samuel Wilderspin', whose interest in infant education was due to his friendship with Buchanan, 'who had come from Robert Owen's infant school at New Lanark – the first established in Great Britain'.[37]

Although, as we have seen, Owen's stature as an educationist was considerably diminished after the mid-1830s, it was never totally swept away. One factor in all this was the continuing importance of the 'proof' represented by New Lanark. As we have suggested, there is a particular problem about Owen's reputation as the founder of infant schools. There is no need for us to examine this controversy in detail, but it is useful to glance at the attitudes it reveals.[38] Wilderspin tried to retract the indebtedness he expressed to Owen in the first edition of *On the Importance of Educating the Infant Children of the Poor* (1823). Owen was probably less than fair in his disparaging remarks about Buchanan in his autobiography. We have already seen evidence of the high quality of the New Lanark schools and of Owen's teachers in general, and also Owen's deep personal involvement in the life of the schools. The nature of the record in the 1830s and 1840s can easily be illustrated. The Central Society of Education, for example, published an article in 1838 ascribing the success of the New Lanark infant school to Buchanan, 'partly with the assistance of Mr Owen'.[39] The *Westminster Review* interested itself in Buchanan's role, on the grounds that 'it is not so much those who with philanthropic objects establish a school, as he who first introduces the plan which makes a school succeed, to whom the country is chiefly indebted'.[40] Wilderspin was telling a select committee in 1835 and *The Times* in 1846 that Buchanan brought from New Lanark a system which amounted to a 'mere assemblage of children . . . a refuge for destitute children . . . but not Infant Schools conducted upon the system now known as the Infant School System'. He denied the contention that 'Oberlin, Fellenberg, or Robert Owen was the Founder of the present Infant School System, with its various arrangements, details, and implements'.[41]

Wilderspin was, of course, right that by his definition Owen was not the founder of infant schools; it is his definition that is interesting, reinforcing the view of infant education we have already seen through inspectorial eyes. The move to assert Buchanan's role as a teacher was important, but it overreached itself in suggesting that Owen himself was not deeply responsible for and involved in all aspects of school planning and activity at New Lanark.

The controversy was not one-sided, and there were educationists who came to his defence, especially Brougham, who in response, for example, to Wilderspin in Select Committee and *The Times*, was deferential to Owen and his role in the history of the infant school. Frederick Hill in 1836 was admitting, on the subject of infant schools, 'the high honour of originating and first bringing into successful operation this important instrument of human improvement and happiness is due to Mr Robert Owen'.[42] A writer in the *National Instructor* in 1850 explained that it was at New Lanark that 'the Infant School originated, and from which all the others have sprung'.[43] Even W. L. Sargant understood that 'the infant school system was an inevitable consequence of Owen's doctrine, as to the vital importance of surrounding human beings with circumstances favourable to their development'. Owen's 'claim to the invention remains unimpeached'.[44]

T. H. Huxley, not otherwise known for any attraction towards Owenism, was invited to take the chair at an Owen centenary commemoration in 1871, and declined in most interesting terms:

> I think that every one who is compelled to look as closely into the problem of popular education, must be led to Owen's conclusion, that the infant school is, so to speak, the key of the position; and that Robert Owen discovered this great fact, and had the courage and patience to work out his theory into a practical reality, is his claim, if he had no other, to the enduring gratitude of the people.[45]

There is no clearer testimony to the way in which Owen's reputation endured outside, and in spite of, the official record.

The memory of Owen's doctrine of character formation was indeed clearly linked with the 'proof' offered by New Lanark. In 1877, for instance, Charles Bradlaugh declared that 'society now adopts the view which Robert Owen was the first to popularise – although not the first to enunciate – that man is better or worse according to the conditions surrounding the parent . . . and those which surround the infant itself'. Owen had 'set an example to all Britain by introducing infant schools in his New Lanark village'. Like John Stuart Mill, Bradlaugh saw how important, if over-simplified, Owen's doctrine of character formation had been: 'the formula that man's character is formed for him, and not by him, does not express all the truth, but expresses much more than is taught by those whose dogma it is that man may will, uninfluenced by events'.[46]

The Owenites, of course, commented persistently on Owen's role as the pioneer of infant education, which they saw as a necessary preliminary to the advance towards a new society. The tone of their comments can be judged from an example in a letter to Owen, written in 1854 when Owen was planning to use a 'panorama' the following year to demonstrate how the human mind could be formed from birth:

How extremely necessary it is that the epoch which commenced infant teaching as a science should be represented in the panorama; therefore your Colony of New Lanark, exhibiting the infant school teaching, begun by yourself, surrounded with those superior conditions, as far as the state of things and of times could permit, should be the starting point.[47]

Within the Owenite movements, and within those working-class and radical movements which owed any kind of debt to him, his educational message was pervasive. It would be impossible here to consider the relationship between Owen's educational views and, for instance, the later Owenite activities, the London Working Men's Association and Chartism, and the educational ideals of co-operation, trade unionism and the labour movement in general.[48] Between the climacteric of Chartism in 1848 and the new socialist organizations of the 1880s, Owen's reputation in the labour movement was keenest among Chartists, ex-Chartists and co-operators. The best-known example from the later days of Chartism is Hetherington's 'Last Will and Testament', dated 21 August 1849. In it he bids farewell to a loathsome social system, expressing his 'ardent attachment to the principles of that great and good man – Robert Owen. I quit this world with a firm conviction that his system is the only true road to human emancipation.' Owen's system was one which 'makes man the proprietor of his own labour and of the elements of production – it places him in a condition to enjoy the entire fruits of his labour and surrounds him with circumstances that will make him intelligent, rational and happy'.[49] Hetherington was one of the pioneer, heroic figures of Chartism. Thomas Cooper, a later recruit to Chartism, considered himself a friend of Owen's,[50] and in 1850 was on the margin of Chartism and publishing *Cooper's Journal*. In that year he published a short article entitled 'Reflections Suggested by the 79th Anniversary of the Birth-day of Robert Owen', by a young Owenite called Thomas Shorter. It reminds readers that Owen

was the founder of the first and most efficient institution ever established in this country for the purpose of infant training . . . Education and employment, – equal rights and liberty of conscience, – the development of all man's faculties and the supply of all man's rational wants: these have been the great objects of his unceasing exertions, and to which his life has been consecrated. His theory of the power of education and surrounding circumstances in the formation of character were submitted by him to the test of practical experiment

... and the wonderful success of that experiment has been attested by evidence of the most incontrovertible character.[51]

This testimony of 1850 (in terms little different from those of, for example, Macnab thirty years earlier) is as revealing in the story of the labour and radical movements as is that of Huxley for educational opinion twenty years later.

In the co-operative movement Owen's educational work was a recurring memory. When A.J. Booth published his *Robert Owen, the Founder of Socialism in England* in 1869, *The Co-operator* published both a short notice of the book and a letter from Booth explaining that he had included a chapter on the early history of co-operation, and that he would be pleased to present a copy to co-operative libraries.[52] Throughout the late 1860s and into the 1870s the same journal contained extensive reference to Owen. An exchange of correspondence between Thomas Hughes and George Storrs on the utility of Owen's works to co-operators took place in 1867–8. Robert Harper contributed two articles on Owen in 1868 (declaring that 'scarcely one of the superior methods of ameliorating human suffering, but was either invented or adopted by him'). Alice Wilson contributed a long poem on Owen in 1868. Henry Travis contributed a series of five articles on 'Education on the Principles of Social Science' (based very largely on Owen's own writings) in 1868, one on 'Education as a Part of the Co-operative Social System' in 1869, and another on Owen in 1871. There is a sense throughout of Owen as major educator, including as 'originator of the rational infant school system', and of New Lanark as the 'greatest of all steps in the onward progress of the human race'.[53]

The revival of interest in Owen's educational work was a feature of the increasing part played by collective social solutions in the national consciousness of Britain in the later decades of the century. The reform, radical and socialist movements helped increasingly after the mid-1860s to confirm the move away from *laissez-faire* modes of thought. H.S. Foxwell in the late 1890s made the points that Owen had in England 'brought socialism down from the study to the street, and made it a popular force', and that popular education and other aspects of social improvement 'either originated in, or were powerfully reinforced by, the Owenite agitation'.[54] Beatrice Webb was only one of those making similar points in the 1890s. Describing Owen as the father of English socialism (a distinctively English socialism, she argued, defined in typically Fabian terms), she associated him with 'beneficent legislation forcing the individual into the service, and under the protection of the State'. The Education Acts are one of her examples.[55] Among educationists, Michael Sadler showed a special awareness of Owen's position in this respect, and in at least three places between 1905 and 1907 he used Owen as the main example of the 'collectivist and authoritarian' nineteenth-century alternative to the 'individualist and radical' current (of the first the 'great figure' was Owen, of the second – Bentham, Brougham and Place).[56] J.F.C. Harrison has rightly argued that too much emphasis has been placed on the view of Owen as socialist pioneer, and by exploring more fully the millenarian and sectarian significance of Owen and Owenism has provided an important corrective to 'over-concentration on a few selected years'.[57] It is also important, however, to establish to what extent outside immediate Owenite circles Owen's reputation (we have been exploring, of course, only one dimension of it) was kept alive in the period between the contraction of his mass base in the late 1830s and the revival of interest in the final decades of the century. Interestingly, the writings of both John Stuart Mill and Harriet Martineau reflect a willingness critically to consider the relevance of Owen's views in the light of the increasing need for 'collectivist' solutions to social problems.[58]

We have suggested that clues to Owen's reputation in the 1850s and 60s can be found in such places as the late Chartist publications, cooperative and other journals, and A.J. Booth's book of 1869. They can be found also in the writings of Marx and Engels. Both were keenly interested in Owen and in the education at New Lanark, Marx principally seeking confirmation of his views on the combination of productive labour and instruction.[59] Engels, in a passage published in German in the 1870s, and in English in 1892, described Owen as 'the inventor of infant schools' where the children 'enjoyed themselves so much that they could hardly be got home again'. In fact, considered Engels, 'all social movements, all real advances in England in the interests of the working class were associated with Owen's name'.[60]

Owen's standing as an educational reformer in twentieth-century British eyes owes most, however, to the relentless enthusiasm with which the Fabians went out of their way to rehabilitate him. Socialists and radicals in the 1870s and 80s (including Joseph Cowen and Annie Besant)[61] had begun the process, but it was the Fabian effort that counted. One of the founding fathers of the Fabian Society, and author of its motto,[62] was Frank Podmore, whose *Robert Owen* is probably the greatest landmark in Owen studies. A pamphlet committee elected in

1884 included Rosamund Dale Owen, Owen's granddaughter.[63] The Society's main work on Owen came after the turn of the century, though indications of the scale of renewed interest can be seen in its, and other, work in the 1890s. Beatrice Webb's *Co-operative Movement in Great Britain* appeared in 1891; a co-operative pamphlet on the history of social conditions in Huddersfield affirmed in 1894 that 'when Robert Owen first directed attention to the early education of infants, he advocated a method of training human character, which our statesmen at length wisely and completely adopted'.[64] Leslie Stephen's famous article on Owen in the *Dictionary of National Biography* in 1895 expressed the certainty that Owen would 'be recognised as one of the most important figures in the social history of the time'.[65]

Of course, not all Fabian writers were equally interested in the restoration of Robert Owen's reputation as an educationist. Sidney Webb, for instance, eager to establish Owen's role in the history of collectivism and socialism, was attracted by that aspect of Owen which related to the growth of state and municipal forms of collective responsibility. But Owen's specifically educational work (apart from his proposals for a national system of education) were not of great interest to Webb himself. To the Fabians generally, however, this was not the case. It was after the turn of the century that interest grew. In 1901 a tract entitled *What to Read* recommended Owen's autobiography and Lloyd Jones's book on Owen (a further list in 1906 added Podmore's biography, published in the same year). Between 1908 and 1917 six Fabian tracts were either about Owen or commented significantly on him. Mrs Hylton Dale's *Child Labour under Capitalism* (1908) considered that Owen 'more than any educationist before or since, recognised that children are like plants, in that they want more than care and attention; they want love'. Mrs Townshend's *Case for School Nurseries* (1909) described Owen's work in infant education as an 'illusory dawn' – with England 'deep in the trough of *laissez-faire* ... one need not wonder that here Owen's preaching fell on deaf ears and produced on permanent results'. B.L. Hutchins's tract on *Robert Owen, Social Reformer* was published in 1912, and C.E.M. Joad's tract on *Robert Owen, Idealist* came five years later. St John Ervine in 1912, in a tract on *Francis Place*, considered that Owen and Place together 'made it possible for democracy to be in England', and Colwyn Vulliamy, in a tract on *Charles Kingsley and Christian Socialism* (1914), turned aside from the main theme to comment on 'the wonderful, almost quixotic, romance of the New Lanark mills, raised wages, reduced hours, free education and amusements' and Owen's 'magnificent schemes for the general organisation of industries and the free instruction of the whole community'.

It was from starting-points such as these that the educational work of Owen came to be built into labour history. From Ramsay MacDonald's *Socialist Movement* (1911), for example, through the work of Max Beer on the history of socialism (his edition of Owen's *Life* appeared in 1920, his *History of British Socialism* in 1919, and *Social Struggles and Thought* in 1925) and that of G.D.H. Cole, emphasis was laid on Owen's part in making it 'impossible for men to refuse to ponder over great fundamental social changes'.[66] The main burden of most of this analysis of Owen as pioneer socialist was not only that he had helped to build a labour movement but that his message had managed to be woven into the fabric of responses to social problems. Thomas Frost, for instance, reflecting in 1880 on the communitarian experiments he had known, commented that though socialism was at that period little heard of, 'the results of its teaching are everywhere around us, and its fundamental tenet, "man is the creature of circumstances", may be recognized in all the legislation of the last quarter of a century'.[67] Holyoake, when summarizing Owen's central doctrine, expressed the view that 'nobody doubts this now'.[68]

There was a growing sense, however, that Owen's specifically educational reputation was inadequate. Podmore's admission that Owen was 'little known' as an educational reformer was echoed two years later by Joseph Clayton, who noted that

> Robert Owen, the founder of infant schools in Great Britain, is still but the shadow of a name, even in circles where Pestalozzi is honoured; and the work Owen wrought for education at New Lanark, unsurpassed in the years that have followed, is still to be apprized at its true value[69]

This appraisal in educational history was to come with a widening of the 'institutional history' of education to incorporate a social-historical approach.

It is an interesting fact that the 'new educationists' of the late nineteenth and early twentieth centuries did not rediscover, or at least did not acknowledge, Owen as part of their tradition. The reason, no doubt, is that his Enlightenment rationalism placed him outside their interests; he was within a tradition which had not broken with reason as the foundation on which to build educational practices. There is a passage in *Democracy and Education* in which John Dewey explains the short-comings of Locke and Helvétius. Their approach to education, including the improvements they advocated in learning processes, remained over-intellectual. At the call of reason 'practice was not so much subordinated to knowledge as treated as a kind of tag-end or aftermath of knowledge. The educational result was only to confirm the exclusion of active pursuits from the school, save as they might be brought in for purely utilitarian ends'. Even object lessons excluded 'the natural tendency to learn about the qualities of objects by the uses to which they are put through trying to do something with them'. The educational reform effected by 'rational-empiricist theories' was confined mainly to 'doing away with some of the bookishness of prior methods; it did not accomplish a consistent reorganization'.[70] Although much of this would be inapplicable to Owen – particularly to the infant school as he created it – he derived his overall theory from the tradition of Locke and Helvétius, and the fact may explain the absence of reference to him in the work of the late-century progressivists. There is no apparent, and perhaps no real, bridge between them.

The position of Owen's reputation in the literature of education depended finally, therefore, on the historians who, in the wake of socialist, and especially Fabian, rehabilitation, attempted to redefine educational history in terms of broader social processes and the history of ideas. Although works like David Salmon and W. Hindshaw's *Infant Schools: Their History and Theory* (1904) helped in the process, it was probably A.E. Dobbs, using a very limited range of sources, who never-theless contributed most to a new approach to nineteenth-century education. In *Education and Social Movements 1700–1850* (published in 1919) he saw education as part of a wider process of social development, and accepted as a legitimate field of inquiry the many relationships between schools and other types of formal and informal education, on the one hand, and social attitudes and realities on the other hand. Both Combe and Owen are given serious attention, and in a chapter entitled 'Education by Collision' Dobbs looks at the educational impact of social movements and programmes. Owen's role as educator was now accessible in a whole new historical environment. J.W. Adamson's *English Education, 1789–1902* (a better book than most of its successors) appeared in 1930, with Owen featuring in a chapter entitled 'Educa-tional Opinion'. The following year came Frank Smith's *History of English Elementary Education 1760–1902*, which bases a summary of Owen's educational work on such sources as Owen's *Life* and *A New*

View, Robert Dale Owen, Podmore and Cole. What Dobbs and Smith, for example, had to say about Owen was in no sense original, but it was necessary and influential, as can be judged from the fact that the Hadow Reports on *The Primary School* (1931) and *Infant and Nursery Schools* (1933) both made emphatic reference to Owen, whose infant school at New Lanark 'had a great influence on the development of infant education'.[71]

Owen's reputation as an educationist in Britain has to be seen, then, in terms of a pattern of educational development, and an accompanying set of historical inclusions and exclusions. Its fate shows how sharply nineteenth-century reputation-makers were able rapidly and effectively to readjust the direction and focus of their lens to suit their educational ideology. It is doubtful whether, as Holyoake appears to suggest, Owen's reputation would have met with any different a fate if he had been more careful in guarding it. It was not Owen's lack of attention, but the administrative system, the 'legitimate educators', the historians of institutions, and various kinds of Victorian indignation in response to Owen's views and activities, that demoted him. It was a new set of social policies and attitudes, radical and socialist revivals, and a wider interpretation of the history of education that rehabilitated him.

Profound and turbulent debates have taken place in the social sciences, particularly amongst sociologists, in recent decades about 'the social construction of reality', and therefore about the nature and content of the knowledge organized by social scientists, about their methodologies and about their place in the social processes themselves. Problems of history as reconstruction of reality have never been far from the concerns of historians, but they have been sharpened by the messages relayed across the social science–history boundaries. The focus on Owen's reputation in this chapter illustrates the double difficulty – the attempt of the historian to interpret himself as reconstructionist, and to do so whilst struggling with data processed through previous layers of reconstruction. Once educational processes are interpreted as being wider than the cumulative legacies of institutions and 'influences', they reveal how complex and uncertain are developments which have often been presented within simple frameworks and with great confidence. The history of education has not allowed itself to be over-disturbed by such historiographic problems. Institutions, organizations and acts – like reputations – have not been subjected to the anxieties which have opened and reopened issues in the social sciences and other areas of history. Education acts, periods, pioneers, schools, ideas, have been carved in historical granite, and only occasionally have changes been noticeable in the surface graffiti.

Notes

1 See, for example, W.A.C. Stewart and W.P. McCann, *The Educational Innovators 1750–1880* (London, 1967), ch. 4, 'Robert Owen and the New Lanark Schools'; Silver, *The Concept of Popular Education* (London, 1965, edition of 1977, with new Preface).
2 Henry Gray Macnab, *The New Views of Mr Owen of Lanark Impartially Examined* (London, 1819), pp. 214–16.
3 Frank Podmore, *Robert Owen: A Biography* (London, 1906), p. 102.
4 James Denholm, *The History of the City of Glasgow and Suburbs*, 2nd ed. (Glasgow, 1798), pp. 265–6.
5 Arthur John Booth, *Robert Owen, the Founder of Socialism in England* (London, 1869), p. 81.
6 Macnab, *New Views of Mr Owen*, p. 214.
7 Charles Gibbon, *The Life of George Combe* (London, 1878), vol. I, pp. 131–2.
8 Letter of 20 September 1828, from John Williamson, Co-operative Union Library collection, no. III. Original spelling and punctuation retained.
9 'Report of a Deputation from Leeds', reprinted in *A Supplementary Appendix to the First Volume of the Life of Robert Owen* (London, 1858), p. 254.
10 Quoted in Lloyd Jones, *The Life, Times and Labours of Robert Owen*, 6th ed. (London, 1919), pp. 106–8.
11 G.J. Holyoake, *Life and Last Days of Robert Owen, of New Lanark*, centenary ed. (London, 1871), p. 19.
12 *Edinburgh Review*, October 1819, p. 454.
13 *Blackwood's Edinburgh Magazine*, April 1821, pp. 88–92. See also ibid., (March 1823) p. 339. The writer was 'Christopher North' (John Wilson).
14 Booth, *Robert Owen*, p. 67.
15 Quoted from 'Characteristics', in Walter E. Houghton, *The Victorian Frame of Mind 1830–1870* (New Haven, 1957), p. 27.
16 Thomas Pole, *Observations Relative to Infant Schools* (Bristol, 1823), p. 11. For the millenarian background to Owenism see J.F.C. Harrison, *Robert Owen and the Owenites in Britain and America* (London, 1969).
17 John Hill Burton, *Political and Social Economy* (Edinburgh, 1849), p. 225.
18 Owen features in Hazlitt's essay 'On People with One Idea'.
19 Charles Bradlaugh, *Five Dead Men whom I Knew when Living* (London, 1877), p. 6.
20 *Report of the Proceedings of the Festival in Commemoration of the Centenary Birthday of Robert Owen* (London, 1871), p. 7.
21 *Life, Times and Labours*, p. 438.

22 Macnab, *New Views of Mr Owen*, p. 213.
23 The Dean of Durham, *Sentiments Proper to the Present Times* (Gateshead, 1848), pp. 3-6.
24 R.W.J. Selleck, *The New Education 1870-1914* (London, 1968), p. 68.
25 Seymour Tremenheere, 'Report on the State of Elementary Education in the County of Norfolk', *Minutes of the Committee of Council on Education, 1840-1* (London, 1841), p. 437.
26 Quoted in W.L. Burn, *The Age of Equipoise* (London, 1964), p. 111.
27 Joseph Fletcher, 'Report on Infant Schools on the Principles of the British and Foreign School Society', in *Minutes* (1845), p. 217.
28 The Cambridge series 'Landmarks in the History of Education', for example, did not include Owen, and only in a new series has it been introduced in 1969 - the first time it has been reprinted in Britain as an *educational* document.
29 *Aberdeen Banner*, 31 December 1842 (MS. copy in University of London, Pare Collection 578, no. 112).
30 Alan Price, 'A Pioneer of Scientific Education: George Combe (1788-1858)', *Educational Review*, June 1960, pp. 219, 227.
31 George C.T. Bartley, *The Schools for the People* (London, 1871). The garbled reference to Owen and New Lanark does not detract from the value of this important book.
32 J.C. Buckmaster, *The Education Question in Parliament. Being a Digest of Proceedings, from 1816 to the Publication of the Revised Code* (London, n.d.).
33 *The Museum, and English Journal of Education*, 1 August 1868, p. 176.
34 Robert Herbert Quick, *Essays on Educational Reformers* (London, 1904 ed.), p. 409.
35 J. Gill, *Systems of Education: A History and Criticism of the Principles, Methods, Organisation and Moral Discipline Advocated by Eminent Educationists* (London, 1876); James Leitch, *Practical Educationists* (Glasgow, 1876). For Leitch the line of tradition runs through Locke, Pestalozzi, Bell, Lancaster, Wilderspin, Stow and Spencer.
36 Sir Charles Reed, in *Transactions of the NAPSS, 1861* (London, 1862), p. 71.
37 H. Holman, *English National Education: A Sketch of the Rise of Public Elementary Schools in England* (London, 1898), p. 41.
38 For twentieth-century commentaries on this controversy see Robert R. Rusk, *A History of Infant Education*, 2nd ed. (London, 1937), and Harold Silver, *The Concept of Popular Education*.
39 Central Society of Education, *Second Publication* (London, 1838), p. 376.
40 See *Westminster Review*, October 1832, p. 407; October 1846, pp. 220-2; July 1847, pp. 484-5.
41 MS. copy of letter to *The Times*, August 1846, Pare Collection, no. 144.
42 Frederick Hill, *National Education; Its Present State and Prospects* (London, 1836), p. 169.
43 'Memoir of Robert Owen', *National Instructor*, 22 June 1850, p. 76.
44 William Lucas Sargant, *Robert Owen and His Social Philosophy* (London, 1860), p. 107.

45 *Report of the Proceedings*, p. 5.
46 Bradlaugh, *Five Dead Men*, pp. 4-5.
47 Letter from Robert Pemberton, 27 November 1854, Co-operative Union, no. 2305. See also no. 1083 (letter from Lord Wallscourt, 1839) and other examples in Harold Silver, *Robert Owen on Education* (Cambridge, 1969), pp. 31-2.
48 For the twenties and thirties see Silver, *The Concept of Popular Education*; for the Owenite movement (although there is little directly on education) see Harrison, *Robert Owen and the Owenites*; for Chartism see Brian Simon, *Studies in the History of Education 1780-1870* (London, 1960).
49 Quoted in Ambrose G. Barker, *Henry Hetherington 1792-1849* (London, n.d.), pp. 59-60.
50 See *The Life of Thomas Cooper Written by Himself* (London, 1872), p. 128.
51 *Cooper's Journal*, 15 June 1850, pp. 370-1.
52 'Robert Owen. - A Liberal Offer', *The Co-operator*, 1870, p. 104.
53 Ibid., 15 November 1867, 22 February 1868, 21 March 1868, 11 April 1868, 11 July 1868, 7 November 1868, 14 November 1868, 28 November 1868, 5 December 1868, 19 December 1868, 2 May 1869. 4 March 1871, 27 May 1871. There is an item on Owen and agricultural co-operation in 12 December 1868, and a reprint of an article from the *Beehive* on 'Robert Owen as a Practical Man' in 30 October 1869. The quotations are from Travis, 5 December 1868.
54 H.S. Foxwell, Introduction to Anton Menger, *The Right to the Whole Produce of Labour*, 1st English ed. (London, 1899), pp. lxxxvi, xciv.
55 Beatrice Potter, *The Co-operative Movement in Great Britain* (London, 1891), p. 16.
56 M.E. Sadler, *Continuation Schools in England and Elsewhere* (Manchester, 1907), p. 5. See also 'The School in Some of its Relations to Social Organisation and to National Life', *Sociological Papers*, vol. II, 1906, p. 124, and *Owen, Lovett, Maurice, and Toynbee* (London, 1907).
57 Harrison, *Robert Owen and the Owenites*, p. 3.
58 See J.S. Mill, *Utilitarianism* (London, 1954 ed.), pp. 52-3; *Autobiography* (London, 1955, ed.), pp. 104-6, 141-6. Also see H. Martineau, *Autobiography*, 3 vols (London, 1877), vol. I, p. 232.
59 See Karl Marx, *Capital*, reprint of English ed. of 1887 (Moscow, 1954), vol. I, pp. 483-4.
60 Friedrich Engels, *Herr Eugen Dühring's Revolution in Science*, reprint of 1934 ed. (London, n.d.), pp. 288-90. This passage occurs in the part of the book (published in German in 1878) which appeared separately in English as *Socialism: Utopian and Scientific* in 1892.
61 See Silver, *Robert Owen on Education*, pp. 37-8.
62 See M. Beer, *A History of British Socialism* (London, 1948 edn), p. 274.
63 See Margaret Cole, *The Story of Fabian Socialism* (London, 1961), pp. 3-5.
64 Owen Balmforth, *Huddersfield Past and Present* (Huddersfield, 1894), p. 4.
65 *D.N.B.* (1895), p. 451.
66 J. Ramsay MacDonald, *The Socialist Movement* (London, n.d. [1911]), p. 204.

67 Thomas Frost, *Forty Years' Recollections: Literary and Political* (London, 1880), p. 22.
68 Holyoake, *Life and Last Days of Robert Owen*, p. 22.
69 Joseph Clayton, *Robert Owen: Pioneer of Social Reforms* (London, 1908), p. 13.
70 John Dewey, *Democracy and Education* (New York, 1966 edn), pp. 266–76.
71 *Report of the Consultative Committee on the Primary School* (London, 1931), p. 3. See also *Report of the Consultative Committee on Infant and Nursery Schools* (London, 1933), pp. 4–5.

4 Education, opinion and the 1870s

A major piece of educational legislation and the controversies surrounding it have long been a favourite focus of educational research. The 1870 Elementary Education Act, symbolizing the belated beginnings of a national 'system' of education, has consistently been given pride of historical place. In 1884 Henry Craik, in his *The State in Its Relation to Education*, suggested that the policies proposed by the Act for filling the gaps in educational provision could 'best be seen through a summary of the discussions which took place during its passage into the Statute Book'.[1] Those discussions were the ones which took place in Parliament itself, and in connection with the two main pressure groups which were involved before 1870 in promoting alternative perspectives on the educational future – the National Education League (NEL) and the National Education Union (NEU). These discussions have been extended backwards in time and outwards in various directions by historians since,[2] but the pattern of analysis has in most historical work remained substantially the same. The theoretical substratum on which the analysis has been based was defined by Graham Balfour in 1898 as follows:

> the times were ripening fast for a more complete change, a change of principle and not of detail. It was evident by this time that the deficiencies in the existing school system could never be overtaken by voluntary effort, and that some more certain basis of support and more responsible agencies were needed than subscriptions which might cease at any time, or schools which might sever their connexion with the State ... At last in 1870 ... a Government Bill for England and Wales was introduced in the House of Commons by the Rt. Hon.

W.E. Forster, and after numerous modifications was passed by both Houses of Parliament.[3]

In what sense 'the times were ripening fast' is clearly a question of the state of 'opinion', of channels of influence and controversy, of social and political pressure points. What was 'ripening', what was 'evident', what could 'never be', what 'were needed', are all clearly matters of the balance of calculations, of rival interpretations, and the question for the historian is how far to look for explanations. It is even possible to challenge the whole process by which the state became involved in educational legislation, and that challenge has been made by E.G. West, arguing that the state *need* not have been involved at all, and that voluntary effort was adequate and misrepresented by statisticians and analysts prior to the 1870 Act. West's 'refutation' (his word) of 'the hypothesis that the industrial revolution brought educational stagnation'[4] is, however, swept along on tides of ideological argument against the state, not on any serious historical analysis, and such an analysis has not been attempted by other historians. We shall see in later chapters how dangerous theory disguised as history can become, whether in this case from the ideological right, or as in later cases, from the ideological left.

What fails to enter the analysis in a presentation such as Balfour's of the almost inevitability of the bill that passed both Houses of Parliament, or such as West's of the conspiracy of the 1860s which needs 'refuting', is the complexity of the reality as seen by contemporaries. An interesting approach to Balfour and to West would be, for example, to examine the nature and extent of resistance to educational legislation prior to 1870, and the weight of outright resistance and alternative strategies in the balance of opinion and policy-influencing processes in the late 1860s. How important, for example, was rural opinion? How did it define and assert itself? An insight can be gained simply by taking a single publication – *Bell's Weekly Messenger* – which throughout 1868 reported meetings of farmers' clubs, chambers of agriculture, and other public and private gatherings.[5] A number of such meetings were willing to accept the restriction of children's – especially girls' – labour in agriculture. The Central Chamber of Agriculture, in London, thought that children under nine years of age should be restricted from employment, but deprecated the establishment of an educational rate or compulsory legislation on the employment of women and children.[6] The Warwickshire Chamber of Agriculture passed a resolution proposing that girls under eleven and boys under ten should not be employed in agriculture.[7] The Hampshire Chamber of Agriculture recommended unanimously that boys under ten and girls under thirteen should not be employed in agriculture.[8]

Although such meetings sometimes heard descriptions of the excessive hours worked by child labour in agriculture,[9] opposition to compulsory legislation and school attendance was clearly widespread. Hereford Chamber of Commerce was told by a speaker on the 'Education of the Agricultural Labouring Classes' that educating two million children at a cost of 30s a year would mean a rate of 8d in the pound.[10] A clergyman told the Shropshire Chamber of Agriculture that 'compulsory education was not likely ever to be a favourite system in England'.[11] Most important, however, was the feeling widely voiced in these meetings that labourers – and not only labourers – did not need education. A report from East Gloucestershire, for example, resisted the notion that it was a duty that the labouring classes should be taught to 'read, write and reckon up their wages . . . experience tells us that many of the best and soberest labourers we have ever had could hardly do either'.[12] Mr C.S. Reed, MP, told prizewinners at the Tunstead and Happing Labourers Association at North Walsham, in 1867, that there was little excuse for taking girls away from school until they were eleven or twelve, as they were seldom wanted for domestic or farm duties below that age. With boys, however, it was different:

> they must bend their back to labour and develop their muscles while they are of tender years . . . I contend that if a boy can read at the age of 9, that is the age at which he should go to field labour, and by attending Sunday schools and night schools, he can retain and, if he will try, improve his education.[13]

A typical resolution, from the Winifrith Farmers' Club, at the Black Bear, Woolmer, agreed unanimously that 'the proposed system of national education is both unnecessary and impracticable in agricultural districts, and that it is the duty of the tax-paying portion of the community strenuously to resist the threatened addition which would be made by its adoption to the poor rate'.[14] That the agricultural labourer was not alone in being better off in ignorance, or illiteracy, or semi-literacy, or that he needed some level of reassurance in that state, was demonstrated by Lord Fortescue, addressing the Barnstaple Farmers' Club on 'Earning and Learning': 'England was great and glorious when affairs were managed according to the lights of past days

– managed very successfully both in peace and war, when the great proportion of the statesmen and generals were unable even to read and write.'[15] Lord Fortescue was clearly unaware that in Germany, the United States, and in sections of Britain opinion, times 'were ripening'. In analysing growing British backwardness in education, industry and other aspects of social and economic structures relevant to international comparison and competition, historians accept that there are points in the 1860s and later decades at which British weaknesses were diagnosed and educational remedies advocated. The story too often fails, however, to take account of forums such as the farmers' clubs and chambers of agriculture, the participants in their debates, and the segments of opinion they influenced and represented. The search for the forums in which opinion was canvassed, moulded, asserted, has been extremely narrow and restricted.

The 1870s become, therefore, a useful case study in the operation and analysis of opinion, one which raises questions about the range and style of the historical analysis that has hitherto been predominant. What, in fact, do historians tell us about the period surrounding the 1870 Education Act, and how reliable and useful is it? The picture is roughly this. There was an Elementary Education Act in 1870, with all the political and social pressures that produced it, after decades of controversy, resistance and delay. There followed the creation of school boards and board schools, rivalry with the voluntary schools, problems about religious worship and teaching, fees and attendance. On the last of these, Matthew Arnold observed in 1869 that the question of compulsory schooling had by then become one of those issues that was 'passing out of the sphere of abstract discussion, and entering into the sphere of practical politics'.[16] The 1870 Act did not make education compulsory for all – the principle was, as Lyon Playfair put it, only 'timidly and hesitatingly put forth'.[17] The principle of compulsion was then strengthened by an Act of 1876, and made universal in 1880. Events of this kind were accompanied in the 1870s by changes in the curriculum, concerns about scientific education – reflected in a royal commission on the subject – and growing, though still limited, concerns of other kinds, including the welfare and opportunities of the children of the poor. An Act of 1869 was followed by changes in the affairs of the endowed grammar schools, and an expansion of education for middle-class girls. Religious tests were finally abolished at Oxford and Cambridge, and a crop of new university colleges sprang up in the decade.

The main weight of historical interest in this period, however, has undoubtedly been on the massive intervention of the state in elementary education, concentrating on its impact on school and pupil numbers, finance, the political aspects of the school boards, their policies, their elections, their meaning in the history of democracy, the growth of the administrative machinery of education, the inspectorate, teacher unionism, local and regional differences in schooling, and the commitment of the labour movement to improving and supplementing the state system.

That, breathlessly summarized, is the received wisdom. The separate ingredients are an understandable selection of what appears, over a century later, to be significant in the education of the 1870s. But it is unsatisfactory for a number of reasons.

First, take the question of compulsory attendance. From most accounts of the period it looks almost inevitable that the Acts of 1876 and 1880 followed that of 1870 – or at least the sequence has not been seen as problematical. But there are difficulties. The 1870 Act included compulsion as an option for school boards, but went no further than that because there was mountainous opposition to compulsory schooling. The Newcastle Commission on the state of popular education had expressed the view in 1861 that Englishmen would never permit state compulsion as in Germany: the Commission thought that it would be too 'great a shock to our educational and social system'.[18] This was a strongly held view in 1870 and even those who approved of compulsory attendance of some kind included a strong contingent who were interested in indirect compulsion through the Factory Acts, wanting to compel employers to take only children who had achieved a certain standard of education.[19] There was also pressure in favour of direct compulsion, from the radical NEL and other quarters, but as a friend of compulsory education confessed in March 1869: 'It may be admitted that not much is to be hoped from the present state of opinion.' He left the question to the reformed Parliament and to the 'unknown future'.[20]

If there was so much hostility to compulsory schooling in and around 1870, nothing that happened afterwards was in the least inevitable. As W.H.G. Armytage has pointed out, there was a 'metamorphosis of opinion between 1870 and 1880'.[21] Gillian Sutherland, in the only extensive analysis of policy changes in the period, comments that 'the politicians led the Department, and public opinion, to a considerable extent, led them'.[22] No one else has even begun to analyse this 'metamorphosis'. It is astonishing that such a major change in Victorian opinion and social consciousness has received so little attention. In the summer of 1877 the *Saturday Review* commented that 'the principle of compulsion, which was denounced not so long ago as revolutionary in the worst sense, is now placidly accepted on all hands'.[23] Why? One might expect that historians of education and of society would have wanted to answer that question, to examine the components of such important changes in Victorian perceptions of government, the school, the family, social class, freedom, and much else that is involved in this development – one of the most important of the period. But their interests have for the most part been elsewhere.

Take a second question – that of the quality of education in the 1870s. Historical attention has been focused in this respect mainly on payment by results from 1862 and for the rest of the century. Other concerns of the 1870s about the quality of education, and about some of its main elements, have not been seriously examined. In fact, how the Victorians saw the quality and value of their education, and what they meant by these, have been only narrowly discussed, and then mainly in connection with the grammar and public schools. In 1874 Matthew Arnold, talking about the quality of the British endowed schools, pointed out that

> we laugh at the French Minister who took out his watch and said with satisfaction that in all French lycées the boys were at that moment doing the same thing. But really, is it so lamentable to think that all schoolboys should at a given moment be reading the fourth eclogue of Virgil; or is it so delightful to think that at a given moment all schoolboys may be reading different pieces of rubbish, out of innumerable and equally accepted collections of it?[24]

Two French observers had in 1868 referred to the science and art department courses available to the working classes, subjects which the public schools 'make the mistake of withholding from the aristocratic classes'.[25] This kind of incitement to consider the content and quality of secondary education in the late nineteenth century has been responded to by some historians. But what about attitudes to the quality of elementary education in the 1870s?

While the nation was congratulating itself on having at last achieved its education legislation in 1870 other tones of voice were being heard. Radical Liberal spokesman John Morley in 1873 delivered an onslaught on the standards of the voluntary schools, notably the Church of

England ones. The education given in the denominational schools, he wrote, 'has been almost worthless'. Everywhere the story told by the inspectors was the same – 'narrow range of subjects, low standards, and lower proficiency'. The schools admitted the children of the working class, he considered, no further than the gates of civilization. And in the 1870 Act Parliament had perpetuated something of little value. 'We are to leave the quality as it is', he said, 'and devote all our efforts to augmenting quantity'.[26] Francis Adams, secretary of the NEL, described the state of education in the 1870s as 'defective and humiliating'.[27] Morley and Adams may have been partisan, but there are other indications of the weaknesses of the voluntary schools in and after 1870. The *Saturday Review*, while rejecting Morley's diagnosis of the clergy as being responsible for the low quality, agreed with him 'as to the worthlessness of much that now goes by the name of education'. The standards through which payment was paid by results represented 'hardly an education at all'.[28] A contributor to the *Contemporary Review* wrote in 1870 that 'the stream of voluntary contributions to the support of education has run thin by degrees, is running most beautifully less, in many, if not most places, and is nearly dried up in some'. Church schools were 'by no means full, nor so effective, as unfailing funds and good management would make them'.[29]

Also in 1870 Lyon Playfair, in a presidential address to the Education Department of the NAPSS, spoke of other nations in Europe having 'spread primary and secondary education in well-organised systems throughout their lands', while 'England had not even laid the foundation-stone of a national system till the present year. And so we have the disgrace of having the worst educated people, as a whole, of any country which professes a high civilisation'. Like Morley, Playfair underlined that the 1870 Act had dealt with 'the quantity of education, but not with the quality' – aspects of which he went on to discuss in detail, attacking payment by results, when the results were 'scarcely worth paying for'.[30]

We know remarkably little about the quality of Victorian education as the Victorians saw it. The history of the classroom is almost non-existent, and we cannot qualify our general statements by reference to practice, good or bad.[31] Opinion about education is less well mapped than the books might suggest, including on the subject of resistance to popular education. Doubts were still being expressed in the 1870s about whether working-class children were being over-educated or educated in the wrong values. Such resistance had been prominent throughout the nineteenth century, and remained so in the 1870s. Just before the 1870 Act one HMI discussed a widespread unwillingness to acknowledge authority. He reported that a clergyman had found it impossible in a large East London elementary school to get out of children 'any idea of what was meant by "betters" in the catechism, "To order myself lowly and reverently to my betters." They plainly expressed by their manners that they knew "no betters".' Since workmen were now going to the same places of entertainment and travelling on the same trains as their employers, suggested the HMI,

> a much more minute attention should be paid in schools for the working-class youth to matters of cleanliness, personal propriety and decorum of language and action, so that the rising generation of the country should attain somewhat of the habits of the gentleman as they are admitted to the political freedom of the citizen.[32]

The same spectrum of opinion remained as had pervaded the century – teach them well as it is their right, or teach them something for safety's sake, or beware of teaching them too much, if anything at all.

Pamphlets were still being written in the 1870s urging, for example, that it was enough to teach boys purely the elements of some trade, such as bootmaking or tailoring, and to teach girls 'to scour floors, to clean and have a general knowledge of systematic arrangement of furniture, etc.; also many other matters which might eventually be required of them in their situations as house servants'. Was it not the duty of the board schools 'to teach the children to be useful in after-life, and not to give them all book-cram?'.[33] In 1871, wrote Playfair's biographer, the 'old fear' cropped up in Parliament that 'there was to be "over-education" of the people'.[34] There is still at least one book, or pantomime or television spectacular, to be written about the long fight to hold back popular education in the nineteenth century – and up to, and including the 1980s.

All of these opinions relate to questions that the Victorians made explicit about the quality of education. So do a whole series of detailed concerns about the content of schooling and the realities of school experience, which remain virtually unexamined. The precise motives of the educators and educationists of the 1870s, their perception of the content and quality of schooling, and of its impact, have not been attractive to historians of this period, and we still make crude but confident assumptions about them. The chairman of the Manchester

School Board, looking back in the 1880s over the first fifteen years of the Board's activities, thought that the aim of the board schools was to promote 'good citizenship', to develop the 'brain power' of the people, to provide people with 'the right to intellectual life, at least to such an extent as to fit its subject for self-culture'.[35] Historians have been too busy with the boards themselves to worry about the cultural meanings of the education they provided.

One central aspect of concern about quality in the 1870s was the relationship between quality of teachers and the quality of education. The history of teachers, as distinct from the history of teacher unionism or of teacher training, hardly exists. How important were questions about the professional competence and effectiveness of teachers in the 1870s? When the occupants of the first two chairs of education were appointed in 1876, not surprisingly they discussed teachers and teaching in their inaugural lectures. For J. M. D. Meiklejohn at St Andrews the 'most important educational question for Scotland and England at the present moment' was what he called 'the culture of the teacher'. The role of the universities was to help turn 'the occupation of teaching into a profession', and to collect and distribute the experience of the best teachers for the benefit of the younger ones.[36] S. S. Laurie, at Edinburgh, saw the same need to weld teachers into a profession, to give education academic standing, and to provide the material conditions for attracting 'able and ambitious' teachers.[37] But men like Meiklejohn and Laurie were not the only ones who saw the question of the teacher as the *most* important educational question of the time. There were those, for example, not only among the women educationists, who saw the situation after 1870 as offering unique opportunities to train and attract high-quality women teachers.[38] For Lyon Playfair in 1870 and afterwards the 'position and qualifications of teachers in our primary schools' was what he called the 'kernel of the whole matter'.[39]

The Liberal campaigners were aware of this. George Dixon, MP, reported in 1872 the words of one teacher who had told him that teachers in Church of England schools were 'anything between a gravedigger and a parson'.[40] John Morley and Francis Adams both amassed information to show that church schoolmasters were often expected to act as grave-digger, beadle, choirmaster and sexton. Morley desribed such teachers as 'upper dependants of the rectory', but that was perhaps a generous description of many teachers whose status was still in fact close to that of the grave-digger and the agricultural labourer.[41] Some teachers, more of them as the board schools were established, acquired a better status. Of the dame or adventure school-teachers, however, the *Saturday Review* wrote in 1871 that 'nothing can equal the dirt of a dirty schoolmaster; his frock-coat the penwiper of half a century, his shirt the same colour as his coat'.[42] Caricatures apart, when there were people who saw the status and culture of the teacher as the *most* important question, it is obviously important to ask how the mid-Victorians approached these questions which touched on the quality of education. This again is a serious matter for historians of education and of society, but they have on the whole avoided such questions.

This whole area of discussion has in fact featured little or not at all in the 'relevant' story of the late nineteenth century. It is immensely relevant, however, if one wishes to see not the bits of Victorians that suit our present purposes, but a much fuller picture of the Victorians in the process of establishing their own patterns of social and cultural relevance. This question of relevance is central to an understanding of why historians have not looked squarely at the 1870s, or why they have maintained any other important historical silence. Relevance to twentieth-century historians of the nineteenth century has, in fact, meant more than anything else a preoccupation with the state. Attempts to explain our modern, industrial, state-ordered society have been uppermost in their historical consciousness. It is important not to detract from efforts to understand the growth and importance of the role of government and the state in the past century, but the fact is that historians have tended to close their eyes to features of social change that have not seemed 'relevant' to those efforts. Historians of education have used the modern industrial state as a touchstone of relevance.

E.H. Carr has referred to the Athenian view of society, warning that it is a pre-selected view, almost the only one available: the Athenian records are not 'objective', they are one view.[43] If there is an Athenian view of Greek society there is also, so to speak, an Athenian view of Victorian society, at least an Athenian emphasis. Historians have too willingly accepted the focus that 'Athenian' spokesmen for the late Victorian state and its machinery came to represent. There are, indeed, 'non-Athenian' views of nineteenth-century society and education – and in the latter case no one has done more than Brian Simon to show us where to find them, how to disentangle them, in looking at the educational implications of labour, radical and popular movements. We need to go further in pursuing other versions of the non-Athenian view if we are to understand mid-Victorian education and society more fully: to do this we need to escape from obsessive concern with what are often the superficialities of the state and its related institutions.

There was no consensus about the nature and extent of the powers of the state in the 1870s any more than there is a century later. We see it as an instrument of capitalist oppression of a whole class, or as a juggernaut crushing the will of the individual, as arbiter, as safety-net, or as many other things – just as people did in the 1870s. Historians have different perceptions of the state when they grapple with the history of modern institutions, including state-supported education. Historians do not share a uniform ideology, in any of the senses we have discussed, but they may share an emphasis, a consensus about what it is important to discuss. British historians of education have widely shared an awareness of the development of the state over the past century, though unlike their European and American colleagues they have found it difficult or unnecessary to make any view of the state explicit. If we look at the established picture of education in the 1870s what we see is mainly the growing state and its works and instruments. It seems to indicate an increasingly 'inevitable' interventionist role in education, and this piecemeal and linear approach has directed attention away from uncertainties and confusions about the state in mid-Victorian society.

Historians of education have therefore found it difficult to situate in any kind of reality Matthew Arnold's magnificent appeal in *Culture and Anarchy* at the end of the 1860s for the state and an established church to be seen as the core of discussion of culture. They have found it difficult to put into the perspective of social and educational change on the one hand T.H. Green's advocacy of the state at the end of the 1870s,[44] and on the other hand the crusade Herbert Spencer was continuing to wage in this period against the state, against free education, against free libraries, and against the whole extension of the state's role in the name of liberalism.[45] The history of state intervention has been written in such a linear fashion that attention has even been diverted away from abortive discussions of the state, such as the incipient demand for it to support and intervene in universities in the 1870s. The two Scottish chairs of education in 1876, for example, were created out of a bequest by the Reverend Andrew Bell. An attempt was made to obtain government money to augment this bequest, and, we are told, this was 'at first favourably entertained. But a very strong opposition came from the authorities of the denominational Training

Colleges', fearing that their monopoly of professional training might be interfered with: 'this opposition received sufficient sympathy from Scottish members of Parliament, and other persons of influence, to induce the Government to recede from its first intention'. This is a most interesting episode at a time when the state was not involved in higher education, and when new English university colleges were being created on the basis of individual and local endeavour.[46]

Another example is the conflict over Robert Lowe's demand in the early 1870s that the state should not only assist but also control the universities, through their examinations, and Lowe defined a university as an 'examining board'. Leading the troops on the other side was Lyon Playfair, who saw the University of London as being 'far more related to the Examining Boards of China than to any European model', but advocated state support which did not infringe upon university autonomy.[47] Such details suggest how far we are from understanding the history of the state in its relation to education if we stick to the history of successful legislation, and omit the bits that may at first sight seem 'irrelevant', or abortive, or inconvenient, but which were important features of the reality as the people who inhabited that world saw it, and which helped to shape the educational and social world we have inherited. The dangers of approaching the history from the starting-point of a *theory* of the state are also great, and we shall return to them in a later chapter.

Historians have to be alert both to the distortions that their own society tempts them into, and to those of the people and time they investigate. The hypnotic attraction of the expanding state has produced such distortion, by encouraging historians to neglect what seem irrelevant dead ends and lost causes – the central theme of other chapters. The fate of reputations is one aspect of this neglect or difficulty, as we have discussed particularly in the case of Robert Owen. There are other examples relevant to this discussion, as was suggested in the last chapter. The Victorians, like ourselves, destroyed reputations: they cooked the books. They massively, as we have done with them, inflated some and diminished others. In the educational affairs of the mid-nineteenth century no one was better known than the phrenologist, educational campaigner and publicist, George Combe – but by the 1870s the Victorians were not just forgetting him, they were deleting him from history. In the twentieth century we have done much the same for the 1870s, and there are two outstanding cases which illustrate the point.

The first is that of Herbert Spencer, who was a towering figure in nineteenth-century scientific, social and educational thought, but who at various points became not just increasingly outdated - as who doesn't? - but also inconvenient to history. His contributions to social and educational thought have been bowdlerized and trivialized. In the 1870s Spencer was still active and influential, propounding an evolutionary model of psychology and education, attacking not just the state but all its works, criticizing educational practice, as he put it in 1876, as 'bad in matter, bad in manner, bad in order' - or, in an alternative description, 'mechanical lessons of stupid teachers'.[48] Spencer's educational ideas, it was said in 1911, had been floated on a prodigious tide of industrial and social change', resulting in acceptance and implementation of his ideas.[49] Spencer's famous essays, *Education: Intellectual, Moral, and Physical* were first published in book form under that title in 1861, and had given him an enormous national and international reputation by the 1870s.[50] In the 1930s the book was described as, after Locke, 'the most widely read treatise on education that England has produced'.[51] But Spencer's highly individualistic views, and even his justification for science as the basis of education, have less and less fitted the historical version of what was relevant and successful in Victorian England. Educational historians have now virtually silenced him. Spencer now seems to me to occupy - almost exclusively on the basis of his 1861 book - a marginal and rather bizarre place in a disembodied history of educational ideas, and no place at all in the history of education itself - except perhaps as an over-enthusiastic contributor to the cause of science education. A rounded picture of Spencer and of his impact in Britain is not available to the reader of most of our contemporary literature.[52]

Lyon Playfair is the second case of someone who was relegated to the margins. Playfair's role as a scientist and educationist in drawing the attention of the Taunton Commission in 1867 to the success of Britain's competitors at the Paris exhibition, and therefore the need for better scientific education in Britain, has been dutifully repeated by educational historians, but it is almost the only part of Playfair's activities that has been. He is to be found in bits of history about the science and art department, and an occasional doff of the hat is made to him as the great chemist who contributed to the science education movement. He is in countless lists. And that, shamefully, is all. Yet in the 1870s, to stick to that decade alone, Playfair was a vital figure in educational discussion - one of the sanest and acutest analysts of education in mid-

Victorian Britain, a major parliamentary figure, an activist on many educational fronts, consulted on education at every level, and making his presence felt in the cause of education as well as science. In 1870 he delivered his powerful presidential address on education to the NAPSS, describing the Education Act of that year as no more than the 'beginning of a mighty work'.[53] In the same year he published lectures on primary and technical education, again indicting England's 'miserable caricature of an elementary education'.[54] Two years later he was publishing his appeal for independent universities supported by the state, and taking a sideswipe at the low quality of primary education, which had 'only produced readers who do not read, writers who do not write, and arithmeticians who do not count'. We had 'bought the complex tools of education, and given them to the working classes, but we have not taught them how to use the tools'.[55] In 1873, in a major speech in Parliament, he was bemoaning the fact that while Scotland had one university student per 860 of the population, Ireland had one per 2800, and England had only one per 3700. He pleaded for university education to be made to bear 'directly upon the occupations of the people, whether these be professional or industrial'.[56] In 1874 Playfair was trying to obtain the appointment of a Minister of Education.[57] In 1877 he was attacking the low status of middle-class education, and chaos in the organization of education in general.[58] In 1879 he moved a parliamentary bill for the registration of teachers.

In Parliament, on the platform, in print, in pressure groups, in private correspondence, he was a formidable campaigner for education, and not just for science education – though even that contribution is distorted, isolated from the other elements of his educational vision. The histories of education mention Playfair in passing, between select committees, royal commissions, and the 'relevant' history of technical and scientific education. On Playfair's activities outside scientific research the *Dictionary of National Biography* recorded in 1901 mainly that he inspected schools of science and art, was active in the cause of compulsory education in 1870, was short in stature, pompous and wordy, and was disliked by many people.[59]

The point is simply that educational and social historians, like all other kinds, operate criteria of relevance, and have no hard core of facts. Their data and their silences are judgements. They are making judgements, and using other people's judgements, even as they get on the bus to the university library or the Public Record Office. Like everyone else, they learn how to dip into history and find what they are mainly looking for. In defining his frontiers of historical relevance the historian exercises choice, under pressures to ask one kind of question rather than another, to make or not to make the state the touchstone of relevance, to ignore or to confront Lyon Playfair.

There are many levels of ambiguity in the word 'relevance'. Do we mean, for example, that which was relevant to the 1870s, and if so to which Athenians or non-Athenians? Or relevant to our desire to explain the present and act in it? We generally use relevance in this latter sense – that which has value for our present motives. Raiding the past for such a purpose has its place, since there are aspects of what is relevant to us now that were not so to the actors at the time. How well did we, as participants, judge the 'relevance' of the jet engine, or the contraceptive pill, or the Mersey Beat, or the creation of OPEC, at the time, and how does that criterion of relevance match up against their relevance to the historian or to all of us even a decade or two later? But simply raiding the past is not understanding it. To use snippets from the 1870s to illustrate how much or how little things have changed is reasonable enough if we realize how limited is the exercise. In 1877, for example, as a century later, education could be described as a 'somewhat wearisome subject'. After all the battles around educational statistics in the early 1870s, the *Saturday Review* could feel that 'alas, there is no longer that divine flame within us which once leapt up around a row of figures, and made a halo around every decimal point'.[60] No doubt when our own current political battles around examination results, or measurable standards or core curricula, or financial cuts, and the rest, have subsided, the press will again find the subject wearisome, and the divine flame will once again, as so frequently, burn low.

In our efforts to make historical sense of a process as crucial and as complex as education, we search, of course, for similarities and differences in the sources and in the historical portraits and narratives and analyses available to us. We search for emphases and messages. It is unfair, however, to point too accusing a finger at the selective use of history as a resource. We are not, after all, bland, neutral people. We have views to stand up for, whether about justice, or Manchester United, or college policy, and we look to the record to help us. We *use* history to help us to convince all the time. This is right and proper, but it is one use of history, and we may learn little of the past through it, getting partial and faulty messages when we imagine that we have got them whole. This is true even on the grand scale: focusing on change, for example, as an American historian has reminded us, may lead us to ignore the historical role of inertia, which 'is responsible for more of "history" than all the campaigns, the movements, the revolutions we readily call to mind'.[61]

The job of the social historian in particular is constantly to emphasize that attempts to explain and buttress the present may actually conflict with attempts to understand the past. In doing so he needs to look for help to the social sciences and especially to sociology, since, with all their controversies and confusions, they can at least alert him to ways of seeing societies and aspects of society, in their complexities, their self-images and their notions of relevance.

There are, then, two levels at which to explore and use history, and it does not help if historians imagine that they are operating at the one when they have slid into the other. Adding bits of information about the past to bits of knowledge of the present may have its interest, but it does not help us to come to grips with the past or with the present, and it is unlikely – to use Keynes's formulation – to emancipate the mind or make it less conservative.[62] The real inroads into conservatism come when people refuse to accept current problems, searches and answers as given, when the past – and the images of the future that we derive from it – strip us of our absolutes. Keynes's use of 'conservative' means 'closed', unable to see the relative, changing conditions that a study of history of opinion conveys. When we look at the 1870s, it is the tension between our opinions and theirs, our ideologies and theirs, that matters most, that enables us to be aware of some of our blindness and its causes. If emancipation can come from a study of the history of opinion, it is not from disembodied intellectual history, not from a mindless record of social events, but from a combination of the two, the history of ideas as they are hammered out and encountered in action.[63]

Interpreting the 1870s, or the history of education generally in the nineteenth and twentieth centuries, means joining James Mill, more than a century and a half later, in attempting to understand why and how 'opinion, of one sort or another, governs the world'.[64]

Notes

1 Henry Craik, *The State in Its Relation to Education* (London, 1884, edition of 1896), p. 90.

2 See, for example, D.K. Jones, *The Making of the Education System 1851-81* (London, 1977); W.P. McCann, 'Trade Unionist, Co-operative and Socialist Organisations in Relation to Popular Education 1870-1902', Manchester University PhD thesis, 1960.

3 Graham Balfour, *The Educational Systems of Great Britain and Ireland* (Oxford, 1898, edition of 1903), p. 18.

4 E.G. West, *Education and the Industrial Revolution* (London, 1975), p. 245.

5 I am indebted for this information to Mr W.J. Petch, Bulmershe College of Higher Education.

6 *Bell's Weekly Messenger*, 9 March 1868, p. 5.

7 Ibid., 21 December 1868, p. 5.

8 Ibid., 7 December 1868, p. 5.

9 For example, ibid., 9 March 1868, Supplement, pp. 1-2, report of a number of speakers at the Central Chamber of Agriculture, London.

10 Ibid., 20 January 1868, p. 5.

11 Ibid., 24 February 1868, p. 3.

12 Ibid., 23 March 1868, p. 3.

13 Ibid., 18 November 1867, p. 3 (reprinted from the *Norfolk Chronicle*).

14 Ibid., 12 October 1868, p. 2.

15 Ibid., 2 March 1868, p. 3.

16 Francis Sandford (ed.), *Reports on Elementary Schools 1852-1882 by Matthew Arnold* (London, 1889), pp. 149-50.

17 Lyon Playfair, 'Address on Education', *Transactions of the NAPSS, 1870* (London, 1871), p. 55.

18 *Report of the Commissioners Appointed to Inquire into the State of Popular Education in England* (London, 1861), vol. 1, p. 200.

19 See Sandford, *Reports by Matthew Arnold* (report for 1869), p. 150; J.P. Norris, *The Education of the People. Our Weak Points and Our Strengths* (Edinburgh, 1869), pp. 19-25.

20 Rev. T.W. Fowle, 'The Application of the Principle of Compulsion to Education', *Sessional Proceedings of the National Association for the Promotion of Social Science for the Year 1867-8* (London, 1868), pp. 249-50.

21 W.H.G. Armytage, 'The 1870 Education Act', *British Journal of Educational Studies*, vol. XVIII, no. 23, 1970, p. 128.

22 Gillian Sutherland, *Policy-Making in Elementary Education 1870-1895* (London, 1973), p. 115.

23 *Saturday Review*, vol. XLIII, 23 June 1877, p. 764.

24 Sandford, *Reports by Matthew Arnold* (report for 1874), p. 183.

25 J. Demogeot and H. Montucci, *De l'enseignement secondaire en Angleterre et en Écosse* (Paris, 1868), p. 293.

26 John Morley, *The Struggle for National Education* (London, 1873), pp. 18, 27-8, 36.

27 Francis Adams, *History of the Elementary School Contest in England* (London, 1882), p. 303.

28 *Saturday Review*, vol. XXXVI, 4 October 1873, p. 431.

29 John Oakley, 'The Attitude of the Church towards Primary Education', *Contemporary Review*, vol. XIV, 1870, pp. 200, 208.

30 Playfair, 'Address on Education', pp. 41, 43–4.
31 David Hamilton, University of Glasgow, has since 1977 been researching aspects of the 'evolution of the classroom system'.
32 Committee of Council on Education, *Report . . . 1868–9* (London, 1869), pp. 129–30.
33 S. Leigh-Gregson, *Progress: Being Remarks on Education as Regards State Aid and the General Systems of School Board, Elementary, Higher, and University Education* (Isbister, 1876), pp. 10–11.
34 Wemyss Reid, *Memoirs and Correspondence of Lyon Playfair* (London, 1899), p. 213.
35 John Watts, 'Fifteen Years of School Board Work in Manchester', Manchester Statistical Society, paper read 14 April 1886, pp. 86, 114, 115.
36 J.M.D. Meiklejohn, *Inaugural Address, University of St Andrews* (Edinburgh, 1876), pp. 1, 10–11, 13.
37 S.S. Laurie, *Inaugural Address, University of Edinburgh* (Edinburgh, 1876), pp. 12, 14.
38 See, for example, James H. Rigg, *National Education in Its Social Conditions and Aspects, and Public Elementary School Education English and Foreign* (London, 1873), pp. 335–6, on opportunities for middle-class women in education; D.R. Fearon, 'Girls' Grammar Schools', *Contemporary Review*, vol. XI, 1869, for a discussion of the limited supply of good governesses and reasons for the poor quality of teachers.
39 Playfair, 'Address on Education', p. 59. See also Lyon Playfair, 'On the Organisation of a Teaching Profession' (Presidential Address to the Conference of Teachers, 12 January 1877), *Fortnightly Review*, vol. XXI, February 1877, pp. 207–13.
40 *Saturday Review*, vol. XXXII, 9 March 1872, p. 291.
41 See Adams, *History of the Elementary School Contest*, pp. 304–5, for extracts from advertisements for church teachers; similarly in Morley, *Struggle for National Education*, pp. 40–1.
42 *Saturday Review*, vol. XXXII, 30 September 1871, p. 426.
43 E.H. Carr, *What Is History?* (London, 1961, edition of 1964), p. 13.
44 See 'On the Different Senses of "Freedom" as Applied to Will and to the Moral Progress of Man' (lecture delivered in 1879), and 'Lectures on the Principles of Political Obligation' (delivered in 1879–80), in R.L. Nettleship (ed.), *Works of Thomas Hill Green* (London, 1886, edition of 1893), vol. II.
45 See Herbert Spencer, *The Man Versus the State* (London, 1884); *The Principles of Sociology* (London 1876; edition of 1885), vol.I, especially pp. 572–3.
46 J.G. Fitch, 'The Universities and the Training of Teachers', *Contemporary Review*, vol. XXIX, 1876, pp. 102–3. For the background to this episode, see William Jolly, 'The Professional Training of Teachers', *Transactions of the NAPSS, 1874* (London, 1875), p. 490.
47 Lyon Playfair, *On Teaching Universities and Examining Boards, Address to the Philosophical Institution of Edinburgh, January 31, 1872* (Edinburgh, 1872), pp. 3–4, including the quotations from Lowe. See also Reid, *Memoirs and Correspondence of Lyon Playfair*, pp. 215–17.

48 Spencer, *The Principles of Sociology*, pp. 572, 761.
49 Charles W. Eliot, Introduction to Herbert Spencer, *Essays on Education and Kindred Subjects* (London, 1911), pp.xvi–xvii.
50 See Robert Herbert Quick, *Essays on Educational Reformers* (London, 1868), for a substantial chapter on Spencer's *Education*.
51 F.A. Cavanagh (ed.), *Herbert Spencer on Education* (Cambridge, 1932), p. xx.
52 Examples of the narrow base on which Spencer has been discussed in this century are: W.J. McCallister, *The Growth of Freedom in Education* (London, 1931), ch. XXV, and J.A. Lauwerys, 'Herbert Spencer and the Scientific Movement', in A.V. Judges (ed.), *Pioneers of English Education* (London, 1952), ch. 7. S.J. Curtis, in *History of Education in Great Britain* (London, 1948, edition of 1949, p. 480) includes as one of the points in his six lines on Spencer that his work was 'riddled with inconsistencies and fallacies'. An attempt to redress the balance is Ann Low-Beer (ed.), *Herbert Spencer* (London, 1969).
53 Playfair, 'Address on Education', p. 62.
54 Lyon Playfair, *On Primary and Technical Education: Two Lectures Delivered to the Philosophical Institution of Edinburgh* (Edinburgh, 1870), pp. 18, 25.
55 Playfair, *On Teaching Universities and Examining Boards*, p. 36.
56 Lyon Playfair, *Speech on Second Reading of Irish University Bill* (Edinburgh, 1873), pp. 4–5.
57 See J.G. Crowther, *Statesmen of Science* (London, 1965), p. 148.
58 Playfair, 'On the Organisation of the Teaching Profession'.
59 *Dictionary of National Biography*, first supplement (London, 1901), vol. 45, pp. 36–7.
60 *Saturday Review*, vol. XLIII, 23 June 1877, p. 764.
61 Robert L. Heilbroner, *The Future as History* (New York 1959, edition of 1960), p. 193. Marc Bloch also comments on views of total change as overlooking 'the force of inertia peculiar to so many social creations', *The Historian's Craft* (English edition, Manchester 1954), p. 39.
62 See p. 10 above.
63 See the discussion in Owen Chadwick, *The Secularization of the European Mind in the Nineteenth Century* (Cambridge, 1975), pp. 11–14.
64 See p. 12 above.

5 Social science and educational reform: Britain and America in the late nineteenth century

The reputation of a reformer such as Robert Owen, we have suggested, has to be interpreted in the light of dominant and changing political and social values. The nature of the social science movements in Britain and the United States in the second half of the nineteenth century, and their relationship to the history of education, offer a broader case study of the same kind. With organized social science in the late nineteenth century we are also concerned with conceptions of social action, including education, and with attitudes to the state. The close relationship between the social science movements in Britain and the United States makes it possible to consider historically the role of parallel and interlocking developments in dissimilar state structures. It is a critically important point at which historical detail and social theory can be seen to intersect.

One important aspect of the history of social science movements is their relevance to the notion of a history of 'opinion', and to 'educational opinion' specifically. If the history of education is to be more than a history of disembodied ideas, or of social movements and processes divorced from will or intention or motivation, it has to locate the ways in which ideas became identified with action. It has to seek the places which shed light on the sources of change, on the origins of power and influence. It is in this connection that the forums of debate assume importance. Historians have found such focal points in parliamentary debate, in pamphleteering wars, in the press, in the records of educational authorities, boards, committees, commissions. Specifically educational bodies, together with the political frameworks of policy-making are, however, only two of the historically visible public chambers of debate. We know, and historians have made inroads into such other territories, that sources of educational energy are to be found in the history of trade union and professional bodies, of women's or industrial pressure groups, of publishing firms, youth movements and the labour market. The emergence of social science as a popularly accessible concept and an organized movement in the second half of the nineteenth century is of crucial importance, both as an 'educational' movement in a direct sense, and as an indication of where historians of education need to look for explanations of how ideas and action come to interrelate. The later emergence of psychology and then of sociology as established disciplines across the middle decades of the twentieth century provide similar indications.

'Social science' and 'educational reform' were related concepts in mid-nineteenth-century Europe and America. The interconnections between Britain and the United States, while sporadic and cautious in many fields, were sustained and significant with regard particularly to social science and its educational implications. Transatlantic educational messages in the nineteenth century were real, multi-directional and complex. The lines run from Prussia to Horace Mann and Massachusetts, and back to England in the 1840s and 1850s. They run from the University of Virginia to the University of London, and from the German universities to the United States and back to England late in the century. If the publications of Barnard and the reports of the commissioners of education relay British and European messages, in return those of the British commissions and committees, and then the Board of Education, exhaustively report American ones - mainly in the fields of mass education and the training of teachers. Samuel Gridley Howe agonized over the models of education for special categories of children in Britain, France and Germany. He and Horace Mann related closely to British phrenology, and at mid-century Mann, George Combe and others represented a transatlantic intellectual community. The messages of Owenism, community, radical and democratic ideals, passed back and forth across the Atlantic.

The terrain has been extensively mapped, mainly in terms of 'influence', and especially the American influence on Britain, and the particular relevance of Massachusetts for English national education.[1] The European impact on United States higher education has been extensively explored. The American adoption of monitorial ideology and practice, and the Owenite and Pestalozzian impact on United States communities and education, for example, have been analysed.[2] The social science movement in the second half of the nineteenth century makes it possible to probe further such parallels and relationships, and to approach some historiographical questions which they raise very sharply.

The National Association for the Promotion of Social Science (NAPSS) was formed in Britain in 1857. It met annually and published its papers in *Transactions*. It also held regular meetings in London, and at various times published a fortnightly journal and pamphlets. It divided its attention among different departments of the social science territory - one of the most central and active ones being that of education. It attracted to its meetings and committees some of the most eminent figures in the world of educational, legal, health and other aspects of reform. Lord Brougham and Edwin Chadwick, Lyon Playfair and Charles Kingsley, Mary Carpenter and a host of others gave its discussions of education considerable importance. John Stuart Mill was on its fringes. Herbert Spencer was largely ignored by the movement, and he treated it with contempt. For three decades it discussed, campaigned, investigated, and promoted its version of social science as the prime analytical and reforming tool of the modern world.

In 1865, from within the Massachusetts Board of State Charities a call went out for an American copy. Intended to be a Massachusetts state body, it was in fact created that October as the American Association for the Promotion of Social Science (usually known as the American Social Science Association). It also held meetings in different cities of the United States, published a journal, and sought to influence the direction of social reform. Like its British counterpart, it made education one of its departments, and like the Education Department of the NAPSS, it discussed the whole range of educational issues relating to the social present and future. It attracted people like William Torrey Harris and Daniel Coit Gilman. It modelled itself explicitly on the British organization, and felt itself part of an international movement, since an International Social Science Association had been formed in Brussels, and national associations or groups of interested people were being established or identified in various European countries.[3] In the United States itself the ASSA encouraged the formation of local and state social science associations. Existing organizations moved into the social science orbit. The ASSA triggered off others. The American Association was pleased to welcome George Hastings, secretary and chairman of Council, from London in 1872, as well as Mary Carpenter. It cherished correspondence from Edwin Chadwick, and one of its first steps was to nominate nineteen English and two Irish corresponding members – and though there was some opposition to the inclusion of Lord Brougham, the list was adopted. The British organization held a special council meeting in 1870 to welcome Samuel Eliot from the American Association, and other Americans addressed the British gatherings. The secretary of the ASSA's Education Department sought and obtained an interview with Charles Darwin. It solicited a letter from him on infant development, made him an honorary member, and officially mourned his death. A.J. Mundella addressed the Philadelphia association on his work in British industry and Parliament for industrial arbitration. The references to Massachusetts education, usually laudatory, were many in the British publications. The references to English education in the American publications were no less frequent, if mostly derogatory.

There is more than a marginal interest in disentangling the early nineteenth-century origins of the terms social science, science of society and sociology. The nineteenth-century origins of sociology, and the routes from Auguste Comte at the end of the 1830s, through John Stuart Mill and others, are familiar.[4] From the beginning of the century Robert Owen and the Owenites were also developing a self-conscious science of society of a different kind.[5] John Stuart Mill used the term social science in an article published in 1836, and Bentham – with less impact – had done so fifteen years earlier.[6] The concept of social science was available before the middle of the nineteenth century, and developed an identity quite different from that associated in Europe and America with the sociology of which Comte and Spencer were the main standard-bearers until the take-off of professional and academic sociology at the end of the century. Mill at mid-century straddled the two terminologies and traditions. In his *System of Logic* he emphasized that it was 'but of yesterday that the conception of a political or social science has existed anywhere but in the mind of here and there an insular thinker generally ill-prepared for its realisation'. The position had now changed with regard to the analysis of social phenomena:

There is nothing chimerical in the hope that general laws, sufficient to enable us to answer these various questions for any country or time ... do really admit of being ascertained; and that the other branches of human knowledge, which this undertaking presupposes, are so far advanced that the time is ripe for its commencement. Such is the object of the Social Science.[7]

Whatever Mill's emphasis on the laws that underlay social science, by the 1850s, when the NAPSS was created, the term combined a sense of the availability of laws, of accessibility of data, and the possibility of reform. It was this development of a reforming social science that, in Philip Abrams's view, frustrated the growth of sociology as a discipline in the mid-nineteenth century.[8]

By the late 1850s in Britain a social science had therefore been constructed by welding together a number of what had come to be seen as related elements: the social philosophy of Mill but only marginally of Comte and the British Comteans; the range of rational or rationalist endeavours that encompassed, for example, Owenite views of social reorganization and Malthusian approaches to 'the social problem'; the investigatory strategies that had led to the creation of statistical societies, traditions of social reporting, and pressure groups and societies promoting the solution of poverty and its attendant evils through national education, charity organization, factory legislation and other reforming social policies; and finally the diverse experience of the correctional, remedial and 'improving' ingredients of what Michael Katz has described as the early 'institutional state'.[9]

The new social science was shaped by and rested on a considerable confidence on the part of influential groups in the Victorian middle class that data, understanding and policy were reaching the point at which the problems of industrial, urban society might be – if not conjured away – at least organized or legislated out of existence.[10] An excellent example of the mood of the moment was the publication in 1859 (anonymously) by George Drysdale, of the third edition of what had five years earlier been named *Physical, Sexual, and Natural Religion*. He now retitled it *The Elements of Social Science*, adding to his previous discussion of poverty, Malthus, population, prostitution and birth control, a section explicitly on social science. In it he explained:

The great want of the age, as has been so admirably shown by Mr. Mill and M. Comte . . . is that there should be a Social Science. By this is meant a body of ascertained laws relating to human society, which, like those that constitute the sciences of mathematics, astronomy, physics, chemistry, or physiology, should be definitely accepted and regarded by all men as beyond dispute. Until there be such a body of truths, universally acknowledged and respected, society must remain in a state of profound disorder . . . the subject should be treated in the same careful and systematic manner, with the same attention to the rules of induction and deduction, as the other sciences.

Not only was this necessary, wrote Drysdale, but he was convinced 'that by far the most important discoveries have already been made and that the science is already sufficiently advanced to meet the greatest practical wants of mankind'.[11] Drysdale published this edition of his book in one of the most extraordinary three- to four-year periods in British intellectual and social history. In 1858 Samuel Smiles published *Self-Help* and Herbert Spencer published the first of the essays which three years later were to form his book *Education: Intellectual, Moral and Physical*. In 1859 Darwin published *The Origin of Species*. All of these were profoundly to affect debate about education and society, and they vividly exemplify the climate of opinion in which the concept of 'social science' was establishing itself.

Central to the concept was the vision of a science which would make society as amenable to analysis and certain kinds of mastery and reform as was the world investigated by the natural sciences. The NAPSS had behind it the model of the British Association for the Advancement of Science (BAAS), which had proved so successful for the popularization and development of science, and had also served as a model in the United States.[12] The degree of confidence in the new science was illustrated throughout the *Transactions* of the new society. It announced its aim as 'to collect facts, to diffuse knowledge, to stimulate inquiry'.[13] The British Association for the Advancement of Science, wrote the secretary of the NAPSS, had demonstrated 'the indivisibility of physical research'. 'Mutual aid' amongst scientists was 'the idea which holds together the British Association. And is social knowledge, the science of promoting the prosperity, happiness, and welfare of the human race, stamped less with the character of unity?'[14] In 1861, Frances Power Cobbe, one of the many women active in the Association, wrote that

> The province of Social Science . . . is simple enough. At the present time our task is nearly the same as that which Bacon commenced for physical science in the Novum Organon. In the first place a vast accumulation of facts and observations, statistics and experiments need to be gathered . . . gradually, by induction, larger generalizations will be reached.[15]

Blackwood's Magazine, torn between information and mockery, called the NAPSS a 'kind of social parliament'. It was different from the BAAS and physical and mathematical science in being also 'benevolent and reformatory'. A human science would be 'the most troublesome' and the NAPSS pursued it in a kind of 'itinerant social and scientific performance', a 'travelling caravan'.[16] Herbert Spencer, pursuing science and truth with quite different criteria in mind, called the Association an 'absurdly self-titled body'.[17]

What the Association did was to bring together under the umbrella of the social science description the reformer and the philanthropist, the earlier Victorian threads of data collection and policy formulation, the experience of factory reform and educational endeavour, interests in law and health and social conditions, and out of them it promoted a comprehensive ideal of social organization and welfare. The NAPSS was organized in departments which, at the annual congresses and between, debated and promoted action in the four or five fields (the number was not constant) concerned. Education was, if not the most influential, one of the – perhaps the – most active of the departments. 'Of all the Departments of Social Science', said Edward Baines in an address in 1871, 'none surpasses, or perhaps equals, that of education, either in importance or difficulty'. It would be the crown of social science, he thought, 'to create an intellectual and virtuous nation'.[18] The links with the main urban centres established by the itinerant congresses, and the wide spectrum of reformers, legislators, inspectors and activists of all kinds that it brought into support from the late 1850s until the 1880s, seemed to provide a platform and even a methodology for social advance. 'Of the practical utility of these Congresses', said the Marquess of Huntly in a presidential address in 1876, 'there can be no question. They bring the worker in the cause of Social Reform and the student of Social Science face to face, and each can aid, instruct, and inspire the other'.[19] The important point is the intense concentration on practical utility and reform. In the context of mid-Victorian Britain, it is essential to underline the role of the movement in focusing attention on legislation and the state. If the starting-point was concern about social dangers, breakdowns and deficiencies, the end product and solution was to be adequate law, parliamentary action, the strengthening of the 'custodial state'.[20] All the efforts of the most prominent and consistent supporters of the Association were directed towards strengthening the state-interventionist side of the community-individual equation. Chadwick, one of the most active people in the Association, was, as one writer puts it, 'the stereotype of this sort of social investigator, intent to discover facts useful for the implementation of social policy'.[21]

Given this overall concern of the Association, and the educational commitments of many of its most prominent and active supporters, it is not surprising that the Association provided one of the most regular and wide-ranging forums of a discussion of education. The educational dimensions of the Association were various. First, the papers presented brought together distinguished educational reformers, experimenters, analysts, and promoters, in a general framework of education-as-social-science. Probably not until the 1960s was there to be another situation in which education was so explicitly linked with a whole range of social policies and reforms. The topics discussed in the first five years, for example, included factory, education and ragged schools, the education of girls, mechanics' institutes, adult education and secular schools, half-time education and workhouse schools, as well as a range of topics to do with middle-class education, educational charities, the training of teachers, and the activities of local, national and government bodies in the field of education. The prime concern was with information and with policy. Secondly, therefore, the Education Department, like the other departments and the Association itself, saw itself and acted as a pressure group. It was probably the instrument for persuading the government in 1864 to establish the Taunton Commission to investigate the endowed schools,[22] and the Education Department was certainly the most important forum for the group of women activists to meet and press the case for improvements in the education of girls. It is likely that from their deliberations there emerged the successful pressure on the Taunton Commission to include the education of girls in their remit.[23] The Education Department was, in fact, the only one of the departments to have women regularly and significantly on its standing committee. In 1867, for instance, ten out of forty-nine members of the committee were women – and these included Barbara Bodichon, Mary Carpenter and Emily Davies.[24] There is evidence that the Department and the Council of the Association, both of which met regularly between congresses, took their pressure group activities seriously.[25] The Association published threepenny and sixpenny pamphlets on education (usually papers delivered to regular meetings in London), and sought to bring pressure to bear on the government and Committee of Council on Education. In 1867, for example, the Council of the NAPSS memorialized for a relaxation of the Revised Code for poor town schools, and in 1869, when the education bill was before

Parliament, the standing committee of the Department memorialized the vice-president of the Committee of Council on the bill, and submitted a petition to Parliament in its favour.[26]

Thirdly, the Department took a strong interest throughout the 1850s, 1860s and 1870s in the question of compulsory education and the means of achieving universal education. There was much discussion in the Association of legislation through education Acts or through an extension of factory legislation. There were regular discussions in the late 1860s, for example, at congresses and at the London 'sessional' meetings, of these and related topics, such as free schooling. These and other educational topics had no more regular or accessible platform for discussion. The movement for secular schools and for the teaching of social science, for example, associated from the late 1840s with William Ellis, W. B. Hodgson, George Combe, William Lovett and others, found – like the women educationists – a forum at the Association that they could not find elsewhere. W. B. Hodgson, one of the key spokesmen for this movement, contributed frequently to the congresses and to other Association and related meetings on the subject.[27]

The fact that the Department and the Association were responsive to issues and trends is visible from the way that the *Transactions* (though not the Association's *Sessional Proceedings*) have been raided for specific kinds of information by historians. What historians have not done is to see all these educational messages and efforts as part of a comprehensive view of social science, as a necessary basis for social action and regeneration. A speaker in 1871 talked of a 'portentous phantom dogging the steps of our prosperity, and it already casts its vast and threatening shadow before it, I allude to the International Society'.[28] Yet again, in the shape of international competition on this occasion, the message was delivered that only an understanding of social laws and correct social action would enable Britain to survive. The message was being delivered this time in a paper on the teaching of social science in elementary schools.

The NAPSS and its departments were active and in varying degrees influential from the late 1850s for something like two decades, declining in support and impact in the final years of existence in the 1880s. For a crucial period of around a quarter of a century it perpetuated and strengthened a particular model of society and social action. The overall impression of its debates and activities is of an unwavering belief in a consensus society, in the rightness of existing social structures, and in the possibility of planning and legislating the problems and weaknesses out of existence. Much of the reforming activity reported by campaigners like Mary Carpenter was explicitly designed to improve the lot of the poor without attempting to tamper with the natural order of society. Mary Carpenter, in 1861, for example, combined a discussion of the need to improve the physical condition of children with the statement that 'there must be nothing to pamper self-indulgence, to raise the child in his own estimation above his natural position in society'.[29] In 1868, in an argument more familiar and strident in earlier decades of the century, Sir William Denison told the Association that the condition of the rural and urban poor was 'miserable in the extreme', but that too much stress should not be placed on education and knowledge as improving forces: 'God has ordained infinite gradations of intellectual as of physical power, and their business was to instruct the working-classes to perform their duties in that state of life in which God had placed them.'[30] An extremely forthright account of these general and educational discussions and assumptions of the Association appeared in *The School Board Chronicle* in 1875 in an anonymous commentary on its recent congress:

> A want of thoroughness in dealing with the question of national education is the usual fault of the Social Science Congress. The points in controversy are generally dealt with in a too compromising spirit. Too much allowance is made for existing conditions which stand in the way of educational work, and in listening to the papers and discussions (with some exceptions) we are led to think that if the National Association for the Promotion of Social Science had the task of national education to perform, they would be so anxious not to interfere with anybody, and to interrupt anything, that, with the very best intentions and excellent resolutions for really doing the work, they would discover in the end that they had done nothing[31]

In this spirit, with the continuing collection of data, and debates which allowed existing conditions to 'stand in the way of educational work', the Association stood relatively still while changes which were to affect and destroy it were gathering momentum. The consensual model of society was being challenged by trade union, radical, socialist and other voices and movements. Other forms of social analysis were developing. Other views of what constituted a social science and indeed a science were being elaborated. The comprehensive, multi-purpose nature of the Association was being undermined, especially from the 1880s, by pressures towards more discrete professional and academic definitions, by the development of social work, of movements towards new versions of political science, economic science, historical science, and a range of other professional commitments which made the Association's structure, purpose and style look increasingly anachronistic.

From the 1850s, therefore, the Association represented a central strand in conceptions of social analysis and action. Its early success in attracting support and making the very concept of social science crucial to the development of educational and social reform, both strengthened the model of social reform that had guided the work of an earlier generation of activists, and acted as a model internationally. The model which combined investigation, information, policy formation and legislative and other action, found a welcome especially in the United States. If the model was accepted, it was because the conditions in which it was to be implemented had major, similar features. Poverty and pauperism, crime and ignorance, insanitary and dangerous urban conditions and out-of-date legislation, ill health and immoral behaviour, ineffective charity and uncertain public responsibilities – all of these were a parallel and familiar context. The British social science and reform model fitted the circumstances of Massachusetts and Philadelphia, Illinois and Indiana, with few adaptations.

The American Social Science Association was in fact modelled on the NAPSS. In 1863 a group of active reformers provoked the creation of the Massachusetts Board of State Charities, and two of the leading figures in its establishment were Samuel Gridley Howe and Frank Sanborn. Both had a profound interest in education, in Howe's case with a strong emphasis on the education of the blind, deaf and mentally handicapped, and in Sanborn's case in the whole range or popular institutions relating to the poor and handicapped.[32] Both were experienced in education, and both saw the concept of social science as the key to a more systematic approach to the alleviation and ending of poverty and all that they associated with it. In 1865, through the Board of State Charities, an invitation was issued to an inaugural meeting of what was intended to be a Massachusetts Social Science Association, but in the event – when it met in Boston in October 1865 – debated and accepted the proposal that it take the title of the American Social Science Association. The circular convening the meeting – by the members of the Board of State Charities, including Howe and Sanborn – explained both the range of intended concerns and the British origins:

Our attention has lately been called to the importance of some organization in the United States, both local and national, whose object shall be the discussion of those questions relating to the Sanitary Condition of the People, the Relief, Employment, and Education of the Poor, the Prevention of Crime, the Amelioration of the Criminal Law, the Discipline of Prisons, the Remedial Treatment of the Insane, and those numerous matters of statistical and philanthropic interest which are included under the general head of 'Social Science'. An association for the consideration of these questions has existed in Great Britain for several years, including among its members many of the most eminent philanthropists and statistical writers of that country. Its published proceedings have been of great service to England and to the world.[33]

Throughout the history of the ASSA there were references by Sanborn and others to the British NAPSS 'after which our own was modelled'[34] (though in his later days, when the NAPSS was already 'long since deceased', Sanborn played down on debt the an organization on which the American one was 'rather distantly modelled'.[35] Samuel Eliot in 1867 referred to the British Social Science Association as 'our namesake and to a great extent our pattern'.[36] The group of 'Corresponding Members' agreed at the first meeting of the ASSA included eighteen in England, one in Scotland and two in Ireland. The English list contained the NAPSS president, Lord Brougham, and the secretary, George Hastings. Other active members of the NAPSS in the list included Mary Carpenter, Frances Power Cobbe and Edwin Chadwick – and, though he was never active in the Association, John Stuart Mill.[37] Chadwick was regularly referred to and quoted from, and he maintained a correspondence with the ASSA.[38] Samuel Eliot, formerly joint general secretary of the ASSA with Sanborn, and now president of the Association, was made a Foreign Corresponding Member of the British organization in 1870.[39] When he visited England in 1870 a special meeting of the Council of the NAPSS was held to meet him at which Chadwick was present, and the following morning Chadwick entertained him to breakfast.[40]

The ASSA was created against the background of urbanizing, industrializing, post-bellum America. Samuel Eliot explained in 1867 that the ASSA was not created too soon for the 'necessities of the time. It began just when war had done its work, and peace, with all its resources, all its powers of repressing error and maintaining truth, was ushering in a new era in our national history.' What was needed for the 'maintenance of truth' was a strategy, an over-arching policy or set of policies – the way of collecting information, reaching understanding and acting upon it that the British organization had demonstrated. It was intended, said Eliot, 'to collect the data of separate efforts, and so to group them, and the inferences to be drawn from them, that general principles might be evolved, and the work of Social Science, wherever it was going on, might be directed and harmonized to the common welfare'.[41] The aim and the deep confidence in a consensual model of social development are identical with those of the founders of the British organization, and draw upon them. The ASSA proclaimed its constitution adopted in 1865 would

> bring together the various societies and individuals now interested in these objects, for the purpose of obtaining by discussion the real elements of Truth; by which doubts are removed, conflicting opinions harmonized, and a common ground afforded for treating wisely the great social problems of the day.[42]

In 1882 a paper on education read to the ASSA described the educational process as 'the whole people, through their common government, watching the growth of American civilization all round this majestic circle of commonwealths'.[43] In 1879 Mrs I.T. Talbot, secretary of the Association's Education Department, concluded her report with the statement: 'free from local and sectional interests and prejudices as the American Social Science Association is, no other associated body can more freely point out defects in our educational system, or better indicate needed reforms'.[44] The model of American society and of the ASSA itself came together in a comment made by Sanborn in 1890, when he talked of the ASSA making its members instructors, censors and instigators, 'but always the servants of the great American people, who are not a populace nor a mob, but a collection of persons having a large stake in the future of their country'.[45]

The aims, assumptions and organizational structure of the ASSA were similar to those of the NAPSS. The ASSA was aware, in its discussions, not only of the British and European social science movement, but also of the similarity of the problems. Indeed there were explanations of the need for the American social science movement in terms of the importation of the problems, and therefore of the solutions. When Sanborn addressed the British organization in Glasgow in 1874 he chose as his theme 'American Poor Laws and Public Charities', but immediately denied the accuracy of his title:

It is hardly correct . . . to speak of the pauperism of New England, or of any part of America, as New England or American pauperism. That evil is and always has been chiefly an imported one. What we have has been mainly grafted upon us from a foreign stock, or bred from an imported seed which African slavery has scattered in our soil. Europe (and chiefly the United Kingdom), along with the Southern States of our Union, are the most prolific sources of pauperism in America.

A 'needy proletarian class', accustomed to alms and charity, had been foisted on the free United States, which until recently had not tended 'to breed this proletarian class'. Sanborn went on relentlessly to hammer the theme, to his no doubt surprised British audience. 'Pauperism', he repeated, 'is not native to America, but imported and continued here'. Emigration, he continued, 'brings with it a sediment of pauperism'. The northern states were unlikely to receive many of the former slaves who would be 'repelled by the climate, as well as detained at the South by other causes', and therefore crime and pauperism were most common in places like New York and New England 'whereon the wave of emigration, rolling across from Europe, first strikes and deposits its sediment'.[46] The whole British structure of the problems and the social science solution were involved in the creation of the ASSA.

The ASSA, in adopting the British model, had to adapt it to American geography, regionalism, state structure and communications. Although the British organization had groups of local activists and met in the major British cities, it did not spawn local organizations. The map of American social science in the two or three decades from the mid-1860s is still far from clear, but local and regional associations, on the model of the American national one, were created, with similar structures, similar emphases, similar aims. The most important of these was created in Philadelphia, and in addition to its pamphlets and occasional publications it found an important mouthpiece in the *Penn Monthly*, which published many of its papers and reports.[47] There were associations in Illinois and Indiana, Galveston and Honolulu.[48] Local associations existed in Massachusetts and elsewhere in New England – including Boston, Quincy and Hopedale.[49] There were at least intentions to create associations in Vermont, California and Kentucky.[50] Other reform organizations considered themselves or were considered to be social science associations in everything but name. In 1879

Sanborn called the New York Charities Aid Association, for example, 'practically a social science body'.[51] Some of the state associations (notably the Illinois Social Science Association) probably had more members than the ASSA (which fluctuated in the late 1860s and early 1870s between 200 and 600 paid-up members).[52]

At the basis of all of these organizations was the connection between social fact and social reform. Philadelphia's Robert Ellis Thompson, who, among various positions he held at the University of Philadelphia, included a professorship of social science, graphically portrayed in a lecture published in 1880 what he called the 'Lessons of Social Science in the Streets of Philadelphia'. In the streets, as in the places where natural scientists did their work, scientific truth was arrived at by 'questioning and cross-questioning facts', by acquiring 'the habit of insight into the meaning of facts'.[53] The ASSA declared its purpose to be 'to collect all facts, diffuse all knowledge, and stimulate all enquiry, which have a bearing on social welfare'.[54] At the foundation of the ASSA, the very first paper read was by Professor W. P. Atkinson, of Cambridge, on education. In the course of it he stressed that education 'can only be pursued successfully as an inductive science . . . We want a body of carefully recorded facts, the results of accurate observation.'[55] The Association was later to try to recruit Charles Darwin's help in obtaining such a body of information, particularly about child development. From the data and interpretation would follow what Eliot called 'collective exertion', dedicated to the prevention and relief of suffering.[56]

In the American as in the British case the extent and strength of the commitment to this process as a science cannot be over-emphasized. The concern with rational, 'scientific' solutions was – if an eighteenth-century legacy – a nineteenth-century conviction. The young Sanborn wrote a college essay on 1853 on the subject: 'Is the utilitarian spirit of modern times less favorable to moral character than the chivalrous spirit of the Middle Ages?' He concluded with a panegyric that could have come from many a millenarian or Owenite, for example, in the early nineteenth century. We are passing, he proclaimed, into an epoch

of Reason as a Science; and already the way grows bright before us. Step by step we shall go on, until we arrive at last at the final development of the race, when all shall consciously desire and will to obey the highest Reason.[57]

Science was the password. Education, said Professor Atkinson in 1867, must be founded 'on a science of the mind'. A paper on social science in relation to penal and reformatory institutions published in the *Penn Monthly* in 1881 refers to 'prison science'.[58] Social science itself, said Samuel Eliot, was 'emphatically a science of reform'.[59] To Sanborn in 1877 it was 'that modern entity, vast and vague, which for lack of a good name we call Social Science'.[60] Throughout the recorded discussions and papers of the Association runs this dominant theme of the science of reform, or reform as science. Reminding the Association in 1879 of its roots in philanthropy and statistics, Sanborn recalled Horace Greeley's definition of social science as 'the diffusion of knowledge, virtue and happiness', a definition which would not, Sanborn commented, please 'the French and English patentees of that recent metaphysical invention which they call "sociology"'[61] (though it should be remembered that Spencer was made an honorary member of the ASSA in 1883). The emphasis was on investigation and method of cure.[62] Huggins, discussing the whole of this relationship between charity and social action on the one hand, and data and method on the other, comments that

> Collection of data was important to the reformers. Statistics became a magic device which would uncover the source of crime . . . But more than this, the emphasis on statistics assumed a natural law determining social action; to do good one needed science rather than sympathy.[63]

So deep was the relationship in the social science movement between data and reform that Sanborn felt moved in 1879 to justify the connection in the foundation of the Association between philanthropy, statistics and social science. 'Perhaps it has been too much the fashion', he protested, 'both here and in England, to regard our new science as but another form of philanthropy.'[64] In the United States, even more than in Britain, Sanborn's 'new science' was, however, on the brink of being challenged and undermined by even 'newer' ones.

The Education Department of the ASSA was very similar to its British equivalent in the range of its concerns, but was unlike it in the capacity to act as a national pressure group and influence educational development, legislation and policy. Its membership included from the outset John D. Philbrick and Daniel C. Gilman. It attracted support and active participation from William Torrey Harris and Andrew D. White. It provided, as in the British case, an important forum for the discussion of compulsory education and the relationship of education to federal and state government, the relationship between education and social and economic progress, the education of the south, technical and college education, kindergartens and the education of the physically and mentally handicapped, libraries and reform schools. It rode a tide of widespread confidence in what a paper to the Philadelphia Association in 1880 called the 'power and promise' of the public school system:

> Do we realize the growing influence of this institution, already affecting the whole Nation, and second in power to the Church only?
> ... The most promising newspaper of one of the most influential religious bodies, a body which largely favors its separate schools, says recently, referring to the connection of public libraries with the schools, 'We have entered, in our school system, upon the *organization of modern society*; we cannot stop half-way.'[65]

Commenting on the Education Department of the British Association, Eliot spoke of education as taking 'of necessity, the prominent place in our considerations'.[66] The *Journal of Social Science* reported during 1870 that the Standing Committee on Education had been active, for example, in connection with the formation of public libraries and art education (both favourite topics in the Association) industrial and nautical schools and the shortcomings of public school text-books. Six years later, when Sanborn reviewed the work of the Association, he commented that in education 'much has been done, directly or indirectly, by our Association since 1865, to call attention to what our country needs, and point out practical ways of attaining thereto'. He cited the work done for art schools and museums, public libraries, a better system of colleges and universities, the health of pupils, half-time schools, the teaching of deaf-mutes and the blind, school inspection, and others.[67] Two papers published in the *Journal of Social Science* in 1880 and 1883 indicate – with a resonance familar in discussions of American education in the 1960s particularly – how broad a definition was given to education, appropriate within an organization with so comprehensive a definition of the work of social science. J.M. Gregory of Chicago, in a contribution on 'The American Newspaper and American Education', suggested that 'All things educate us. Country and climate, scenery and society, business and pleasures, life's daily doings and daily encounters, all environments of matter and mind exert upon us silent, it may be, but plastic power.'[68] William Torrey Harris, in similar vein, told the Education Department that it recognized

other institutions besides the School as instrumentalities of culture
. . . I have attempted to define the scope of Education as a training
given to the human individual by the institutions of society. These
institutions are the Family, Civil Society, the State, and the Church.
They all educate the mind quite as essentially as the School does.[69]

It is not surprising that education should be seen as central to the work
of social science and reform, or that its power and pervasiveness should
be so underlined. What is important is that the American Association,
as in Britain, produced a comprehensive pattern of analysis, and for the
most part rejected incorherent, unsystematic, voluntary approaches to
reform, in favour of systematic public provision, coherent public policy, rational government intervention. Andrew D. White argued that
'the main provision for advanced education in the United States must
be made by the people at large acting through their legislatures'.[70] General Logan, discussing the free school system in the south in 1877,
argued against the Spencerian 'fallacy' of non-interference by governments, ascribed Britain's comparative industrial decline to the free
school system of other nations, and held that, in spite of the political
dangers of so doing, 'the industrial necessities of the age force every progressive government to educate the people'.[71] Following a paper read to
the Education Department on 'National Aid to Education' in 1882, the
ASSA presented a petition to Congress calling for national funds to be
'distributed for a limited period, to the common schools of the States
and Territories, on the basis of illiteracy, and in such manner as shall
not supersede nor interfere with local efforts'.[72] The approach to
national legislation and intervention was obviously different in
emphasis and detail from the British equivalents, but the commitment
to national action, using education as an instrument of policy, and
within the context of a comprehensive social science analysis, was
roughly the same.

It is important to underline that in all of these discussions, as
throughout the work of the ASSA, the transatlantic dimension
remained – if not prominent, at least constant. The ASSA welcomed
and lionized Mary Carpenter, and the *Journal* wrote that 'the cause of
education and reform has been greatly strengthened . . . by the presence
of Miss Carpenter'.[73] The Education Department sent congratulations
to the NAPSS on a successful visit by Mary Carpenter to India, which
was the direct cause of the establishment of a Bengal Social Science
Association, and which the Americans described as 'a stimulus afforded

to social progress'.[74] British speakers appeared at ASSA meetings (including one from St Andrew's University, Scotland, whose main message was that the Americans and the Scots both had too many colleges and universities).[75] The secretary of the NAPSS not only visited Boston in 1872 'for the express purpose of showing his interest in the Association', but he also returned home with a useful piece of experience. Hastings had been elected to the new school board in Worcester, and as its chairman he was interested in Boston's efforts in relation to truancy, a scheme 'to look after the children, see that they are at school, and report the absentees'. In May 1873 Worcester accordingly appointed a similar 'School Board Agent'.[76] The contacts with Britain were two-directional. Sanborn in Glasgow and Hastings in Boston symbolize the relationship. The secretary of the ASSA's Education Department was deputed to visit Charles Darwin in Orpington in 1881, and at his death in 1883 the ASSA held a commemorative session, hoping that Herbert Spencer, then in the United States, would be able to attend. He could not do so, but was immediately made an honorary member – having had no previous known contact with either the ASSA or the NAPSS.[77] The papers and discussion at the ASSA constantly refer to European and especially British experience, sometimes in derogatory fashion, sometimes to indicate useful models, increasingly to detect American influence (as when Gilman, in 1879, suggested that it was 'not difficult to trace in the modern school-laws of England, the study of American experience').[78]

The ASSA shared ultimately with its British counterpart an inability to sustain the stance derived from its conception of social science. Neither of the two associations was ever fully aware of how and why it was being overtaken by events and alternatives, but the ASSA was more able to make realistic judgements because it had itself more visibly contributed to its own destruction. From the very beginning the ASSA had acted as convenor and sponsor for other, specialist, developments. It had originated, for example, alongside its own meetings, what was to become the National Conference of Social Work, and in 1872, together with the NAPSS, sponsored an International Penitentiary Congress in London.[79] From its ranks emerged the American Economic Association, the American Historical Association and others, in ways that have recently been mapped by Thomas Haskell and Mary Furner.[80] Sanborn looked sadly at all of this when he reviewed 'The Work of Twenty-Five Years' at the quarter-centennial meeting of the ASSA in 1890. The now defunct British Association had been for thirty years, he explained, 'a guiding and stimulating force', but in Britain as in the United States

> the movements originated by the parent society weakened the parental vitality; and the British Association practically ceased to exist some years ago, leaving other organizations to carry on the same work by specialization. Our Association also has given birth or furtherance to the National Conference of Charities, the National Prison Association ... the American Public Health Association, the Economic Association, and other bodies now in active life; but, in the process of extending and specializing our work, the vigor of the parent society has been somewhat diminished.[81]

Although the ASSA survived until 1909, it had been overtaken by new social and political situations, by specialism and by sociology. Sanborn's explanations of weakened parental vitality go part of the way towards understanding the new contexts and styles of social analysis, and the attempts of new 'scientific' approaches to break free of the reforming legacy of which the ASSA was a paramount example.

The appearance of the new economic, historical and other organizations marked both a changed map of academic organization, the new contours and definitions of professional allegiances, and hopes of a purer science. Typical of the new spirit was the creation in Philadelphia in 1890 of the American Academy of Political and Social Science, which at its first meeting was reminded of the history of the Philadelphia Social Science Association, but was clearly setting out in quite a new direction. The description of its inauguration has an interesting vocabulary. Nowhere more than in America was there 'a more hopeful outlook for scientific work'. The new, small institutions of higher education scattered across the United States were 'increasing our stock of scientific capital'. The 'growing stock of technical or professional literature' was evidence of the growing interest 'in the scientific aspect' of these specialist problems. There was a growing 'scientific spirit' and co-operation 'among scientific workers', but the 'spirit of scientific co-operation' had not found adequate expression (and the ASSA was one organization mentioned as not adequate to the new task). The new Academy would offer students of economics, politics and sociology (they are the three disciplines mentioned) opportunities for publication enjoyed 'in a similar field by the various academies of natural science'. After a three-page report on all of this new 'scientific' commitment, the new Academy is described as having begun its monthly meetings,

described as 'Scientific Sessions'.[82] Science, or at least scientific
pretensions, professionalism and specialization went hand in hand.
Social work was cutting adrift from the all-purpose reform activities of
organizations like the ASSA, and although in 1915 Abraham Flexner
was to deny that social work met the criteria required for a profession,[83]
that was the direction the activity was heading from the last decades of
the nineteenth century. It was not just that the parents were weakened
and the children were stronger – the aims and definitions of the new
bodies were different. They found different homes, especially in the
new universities – on quite a different basis from earlier attempts to find
the ailing ASSA a home in one of the new universities, notably Johns
Hopkins, or a university base for Sanborn at Cornell. Sociological
societies were created in Britain and the United States in the mid-
1900s, though the firm academic basis of sociology was laid in many
American institutions and publications in the 1890s. In both countries
the all-purpose social science organization was replaced by discrete
professional and academic institutions. What was happening to social
science as a concept and a movement was also happening to moral
philosophy as a university and college discipline. They were both
dismantled into the social sciences.

The whole Anglo-American relationship and parallel in this social
science context points to some familiar – and none the less intriguing
for being familiar – problems of analysis and judgement. The aims and
styles of action of the two bodies were very close in a period when the
social problems and their causes were viewed similarly. The ASSA, in
borrowing from Britain the model of operation, did not need to borrow
traditions of philanthropy or pragmatism or social engineering, but
obviously the centralizing and systematic portrait presented by the
NAPSS was immensely attractive. The times, as we have suggested,
seemed to demand a similar American approach. Behind the British
model lay the authority of internationally known work by Chadwick in
a range of areas, including public health; of Mary Carpenter, and
British efforts towards the reform of attitudes to the young offender; of
the factory inspectors who were prominent in the NAPSS. Prominent
educationists like George Combe, Louisa Twining, the Seniors, and
school inspectors and assistant commissioners like the Rev. James
Fraser and J.G. Fitch, either became honorary members of the ASSA or
were points of reference in the American discussions. It is not unimportant that part of the social science tradition derived from Owenite
and phrenological sources, from earlier forms of alliance between

analysis, correction and ideal - and in men like Samuel Howe in America and W.B. Hodgson in Britain similar traditions were carried into the new setting.

But it was above all in the similarity of the reforming endeavour that the closest parallel link lies. Sanborn, in one description, 'achieved distinction as the leading social worker of the day'.[84] He linked across to all those Concord eminences whom he knew, whose philosophical dialogues he shared, and whose biographies he wrote. He was known as a radical (and in some connections even a dangerous one) and for nearly forty years was associated with the prominent liberal journal, the Springfield *Republican*.[85] In his life of Howe, Sanborn describes Howe's taking on the presidency of the Massachusetts Board of State Charities as another of his long campaigns against 'false methods and hurtful conservatism'.[86] The American honorary members of the ASSA included Henry Barnard, Henry C. Carey and A. Bronson Alcott, of whom Sanborn and William T. Harris jointly wrote a biography. After making allowance for transatlantic differences, the circle that these people represented, liberal, educationally radical, with occasional thrusts of deeper radicalism and threads of political and social conservatism, is not very different in profile from that of the leading figures we have mentioned in and around the NAPSS in Britain. In many other respects, especially the content of educational discussion and the conception of education–society links, the similarity is close. It is likely that the same is true of the role of women in the two movements, although the position is less clear in the United States given the scattered nature of the movement and the lack of local records. What we do know is that women appeared as officers of the ASSA. Of 189 'regular members' in 1867, 23 were women.[87] The British corresponding members of the ASSA included Mary Carpenter and Frances Power Cobbe (but it is interesting that there is no woman amongst the corresponding members in the other European countries). What is perhaps more important in the American context is the extent of female participation in the offspring and related organizations of the ASSA (though for all its concerns, the National Conference of Charities and Correction only had two women presidents before it became the National Conference of Social Work in 1917 - Jane Addams being the first in 1910). There is evidence, however, that women were active locally in the social science organizations. Sanborn, in 1877, referred to a number of aspects of the training of women for careers, and mentioned two organizations recently formed to promote the education of women – a 'Society for Promoting Study at Home' and the 'Massachusetts Society for the University Education of Women'. He went on to comment:

> These are but examples of hundreds of useful and almost unobserved agencies for carrying onward the practical work of social science; most of which depend, first or last, upon the interest taken in them by women . . . although the *theory* of social science has been framed by men, its *practice* can only be advanced by the co-operation of women.[88]

Taken alone this could simply mean that whatever Sanborn approved of was social science, and that women were on the fringe of the social science movement as 'co-operators'. In 1879, however, Sanborn referred to the new social science associations in Illinois and Indiana, and to the New York State Charities Aid Association, adding: 'these three State societies are all managed by women, and they are at present constantly more active than our own Association, which may be regarded as their parent'.[89] In Britain there is no doubt that the NAPSS was vitally important to the developing women's movement, especially in the field of education, and although there are obviously parallels the precise nature of the American developments is uncertain.

All of this points mainly towards three kinds of question which would merit fuller discussion. *First*, there is the question of why the social science movement has been relatively neglected in both Britain and the United States. In Britain, there are three published works in which the NAPSS can be said to be seriously analysed, and of three theses on British social science, two were produced in the United States.[90] None has any interest in the educational work and content of the movement. In the United States, until recently, most published references to the ASSA derived from the book by the Bernards on the *Origins of American Sociology* published in 1943, though the recent books by Haskell and Furner have carried the analysis very much further. The same statement must, however, be repeated: none has any interest in the educational work and content of the movement.[91] The only minor exception on either side of the Atlantic has been Michael Katz's *The Irony of Early School Reform*, which is not *about* the movement, but engages seriously with some of its constituent elements in an analysis of urban conditions, poverty and juvenile reform. The first question, then, would be to account for this neglect.

The *second* would be to find an acceptable way of explaining the organizations, their self-definitions and purposes, and their ideological and conceptual commitments. Charles H. Hopkins, in his *The Rise of the Social Gospel in American Protestantism*, traces the major intellectual debt of the social gospel to 'those enlightened conservatives who faced with open minds both the new science and the new industrial order of the later half of the nineteenth century'.[92] That would be a helpful starting text, but it would lead straight into the controversies of American historiography of the 1960s and 1970s, with all the difficulties of handling concepts like conservatism and liberalism, new industrial order and the corporate state, and every other concept that has been argued over in relation especially to social and educational reform in the late nineteenth and twentieth centuries. Were the reformers merely puppets of some deeper, hidden and manipulating forces? To what extent are we engaged as historians with the declared, secret or unsuspected motives of the reformers? Two extreme positions make it difficult to write the history of motivation. The first is simply to encapsulate the motives of the historical actors with their own emphases and understandings. The second is to deny the relevance of the actors' own perceptions and to place them in the context of imprisoning structures or deep, underlying historical forces continuing their own relentless paths and ultimates. The first results in description, phonographic representation, history which offers no historical analysis, and ascribes no ideological or theoretical place to the historian. The second makes off towards functionalist abstractions or structuralism, and leaves little or nothing for the historian to do except illustrate theory. Both, if caricatures, represent real movements in the world of historical debate, and we can pin names on both of these and their variants. Both have been and are operational, and they have identified historical motivation as suspect, dangerous or simply to be avoided.

The history of social science as of all reform movements cannot for ever avoid the issue, and cannot for ever go on seeking and finding momo-causal explanations and endlessly ephemeral vocabularies. We cannot deny the actors a voice, and we cannot drown their voices in our own raucous search for comforting explanations. The historical actors are probably telling at least part of the truth, and *suggesting* the other part. They are neither blind puppets nor congenital liars. They place an emphasis on a purpose, and what they *assume* – what they *inform* us that they assume – indicates other purposes. They have to be listened to. The first problem is to detect in their statements and actions the purposes they reveal that are additional to the ones they make explicit. The second problem is to be constantly aware, amongst the explanations we construct, of our own basis of selection. Almost any of the instances quoted or referred to in this chapter would serve as an example of how to proceed.

Take the previously quoted passage from the 1883 paper on national educational policy read to the ASSA, in which the speaker described

> the whole people, through their common government, watching the growth of American civilization all round this majestic circle of commonwealths; in ordinary times doing enough to vindicate the precedent, in the days of emergency coming in with irresistible power to stimulate home action, and arouse the people to their duty by the potent inspiration of national encouragement and material aid.[93]

This can be accepted at face value within the context of the educational and social policies of the speaker and the Association. It can be dismissed as rhetoric, or explained in terms totally outside the immediate vocabulary and conceptual machinery – for example in terms of class society or industrial needs. The explanation can be organized within later, superimposed sociological or historical concepts – including social control and the capitalist state, or extensions into the analysis of racist or other structures and practices. The paper from which this passage is extracted is a complex argument, and there is something important in it and in the passage. Whatever the *declared* motives of extending national aid to education, and whatever the surrounding explanations that may be imported to extend them, there are within the passage itself important clusters of vocabulary which tell us more about motive, and which the speaker took for granted. The generalized vocabulary accumulates – 'national policy', 'nation', 'whole people', 'common government', 'American civilization', 'the people', 'national encouragement', and so on. From *within* the passage we can search for the meaning of this accumulation and it obviously lies in this case in a version of social consensus, actual or desired. The passage may not have been designed consciously to be *about* that, but its vocabulary tells us – practised in seeking such nineteenth-century meanings – about the underlying purpose to which the speaker *assumes* education is directed. There may be other meanings to which the analysis will lead, but the question of motivation starts with the speaker, the actor. Obviously, we select passages and put weight on words. In doing so we ascribe *priority* motives, and obviously we are intent on doing more than interpret a sentence or two written and spoken by a Boston clergyman in 1882. The historian is negotiating something with the Rev. A.D. Mayo.

Mayo, and Sanborn and anyone else we have brought as witness to the reform process, tell us the shape and values of the society towards which they reach. The emphasis we detect is important in understanding the motivation of the people, of the organization, of the social movement to which we attach meaning. We do not discard our own ideological baggage in doing that, but if there is to be any possibility of approaching historical motive, we need to allow our machinery to engage with that of Mayo or Sanborn and begin with what they tell us. If we don't, the historical exercise will disappear into antiquarianism or theory; we shall have avoided the problem and left ourselves with a display of antiques or theories. We pay heavily in retreating from motive.

The *third* question is implied in the whole of this argument. Were the social science developments in Britain and the United States instances of parallelism or superficial connections, or are there important questions about a real transfer of cultural messages, ideologies and social practices? I suspect that the latter is true in this case, not because the people concerned were all reformers or liberals or social engineers in a convenient historical category, but because their ideals and meanings drew similar strength from similar perceptions of similar situations. If Owenism or phrenology produced one kind of intellectual and cultural interchange earlier in the century, social science now produced another. The transatlantic issues relate directly to the other unanswered questions about historical neglect of the territory, and educational historians' paralysis in the presence of questions of motivation.

What was shared was confidence in a new-found framework within which to investigate change, understand cause, and act. There may, on our bigger canvases, be room for analysis in terms of manipulation, or the protection of the status quo, or the advancement of a liberal-capitalist model of society, or the healing of civil war wounds in the service of the nation state – or any of these in combination, or others. Those are not sufficient explanations, however, until we have laboured over the parts and intimate processes. Where people draw their ideas and inspiration and confidence from, their hesitations and responses to criticism, their definition of the strategies they adopt or reject, are equally – and at this point in our understanding perhaps more – important.

If all of these questions are germane to the history of social science and the location of sources of stability and change in social policy in general, they are equally so to the history of education. The history of late nineteenth-century education in both Britain and America is the history of how education was perceived – differently by different people and groups at different times – within definitions of society and of an acceptable social policy. What was being debated in the social science organizations was an appropriate direction for an 'educated society', appropriate levels and forms of provision for the intended future. Historians return to these debates armed with explanations in terms of progress or capitalism or industrialization or social control or reform. Unless history becomes abstract theory or the story of human puppetry, however, the debates have to be heard clearly and dissected with care. The dissection is important to the history of education because social processes have always been subject to controversy and debate, and without the messages from social science and other contexts it remains the story of isolated figures and institutions. Education is what people thought it was and intended it to be, as well as what they constructed and experienced.

The social science story is also directly relevant to the interpretation of educational developments in the late nineteenth century in pointing to the directions from which the participants in educational debate came. They were not only schoolteachers and politicians, clergymen and philanthropists. The pattern of the reform enterprise includes philosophers and statisticians, administrators and a variety of spectators of social change and speculators about the future and the agencies by which to arrive there. They were 'social scientists'. It was to be crucially important to education in the twentieth century that from the end of the nineteenth 'social scientists' were to become sociologists and psychologists, economists and a range of other social scientific specialists, in new professions and changed academic settings. Social science as a movement and a concept leads into historically important features of higher education, as well as new debates and forums of debate about children and adolescents, schools and curricula, the politics of finance and the purpose of reform, policy and practice.

Notes

1 See for example W.H.G. Armytage, *The American Influence on English Education* (London, 1967); Frank Thistlethwaite, *The Anglo-American Connection in the Early Nineteenth Century* (Philadelphia, 1959); Peter N. Farrar, 'The Influence of the Massachusetts System of Education on the

Movement for a National System in England and Wales in the Nineteenth Century', Liverpool University MA thesis, 1964.

2 See for example Carl F. Kaestle, *Joseph Lancaster and the Monitorial School Movement: A Documentary History* (New York, 1973); Arthur Eugene Bestor Jr, *Backwoods Utopias. The Sectarian and Owenite Phases of Communitarian Socialism in America, 1663-1829* (Philadelphia, 1950); Gerald Lee Gutek, *Joseph Neef: the Americanization of Pestalozzianism* (University, Alabama, 1978).

3 American Social Science Association, *Constitution, Address, and List of Members* (Boston, 1866), p. 12.

4 See Victor V. Branford, 'On the Origin and Use of the Word Sociology', *Sociological Papers* (London, 1905).

5 See Eileen Margot Yeo, 'Social Science and Social Change: A Social History of some Aspects of Social Science and Social Investigation in Britain 1830-1890', University of Sussex PhD thesis, 1972, ch. II.

6 See Peter R. Senn, 'The Earliest Use of the Term "Social Science"', *Journal of the History of Ideas*, vol. XIX, 1958, pp. 568-70; J.H. Burns, 'J.S. Mill and the Term "Social Science"', *Journal of the History of Ideas*. vol. XX, 1959, pp. 431-2; J.H. Burns, *Jeremy Bentham and University College* (London, 1962), p. 8.

7 Ronald Fletcher (ed.), *John Stuart Mill: A Logical Critique of Sociology* (London, 1971), pp. 132-4.

8 Philip Abrams, *The Origins of British Sociology: 1834-1914* (Chicago, 1968), pp. 46-9.

9 Michael B. Katz, 'Origins of the Institutional State', *Marxist Perspectives*, vol. I, no. 4, 1978.

10 For the fullest discussion see M.J. Cullen, *The Statistical Movement in Early Victorian Britain: The Foundation of Empirical Social Research* (Hassocks, Sussex, 1975).

11 George R. Drysdale, *The Elements of Social Science; or Physical, Sexual and Natural Religion ... by a Doctor of Medicine* (London, 1854), 3rd ed. 1859, enlarged ed. of 1881, pp. 451-2.

12 Sally Gregory Kohlstedt, *The Formation of the American Scientific Community: the American Association for the Advancement of Science 1848-60* (Urbana, Illinois, 1976).

13 *Transactions of the NAPSS, 1857* (London, 1858), p. xxviii.

14 Ibid., pp. xxi-xxii.

15 Frances Power Cobbe, 'Social Science Congresses, and Women's Part in Them', *Macmillan's Magazine*, vol. v, 1861, p. 84.

16 'Social Science', *Blackwood's Magazine*, vol. 88, 1860, pp. 701-6; 'Social Science', *Blackwood's Magazine*, vol. 90, 1861, p. 463.

17 J.D.Y. Peel, *Herbert Spencer: The Evolution of a Sociologist* (London, 1971), p. 228.

18 Edward Baines, 'Address', *Transactions of the NAPSS 1871* (London, 1872), pp. 76, 84.

19 The Marquess of Huntly, 'Opening Address', *Transactions of the NAPSS 1876* (London, 1877), p. 2.

20 Abrams, *Origins of British Sociology*, p. 49.
21 Peel, *Herbert Spencer*, p. 83.
22 Brian Rodgers, 'The Social Science Association, 1857-1886', *The Manchester School of Economic and Social Studies*, vol. XX, no. 3, 1952, p. 295; 'Report of the Standing Committee of the (Education) Department', *Transactions of the NAPSS 1864* (London, 1865), p. 319; 'Report of the Standing Committee of the (Education) Department', *Transactions of the NAPSS 1865* (London, 1866), p. 263.
23 See Josephine Kamm, *Hope Deferred: Girls' Education in English History* (London, 1965), ch. XIV ('The Schools' Inquiry Commission, 1864-67').
24 *Social Science, Being the Journal and Sessional Proceedings of the National Association for the Promotion of Social Science*, vol. I, no. 19, 1867, pp. 311-12.
25 For a sarcastic attack on the Association as a vehicle for the women's pressure group see 'Social Science', *Blackwood's Magazine*, 1861, pp. 468-71.
26 *Social Science*, vol. I, no. 5, 1867, p. 82; *Sessional Proceedings of the National Association for the Promotion of Social Science* (formerly *Social Science*), vol. II, no. 30, 1869, p. 677.
27 See, for example, *Transactions* for 1865, 1867, 1873. He was present at an Association meeting held at the Society of Arts in 1868 'to appoint a committee to diffuse information as to the natural laws regulating wages . . . and to promote industrial partnership . . .' (*Sessional Proceedings*, vol. I, no. 26, 1868, p. 389).
28 Whateley Cooke Taylor, 'On the Teaching of Social Science in Elementary Schools', *Transactions of the NAPSS 1871* (London, 1872), p. 392.
29 Mary Carpenter, 'The Application of the Principles of Education to Schools for the Lower Classes of Society', *Transactions of the NAPSS 1861* (London, 1862), p. 348.
30 Report of a paper 'On the Bearing of Our Social System on Questions Connected with the Education of the Labouring Classes' by Sir William Denison, *Transactions of the NAPSS 1868* (London, 1869), p. 456.
31 *School Board Chronicle*, no. 244, 1875, p. 381.
32 For Howe see especially Harold Schwartz, *Samuel Gridley Howe: Social Reformer 1801-1876* (Cambridge, Mass., 1956), and F.B. Sanborn, *Dr. S.G. Howe: The Philanthropist* (New York, 1891). The best approach to Sanborn is through his numerous contributions on social science to the *Journal of Social Science*.
33 'Circular of the Massachusetts Board of Charities', 2 August, 1865, *Constitution, Address, and List of Members*, pp. 10-11.
34 *Journal of Social Science*, no. VII, 1874, p. 387.
35 Ibid., no. XXXV, 1897, p. 23.
36 American Social Science Association, *Documents Published by the Association, Part II: Address . . . by Samuel Eliot, to which Are Added Lists of Papers, Members, etc.* (Boston, 1867), p. 72.
37 See, for example, *Constitution, Address, and List of Members*, pp. 49-50.
38 *Journal of Social Science*, no. XI, 1880, p. vi (quoting Chadwick's advice to the Association in 1866).

39 *Sessional Proceedings*, vol. IV, no. 1, 1870, pp. 25-6.
40 American Social Science Association, *Extract from the Sessional Proceedings of the British Association for the Promotion of Social Science* (Boston, 1870), pp. 1-8.
41 Samuel Eliot, 'Address', in *Documents Published by the Association, Part II*, p. 67. For a discussion of social science in the post-bellum period see L.L. and Jessie Bernard, *Origins of American Sociology: The Social Science Movement in the United States* (New York, 1943), pp. 559-94.
42 *Constitution of the American Association for the Promotion of Social Science* (adopted in Boston, 1865; amended at New Haven 1866), p. 1, item II.
43 Rev. A.D. Mayo, 'National Aid to Education', *Journal of Social Science*, no. XVII, 1883, p. 7.
44 In ibid., no. X, 1879, p. 42.
45 *Journal of Social Science*, no. XXVII, 1890, p. xlviii.
46 F.B. Sanborn, 'American Poor Laws and Public Charities', *Transactions of the NAPSS, 1874* (London, 1875), pp. 879-80.
47 The Philadelphia Social Science Association was established in November 1869 - see *Journal of Social Science*, no. V, 1873, pp. 202-5. In its publication of Simon N. Patten, *Principles of Rational Taxation* (Philadelphia, 1889), it appends a list of papers read before the Association to that date.
48 Illinois and Indiana are mentioned by Sanborn in *Journal of Social Science*, no. XI, 1880, p. vi. The Bernards' list contains Boston, Quincy, New York, New Haven, Detroit, St Louis, Chicago, San Francisco, Galveston, Indianapolis and Cornell University (*Origins of American Sociology*, pp. 553-8). The Western Social Science Association was organized in Chicago in 1868 and published a statement entitled *Social Science Defined* (the first secretary lived at Springfield, Illinois, and the president at Detroit, Michigan).
49 The *Constitution, Address, and List of Members* mentions local associations in Boston and Quincy (the former of which issued publications). The Hopedale Association is mentioned in ibid., p. 55.
50 See ibid., p. 14.
51 *Journal of Social Science*, no. XI, 1880, p. vi.
52 Ibid., p. vi.
53 Robert Ellis Thompson, 'Lessons of Social Science in the Streets of Philadelphia', *The Penn Monthly*, vol. XI, 1880, pp. 920-1. For Thompson, see James Donbrowski, *The Early Days of Christian Socialism in America* (New York, 1936), p. 12n.
54 *Constitution, Address, and List of Members*, p. 15.
55 Ibid., p. 32.
56 *Documents Published by the Association, Part II*, pp. 67-9.
57 The essay is in the Sanborn papers, Library of Congress, Washington DC (the quotation is from the last page).
58 *Penn Monthly*, vol. XII, 1881, p. 18.
59 *Documents Published by the Association, Part II*, p. 74.
60 *Journal of Social Science*, no. IX, 1878, p. 1.
61 Ibid., no. XI, 1880, pp. vii-viii. In 1868, it should be noted, the Western

130 Education as history

SSA used the terms 'social science' and 'sociology' interchangeably (*Social Science Defined*, pp. 1-2).

62 See, for example, a 'Report from a Department Sub-Committee on Kindergartens', *Journal of Social Science*, no. XII, 1880, p. 9: 'social science seeks to discover the sources of evil in civilization, and the best methods of eradicating those evils'.

63 Nathaniel Irvin Huggins, *Protestants against Poverty: Boston's Charities 1870-1900* (Westport, Connecticut, 1971), p. 72.

64 *Journal of Social Science*, no, XI, 1880, p. vii.

65 James S. Whitney, 'Public Schools in their Relations to the Community', *Penn Monthly*, vol. XI, 1880, p. 414.

66 *Documents Published by the Association, Part II*, p. 73.

67 *Journal of Social Science*, no. VIII, 1876, p. 35.

68 Ibid., no. XII, 1880, p. 63.

69 W.T. Harris, 'Address on Education', in ibid., no. XVII, 1883, p. 133.

70 Andrew D. White, 'The Relation of National and State Governments to Advanced Education', in ibid., no. VII, 1874, p. 302.

71 General T.M. Logan, 'The Opposition in the South to the Free-School System', in ibid., no. IX, 1878, pp. 93-4.

72 Ibid., no. XVII, 1883, p. 23.

73 Ibid., no. V, 1873, p. 160.

74 For details of this Association see *Transactions of the Bengal Social Science Association*, vol. I (Calcutta, 1867). For Mary Carpenter's visit see *Documents Published by the Association, Part II*, p. 72 and *Sessional Proceedings*, vol. I, no. 11, 1867, p. 209.

75 Report of contribution to discussion by Dr Tulloch in *Journal of Social Science*, no. VII, 1874, pp. 319-20.

76 Letter from George W. Hastings, in ibid., no. VII, 1874, pp. 339-40.

77 Ibid., no. XVII, 1883, pp. 156-61.

78 D.C. Gilman, 'American Education, 1869-1879', in ibid., no. X, 1879, p. 19.

79 Frank J. Bruno, *Trends in Social Work as Reflected in the Proceedings of the National Conference of Social Work 1874-1946* (New York, 1948), pp. 4-5.

80 See Mary O. Furner, *Advocacy and Objectivity: A Crisis in the Professionalization of American Social Science, 1865-1905* (Lexington, Kentucky, 1975); Thomas L. Haskell, *The Emergence of Professional Social Science: The American Social Science Association and the Nineteenth-Century Crisis of Authority* (Urbana, Illinois, 1977).

81 *Journal of Social Science*, no. XXVII, 1890, p. xlvi.

82 American Academy of Political and Social Science, *Annals*, vol. I, 1890-1, pp. 132-7.

83 Abraham Flexner, 'Is Social Work a Profession?', *Proceedings of the National Conference of Charities and Correction* (Chicago, 1915).

84 Arthur Mann, *Yankee Reformers in the Urban Age* (Cambridge, Mass., 1954), p. 17.

85 Bruno, *Trends in Social Work*, p. 11.

86 Sanborn, *Dr. S.G. Howe*, p. 291.

87 *Sessional Proceedings*, vol. I, no. 19, 1867, pp. 311-12.

88 *Journal of Social Science*, no. IX, 1878, pp. 12-13.
89 Ibid., no. XI, 1880, p. vi.
90 Brian Rodgers, 'The Social Science Association'; Abrams, *Origins of British Sociology*; Donald G. Macrae, *Ideology and Society* (London, 1961); Robert Pemble, 'The National Association for the Promotion of Social Science, 1857-1886: Some Sociological Aspects', Nottingham University MA thesis, 1968; Lawrence Ritt, 'The Victorian Conscience in Action: The National Association for the Promotion of Social Science, 1857-1886', Columbia University PhD dissertation, 1959; Yeo, 'Social Science and Social Change.
91 The point is elaborated in Harold Silver, 'In Search of Social Science' (essay review on Furner and Haskell), *History of Education Quarterly*, vol. 19, no. 2, 1979.
92 Charles Howard Hopkins, *The Rise of the Social Gospel in American Protestantism 1865-1915* (New Haven, 1950), p. 18.
93 Mayo, 'National Aid to Education', *Journal of Social Science*, no. XVII, 1883, p. 7.

6 From social science to the social sciences: reordering higher education

In Europe and America, mainly from the 1880s, the discrete social sciences as we now know them established their autonomy in academic and professional arenas, and with new institutional machineries. We have seen, in the later history of the social science movements, the roots of disintegration of older attempts to see society whole through wide lenses and comprehensive strategies. The history of schooling and of educational processes such as testing and examinations, the school leaving age and the organization of the curriculum, obviously contains – amongst other crucial factors from the end of the nineteenth century – central contributions from the new psychology, the 'scientific' study of children and of teaching and learning, the 'application' of psychology to pedagogy, the understanding of children's cognitive and emotional growth, and the construction and phasing of elements of the curriculum. Sociology, slower to establish itself in Britain, was to become by the second half of the twentieth century, a rival as major contributor to explanations of children's levels of achievement, as well as a basis on which to rest explanations of the roles of education in social differentiation and mobility, and the persistence of inequalities, discrimination and privilege. 'Educational foundations', as a fundamental ingredient in educational analysis and teacher education, emerged strongly in the second half of the twentieth century as a territory to which these modern social sciences made their separate (though, it was hoped, related) contributions. Philosophy, anthropology, economics, history, played their discrete roles alongside psychology and sociology - all of them having established their academic bases and respectability in higher education at the end of the nineteenth century and in the early decades of the twentieth. Their history is basic to that of higher education in the twentieth century, and to that of education generally.

This reordering of higher education, and its relationship to a variety of educational and social processes, is still a neglected area of the history of higher education and of relationships between knowledge and its professional embodiments, on the one hand, and wider social changes and processes on the other hand. There is no social history of the social sciences, and their position in higher education has been viewed largely in relation to the history of ideas and ideologues and founding fathers, of curriculum content and subject methodologies. As in the last chapter, problems in the history of education need to be seen as shared with and illuminated by other historical processes. Education rightly relates not only to social science and social science organizations, but also to the structure of university departments and the management of academic learning. The history of American school curricula relates to that of expectations of and by the changed pattern of higher education in the late nineteenth century, and in turn to the social groups for which higher education catered, and the social and economic structures to which it contributed and from which pressures were felt. The history of school curricula in England relates similarly to elements in and surrounding higher education, but ones which were differently ordered and differently felt, contained different emphases and had different outcomes. The visible differences between schooling in England and the United States, therefore, include different statuses of subjects, different levels of student choice, different approaches to curriculum content, structure and sequence, and different structures of assessment, guidance and rewards. Less visible are such areas as differences in channels and expectations of accountability. The nature, extent and availability of higher education, and the changing relationship of the whole educational system to the labour market, are major ingredients of the history of education at any level. The establishment and strengthening of the separate social sciences is a case study in these complexities.

The social sciences, as we have seen, grew out of more amorphous disciplines, including, and notably, moral philosophy. Out of the fragmentation of the old disciplines, and in response to newly defined areas of knowledge and newly expressed social and political needs, appeared not only the new 'academic' disciplines – scientifically conceived and often labelled as science – but also areas of professionally related study claiming a legitimate place in the structure of higher education. Social administration and social work, for example, entered the arena, as – in the United States primarily – did business studies and other specialisms related to commercial, industrial or administrative life.[1] Old disciplines like history were transformed.[2] A substantial part of the explanations of changes in the social scientific map of higher education lies outside the system and the institutions. The analysis must allow for major differences between Britain and the United States, especially in the rate and nature of change in higher education – though there are some interesting similarities between the new American land grant colleges and newly founded universities and the British university colleges of the later nineteenth century.

The concept of a social science was, as we have seen, available primarily from the late 1830s, as used by John Stuart Mill – though it had been used in either that or a similar form by Jeremy Bentham, Robert Owen and the Owenites. In the second half of the century it acquired particular connotations and an organizational base on both sides of the Atlantic, and in both cases was seen – at least implicitly – as in opposition to the 'sociology' of Comte and the Comteans, Spencer and the Spencerians. The social science associations did not establish or seek to promote a body of theory. The NAPSS in Britain, and the ASSA, no doubt derived from Mill and others in the 1850s and 1860s a sense of society as being amenable to scientific analysis, and combined with it a commitment both to the accumulation of data relating to social problems, and to appropriate action to cure them. In this form – pragmatic, philanthropic, reforming – social science stood outside the academic traditions of British and American universities – though in a number of American cases, notably the land grant colleges and universities like Cornell – attempts were made to import it amid a range of new, practically oriented courses. Any such importation, however, had to compete with rival pressures towards the protection or enhancement of academic, scholarly values. In the United States this contrary set of pressures focused on the influence of German scholarship, and especially the movement towards graduate and research-based departments and institutions. In both Britain and the United States, in their different ways, the history of the nineteenth-century higher education curriculum is one of fundamental and continual conflict. The emergence of a social science outside the established academic institutions therefore made its acceptance, and the acceptance of courses of study or professional activities associated with it, the more difficult in university and college structures. Philip Abrams has expressed the view that in Britain this social science largely prevented the growth of sociology as an established discipline in the second half of the nineteenth century,[3] and he is probably right both for Britain and the United States. Since moral philosophy contained elements of the same commitment to social reform and action, especially in the later decades of the nineteenth century, the emergence of a different version of social 'science' presented two underlying problems. First, it had to establish its 'scientific' credentials. Second, it had to abandon or to redefine the moral and reforming purposes associated both with moral philosophy and other disciplines (including even history), and with the social science movement itself. It met major obstacles both inside and outside higher education in doing so.

Mid-nineteenth-century social science was widely acceptable as a strategy and even as a substitute for an explicit theory mainly because it brought together groups of activists looking for a common forum, a common cause and above all a common confidence. Society had created, and failed to solve, an enormous range of problems. The problems themselves and the irrational responses and behaviour they provoked threatened the bases of social harmony and progress. The confidence needed and sought was in the possibility of solutions to visible, tangible problems. The search was therefore for closer understandings of the problems, suitable bases on which to construct solutions. These nineteenth-century reformers felt no need

> to set up elaborate sociological hypotheses. All around them were poverty, slums, crime, disease, illiteracy, drunkenness, immorality. As they saw it these things were caused by man and it was man's duty to get rid of them ... diagnosis was hardly necessary; it was the remedies that must be urgently sought.[4]

In Britain, therefore, the social science movement brought together Brougham and Chadwick, factory and school inspectors, distinguished figures in the fields of law reform and urban, sanitary and health reform, clergymen and campaigners for women's rights, Charles Kingsley and Lyon Playfair. In the United States it brought in similar groups, but reached out more successfully to higher education, including to university presidents like Andrew White and Daniel Coit Gilman. The movements shared assumptions about social consensus, progress and the inductive road to truth. By the 1880s and 1890s the assumptions and the strategies were being challenged by new versions of 'science', in a period when the academic and social respectability of a discipline was becoming increasingly dependent on the label. From the 1880s, we see the appearance of strong emphases on such new labels, either for old subjects or for new ones – including economic science, political science, historical science or the science of history, the science of the mind, linguistic science, and the rest. Men like Graham Wallas in Britain were pursuing a new science of politics.[5] In 1885 Sir John Seeley announced to his Cambridge students that what had previously been the Political Philosophy on which he lectured was henceforward to be called Political Science.[6] Seeley assumed that 'the materials of social and physical science were identical in that they consisted in a mass of unchanging facts in no way influenced by those who investigated them'. He was engaged in studying political phenomena 'scientifically', producing a 'scientific' history.[7] When the Sociological Society was created in London in 1904 it received and debated a paper from Durkheim, the summary of which that was read to the members began: 'The prime postulate of a science of society is the inclusion of human phenomena within the unity of Nature. Thus only can social phenomena be subjected to those precise observations which may be resumed in general formulae called natural laws.' He traced the contributions made to the development of such a science by Comte and Spencer, the latter of whom had 'opened the way for those taxonomic studies necessary for a scientific classification of human societies'.[8] Knowledge was becoming acceptable only if the model on which its accumulation and structure were based was recognizably scientific. The internal ordering and development of that knowledge are obviously critically important to its history, but the emergence of the social science *disciplines* as acceptable, institutionalized forms for the control and manipulation of such knowledge, is dependent for explanations on the social changes that were making the search for scientific laws and definitions so central.

It is important to emphasize that the pursuit of science ran in parallel, in both Britain and the United States, with the pursuit of – if not a scientific basis for social work, social reform and social service – at least a rigorous 'professional' basis for such forms of action. This is true in Britain of the late nineteenth and early twentieth-century move towards new conceptions of social work, and the move of social work and social administration into university environments – at the London School of

Economics and Liverpool Universities.[9] The ASSA not only spawned specialist groups from the 1880s which became specialist organizations of economists and historians, for example; it also produced groups and organizations devoted to specialist forms of social action – from the 1860s – in fields such as 'prison science' and 'charities and correction' (the National Conference of Charities and Correction retained that title from its inception in 1874 until it became the National Conference of Social Work in 1917). The pressures for the fragmentation of the university and college curriculum therefore came from many directions, inside and outside, including organizations which rested in some way on a basis of academic expertise and carried their battles into the established institutions or sought to create new ones. Church, Haskell and Furner have documented some aspects of these complex changes for the United States, outstandingly for economics,[10] and it is clear that the story of the social sciences in general cannot be told by reference solely or even predominantly to the institutions themselves. Reba Soffer has underlined the role of Alfred Marshall, for example, in transforming British economics from a 'science of wealth' to a 'science of welfare', but she has also underlined the context and the motivation:

> In 1903 Marshall was pleased to report to the Royal Commission on the Aged Poor that the 'best educated and most intelligent minds in England, the students at Oxford and Cambridge,' were becoming informed social reformers. Marshall's ambitions for university students were fulfilled to remarkable degrees. Unprecedented numbers of economists, statesmen, civil servants, educators, and writers went forth from the universities to attack social problems vigorously and successfully. University-trained specialists replaced their amateur predecessors in finance, government, and journalism with an authority that was rarely challenged.[11]

The notions of 'informed', 'trained' specialists with 'authority' are what differentiate such a picture from that of the membership of the NAPSS. The explanations of the new university-based curricula and definitions do not lie simply in outside penetration of the system, or the motives and reforms of individuals within it. They lie also in changing interpretations of social problems and phenomena, changing attitudes towards solutions and towards responsibility for solutions, changing views of the role of the state and of the management of social conflict and consensus. The creation of the London School of Economics and Social Science, and the stress it laid on training in the methods of social investigation, cannot be explained without reference to such wider changes, as well as to other more directly related questions of social theory, policy and analysis. The transformation of psychology, for example by William James, cannot be separated from wider debates about reason and its application to human affairs, from the relationship between reform and people's ability to understand their own motives and behaviour.[12]

Why economics or psychology emerged from moral philosophy, why social science abandoned the field to the social sciences, why social work entered the university arena – these are questions which reach into all corners of social and political experience. If the non-university base and structure of social science is an important preliminary to the new definitions of the 1880s and 1890s, so also, for example, is the changing professional context in which they emerged. Burton Bledstein's argument is that the expanding American middle classes in the late nineteenth century used the new college and university to enhance and solidify their power,[13] but it is also true that the curriculum changes, their confusion, fragmentation and realignments, depended on the forms taken by these moves towards the restructuring of social and political power. This is particularly true of the end-of-century establishment of forms of professional solidarity and power, forms of expertise and specialism that have become the subject of extensive historical interest.[14] The growth of professionalism, even given the conceptual and historical difficulties surrounding the term and the process, involved features which influenced the development of the social sciences in higher education. Economics, comments Reba Soffer, was not a profession until Marshall made it one.[15] Furner places the whole discussion of the development of social science and economics in late nineteenth-century America in the context of 'professionalization'.[16] All the activities and struggles of incipient academic groups, departments, associations in the new social sciences can be interpreted in terms of the self-definitions, subject definitions, career defence and collective control and action which belong in the discussion of professions. The history of social work and some related areas – such as hospital almoners, for example – illustrates at one level the transition towards the professional association and away from the learned society, a process that American historians such as Kohlstedt, and Oleson and Brown have discussed.[17] Attached to the concept of a professional or would-be professional activity were the conference and the committee; the information bulletin and publication machinery – including the analytical pamphlet and the campaigning leaflet; the concern to influence policy; the preoccupation with training and with the institutions where the training was to take place; the actual or metaphorical badges of the profession; the identifiable signs of belonging and the continuing negotiation over rights of membership amongst those who belong, and between them and those who seek to belong; and ultimately the concern with collective bargaining and self-defence, with the ambiguities of relating to working-class trade unionism or of distancing the organization from it. The American Economic and Historical Associations carried into the universities the search for all these accoutrements of professionalism, and extended them into the establishment of learned journals, specialist libraries, and styles of work – along lines that A. E. Bestor has described.[18] When James Bryce gave the introductory address to the new Sociological Society in 1904, he summarized the purposes of the new body as being primarily to bring together 'many incipient branches of social study' important to a sociological society; to establish close relations amongst cognate societies and associations already working along parallel lines; to break down the isolation of workers in such fields and help specialists to 'meet and compare notes more often'; to foster 'the development of the theoretical side of systematic inquiry into the sciences connected with human progress'; to accomplish certain immediate and practical objectives – including 'better provision for the teaching of the theory of all branches of social inquiry than exists in our universities or other educational institutions', the establishment of chairs, and the provision of libraries better equipped for sociological research. All of these elements are classic indicators of the moment of professionalization. It is important in this connection that Bryce rounded off all of these imperatives for the new body with a strong statement about the 'scientific' climate which made them necessary:

> Finally, let me refer to what in the largest sense may be said to be the general aim of the Society. It has become a commonplace to say that the great change – the greatest of all changes perhaps – that has passed over the world during the last 150 years has come not only from the material developments arising out of the progress of the physical sciences, but even more from the effect these sciences have produced upon the minds of men, and upon the investigation of all other subjects. The very idea of science . . . has now become immensely potent and so universally disseminated as to mark an important stage

in the development of the human mind . . . All the human sciences, from history and ethics downwards, have not yet been brought as fully within the grasp of this idea as ought to be the case. Therefore, a sociological society has a great and useful task before it in endeavouring to interpenetrate every department of human investigation with the scientific idea.[19]

The coupled notions of science and profession are important pointers to the nature of the historical process with which we are here concerned.

It would not, of course, be true to suggest that these were pressures purely external to the universities, and not taking shape there before the new specialisms appeared in the outer world. It is clear that the new associations appeared in the United States, for example, because there was a multi-purpose base on which they had been operating and which produced dissatisfaction and rivalries. It was also, however, because the problems to which the new groupings began to address themselves related to new channels of activity, new expectations and pressures, and obstacles within the existing curricula and structures of higher education. If the ASSA did not and could not respond adequately to new demands and expectations, the colleges and universities could be seen to be already engaged in versions of the same conflict. The nineteenth-century university controversies about the nature of a liberal education, about the position of technology and the utilitarian subjects in higher education, about examinations and standards, vocationalism and electives, the very conception of a 'university' – all included elements of the same conflicts as were producing the newly defined social sciences and related activities in other contexts. The professional groups and associations and the institutions of higher education all came to face a similar set of increasingly crucial problems in the last two decades of the century. The concern was less and less with semi-legislative or semi-private stategies for reform and the solution of piecemeal problems, and increasingly with ways of providing the state and the social order with expert information and advice, with qualified manpower, with people prepared academically ('scientifically') to contribute to increasingly elaborate machineries of economic and social planning and policy implementation. It was no longer that society needed well-informed activists, but that governments (and empires) needed expert, professional assistance in establishing and sustaining the economic and social machines. The experts therefore responded to mounting pressure to establish and sustain their own 'professional' organizations, training requirements and public signals of their qualification and authority to advise, to decide, to manage, to produce objective ('scientific') information, advice and decisions. David Noble has pointed out in the case of engineering, however, that it is wrong to see the specialist as in the grip of industrial and economic forces. They themselves had positive, decision-making capacities, often thrusting their specialisms and requirements into the consciousness of universities and colleges, in their attempts to tame technology for a social order which they helped to design, and for which they recruited the university curriculum.[20] A similar interrelationship can be pursued between higher education and the worlds inhabited by the potentially self-contained groups of social scientists.

A number of overlapping considerations have now begun to come together. First, the attempted transition from what Smelser – discussing the changing position of the social sciences in the college curriculum – describes as a transition from normative moral and political philosophy to more cognitive science ('attempted', because Smelser's picture underestimates the degree of moral or normative content in the new 'cognitive' or scientifically based disciplines). Secondly, the changing organizational base. Thirdly, the emergence of professional definitions directly related to the growing need for authoritative, expert analysis and advice. Fourthly, the changing structures and conflicts inside higher education.

At the back of all of those elements there is also, of course, the underlying responsiveness of higher education institutions and social scientists old and new to the challenges of social and political change. In particular, there is their awareness of social tension, conflict, violence, the irrational. There is the complex motivation discussed in the last chapter which points towards reform, social reorganization to conserve the social order or to change it marginally or fundamentally. The new social scientists of the late nineteenth century were, in Soffer's words, 'liberals who believed that informed reason and goodwill could overcome even the most intractable obstacles to social justice'.[21] The history of the curriculum cannot be written in terms of direct correlations between higher education and economic and political realities – though there are obviously important moments of such direct and observable interaction.[22] Nevertheless, the challenges and the threats and the pressures do form part of the consciousness and the policy-making processes of higher education, as of any other process or institution. Curriculum change in higher education has often been the product of such sensitivities, including existing or potential competition from other institutions - as was the case in both Britain and the United States from the 1880s. In the United States the main features of higher education in the period between 1870 and the beginning of the twentieth century constituted what Laurence Veysey portrays as an academic revolution: 'the American university of 1900 was all but unrecognizable in comparison with the college of 1860. Judged by almost any index, the very nature of the higher learning in the United States has been transformed.'[23] The social and curricular changes intended to be produced by the Morrill Act and the creation of the land grant colleges from the early 1860s gathered momentum in the 1870s and 1880s and made their real impact in the 1890s. Also from the 1870s, the creation of universities with newly conceived curricula - notably Johns Hopkins and Cornell - had their main effect later in the century. The lessons or adaptations of the experience of German scholarship took new shapes in the changing urban, industrial and commercial landscapes of the last two decades of the century (and had gone far enough by the First World War to provoke the imperial wrath of Thorstein Veblen).[24] American government, industry, commerce, were no longer the same in the end-of-century period of reform, social efficiency and the corporate state. The proliferation of university departments was a response at several removes. The denominational college had been thrust into new responses in order to survive. The new social science departments did not just appear by a process of fission from older ones under the impact of the extension of knowledge, important though this was. The new academic frontiers within the social sciences in higher education have also to be explained by struggles to achieve new legitimacies, which in turn were aimed to serve new needs.

The features we have so far underlined need to be extended, but it is possible here to underline only two of them. The first relates to the invasion of higher education by the new forms of vocational training that we have discussed, and which helped to influence the social science developments. Cheit describes the period 1880-1900 in the United States as the 'pioneer' period of business administration, for example.[25] In Britain, the end of the century saw the acceptance of social administration and social work into the university community out of the tradition of the Charity Organization Society and then family case work. The new 'professions' for which such university bases were found did not, in Abraham Flexner's view in 1915, meet criteria required for classification as a 'profession' – including the possession of an adequate intellectual base, having a relationship with knowledge that could be learned, and having both altruistic and practical features. On this basis Flexner excluded pharmacy, business and social work from his definition of 'professional'.[26] Social work, however, had developed in parallel with or as the child of, the earlier social science. If it was not seen as 'professional', this was in large measure because it had been fostered as a possible career for women, including the kind of women who had debated at the NAPSS in Britain, and had helped to organize regional and local organizations of the ASSA in the 1860s and 1870s. They were women who in Britain were typified by Octavia Hill and the women of the Charity Organization Society, and in America by those of the National Conference of Charities and Correction. The problem of 'professional status' was to a considerable extent one of the changing status of women and their move from charitable action to employed social work – an issue which Flexner did not confront.

In moving into the fringes of higher education, therefore, social work and its close relations influenced and strengthened the move of the academic social sciences towards academic, departmental purity, and away from the overt charitable impulse, the atheoretical basis, the low-status, prehistorical identity they associated with the old social science and the new activities which were its legatees. The social sciences wished to be free of the associations with the past, and to be seen to be separate from the service, applied company that began to join them on university campuses. Separateness was necessary for status, survival and advance.

The last element to be underlined, one which has been mentioned at a number of points, was the arrival of sociology, and its attempts at the beginning of the twentieth century to find its base in the theories and models provided especially by the new biological science. If sociology was establishing itself in the universities and on the printing presses of the 1890s, it was in the first decade of the twentieth century that the British and American sociological societies were created. The early papers of the British organization are full of discussions of eugenics and topics such as 'the biological foundations of sociology'. An American professor of philosophy came to the Sociological Society in 1906 to 'give some idea of the difficulties which have been encountered in the United States, under its peculiar set of conditions, in advancing the subject to its due place amongst the others of the curriculum'.[27] The problem was at heart one of academic balkanization. Sociology, in attempting to define its place in the academic sun, provoked the resentments of the other, already established disciplines, including economics, history, political science and social psychology. The departmental frontiers were therefore guarded ever more heavily, and sociology had to win its institutional freedom from economics or philosophy almost as soon as these had recovered from their own battles to free themselves from moral philosophy or moral science – or they had to penetrate the curriculum from outside. The myriad subdivisions of sociology or history were to follow the same sort of path in later decades of the twentieth century. None of the newly triumphant social sciences of the late nineteenth and early twentieth centuries found their new autonomy to be free from internal conflict and controversy, but this was to be particularly true of sociology. It was not long, in the Sociological Society, before H. G. Wells was denying that sociology was a science and was, if anything, the pursuit of utopia.[28] A month earlier Beatrice Webb had begun a paper on 'Methods of investigation' as follows:

> What we have to do in social science is to apply the scientific method to the facts of social life. There is only one scientific method – that used in physical science . . . the application of that method is a technical matter . . . And so in the case of sociology, which is the science of men in combination, the application of scientific method needs the use of certain technical instruments.[29]

For Sidney and Beatrice Webb, in Donald MacRae's words, 'sociology was a perfect card index of all unique social facts' (he goes on to describe this as 'barren philistinism').[30] There were to be different ways of interpreting Bryce's appeal for 'the development of the theoretical side of systematic inquiry'!

The American sociology of the turn of the century drew on different sources and produced its own varieties and conflicts, but it is interesting that in reporting the emergent discipline to his London audience, the American professor suggested that his country was 'open to sociology in a way in which it is impossible to be open in this country'. America was 'continually confronted by sociological literature' because of its demographic and urban realities: the varieties of immigrants, the growth in population, the 'rush to the cities', the race questions in the south, the pioneer life, the 'American character'.[31] In many ways these issues – and the parallel catalogue of British nineteenth-century problems – were the justification for the creation of the NAPSS and the ASSA in the 1850s and 1860s. What was new, and what the professor did not mention, was the changed way of perceiving the problems, and above all the changed ways of considering the management of possible solutions. The history of why Britain or America was at any point 'open to' one of the new social sciences has to approach its witnesses with some care. The vocabulary of the social sciences, of higher education and its curriculum, and the language of their debates, needs to be approached with caution.

In spite of the differences between the two countries, therefore, there are important historical features of the position of the social sciences in higher education that can benefit from an overlapping analysis. The role of the expansion of knowledge, and of perceptions of its importance, are crucial elements in both historical analyses. In both cases we find the social sciences defining and defending themselves against established organizational, intellectual and social definitions. They found their theory and practices in situations heavily influenced by changes in the operation of the economy, of government, of the state, of professional groups and organizations. In putting up the flags and mounting the defences round their new departments, organizations, conferences, journals and the like, the new social scientists were doing more than follow a logic imposed by changes in the structure of knowledge of higher education. The transition from social science to the social sciences has also to do with the economic and political, social and intellectual processes which we have discussed and which would form the elements of the sustained social history of these aspects of knowledge and of higher education that is lacking.[32]

What is most needed in this area of educational and social history is an escape from the history of intellectual pedigrees, from house histories, from common-sense assumptions about the nature of and reasons for institutional and curricular change. The story needs to include more searching investigations of the professional pressures, the relationship between higher education and emergent categories of employment, the tension between liberal and emergent socialist solutions, the nature of the conflicts with the rearguard and against options that were unsuccessful or lost. It is in this sense that the necessary social history of these disciplines in this period becomes a case study of historical weaknesses and possibilities. It also offers an important glimpse of the late nineteenth-century roots of some twentieth-century educational developments. The establishment of the social sciences, their definitions and frontiers, their territorial ambitions and relationships with training, public policy and the power structures of education, are as central to the history of educational systems and ideas as are more familiar institutions in the historical landscape.

Notes

1 Earl F. Cheit, for example, discusses agriculture, engineering, business administration and forestry in his *The Useful Arts and the Liberal Tradition* (New York, 1975).
2 See J. Franklin Jameson, 'The American Historical Association, 1884–1909', *The American Historical Review*, vol. XV, no. 1, 1909.
3 Philip Abrams, *The Origins of British Sociology: 1834–1914* (Chicago, 1968), p. 44.
4 Maurice G. Kendall, 'Measurement in the Study of Society', in William Robson (ed.), *Man and the Social Sciences* (London, 1972), p. 136.
5 See Reba N. Soffer, *Ethics and Society in England: The Revolution in the Social Sciences 1870–1914* (Berkeley, 1978), ch. 9, 'Graham Wallas and a Liberal Political Science'.
6 Sir J.R. Seeley, *Introduction to Political Science: Two Series of Lectures* (London, 1896), p. 1.
7 Deborah Wormell, *Sir John Seeley and the Uses of History* (Cambridge, 1980), pp. 34, 39, 124.
8 Abstract of a paper by Durkheim, 'On the Relation of Sociology to the Social Sciences and to Philosophy', in *Sociological Papers 1904* (London, 1905), pp. 197–8.
9 For a comparative history of the development of social work from charity organization see Kathleen Woodroofe, *From Charity to Social Work in England and the United States* (London, 1962).
10 Robert L. Church, 'Economists as Experts: The Rise of an Academic profession in America 1870–1917', in Lawrence Stone (ed.), *The University in Society* (Princeton, 1975), vol. II; Thomas L. Haskell, *The Emergence of Professional Social Science* (Urbana, Illinois, 1977); Mary O. Furner, *Advocacy and Objectivity* (Lexington, Kentucky, 1975).
11 Soffer, *Ethics and Society in England*, pp. 69, 86.
12 Ibid., p. 116.
13 Burton, J. Bledstein, *The Culture of Professionalism: The Middle Class and the Development of Higher Education in America* (New York, 1976).
14 See particularly ibid., and Christopher Lasch, *Haven in a Heartless World: The Family Besieged* (New York, 1977).
15 Soffer, *Ethics and Society in England*, p. 87.
16 Furner, *Advocacy and Objectivity, passim* but see for example chs 12 and 13.
17 Sally Gregory Kohlstedt, *The Formation of the American Scientific Community: The American Association for the Advancement of Science 1848–60* (Urbana, 1976).
18 Arthur E. Bestor Jr, 'The Transformation of American Scholarship, 1875–1917', *Library Quarterly*, vol. xxiii, 1953, pp. 164–79.
19 James Bryce, Introductory Address on 'The Use and Purpose of a Sociological Society', *Sociological Papers 1904*, pp. xiv–xviii.
20 David F. Noble, *America by Design: Science, Technology, and the Rise of Corporate Capitalism* (New York, 1977), *passim*, but see particularly Epilogue.

21 Soffer, *Ethics and Society in England*, p. 217.
22 See Tony Mansell and Harold Silver, 'Themes in Higher Education: Britain, America and Germany', in W.E. Marsden (ed.), *Post-War Curriculum Development: An Historical Appraisal* (Leicester, 1979).
23 Laurence R. Veysey, *The Emergence of the American University* (Chicago, 1965, edition of 1914), p. 2.
24 Thorstein Veblen, *The Higher Learning in America: A Memorandum on the Conduct of Universities by Business Men* (New York, 1918). The influence of German scholarship is a common theme in the literature, but an important account of its early domestication in the United States is Carl Diehl, *Americans and German Scholarship 1770-1870* (New Haven, 1978).
25 Cheit, *The Useful Arts and the Liberal Tradition*, p. 84.
26 Abraham Flexner, 'Is Social Work a Profession?', *Proceedings of the National Conference of Charities and Correction* (Chicago, 1915).
27 R.M. Wenley, 'Sociology as an Academic Subject', *Sociological Papers 1906* (London, 1907), p. 281.
28 H.G. Wells, 'The So-Called Science of Sociology', in ibid., pp. 357-69.
29 Mrs Sidney Webb, 'On Methods of Investigation', in ibid., p. 345.
30 Donald G. MacRae, 'The Basis of Social Cohesion', in Robson, *Man and the Social Sciences*, p. 50.
31 Wenley, 'Sociology as an Academic Subject', pp. 286-9.
32 The American research has gone much the furthest in this direction. The work on Harvard has been the most far-reaching, including Robert Church's 1965 Harvard PhD, 'The Development of the Social Sciences as Academic Disciplines at Harvard', and Paul Buck (ed.), *Social Sciences at Harvard 1860-1920: From Inculcation to the Open Mind* (Cambridge, Mass., 1965), to which Church contributed a chapter on 'The Economists Study Society: Sociology at Harvard, 1891-1902'.

Part Two

Twentieth-century studies

7 The liberal and the vocational

In the early decades of this century there were many commentators who, like A.N. Whitehead, believed that 'the antithesis between a technical and a liberal education is fallacious'.[1] In 1919, two years after Whitehead published the remark, the Adult Education Committee of the Ministry of Reconstruction published a report in which it discussed at length the relationship between 'Technical Education and Humane Studies'. In it, the committee favoured establishing a division between technical and vocational instruction on the one hand, and non-vocational and humane studies on the other, thinking the distinction a useful one – 'more especially because the distinction is one which exists in the popular mind and has taken root in practice'.[2] Historical discussion of the various concepts and distinctions involved here has tended to focus on those points in the nineteenth century when they were most sharply thrust into public debate. There is a considerable literature tracing the fortunes of the concept of liberal education from Aristotle to Matthew Arnold, Cardinal Newman and the disputes over science and technology in the last decades of the nineteenth century. What has not interested historians is the way in which the 'fallacious' antithesis was projected through the twentieth century, and the forms in which it persisted in 'the popular mind'. The arguments surrounding the views of an Arnold or a Huxley do, of course, reflect the 'popular mind' in some way, and they are not merely the pinnacles of debate. Historical accounts have often, however, treated them as such, and the sources tend to remain Newman's *The Idea of a University*, J.S. Mill's inaugural address at the University of St Andrews, Arnold's *Culture and Anarchy* and the essays of T.H. Huxley. Historians of education have ranged more widely, to the reports of the Clarendon and Taunton commissions, and sources relating particularly to the decision-making processes of Oxford and Cambridge, but the popular sources of or support for the liberal–vocational antithesis have not been explored. The attitudes of students, employers, politicians, the press and others have been more assumed than investigated.

Social scientists are used to analysing the situation, reactions, attitudes of clients, tenants, recipients, voters, victims. The literature of the sociology of housing or social work, the social services or prisons, grapples with the problems of taking account of the perceptions of those 'to whom it is done'. A range of methodologies and theories have surfaced and transformed the disciplines, precisely as a result of attempts to solve the problem. Sociologists of education have in general avoided the ground. Exceptions are important, and Paul Willis's *Learning to Labour* would be one. But the educational literature of the client and the victim has been mainly of a different order, less 'academic', more 'literary' or campaigning, proclaiming death at an early age, children born to fail, kids oppressed. If social scientists have on the whole avoided entanglement with the beneficiaries of education, historians have the more so. Historians of social work and penitentiaries and asylums have felt impelled towards the 'victims', even if the histories have eventually said more about the historians' theories of social control than about the victims. Historians of schools or colleges or early childhood education or the curriculum have made little effort to see the story from below. Much brouhaha is, of course, evident in the field of oral history, and historians of the more recent past have been able to pursue 'victims' of many kinds. Life is less easy for the historian of ancient Athens or Carolingian Europe or colonial America or Regency England – though there have been historians who have been teaching us how.

It was suggested in 1962 that if 'educational science' were to evolve its own language it would very likely consist primarily of psychological terms – certainly at that time its terms were felt to be mainly psychological.[3] Even that tradition, however, had not injected into educational analysis any concern with the participant's view, as distinct from perceiveḍ or measured behaviour. All the main vocabulary and structure of analysis in the history of education and related processes have been defined from the top, and the most persistent controversies have been sustained by interpretation and reinterpretation of definitions from the top. Of nothing in education has this been more true than the continuing debate about a 'liberal' or 'general' or 'humane' education, and its opposites. The intention here is to suggest a framework for such an approach to this important element in the history of education in the early decades of the twentieth century, when the vocabulary of the debate was still fluid, and interesting areas of definition and decision were opening up. The most critical period in Britain for the fate of the concepts of liberal and vocational or technical, in relation to schooling, was probably the 1920s, and a clarification of the issues involved in and around the 1920s is necessary for an understanding of the debates about the curriculum, about school and work, about education and the economy, which developed later in the century – outstandingly in the late 1970s.

The distinctions involved in these concepts have bedevilled twentieth-century discussions of every level and type of education, and every strategy of planning and reform, but attempts to clarify the meanings of the vocational and the liberal, and their roles in educational practice, have been left mainly to philosophers. These distinctions have later in the century become central features of policy discussion, especially as – in the late 1970s and early 1980s – the Department of Education and Science and others attempted to define with increasing urgency the 'core curriculum' and the responses of the educational system to economic pressures. A study of the vocational–liberal distinctions and efforts to establish or dispose of them, levels of disagreement about meanings and their relation to debates about social and political change, about childhood and adolescence, about moral values, indicates how great is the unexplored historical gap between nineteenth-century analyses and the agonies of the late twentieth century. The directions of attention that would need to be followed to explore the early twentieth-century genesis or refashioning of later concerns have not proved attractive ground partly because it would be necessary more than anything to explain the distinction 'which exists in the popular mind' and had 'taken root in practice'. What happened to the concepts in the developing system and practice of the early decades of this century cannot easily be reached by reference to the writings of some Matthew Arnold, or to a neat and widely acceptable version of nineteenth-century social class, or a concern with easily presentable narratives of 'progressive education', or the growth of subjects or the classification of institutions.

In the next chapter we shall be tracing some, mainly later, twentieth-century attitudes to higher education in Britain. That study, like any study of educational opinion, involves assumptions, dichotomies, popular and expert understandings, which present apparent clarities and fundamental uncertainties. We cannot here trace those complexities at all levels across the century, but we can take soundings in the period particularly after the First World War. Important contexts had already been established. Relationships between education and the industrial and economic fortunes of the country had already been under scrutiny for several decades as a result of increasingly successful economic competition from the United States and Europe. Apprenticeship and industrial training had become matters of concern as comparisons were made with more systematic educational structures elsewhere. As the labour market changed and juvenile employment declined, the moral, social and intellectual health of the adolescent had become a matter of mounting public concern, and the prolongation of school life of increasing urgency. The structures of schooling, the nature and accessibility of secondary education, the content of the curriculum, the 'relevance' of subjects, alternative job-related schools for the 'non-academic' adolescent, had become pre-war concerns that were intensified in wartime conditions. The family, Christian values, social stability, were as threatened by prospects of juvenile unemployment and delinquency, loss of parental authority and of traditional patterns of church-going, as by war itself. Discussions about the content and structures of education had already become deeply enmeshed with concerns about economic and industrial, demographic and moral transformations.

An important ingredient of these changes had been the persistent attempts, particularly in the last three decades of the nineteenth century, to respond to international and domestic pressures towards scientific and technical education. However slow and inadequate the developments have seemed with hindsight, and to many contemporary commentators in the late nineteenth century, changes in the elementary and secondary, further and higher, structures had made significant inroads into previous consciousness and practice. In 1900 Her Majesty's Chief Inspectors of Schools, for example, were commenting that 'nothing in English education is more remarkable than the manner in which special institutes for the purposes of science, art, and technical work have sprung up all over the country during the past twenty years', and that the 'school of science' scheme had 'proved itself adaptable to very varied types of schools – technical schools, grammar schools, rural agricultural schools, board schools and girls' schools'. Detailed, confident and optimistic accounts were being made by the inspectorate of all of these developments, despite the weaknesses they were recording in content, relationships with employers, and especially finance.[4] At this stage the inspectors are not concerned about the battle over vocational and non-vocational; their assumption is that technical, scientific, art and craft needs have to be met, and that one expedient is virtually as good as any other to achieve the desired end. There is a sense in these reports of an openness to change, an indistinguishable potential for development within existing institutions and in newly created and separate institutions. The only underlying policy pressure is for a sound general elementary education on to which technical education can be built. A major component of these developments had been the higher grade schools, in which – out of an elementary, not a grammar, school tradition – experimental curricula based on technical, scientific and applied subjects had been constructed. Historians have differed in interpreting the role of Robert Morant and the 1904 Regulations in preventing the emergence of an 'alternative' secondary school tradition, but there is no doubt that many contemporaries saw the model of secondary education that triumphed in the 1900s as an opportunity lost. The Spens Report on *Secondary Education*, in 1938, accepted this historical judgement in no uncertain terms, even italicizing the passage:

The most salient defect in the new Regulations for Secondary Schools issued in 1904 is that they failed to take note of the comparatively rich experience of secondary curricula of a practical and quasi-vocational type which had been evolved in the Higher Grade Schools, the Organised Science Schools and the Technical Day Schools. The new Regulations were based wholly on the tradition of the Grammar Schools and the Public Schools.

The Report went on add a crucial general commentary on the implications of the 1904 decisions:

the concept of a general education which underlies these Regulations was divorced from the idea of technical or quasi-technical education though in reality much of the education described as 'liberal' or 'general' was itself vocational education for the 'liberal' professions.[5]

Between those first few years of the century and the judgements of 1938 and historians of later decades attitudes had hardened and concepts had congealed. What has not been noticed, however, is that the controversies around the issues of 'practical', 'quasi-vocational' and 'liberal' education and the 1904 Regulations were not the end of debate, but one of the first signals of a sustained and confused battle.

One of the contexts for the controversies was the emergent structure of technical education in the period after the 1902 Act, and particularly the search for new, post-primary or alternative secondary forms of schooling. It is a common feature of British educational history that problems of this kind result in new institutions. Existing institutions either fail to adapt or adapt slowly and inadequately, and the creation of new, lower-status institutions protects and even enhances the status of the existing structures (examples would include the 'purification' of the grammar schools when the monitorial schools were created in the early nineteenth century, and the protection of existing university values by the creation of new institutions in the second half of the nineteenth century and in the late 1960s, including both generations of 'polytechnics'). The establishment of junior technical schools in the early twentieth century was one such mechanism, diverting pressures for practical, vocational and job-related forms of schooling away from the grammar schools as defined in the period 1902–4. Eighty-six junior technical schools were in operation in 1922–3, and by 1938 there were 224, offering courses in building and engineering, art and commerce, and a range of other practical courses.[6] They were seen as an alternative to the grammar school for elementary – that is, predominantly working-class – pupils, and the Spens Report, for example, discussed them as such, suggesting policies for elevating them in status (to technical high schools), taking their pupils at eleven instead of their existing common entry age of thirteen.[7] John Graves, discussing these schools in 1943, described their handicap – the best brains being creamed off to the grammar school, and the 'greater social prestige' being attached to the latter.[8]

Previous failures to reconcile strong new pressures for structural and curriculum change with existing values and practices led to a continuous search in the 1920s and 1930s for institutions, 'sides' and courses which would provide discrete responses. The view most commonly expressed in the early decades of the century was that technical education was end-on to an initial general education, though there were disputes about whether this meant that it followed on 'elementary' or 'secondary' education. Since it was widely agreed that technical education or instruction was not yet – in the words of the Newbolt Committee on *The Teaching of English in England* – 'rightly "education" at all',[9] it was best postponed until the general education groundwork had been completed. What was at stake, therefore, was the structure of the educational system itself, the whole debate about access to secondary education which pervaded the period between the wars. Technical education, suggested the Ministry of Reconstruction Adult Education Committee in 1919, was 'based upon inadequate foundations. It is built upon elementary education; it should be built, in our opinion, upon secondary education.'[10] The question, then, was one of access, of definition and of length of school life. Attitudes to the technical and the vocational related to attitudes about the total educational system. At what age, and for which children, was there a dividing line between the general and the specialized? The argument for delayed attention to the vocational was perhaps most strongly pressed by those who had resented the emergence of higher grade schools or other forms of science-based or practical schooling:

Few educationists to-day believe in the possibility of producing a wide and catholic mind by means of specialised school instruction . . . While few enlightened teachers would advocate for pupils under sixteen a merely mathematical or scientific or linguistic training, in practice this tendency is often seen. The State itself some years ago encouraged this tendency, and by its large grants to the Organised Science Schools handicapped to a disastrous degree the literary and linguistic curriculum. Its repentance is, however, thorough[11]

The estimate of 'few' may be misleading in both connections, but the arguments for a school system in which 'specialised school instruction' was either discrete or delayed were powerfully advocated. Antagonism to a science-based alternative to the traditional curriculum, expressed here in 1922, continued to be strong and vocal. In the following year it found further expression in a Board of Education consultative committee report on curricula for boys and girls: 'A considerable number of the Higher Grade or Higher Elementary Schools, taken over by local education authorities from school boards as secondary schools, had become so dominated by Natural Science as to imperil the wider conception of a liberal education.'[12]

One outcome, therefore, was the widespread acceptance of diversity of institution to meet diversity of need and of talents, and such acceptance was to be found in all areas of opinion. A typical and lucid statement by a supporter of new and imaginative approaches to vocational education, of combating the 'wordy spirit of the pedagogue' and desk routines, and of bringing the 'spirit of the workshop' into the schools, proposed that:

> The diversity of practical aims can roughly be met by organizing the following types of school:
>
> 1. Primary artisan schools for pupils entering the unskilled and skilled manual occupations.
> 2. Primary schools with a commercial bias for pupils who will become clerks or small traders.
> 3. Secondary schools having three sides:
>   (a) A commercial side for pupils desiring to enter commercial life.
>   (b) A technical or industrial side for pupils desiring to enter industry.
>   (c) A side preparatory to the university for those desiring to enter professional life.[13]

Some such attempt to divide pupils by school or 'side' is common in educational policy formulations throughout the late nineteenth century and twentieth century. It was present in the discussion of secondary education by the Taunton Commission in the 1860s, and was most vigorously expounded by the Norwood Committee on *Curriculum and Examinations in Secondary Schools*, which in 1943 detected three kinds of children to match its proposed tripartite structure of secondary education. Even R.H. Tawney's policy document for the Labour Party in 1922, *Secondary Education for All*, is cautious and ambiguous about alternatives to the existing grammar schools. In a discussion of central schools, defined by the London County Council as 'providing for certain specially selected boys and girls from the age of eleven upwards a four years' general course of instruction with a definite commercial or industrial bias', Tawney rejects not the idea of different kinds of school but the interpretation of central schools as sub-standard and inferior.[14] In Britain, as in the United States, controversies around the curriculum therefore reflected deeper concerns about educational provision in general.[15] Technical education was a point of entry to debates about social class differentiation in the educational system.

The importation of the 'spirit of the workshop' into the school, pressures for vocational developments in the curriculum – especially, but not solely, for working-class children – were a response, amongst other things, to changes in industry and employment. Traditional forms of apprenticeship were being modified or abandoned amidst changing economic conditions and the awareness of new needs for skill and training. Underlying some of the calls for vocational preparation in schools was a nostalgic search for a substitute for craft-based apprenticeships, for the romantically conceived wholeness of the workshop. Educationists were aware of the impact and implications of changes in apprenticeship. A discussion of 'modern views on education' at the time of the First World War complained that vocational courses were only partially supplying a need which had become 'increasingly marked of late owing to the very general abandonment of the apprenticeship system by employers'. It called for the matter to be approached 'more frankly' since the advantages of a broad, liberal education did not amount to much if a boy could not afterwards earn bread and cheese.[16] J.J. Findlay, in a book on the foundations of education, argued strongly in 1927 for an enlightened approach to technical education for the masses, between the ages of twelve and eighteen. Defending the proposition against the charge of seeking to make workmen more efficient and contented, he advocated a form of technical education which would respond to the needs of 'the rational mind, the aesthetic mind'. The modern educator needed to revive the principle of apprenticeship, in new forms:

> The apprentice was a learner rather than a wage-earner; his master undertook to acquaint him with all sides of his craft . . . The things to be learnt are different and they can no longer be taught by the master alone, but the cardinal impulses of youth have not changed: all young people, the most unskilled as well as the finest minds, need both the social control of an apprentice system and the intellectual and aesthetic culture which characterized the old apprentice systems in the heyday of their prosperity.[17]

Progressive educators were looking for ways of adapting structures and curricula to achieve such an end.

A stronger relationship between curriculum and employment raised anxieties. How specific, for example, could a vocational, school course be? The answer to this question was explored most influentially in T. Percy Nunn's *Education: Its Data and First Principles*, first published in 1920, constantly reprinted, and the most read and representative text of the progressive education movement between the wars. Nunn's view was that there was an acceptable and an unacceptable linkage between vocational training and employment. Basing his arguments on what he saw as 'purely educational grounds' (rejecting the claim that behind vocational education was the 'hand of the exploiting employer') Nunn chose two sets of possible employment. The first included, for boys, that of policeman and tram-conductor, and for girls, cardboard box-making. It was 'useless' and 'wrong' for schools to train for such occupations. It was different with the second set of employments – naval officer, mariner, engineer, cabinet-maker, builder, farmer – because these latter occupations met 'no trivial or transient needs. They have behind them a dignified history and a distinctive moral tradition . . . They have . . . given scope to noble intellects and splendid practical powers.'[18] Eighteen years later, with Nunn as a co-opted member of its curriculum sub-committee, the Spens Committee drafted a chapter on the curriculum for which Nunn contributed a memorandum on principles. This chapter repeats Nunn's 1920 vocabulary of 'no trivial or transient needs', and lists four of Nunn's previous examples of occupations which gave scope, in the Spens version, for 'originating minds and great practical powers'.[19] At this level of discussion the issue was not so much what was vocational, as the values and traditions on which acceptable versions of the vocational could be constructed. If the vocational was not to point towards such trivial and transient occupations as the police, the justifications for vocational content in curricula had to be wide, almost 'liberal'.

The most widespread form in which 'the vocational' was translated into acceptable school practice was as 'the practical', seen less as directly related to employment, as 'pre-vocational'.[20] The Hadow Committee insisted repeatedly in its report on *The Education of the Adolescent* that it was in favour of a 'practical bias' in the curriculum of modern schools and senior classes, an emphasis on the 'practical aspects of certain subjects without involving work in the technicalities of any one specific trade or occupation'. Courses of instruction in the last two years of post-primary schools should 'not be vocational', but the treatment of subjects such as history, geography, elementary mathematics and a modern language 'should be "practical" in the broadest sense, and directly and obviously brought into relation with the facts of every day experience'.[21] The Board of Education's *Handbook of Suggestions* for teachers in elementary schools suggested in its 1927 edition that handwork was of value for people with 'little power of abstract thought', and for children in particular could 'add reality to almost every subject of the curriculum'.[22] Handicraft had by the 1920s established itself in elementary schools 'as the result partly of the theory that up to the age of adolescence the instincts of children incline to the practical side'.[23] From the late nineteenth century, particularly in connection with the advocacy of 'Sloyd' as 'educational handwork', there had been consistent support for the idea that manual training 'was not a mere training of the hand for industry, but a training of the mind through the hand'.[24] Some educationists, including Findlay, had to work through the difficulties of justifying manual training (were they merely, for example, imitative of adult pursuits?) before coming down in its favour, and text-books galore advised teachers to treat handicraft as a source of accuracy, ability to plan, as 'headwork and heartwork as well'.[25]

However interpreted, the vocational, the manual, the practical, were seen as entering or overlapping with the traditional territory of the liberal or general curriculum, and were often perceived as enhancing its purposes - notably with those pupils who required additional motivation. Again Nunn's 1920 ideas and influence offer an insight into the thinking, the curriculum and the system. Nunn had also been co-opted on to the drafting committee of the Hadow Committee, and had 'rendered invaluable help in the preparation of the Report'. The report, for all its preference for 'the practical', conceded that a vocational education could give a pupil's studies a 'definite direction', and - repeating the 1920 formulations - it felt that for many pupils it would offer the best form of personal development, since 'it not infrequently releases the finer energies of mind, which more general education would leave inert'.[26] Six years earlier Nunn had seen schooling, if directed towards traditional occupations, as carrying a pupil towards a goal, unlocking 'the finer energies of a mind which a "general" education would leave stupid and inert'.[27] This sense of the dignity and power of vocational education, and the possibility of its being conducted in a liberal spirit - once released from the narrow interpretations imposed on it by industry and others - not only follows Nunn from the 1920 book, through the Hadow Committee and the Spens Committee. By 1938 *Education: Its Data and First Principles* had been through a second edition and twenty-two reprints. The Spens Committee, in reasserting that vocational education could give pupils a 'directly envisaged goal', important for those minds 'whose energies are released' only by such studies, was also reasserting that 'vocational education is in the fullest sense also liberal'.[28] The repetition is more than a tribute to Nunn's ubiquity, it is an indication of how strongly the principles he had espoused were continuing to find support.

The importance of this approach lies not only in its explanation of a psychological dimension to vocational content, but also in its relationship to the wider context of schooling. Elementary school provision was now universal, attendance had been made compulsory, the minimum age of school leaving was rising and had oeen standardized at fourteen by the 1918 Education Act. Disquiet about the problems of adolescence was being widely voiced and they were being increasingly defined and investigated. Juvenile unemployment had become a major social issue. The motivation of, particularly, working-class children, being retained for longer periods in school and with worsening prospects of future employment, was more than a question of pedagogy and creative school experience. Changing economic and social conditions and needs weighed heavily on the concepts handled by Nunn and his contemporaries.

The motivation of the reformers must not, however, be oversimplified. They had inherited dichotomies inherited from, and deepened by, the nineteenth century. However ancient some of the concepts and controversies may be, the nineteenth-century industrial world crystallized a version of 'the liberal' which was strongly to influence the curriculum debates of the twentieth century. Older traditions of 'vocational' preparation for the professions were reinterpreted in Europe and America with new emphases on the general, liberal education which provided access to certain values and cultural characteristics. The reinterpretation was intended to sustain and protect élite positions, to justify the shape and content of the British public school, the German university. Jurgen Herbst summarizes the change in both Europe and the United States: 'in the nineteenth century a liberal education was the intellectual and moral cultivation in academic-preparatory schools, colleges, and universities reserved for the male children of a country's social elite.'[29] The reformers of the early twentieth century juggled with all the concepts and arguments we have outlined, and gave different priorities to economic and psychological, social and educational considerations. Many of them saw the possibility that their proposed new curricula might go hand in hand with industrial and social reforms of other kinds. They often shared in the kind of analysis conducted by the 1919 Adult Education Committee. In wishing technical education to become a 'medium of humane education' the Committee was aware of the weaknesses of technical education as it existed, weaknesses which derived from the fact that 'vocational instruction has inevitably taken its colour from the industrial system, which has pressed education into its service'. Technical and nontechnical education would in future overlap: 'in a better social order, with a nobler conception of industry and a broader view of the meaning and purpose of education there would be a considerable amount of common ground'.[30] Pressures for vocational education came not only from industry (and the Hadow Committee discovered that employers were in fact not particularly in favour of vocational studies in the elementary school) but were also directed against industry. The Newbolt Committee saw the history of educational thought since the Renaissance as one in which the commercial and industrial facts of the modern world had been either despised or ignored, and the result had been 'a cleavage, disastrous both for education and industry'.[31] Debates about the vocational and the technical in the 1920s continually reopened questions that nineteenth-century changes, the creation of new institutions, the 1904 Regulations, had been intended or had appeared to settle.

The Newbolt Committee talked about that 'thronged but ill-built structure, behind the main educational facade, known as technical education'.[32] In doing so it reflected widespread understanding amongst educationists that existing principles and practices, curricula and courses, school and higher education structures, did not answer the need. In spite of this awareness the vision of a practical, technical or vocational education which could compete with, overlap with, become a part of, remodel, the liberal curriculum, was widespread and strong. A.N. Whitehead, sharing the Adult Education Committee's ideal of changes that would result in work being 'transfused with intellectual and moral vision', producing 'workmen, men of science, and employers who enjoy their work', also saw that

> alike for masters and for men a technical or technological education, which is to have any chance of satisfying the practical needs of the nation, must be conceived in a liberal spirit as a real intellectual enlightenment . . . In such an education geometry and poetry are as essential as turning laths.[33]

The 1920s and 1930s abound in expressions of this kind of view, projected into national debate around and during the First World War. Many of the participants argued that the distinction between the technical and vocational on the one hand, and the liberal and the humane on the other hand, could not be ascribed to content: the distinction had become associated historically with differences of approach, of treatment. There were voices in the late nineteenth century proclaiming that 'the difference between technical instruction and general instruction lies not in the subject, but in the method and purpose of the course of study'.[34] Nunn looked to vocational education 'conducted in a liberal spirit'.[35] The Hadow Committee warned of the dangers both of too isolated and narrow a school curriculum and of too responsive a curriculum to the specific needs of later life – it sought instead a well-balanced curriculum that combined the two conceptions in what it called 'social individuality'.[36] The Newbolt Committee wanted technical instruction to be 'supplemented and informed with the humanities' and thereby to become technical *education*.[37] F.S. Marvin, formerly one of His Majesty's Inspectors, wrote in 1933 that 'in an age when the application of Science is the predominant force the study of Science and practical aptitude cannot long be considered "uneducational"'.[38]

A number of processes were therefore becoming interwoven at this point in the period around the First World War and through the next two decades. Tawney, the Labour Party, the unions, were pressing for a restructuring of the system to open up access to secondary education of some kind to all. Some educationists, prominent amongst them J.J. Findlay, were resisting the 'older type of technical school' and looking for what Findlay in 1911 called 'a prolonged experience of general liberal culture at school and college' as a sound introduction to 'the specialised duties of adult life'. In 1927 Findlay was arguing that what used to be called 'Liberal Education' and was now being called 'Education for Leisure' was being recognized as appropriate to the 'children of poverty', a development which was 'novel to our epoch and springs from the general philosophy of equality or democracy'.[39] The uncertainties of the status of the technical and vocational accompanied these uncertainties about the structures of schooling and of the curriculum as a whole, or of appropriate differentiated curricula. One former director of education argued in 1929 that 'the keenly, almost angrily, debated question of "vocational training"' would be unnecessary if the phrase were defined – as a specific training for a trade, a preliminary training as a basis for all crafts, or the ordinary school subjects being responsive to local industry and conditions.[40] Implications and agreement depended on the selection of meaning. Committees, educationists, the writers of text-books on teaching and the curriculum, were seeking to respond to the sense that the schools were 'out of touch with the interests of practical life' – a charge explicitly considered by the Spens Committee and declared 'not ill-founded'.[41]

That judgement, at the end of the 1930s, echoed that of the Newbolt Committee at the beginning of the 1920s: 'in the general course of our inquiry it has been borne in upon us time and again that our educational system is too remote from life'.[42] In all of this combination of concerns there were advocates and possibilities of radical new interpretations of the vocational–liberal divide, and radical new approaches to the curriculum. There were choices to be made, but resistance or uncertainty or confusion proved too strong for Britain to achieve at this stage what had not been achieved in the battles over science and technology in the late nineteenth century. What Herbert Spencer, the Devonshire Commission, T.H. Huxley, Lyon Playfair and others failed to secure in the 1870s and after – an adequate institutional and curricular status for science, the spokesmen, committees and participants of the 1920s and 1930s similarly failed to secure – an adequate space for new interpretations of the technical and vocational in the emergent structures of post-elementary and higher education.

It is interesting that in the debates of these decades, especially in the important British phenomenon of the consultative committee, attempts were made to use the earlier American experience as evidence and support. The main period of enthusiasm for vocational education in the United States culminated in the passing of the Smith–Hughes Act in 1917, providing federal support for vocational training schemes. Across almost three decades of pressures for and promotion of vocational education, the American debates had covered similar but wider ground, involving the unions, professional associations, and public involvement at a level not reached in Britain. The secretary of the National Society for the Promotion of Industrial Education wrote that 1912 and 1913 had been the 'harvest time for the cause of vocational education in the United States'. The press was teeming with editorials and articles

> which indicate an overwhelming sentiment in favor of enlarging and extending the scope of education in this country to include the training of the great mass of our workers for wage-earning occupations of every kind. The friends of antichild labor have joined hands with the friends of industrial education.

Educators had seen in the vocational education movement a means 'to reduce the waste pile of human life, to reach groups of children long neglected, and to democratize the public schools in the country in a true sense'. The article appeared in the annual report of the Commissioner of Education, who himself wrote, somewhat less optimistically, that the pioneers of the movement were encountering resistance, partly because some people thought that vocational propaganda pointed towards 'social cleavage', and partly because there was suspicion of a foreign, mainly German, practice.[43]

The important period, therefore, for the American debates about the nature, purpose and desirability of vocational education was already reaching its climax before British interest grew in the period between the wars. The consultative committees were able to look for American evidence in their discussions, and they regularly used it. At one level, the committee under Sir Henry Hadow, when producing its report on *Psychological Tests of Educable Capacity* (1924), outlined the 'rapid and remarkable expansion' of the movement for vocational aptitude testing, vocational guidance and vocational selection, pioneered in the United States in the 1900s.[44] Guidance and testing in Britain assumed different forms from the American ones, and also had other roots. Vocational education was firmly related, however, to American ideas and practice. The Newbolt Committee on the teaching of English looked to the United States for the demonstration that English could and should – even in the case of literature – be given a vocational bias, in the sense of relating directly to the 'life and work of those who study it'. The experimental basis for their confidence had been conducted by Frank Aydelotte, formerly a Rhodes scholar at Oxford, and by this date Professor of English at the Massachusetts Institute of Technology. The committee reprinted three pages of an essay by Aydelotte describing how engineers were encouraged not 'to be ashamed of being engineers, but we do ask them to be ashamed of being narrow, one-sided engineers'. To understand the value of English, it was first necessary to understand what was meant by engineering, to develop 'a thoughtful outlook on life and his profession'. They were asked to read essays by nineteenth- and twentieth-century engineers and scientists, both on engineering and on wider topics, including the relation between science and literature. By this means students were brought to an interest in literature, ready to find in it 'something which they can relate to their own problems'. The committee saw the need to extend this approach to include social and industrial history, but thought the principle excellent and adaptable to technical schools and colleges.[45]

The Spens Committee quoted approvingly from a memorandum submitted to it by Dr J.L. Tildsley of the New York Board of Education: 'there is no subject in the curriculum of any type of vocational school for any age of boy or girl that might not be liberalised while at the same time furnishing the highest degree of vocational effectiveness'. Members visited British junior technical schools, reported that they were satisfied that the schools aimed to liberalize all subjects in their curriculum, and juxtaposed that view alongside Tildsley's stress on the ability of any subject 'whether in conventional terminology, it is called academic or technical, liberal or vocational' to unfold all the powers of man and make them usable to the utmost 'in the special phase of production or the special phase of living in which he may chance to engage'. The discussion was reinforced by the inclusion in an appendix of a memorandum on the secondary school curriculum by I.L. Kandel, which, though discussing the curriculum and vocational education in general terms and without specific reference to American experience, lent to the whole analysis the authority of Kandel's influential position at Teachers College, Columbia University, New York.[46]

In Britain the technical–vocational remained uneasily low status in curricula at every level until economic pressures in the 1970s and 1980s returned the concepts and controversies to centre stage. It was not only the nature of the distinction between the vocational and the liberal that continued to be problematic, but also the direction in which reform needed to be channelled. There continued, beyond the 1930s, to be firm expressions of belief that the vocational did not necessarily mean narrow – the Norwood Committee in 1943, for example, repeated earlier commitments to technical school courses which were specialized but also 'broad in conception'.[47] From this point on, however, the direction of attack was simultaneously towards broader conceptions of the technical and vocational and towards a curriculum balance in which the vocational and the liberal, separately conceived, complemented each other. Remarkably little discussion about these issues took place in Britain – or in other countries – in the immediate post-war years, as attention was focused on changes in the system, new structures, expansion, and developments in further, technical, college and university education. The whole tone of the discussion changed. Proposals from the Council for Curriculum Reform in 1945 talked about common-core studies between ages five and sixteen gradually diminishing in the secondary school to allow for 'the inclusion of vocational or academic specialisation according to the type of school and the child's needs'.[48] In 1949 Eric (later Lord) James was anxious to define the 'bare minimum of knowledge that should be possessed by an educated citizen', but wished the study of science and other specialist subjects to encourage the clarity and sense of creation associated with languages and the arts. At the same time Sir Walter Moberly was demonstrating the 'parasitical' nature of 'liberal education', and the association between technology and the wider, more democratic constituencies entering higher education in Britain and elsewhere.[49] Under such pressures, liberal attitudes to the technical were being expressed by Eric James and others in Britain, and by the Harvard Committee's *General Education in a Free Society*, stressing that 'a general education is distinguished from special education, not by subject matter, but in terms of method and outlook'.[50] As emphasis on technical, post-school education increased, however, the debate in Britain turned more towards 'liberal studies', additions to the curriculum and sixth-form minority studies. An influential Ministry of Education circular on *Liberal Education in Technical Colleges*, in 1957, continued to stress that the liberal element in a course 'depends as much on *how* subjects are taught as on *what* is taught', and that teachers of scientific and technical subjects were in the best position to 'inculcate habits of reflection and free enquiry which are the mark of an educated and liberal mind'. At the same time, however, it discussed the additional *subjects* that would help to liberalize the technical curriculum, and from this point in the 1950s, as technical courses expanded, liberal studies additives were incorporated in college courses – including as a compulsory element in those of the National Council for Technological Awards.[51] The Crowther Report, *15 to 18*, tried two years later to tread the same tightrope: it wanted to make vocational subjects less instructional, more attractive, but at the same time looked for 'a balanced education'. Although this need not be achieved only, or even mainly, 'by the addition of courses in the humanities . . . there should be some movement in that direction'.[52]

The ambiguity is important and its roots are in the 1920s and 1930s. Kandel drew attention in the 1930s, in a comparative study of American and European secondary education, to the fact that the curriculum of the English secondary school was 'determined by the aims and purposes of a general, liberal education, to the exclusion of any consideration of vocational preparation'.[53] Attempts to allay fears about the vocational were in British conditions relatively unsuccessful, and the result was, as in the past, a continuous search for differentiation, by college, by school, by 'side', by curriculum, by children, by sex. For most of this century the main debates have, in fact, been about differences, at every level of the educational system. The advocacy of a pervasive liberalization of all aspects of vocational education, and of the vocationalization of the traditionally liberal, did not in general produce those results. It produced, from the late 1920s, commitments to differences in schools, different types of curricula, and in fact a strengthening of the status divide between the liberal and the vocational. Disputes about curriculum models resurfaced significantly in the 1960s, mainly in terms of secondary schools, because of the accelerating comprehensive school movement, and the awareness of new clienteles requiring adaptations to traditional assumptions about teaching, about assessment, about the curriculum. Under the impact of economic recession, structural unemployment, international competition, and an acute awareness of major, unresolved economic and social problems, pressures for vocational interpretations became more vigorous. The search was on in the late 1970s for a core curriculum, under ministerial and official pressures.[54] In the early 1980s the Department of Education and Science was relentlessly pursuing a school curriculum which prepared children to relate to adult needs: 'parents, employers and the public rightly expect the school curriculum to pay proper regard to what the pupils will later want and be called upon to do'. The curriculum sought would measure up to national and local needs and allow for local developments.[55] Her Majesty's Inspectors were at the same time looking for a curriculum which would respond to the implications of social changes, the advent of micro-electronics, and the problems of energy conservation.[56] The Schools Council was in pursuit of a 'minimum curriculum' and a range of basic skills through *The Practical Curriculum*.[57] All of these reflected the uncertainties of earlier debates about definitions and direction, and failures in the 1920s and 1930s – as in the second half of the nineteenth century – to respond to pressures to reinterpret the vocational and the liberal outside the narrow frameworks and status structures of the nineteenth- and twentieth-century British educational system.

What the 1920s and 1930s reveal is a crucial moment of tension and possibility, reflected in committee reports, the pronouncements of educationists, textbooks for teachers, school inspectors, and the sources they reveal. A study of the relationship between opinion and emergent policy, compromise and evasion, would require historians to go considerably further. It would need to bring teachers and employers, civil servants and the press, professional journals and conferences, trade union and student expressions of view, more centrally into the analysis. A clearer picture of the 1920s in this respect means a clearer picture of weaknesses and processes in contemporary Britain.

Notes

1 A.N. Whitehead, *The Aims of Education and Other Essays* (London, 1932, edition of 1970), p. 74. The essay on 'Technical Education and Its Relation to Science and Literature' was first published in *The Organisation of Thought* in 1917.

2 Ministry of Reconstruction, Adult Education Committee, *Final Report* (London, 1919), p. 149.

3 British Psychological Society and Association of Teachers in Colleges and Departments of Education, *Teaching Educational Psychology in Training Colleges* (London, 1962), p. 5.

4 See especially reports by Chief HMIs C.A. Buckmaster and H.H. Hoffert on the Central and Western, and Southern and Eastern Districts, respectively, *Report of Board of Education, 1900-01* (London, 1901), vol. II, pp. 248-64, 265-77.

5 Board of Education, *Report of the Consultative Committee on Secondary Education* (London, 1938), pp. 66-7. For the case against Morant and the 1904 Regulations see Eric Eaglesham, *From School Board to Local Authority* (London, 1956) and *The Foundations of 20th Century Education* (London, 1967). For a more sympathetic view see Olive Banks, *English Secondary Education* (London, 1955).

6 John Graves, *Policy and Progress in Secondary Education 1902-1942* (London, 1943), p. 142.

7 Board of Education, *Secondary Education*, p. xxvii.

8 Graves, *Policy and Progress*, pp. 142-3.

9 Board of Education, *The Teaching of English in England* (London, 1921), p. 153.

10 Adult Education Committee, *Final Report*, p. 150.

11 W.G. Sleight, *The Organisation of Curricula in Schools* (London, 1922), p. 103.

12 Board of Education, *Report of the Consultative Committee on Differentiation of the Curriculum for Boys and Girls Respectively in Secondary Schools* (London, 1923), p. 38.

13 W.P. Welpton, *Primary Artisan Education* (London, 1913), pp. 6-7, 48.

14 R.H. Tawney, *Secondary Education for All* (London, 1922), pp. 104-9.

15 For a discussion of the American junior high school curriculum in relation to new social pressures and constituencies of students see John H. Woodburn and Ellsworth S. Obourn, *Teaching the Pursuit of Science* (New York, 1965), ch. 15.

16 Thiselton Mark, *Modern Views on Education* (London, n.d.), pp. 156-7.

17 J.J. Findlay, *The Foundations of Education: A Survey of Principles and Projects*, vol. II: *The Practice of Education* (London, 1927), p. 323.

18 T. Percy Nunn, *Education: Its Data and First Principles* (London, 1920), pp. 204-5.

19 Board of Education, *Secondary Education*, pp. xv, 161.

20 Frank Smith and A.S. Harrison, *Principles of Class Teaching* (London, 1947), p. 88.

21 Board of Education, *Report of the Consultative Committee on The Education of the Adolescent* (London, 1926), pp. 88, 121.

22 Board of Education, *Handbook of Suggestions for the Consideration of Teachers and Others Concerned in the Work of Public Elementary* Schools (London, 1905; edition of 1927), p. 329.

23 Board of Education, *Report of the Departmental Committee on the Training of Teachers for Public Elementary Schools* (London, 1925), p. 123.

24 T.G. Rooper, *School and Home Life: Essays and Lectures on Current Educational Topics* (London, [1896]), p. 432. See particularly the chapters in this book 'On the Relation of Manual Occupations to Other Studies in Elementary Schools', and 'A Plea for Sloyd'.

25 J.J. Findlay, *Principles of Class Teaching* (London, 1902), ch. III, 'The Nature of the Pursuits Selected for Class Teaching', especially pp. 80-7; James Welton, *Principles and Methods of Teaching* (London, 1912 edition), pp. 520-9.

26 Board of Education, *The Education of the Adolescent*, pp. xvii, 120.

27 Nunn, *Education: Its Data and First Principles*, p. 205.

28 Board of Education, *Secondary Education*, p. 162.

29 Jurgen Herbst, 'The Liberal Arts: Overcoming the Legacy of the Nineteenth Century', *Liberal Education*, no. 66, 1980, p. 30.

30 Adult Education Commitee, *Final Report*, pp. 152-3.

31 Board of Education, *The Teaching of English in England*, p. 165.

32 Ibid.

33 Whitehead, *The Aims of Education*, pp. 67-70.

34 Rooper, *School and Home Life*, p. 430.

35 Nunn, *Education: Its Data and First Principles*, p. 205.

36 Board of Education, *The Education of the Adolescent*. p. 101.

37 Board of Education, *The Teaching of English in England*, p. 165.

38 F.S. Marvin, *The Nation at School* (London, 1933), p. 167.

39 J.J. Findlay, *The School* (London, 1911), p. 154; *The Foundations of Education*, vol. II, p. 324.

40 Bolton King, *Schools of Today: Present Problems in English Education* (London, 1929), pp. 69-70.

41 Board of Education, *Secondary Education*, p. 163.

42 Board of Education, *The Teaching of English in England*, p. 165.

43 *Report of the Commissioner of Education for the Year ended June 30, 1912* (Washington, 1913), vol. I, pp. 21-2: C.A. Prosser, 'Progress in Vocational Education', in this *Report*, pp. 281, 287. For the history of the American debates see Marvin Lazerson and W. Norton Grubb, *American Education and Vocationalism: A Documentary History 1870-1970* (New York, 1974). For a number of contributions, notably stressing the importance of the Smith-Hughes Act, see Harvey Kantor and David Tyack (eds), *Work, Youth and Schooling: Historical Perspectives* (New York, 1982).

44 Board of Education, *Report of the Consultative Committee on Psychological Tests of Educable Capacity and Their Possible Use in the Public System of Education* (London, 1924), pp. 47-51.

45 Board of Education, *The Teaching of English in England*, pp. 161-5.

46 Board of Education, *Secondary Education*, pp. 269–70, 415–28.
47 Board of Education, *Curriculum and Examinations in Secondary Schools* (London, 1943), p. 20.
48 Council for Curriculum Reform, *The Content of Education* (Beckley, Kent, 1945), p. 54.
49 Eric James, *An Essay on the Content of Education* (London, 1949), pp. 74–5; Sir Walter Moberly, *The Crisis in the University* (London, 1949), pp. 47, 167.
50 Harvard Committee, *General Education in a Free Society* (Cambridge, Mass., 1945), p. 57.
51 Ministry of Education, *Circular 323: Liberal Education in Technical Colleges* (London, 1957).
52 Ministry of Education, *15 to 18: A Report of the Central Advisory Council for Education* (London, 1959), vol. I, pp. 369–70.
53 I.L. Kandel, *History of Secondary Education: A Study in the Development of Liberal Education* (Boston, 1930), p. 363.
54 Especially pursued by Shirley Williams as Secretary for Education – see, for example, her speech to the North of England Conference, 1977 (*Times Educational Supplement*, 14 January 1977, p. 8), and the section 'Curriculum' in the Green Paper published the same year – *Education in Schools: A Consultative Document* (London, 1977).
55 Department of Education and Science, *The School Curriculum* (London, 1981), pp. 1–2.
56 Department of Education and Science, *A View of the Curriculum* (HMI Series: Matters for Discussion, 11), 1980, p. 5.
57 Schools Council, *The Practical Curriculum* (Schools Council Working Paper 70) (London, 1981), pp. 14, 22–4.

8 Expectations of higher education: some historical pointers

Whilst preparing its report on *The Education of the Adolescent* the Hadow Committee took evidence from the Federation of British Industries and a large number of representatives of industrial and commercial firms. The report summarized their responses to the question: 'What kind of qualification is most desirable in your work, e.g. scientific, mathematical, mechanical, artistic, literary or linguistic?' Engineering firms emphasized elementary mathematics and science, together with 'a literary training' to enable apprentices to express themselves properly. 'Intelligence was more valuable than previous experience.' Textile manufacturers emphasized various technical and clerical skills for various categories of employee, and added that 'for buyers and for commercial travellers quick observation, a power of reasoning, and a high grade of general intelligence were necessary'. Chemical and soap manufacturers 'thought that pupils who remained at school the longest stood the best chance of becoming efficient workers later'. Cocoa manufacturers stated that 'the most important qualifications for their purpose were receptivity of mind, keenness of observation, application to work, adaptability and general intelligence. Acquired knowledge was subordinate in importance to these qualifications.' A firm of boot and shoe manufacturers thought that no special qualifications were necessary, but thought the elementary school course was too short to develop the right qualities of initiative, resourcefulness and ambition. Farmers and agriculturalists wanted more practical and less book work; some employers emphasized the need for closer cooperation between school and employer; and 'several great distributing firms stated that a good general education was the best foundation on which to build, though after 14 years of age some training in commercial methods might be of advantage'.[1] In these comments lie all the dichotomies, tensions and uncertainties we have discussed in the last chapter, and they are a reminder of the problems of 'general' and 'specific' or 'practical' training as perceived by one section of the community interested in schooling processes. With the raising of the school leaving age to fifteen and then sixteen, with the restructuring of the educational system so as to provide 'secondary education for all', and the expansion of the systems of further and higher education, it is important to examine how employers' and others' attitudes have developed towards these new structures. Since the age of transition from school to work has changed, since higher proportions of pupils have been staying on at school for longer periods in recent decades, and since opportunities for education and training beyond the minimum leaving age have expanded, the kind of discussion pursued by the Hadow Committee has been transferred to older age groups and institutions with different histories and purposes.

Higher education, and its relationship to the professions, to employment, to technology, to commerce, to industry, to public service, has in the twentieth century been a major focus of attention in controversies about the liberal and the vocational. Newman and others defined the boundaries of the discussion as twentieth-century Britain inherited it, but they did not close the discussion. An historical approach to opinion in many fields is difficult, given the lack of usable historical documentation, but in a field such as higher education it ought to be possible to find a foothold on popular attitudes, on the expectations of individuals and groups who relate to the institutions or to the employment of graduates. This chapter is an attempt at a case study in how such history might be written, and is therefore more than anything a search for ways of approaching concepts like liberal, professional or vocational from directions other than those provided by the most articulate, the most passionate, the most visible historically.

When University and King's Colleges, London, were created in the late 1820s, there were hopes and intentions of securing a charter for a University of London. The House of Commons carried a resolution in 1831 requesting that such a charter be granted, and the government announced its intention later that year to create a university which would be an examining body and would 'confer degrees on candidates from all parts of the United Kingdom, and from every seminary of education'. One defence of this broad definition of the new institution contained the following passage, commending the government for this first act of government initiative in promoting 'the advancement of general education':

> The Government for the time being had, indeed, occasionally rendered a reluctant assistance when it had been, as it were, *compelled* to do so; but the question with it was never 'how may the interests of science be most promoted,' but 'with how small a concession to public opinion can we escape for the present': never, 'in what way can we best advance the education of the people', but 'with how little can we satisfy this or the other body of men'.[2]

That, at an important moment in the history of new nineteenth-century departures in university education, neatly illustrates the dilemma of historically relating opinion and policy. How do government and public interests differ? In what circumstances does government 'concede', and how does public opinion express itself forcefully enough to obtain concessions? At each step along the historical path such questions change their shape, not merely because governments change, but because opinion and its organization by 'bodies of men' change, and the relationships of all the elements in this complex diagram change. In terms of higher education across the past two centuries, such historical analysis involves clearly distinguishable, if changing, constituencies with a stake in its scale, shape, content, aims, products – government, church, bureaucracy, industrial and commercial employers, parents, local communities, students. The changing content of the total exercise of higher education – including the twentieth-century emergence of the supervised doctorate, research funded from within university budgets and from outside bodies, and the universities' involvement in school examinations – has itself fed back into the pattern of expectations of these constituencies.

Twentieth-century attitudes towards higher education are for the moment more easily grouped and understood in terms of theme and concept than in strict chronological progression. In disentangling opinion or expectation it is at this stage of the historiography important to outline not so much the progression overall, as the means of thematic organization and the emphases discernible within each of the themes. In a case study of this scale, the total pattern has to be broken down into manageable pieces.

Historians have shown little interest in the expectations of higher education expressed by the constituencies concerned. Historical interest in institutions has not been concerned with their responses – or lack of them – to popular expectations, except in broad terms to the religious and political contexts of university change in the nineteenth century. Histories of higher education in Britain have tended to focus either on the internal development of institutions, or on policy and policy-related opinion – mainly of or surrounding government and its committees and commissions. Only in rare cases such as Michael Sanderson's *The Universities and British Industry 1850–1970* and Sheldon Rothblatt's *Tradition and Change in English Liberal Education* has the sweep become more wide-ranging and complex.

An approach to twentieth-century opinion about higher education has to be based, therefore on unsystematically explored materials of various kinds – speculative, prescriptive, campaigning, impressionistic, auto-biographical, research-based on various scales and at one or another level of sophistication, together with policy statements by individuals and official and unofficial bodies. The material does suggest some consistent themes, which could be grouped around a number of key words – for example, the expectations of different constituencies in terms of *profession, vocation* and *relevance; a general, liberal, broad* or *specialized* education; *excellence; national, regional, local, social, economic* and other *needs* and *wants.* In British debates around higher education in recent decades it is natural that dominant themes should have been industrial and technological expectations of higher education, and the nature and place of the appropriate studies in old, adapted or new institutions. The impact of economic, technological, industrial and wider social changes and dilemmas has heavily underlined issues of institutional scale, scope, structure, curriculum and values. Even in periods of expansion, when apparent consensus has been most easily reached about possible and substantial responses to the challenges involved, underlying conflict about aims and strategies has never been concealed. Debates about, for example, the binary system, or the nature and acceptability of 'technological universities', or about expansion itself, have been more than technical discussions about tactics, but have been essentially conflicts of values, highlighting attitudes towards every aspect of the higher education system and beyond. For these reasons, the emphases reflected in this chapter tend to be on issues connected with the place of technology and the 'applied' subjects, and on the nature of the differences between curricula and institutions as perceived from the starting-point of national economic and industrial pressures.

THE NINETEENTH-CENTURY LEGACY

The main purposes and hesitations of the nineteenth-century university have been extensively discussed by historians and others, and have been presented with a variety of emphases. Oxford and Cambridge had traditionally served a number of professions – mainly the law, the church and government – and, as monopoly institutions in England until the University of London was created in the late 1820s, were central in producing the nation's professional, administrative and political élites.[3] Such underlying purposes were not incompatible with their other role – that of serving what the University Grants Committee called 'a leisured and privileged section of society', with no apparent concern for professional requirements.[4]

Leisure, privilege, a cultural context and professional preparation were not the discrete categories of a later age. The pressures of the nineteenth century produced both adaptations in these universities and the creation of new institutions – some to become university colleges and universities, others to become technical colleges or the first generation of 'polytechnics' at the end of the nineteenth century. One adaptation resulted, for example, from changes in recruitment for the civil service, and the need for the universities to extend the range of professions or vocations for which they prepared.[5] One of their main functions, of course, had always been to reproduce the universities themselves, by the preparation of future academics. With the emergence of an increasing number of 'disciplines' and a new emphasis on research, the harnessing of the universities to the learned and academic 'professions' become increasingly important. Various kinds of specialized training were beginning to sit uneasily alongside traditional forms of general education and demands for wider and more democratic access to higher education.

Nineteenth-century pressures to extend the traditional curriculum produced slow or unsystematic responses from Oxford and Cambridge which resisted the introduction of, for example, history and physical science[6] and were in general resistant to extensions into what were perceived as more directly 'vocational' studies.[7] Science retained its largely semi-amateur status at both universities, and they resisted or responded cautiously to new interests in learning and research.[8] Science only slowly 'crossed the channel', and 'the most powerful argument for founding new colleges was the reluctance of the older universities to train the middle class in science applied to industry'.[9] Institutional resistance of another kind highlighted the vocational or professional element in the existing and emergent patterns of higher education – resistance to higher education for women. Although there was growing support in late Victorian England for the view that women had a right to access to at least some of the traditionally male occupations, the view was widely and firmly held, first that universities were a form of 'occupational training', second that women had no place in those occupations for which the universities were a preparation, and third, therefore, that the vocational education provided by the universities was 'inappropriate for women's role'.[10]

The new university colleges and polytechnics of the second half of the nineteenth century were to a considerable degree a response to overseas economic and industrial challenge – and were at the time often described as such. They were created by local philanthropy and effort in precisely those geographical areas most likely to be sensitive to this challenge, and to have precise expectations of the new institutions. Until the last third of the nineteenth century industrialization had been only minimally indebted to English higher education,[11] though the debt to Scottish and European higher education, through the overseas education of English nonconformists and the immigration of Scots, was no doubt considerable and has yet to be properly evaluated. From the founding of Owens College, Manchester, in 1851, but especially with other new provincial foundations from the 1860s, the response to the international challenge began to be made in earnest,[12] though the 'functional' roles of the new institutions must not be exaggerated. The University of London, at the beginning, was against engineering and 'technical Chemistry', and in Sanderson's view taught relatively little 'useful knowledge'.[13] The later northern and midlands foundations soon, if not from the outset, abandoned narrow definitions of themselves as higher technical schools. Even T.H. Huxley doubted whether the universities were the place 'for technical schools of Engineering or applied Chemistry, or Agriculture'.[14] This was to remain a twentieth-century issue. The Federation of British Industries was warning in 1950, for example, that in teaching applied science universities must 'avoid the danger of being converted into superior technical colleges'.[15]

Civic consciousness and pride played an important part in these northern and midlands foundations.[16] However, the university colleges (in ways not unlike the development of some of the American land grant colleges from the 1860s) did not always respond immediately, directly, whole-heartedly and functionally to the intentions of the founders.

They had 'prodigious, antagonist forces' to meet in the industrial cities,[17] especially from people anticipating that they would result in lower standards and utilitarian narrowness. University teachers, on the one hand, and the 'captains of industry' on the other hand, operated on the basis of quite different values.[18] There were élites other than industrial ones to be trained, and older traditions to be reasserted and adapted. The secularization and diffusion of higher learning brought it into an increasingly direct and complex relationship with government and other social agencies and the processes of economic and social change. It was increasingly involved, whether or not willingly or explicitly, in an expanding process of occupational selection, training, guidance and placement.[19]

How the new institutions responded to these local pressures and expectations can be seen from the analysis conducted by Abraham Flexner at the end of the 1920s, comparing the British provincial universities and their local roles with those of their American counterparts. 'The provincial universities sprang from the soil; they obtain part of their support by heeding local needs. Thus technological activities, varying with the locality, are highly, in places, too highly developed, and, for a university, too highly specialized.' Having expressed reservations about the British institutions, however, Flexner admitted that local factors had been 'balanced against other factors. The older and more solid disciplines are therefore represented not only in the curriculum, but in the management.' The universities had not 'run wild, as have our American institutions'. Even the School of Commerce which Joseph Chamberlain had obtained through local support for the University of Birmingham was undertaking 'little or nothing that could not without propriety be done in the same fashion by the faculty of arts'.[20] The Victorian debates about the meaning of culture were often a response to such developments, with some protagonists arguing like John Stuart Mill against the professional training role of the universities. Sir Joshua Fitch, for example, distinguished inspector of schools and long associated with the University of London, was arguing at the turn of the century that universities were not places of useless learning but providers of 'instruments of culture and intellectual power' and needed to enlarge that tradition by harnessing it to new social needs. One such need was 'to ennoble and liberalise the higher employments of life' - as had long been the case with law and medicine, for example - by extending university curricula to embrace engineering, chemistry, electricity, architecture, textile manufacture, agriculture, banking and commerce. The London School of Economics was in his view a model – 'broader and more comprehensive than any academic institution hitherto known in England'. Annexing such new subjects to academic curricula would remove from them – as in the case of the commercial subjects – the stigma of being 'in the hands of empirics and utilitarians'.[21]

The legacy of the nineteenth century, therefore, was an attempt by established and new institutions to cope with the ambiguities and dangers of strong pressures of various kinds. Industrial, economic and social demands of higher education were resulting in slow curricular responses and the creation of new institutions. The new provincial university colleges and universities had a local and regional context which only partly shaped their activities – with other contexts providing countervailing pressures (including demands for a liberal curriculum emanating from within the institutions themselves and from elsewhere – including their academic patron, the University of London). The technical colleges and polytechnics of the final decades of the century were lower in status and more directly a product of demands for the training not so much of 'captains of industry' as the lower ranks of technically qualified industrial and commercial manpower. The twentieth century inherited conflicting views about what was appropriate for a university, but also distinctions amongst universities and between universities and other emergent forms of higher education.

UNIVERSITIES AND SOCIETY

Only in the twentieth century has 'higher education' really extended beyond the universities (although the earlier history does include other institutions and processes – for example the Inns of Court). Higher technical education, the polytechnics (Mark I, as created in the 1880s), teacher education, art and commercial education, only became visible and definable as 'higher education' at various points in the twentieth century. It is inevitable, therefore, that this discussion begins with the universities alone. Across the centuries public criticisms of the universities have related to every aspect of their activities, and have come from opposing directions: they have been condemned as isolated from the 'real world', and for their 'worldliness', as supporters of Establishments and of seditious, rebellious and revolutionary causes, for their commitment to narrow principle, and for being too easily tempted into expediency. They have been arraigned for failing to do the bidding of kings, or to respond to the economy's need for manpower, or to industry's need of relevant research and skills.

Sanderson has expressed the view that 'the increasing involvement of the universities with industry is perhaps the most important single development in the history of the British universities over the last hundred years',[22] and yet there has been a continuous stream of accusations levelled against the universities that they have failed to respond to industry's and other social needs. The universities have, in this connection, been seen as 'ivory towers', as concerned with knowledge, argument, issues, standards and values with little relevance to or few implications for the outside world. This is, of course, both an oversimplification and an exaggeration of many of the criticisms, let alone of the reality, but it reflects the level at which the accusations have frequently been made. Clearly, as has often been recognized, such a one-directional critique indicates in fact a two-way process. There had long been criticism, including from within industry itself, that employers were failing to recruit graduates. Sir Miles Thomas, for instance, pointed out in 1949 that the motor industry, the banks and the co-operative societies recruited hardly any at all.[23] When *Nature* was suggesting in 1960 that industry had traditionally been badly served by the universities and the schools, it went on to point out that industry had until recently resisted recruiting intellectual quality as distinct from skill (although it quoted Vice-Chancellor Christopherson to indicate that industry had changed more than the universities in recent years).[24] Similarly, six years later, the *Times Review of Industry and Technology* talked about the failure of communication between industry and the universities, with both sides having outdated ideas about the other, and even (quoting a director of industrial studies at Liverpool University, seconded from ICI) 'about their own sphere'.[25] When the Finniston Committee reported in 1980 on *Engineering Our Future* it pointed not only to the poor quality of entrants to engineering, but also to the fact that until the 1960s most engineers obtained their formal education via part-time study or block release while working in industry.[26] Finniston himself had written in 1967 that industry often saw the universities as unapproachable, while the universities believed industry was not playing its proper role in determining what form the training of students for industry should take. The boards of companies spent a lot of time on the specifications and acquisition of machine tools, but little time on the specifications and hiring of qualified manpower. Although industry was aware of the need for graduates, 'what is at fault is that until very recently neither industry nor the universities gave the time and effort to define more closely what industry required of the manpower . . . output of universities for more effective use in and by industry'.[27]

Although we are for the moment concerned with one direction of criticism, the more complex flaws in relationships have to be borne in mind. So much is this the case that, in relation to the Finniston Report the Engineering Employers' Federation felt it necessary to comment that the report had overstated the extent to which professional engineers 'may be regarded as responsible for the economic situation in the UK'.[28] Blame is seldom as simple as it is convenient to apportion it.

Such critiques of the university have, of course, been one strand in a continuing debate about the purposes of a university, and increasingly of higher education more widely. We shall return to a discussion of the purposes of other forms of higher education in a later consideration of the perceived differences between a university and polytechnic education. Here we are concerned with the longer nineteenth- and twentieth-century discussion of outside pressures and university responsiveness. There is also an unbroken line of opinion in the twentieth century, of course, that universities should be either unresponsive or extremely cautiously responsive to the 'needs of society' which may undermine the autonomy and distinctive role and standards of universities, and we shall return to this also. Representative voices of this tradition would be Flexner in 1930 arguing that 'a university should not be a weather vane responsive to every variation of popular whim. Universities must at times give society, not what society wants, but what it needs',[29] and Minogue in 1973, describing the universities as 'cities under siege' from outside forces seeking to dress up enthusiasms as academic beliefs.[30]

Whatever the reasons for the universities' reluctance to deliver, expectations that they would respond to felt needs and demands have been strong, and the disappointments sometimes great. In a famous lecture in 1964 the then chariman of ICI, Sir Paul Chambers, accused the universities of producing men who were 'timid and irresolute', the product of 'intellectual and inconclusive discussions', which were 'a bad training for the real world'.[31] This was not the first time, however, that such criticisms had been levelled against the universities. Almost a decade earlier, a Conservative Bow Group author had commented in similar terms, answering the question – what should university education seek to provide?

Probably the most important attributes are straight thinking, original thinking, and a capacity to make decisions ... At the university ... the undergraduate is encouraged to question everything, to criticize the authorities and to respect ability. He is taught to discuss, and encouraged to dispute. At the extreme his questioning may lead to a destructive rather than a constructive outlook.[82]

Not everyone outside the universities agreed with such criticisms (Lord Butler, for example, disagreed with Chambers in discussing how university education benefited the community),[33] but this is not the issue here. What is important is the extent of the consensus amongst critics and supporters alike as to the desirable 'vocational' relationship between the universities and the outside world.

This consensus underlay much of the support for higher education (including university) expansion in the 1960s. Even the Bow Group author, in 1955, while criticizing the universities, accepted an incipient 'Robbins' principle of increased access: 'we have established the social doctrine in this country that no barrier – poverty or otherwise – to higher education shall remain in the path of any young person who has the ability to profit by it'. She reminded industry at the same time that firms needed to make adjustments as a consequence – 'It is to the universities that industry must now look to fill its future vacancies in these middle and lower positions; not to the seventeen-year old school leavers, as in the past.'[34]

What the Robbins Report was about was, of course, the need to remove such barriers to higher education, but also the structures and strategies most appropriate for the new and extended categories of students to be attracted into the system, once the concept of a restricted 'pool of ability' had been abandoned. Much of the evidence to the committee was concerned with the right kind of institutional structures and curricula for the new clienteles. The Ministry of Education, for example, suggested to the committee that wider, more general degree courses were perhaps appropriate for the kinds of students who would be admitted to higher education in conditions of expansion.[35] The committee itself, as indeed the 1950s sociologists of education on whose work it drew, had no difficulty in justifying its recommendations in terms both of egalitarian principle and of national economic benefit.[36] One caustic comment on this aspect of the Robbins recommendations and general trends in higher education in the 1960s considered that although universities had failed to prepare students for the outside world, 'the expansion of higher education has been legitimated largely in vocational terms'.[37]

The pursuit of expansion seemed inevitable and inevitably continuous in the early and mid-1960s. Brian Chapman, writing in *Nature* in 1964, thought that 'the expectations of parents, schoolteachers and pupils have now been raised to a point where no Government could safely jettison the Robbins Report before making a more than token effort to get it under way'.[38] Nevertheless, criticism of the universities has continued in many quarters over the past two decades, directed against their remoteness and unresponsiveness to 'changes in social environment'.[39] Even more, it has been suggested that universities actively discourage graduates from entering business and industry;[40] 'The historical development of the universities', suggests a professor associate of chemistry out of industry, 'has shown the strong anti-technology attitudes and dislike of the utilitarian approach'.[41] Intellectuals, it has been suggested, are opposed to the business ethic, increase their students' antipathy to entering business, and are too remote from industry and commerce.[42] The GKN group was extremely specific and explicit in a submission to a House of Commons committee in 1972: 'industrial requirements are insufficiently recognised in the academic world, e.g. . . . the importance of the profit motive as the heart beat and the generation of cash as the life-blood of private enterprise industry is insufficiently understood'.[43] Over recent decades dissatisfaction has also been widely expressed with the mismatch between the curriculum provided and the actual needs of specific professional groups and industries – for example professional engineers[44] and professional scientists. In the latter case, a survey in 1969 found that 'a large body of professional scientists feel that the graduates of such (traditional) courses are inadequately prepared for a career in industry'.[45] Here again, GKN had very precise criticisms to make in 1972: 'it appears that, in the case of engineers, university curricula encourage narrow specialisation and fail to develop the more generally needed skills such as the ability to verify the validity, relevance and significance of information'. Against such criteria GKN had 'experienced a growing disenchantment with graduates'.[46]

Dissatisfaction of a different kind was revealed in 1971 when parents of undergraduates were asked what they, the parents, prized most highly in a university education. Their choices went strongly towards such categories as 'concentrated and highly specialised degrees' and hard work, but the survey concluded that 'parents are least satisfied that universities are catering for their highest priorities'[47] (although it had been suggested in the social survey of 1945 that 82 per cent of parents with children still under twenty in higher education were satisfied with the education their children were receiving).[48] In different, and often contradictory, ways there is a long-standing critique of the universities as unresponsive to the real needs of the society which supports them – including those of the school leavers who enter them – a topic to which we shall return.

The critique has obviously been most acute in the second half of the twentieth century in relation to the responsiveness of the universities to industrial requirements, and for two main reasons. First, the demands from industry appear at first sight to be very precise, and they have apparently not been met for reasons of suspicion and hostility on the part of the universities. Second, the industrial demand is frequently made on behalf of a larger constituency – that is, industry appears to speak on behalf of the nation itself, an appeal it makes most sharply when the economy is under particular threat. Again the discussion highlights a view and expectation of the university (often, as we shall see, with different implications for different institutions). The university – industry link is a question not just of for and against, but also of evaluating the degree of need and 'success' in the relationship, and the determinants of that 'success'.

Although the industry–university relationship has generally been held to be a difficult one, with mutual suspicion being expressed of the dominant values of the other side, the need for a closer understanding – and for the benefits to accrue from it – have been constantly expressed in past decades. At a conference sponsored jointly by the Association of University Teachers and the *Times Higher Education Supplement* in 1978, for example, one speaker indicated how difficult industry–university communication had been, and another emphasized that university responsiveness to industry and commerce was both necessary and beneficial to the universities, without impairing their autonomy.[49] As long ago as 1943, however, the president of the National Union of Students had underlined how 'indispensable' was the social, industrial and professional service which the universities gave to the community.[50] If the conflict of values between the university and industry had lessened by the 1960s, mutual suspicion had not been dispelled. Industry had mistrusted the intellectual's passion for abstraction, but, as Chapman points out, industry had come to realize that intellectual abstraction might have applications, and university and industrial values had come closer together.[51] By the 1960s, indeed, industry had come to rely on higher education expansion to supply its much-needed high-level manpower[52] – and in some cases to replace the 'brain drain' of qualified personnel to more lucrative employment overseas. Uneasy glances were being cast at those countries like the United States, Japan and Federal Germany, where it seemed to be no accident that success in technological and industrial performance was accompanied by intensive development of higher education or intensive use of highly qualified and highly paid manpower.

By the 1960s those parts of British industry that had not yet done so were learning that they had to look to the universities for the manpower they had once recruited from the secondary schools. There was a scarcity of school leavers – and in spite of the Chambers criticism of the university graduate, ICI recruitment of university graduates was rising.[53] A revealing editorial in *Nature* in 1954 summarized the post-war position very clearly. Since the late 1940s relations between the universities and industry, it suggested, had been steadily improving (with five conferences on the subject arranged by the Federation of British Industries between 1948 and 1954). There was still, however, much ignorance amongst parents and teachers about careers in industry, and the FBI had recently published two handbooks – one for students and one for industry – about graduate careers. It was still at that stage necessary 'to bring home to industry, and particularly to firms which do not at present employ university graduates, even in science or technology, the importance of a high standard of education and personality in management'. It emphasized the 'serious extent to which industry's direct recruitment of the cream of school-leavers is now limited'. The FBI itself had pointed out that to continue to rely on intelligent school leavers was 'to risk disaster'.[54] It has been important to underline this post-war situation in order to put into context the more recent criticisms, and the kind of relationships within which they have been formulated. University 'responsiveness' clearly needs to be examined against the complex attitudes outside as well as inside the universities.

Since their foundation it has been the civic universities that seemed best fitted or most likely to respond to outside demands and pressures. In 1949, for example, the vice-chancellor of the University of Birmingham, stressing that such universities formed part of the industrial world they served, also thought that they were the 'natural home of certain applied subjects'.[55] It is interesting to note that in 1972 Crouch and Mennell thought that while the universities might initiate links with industry, 'the more natural centres for projects of this kind should be the polytechnics'. They also laid stress on the view of Harold Wilson and the National Executive of the Labour Party in the period 1963–5 that universities should be sited in industrial areas where, in Wilson's words, they could 'reflect the pulsating throb of local industry'.[56] As in developing countries today, the expectation was that the universities would make a direct and substantial contribution to national or regional economic development.[57]

Such references indicate the level of confidence that has been expressed in the university as a contributor to industrial and economic growth. The picture can be extended to include the confidence placed in this century in the university as a participant in local development, for example in the cases of the universities of Leicester and North Staffordshire at Keele.[58] It can include the view expressed by the Trades Union Congress in 1956 that the university should provide for the needs of industry, which

> are not limited to scientists and technologists. There is some demand for graduates in Arts subjects for administrative and executive posts, particularly in the field of personnel management, while the development of scientific management techniques requires the recruitment of specialist staff suitably qualified in statistics, applied economics and accountancy.[59]

It can include the view of a vice-chancellor in 1964 that it was part of the business of a university to produce the increasing number of highly trained people on whom society depended to win new knowledge and to put it to practical use.[60]

Against this general expectation that universities would respond to appeals for their expert help, there have been alternative views, of which only an indication can be given here. A functionalist argument might assume that the university would in some direct way respond to the requirements of the twentieth century, but doubts have been expressed about the possibility of describing the history of higher education in these terms.[61] Hull University College, for instance, seems to have resisted local and even national blandishments (from the local founders and national financial temptations) by keeping technological developments at arm's length at and after its creation in the 1920s[62] and in so doing it seems to offer an example of 'dysfunction'. In addition to the cautionary advice of commentators from Flexner to Minogue to resist the zig-zags of outside influence, there have been other views of what a university should and should not provide. Two main variants can probably be detected. First, there have been views like those of Lord Todd in his presidential address to the British Association in 1970, suggesting that a technological society needs only a small number of 'creative scientists and technologists to generate new ideas',[63] and therefore that the majority of the technicians required can be produced elsewhere. This is a theme that runs through the debates of the decades since the Second World War, and underpins the ideology of the binary structure. Second, there is the sense of threat to university independence and academic freedom, a theme which has been basic to discussions of the university internationally since the 1950s. In the United States this debate has centred around the themes of federal funding of university research, and of links with the big corporations – the latter featuring prominently in radical student attacks on university allegiances in the late 1960s. In Britain there have been weak echoes of both of these kinds of argument, together with some suspicion of industrial influence on research and teaching in higher education. The National Union of Students, for example, told the Robbins Committee that many students thought the vocational emphasis in higher education was now too great, and that students complained about excessive emphasis on technical subjects on those courses (for example, sandwich courses) where large firms supplied a major proportion of the students and directly influenced syllabuses. Nineteenth-century higher education had benefited from the generosity of local industrialists, but increasing links were now distorting the pattern of higher education, and firms were now over-influencing developments in particular institutions.[64]

The issue of university independence has, of course, taken other and sometimes more public forms, including wartime and post-war state financing and intervention, new forms of accountability, the undermining of the relatively independent role of the University Grants Committee, and direct political pressures on the university. Even the proposal to set up what became the Robbins Committee, established by the Prime Minister to investigate higher education, seemed to some to constitute a threat,[65] and the notion of expansion itself provoked, particularly among some academics, a sense of danger to established standards and autonomous decision-making.

In the late nineteenth and early twentieth centuries the threat to the established university order lay not only in applied science and technology, but also in the rise of history and the establishment of English, the encroachment of social science and its division into the social sciences, the creation of a university base for new areas of 'professional' training – including social work, social administration and teacher training. Increasingly, however, the debate about public expectations of the university – and of other, new institutions of 'higher education' – revolved around the nature, position and status of applied science and technology.

TECHNOLOGY AND HIGHER EDUCATION

Pressures for a greater university involvement in the training of technologists, engineers, applied scientists and related professions (including managers and people skilled in various economic and business skills) have steadily increased in this century – especially since the Second World War. At the same time there have been repeated criticisms of industry itself, and its failure both to make clear what its requirements were and to take advantage of the qualified scientists and technologists being produced. This failure was ascribed in the period after the Second World War partly to a lack of proper communication networks between the two sides, and this has resulted in recent decades in attempts to establish standing machineries and *ad hoc* conference and other platforms for the clarification of views and problems. While the nineteenth-century university neglect of applied science was a real inheritance, it was equally common ('more common' in Sanderson's view) that industry failed 'to employ men of higher scientific education' in the late nineteenth century.[66] In 1950 a professor of civil engineering and dean of a faculty of applied science summarized the history of employers' attitudes as follows:

> Welcome by the Region of the products of the University has not always been accorded in the field of applied science. To become a graduate in technology, for example, was for decades an unorthodox approach to industrial work, and the young graduate engineer faced even harder tests of personality and ability than did his fellows. It is not an exaggeration to say that in his early years his University degree was as much a handicap to the young technologist as it was an advantage.[67]

The next sentence began: 'This is now changed . . .' but how completely this has changed is open to question.

In 1969 the vice-chancellor of the University of Warwick conceded that there had for a long time been sympathy between the universities and public service, but expressed the view that

> we are only now beginning to witness a revolution in industry's attitude towards men and women of high ability and advanced training. For too long in industry, I think, nepotism, the strength of the family, has prevented the ablest from rising to positions of responsibility. And throughout industry there has been too great a tendency to reject ability . . . industry and commerce have for years been wasteful of talent.[68]

Even when industry recruited science specialists for research, its record of dealing with them was long subject to criticism.[69] Complaints about the low status of engineering form a clear and continuous thread in post-war British industrial history.[70]

Industry's expectations of the universities were coloured for generations by such attitudes. Even when graduates have been recruited for industry and commerce the relative statuses of different higher education institutions and of different faculties within them have played a large part in determining the nature of that recruitment. Lord Hailsham, opening the first Gulbenkian conference on higher education in 1960, suggested that the British two-tier system of universities and technical institutions had some benefits but 'gave colour to the extremely dangerous heresies that some studies are more gentlemanly than others'.[71] A discussion of ambiguous expectations of the vocational aspect of higher education will follow; for the moment it is the particular problem of the status of science and technology in the universities that is important.

In the late nineteenth and most of the twentieth century there has been anguished discussion of the position of applied and pure science in the universities, and this discussion has also been crucial to the increasingly diverse expectations of different categories of institution in the higher education system. Science, said Lord Hailsham at a meeting to support the creation of a university in Brighton, is 'a vocation of universities',[72] echoing generations of debate about what *kind* of science was appropriate to a university. Sir Lawrence Bragg, in 1949, based his whole case for the creation of separate high-level technological institutions on the distinction between applied and pure science, and the greater appropriateness of the latter to the university.[73] Bragg's distinction between applied and pure science and the inference he drew from it, were hotly challenged at the time, and the controversy has never fully disappeared.[74] In 1950 the *Times Educational Supplement* took up the same theme as Bragg and argued 'The Case for the Technical University',[75] using MIT and the Technische Hochschulen as models. Lord Butler reflected in 1968 that 'it has been to our disadvantage that nothing in England was ever instituted to compare with the Grandes Ecoles Polytechniques in France in 1794 or with the Technische Hochschule in Zürich.[76] This has been an ongoing debate in Britain, with support often being expressed for the separate technological institution, either because technology was inappropriate in the university, or because it would never be able to obtain its proper status there.

The view has been consistently expressed in this century that applied science in the universities (or in *some* universities) meant a lowering of standards[77] and the argument has been presented that the new universities of the 1960s based themselves at least initially in the humanities, social sciences and pure science in order to achieve an image of quality that would enable them to compete with Oxford and Cambridge.[78] It should be added, however, that the decisions of the new universities were taken under strong encouragement from the University Grants Committee, itself seeking means of producing fewer 'specialist' graduates, and urging the new bodies not to introduce applied science at an early stage of development – and if they wished to include engineering, then to make it engineering science.[79] The vice-chancellor of the University of Birmingham argued in 1949 that the civic universities were the 'natural home' of applied science.[80]

Views and pressures such as this form part of the diverse pattern of snobberies, heresies, distinctions and hierarchies which make 'expectations' of higher education complicated. They make it necessary to differentiate between subjects, degree patterns, individual institutions within sectors of higher education, and the sectors themselves. The responses of the universities and other higher education institutions have been conditioned at different times by ideals and definitions, and by necessity and the simple need to survive.[81] The universities have since the Second World War compromised in the face of diverse pressures, and have, in the view of the UGC, compromised also between the general European model of locating technology in high-status separate institutions, and the American model of admitting technology into the universities.[82] The British universities have sought to admit technology on terms, and to differentiate between their approach to technology and applied science, and that of 'technical' or 'technological' institutions.

The legacy is therefore a general sense of technology as 'inhuman'[83] – though with important exceptions – and needing in one way or another to be 'liberalized'. The universities have tried to find ways of replacing 'vocationally taught' engineering or technology by engineering science,[84] and with much confusion and controversy the colleges of advanced technology tried to pioneer a 'liberal studies' element in technological courses. The result has been a continuing ambiguity about the status and appropriate structure of 'applied' courses of all kinds in higher education, with the central uncertainty being about the position of 'mere' technology. The ambiguity is clearly expressed in a study of the attitudes of students to their education in colleges of advanced technology in the 1960s:

> It is apparent from the inquiry that there is a certain dissatisfaction in the minds of many students concerning the purpose to be served by the kind of training which they are undergoing at the college of advanced technology. They resent the idea that they are to be turned out merely as technologists and there is a reaching towards something which measures up more nearly to the ideal of the educated man . . . Many feel, perhaps without justification, that their needs would have been better met at a university.[85]

Any analysis of expectations by students and others of what higher education has to offer has to be seen at least to a large extent against such a background of the interpretation of the divide between 'pure' and 'applied' (as well as between arts and science or other distinctions that are easy to express but difficult to define). There is a substantial literature which extends and discusses further the pure/applied distinction made by people like Bragg, and spells out the institutional implications.

The Percy Committee on Higher Technological Education in 1945 serves as a base point for this literature over the past few decades. The Committee proposed the selection of a limited number of technical colleges for the development of technological courses 'of a standard comparable with that of University degree courses'. In doing so, it emphasized the basic view that it was the universities' job to produce scientists, and that of the technical college to operate mainly at the technician level, however much the two institutions might need to share the responsibility for some categories of manpower needed by industry:

Industry must look mainly to Universities for the training of scientists for research and development, and of teachers of science; it must look mainly to Technical Colleges for technical assistants and craftsmen . . . both Universities and Colleges must share the responsibility for educating the future senior administrators and technically qualified managers of industry.

The Committee pointed approvingly, however, to the commitment of university courses to an emphasis on academic study, in which work experience played no formal part, and to that of technical colleges with their tradition of concurrent work practice.[86] Whatever the changes since the 1940s may have been, such distinctions have remained part of the consciousness of schools and of intending students. A study in 1963 demonstrated that the most able science sixth formers were attracted and encouraged towards pure rather than applied science courses in higher education, whilst the less able were encouraged towards technology and engineering. The central issue was the 'image' of technology and applied science, and the tentative conclusion of the research was that 'the special pattern of recruitment in England arises not as a direct result of early specialization, which does not differentiate between the future scientist and the future technologist, but because of the public "image" of the two careers'.[87] An analysis of university science students' choice of pure or applied science in 1973–4 discovered that some 30 per cent of science students felt that they had been subject to encouragement or discouragement from their schoolteachers. A majority of these, both pure and applied science students, said that they had been encouraged to study pure rather than applied science.[88] When the Barlow Committee on scientific manpower reported in 1946 and echoed the findings of the Percy Committee, it reflected that 'it is only to the Universities that we can look for any substantial recruitment to the ranks of qualified scientists . . . Generally speaking, the university is an essential stage in scientists' education'.[89] There is a direct line of explanation from the foundation of institutions in the nineteenth century, to such views in the 1940s, and to the expectations of certain categories of students of what is appropriate in higher education in the final decades of the twentieth century.

PROFESSIONAL, PRACTICAL, RELEVANT

Although there is a deeply rooted tradition which has defined the purposes of higher education in terms of values disconnected from direct considerations of profession or relevance to a specific vocation or calling, there is, as we have seen, an equally strong affirmation of the history of higher education as serving professional purposes. Lord Boyle, speaking in 1978, echoed a view expressed by many historians:

> we in the universities see no inconsistency between a strong commitment to academic disciplines and, at the same time, a recognition of the need to think also about the educational requirements of those who are going to enter industry or the professions. Universities do far more professional training than is often realised.[90]

Flexner, earlier in the century, was eager to rid the universities not so much of 'professions' as what he saw as pseudo-professions, and his analyses and definitions were aimed to show that various aspirants to university status – such as business and social work – were not in fact professions.[91] Professions and professional roles and values are, of course, defined variously at different times and in different ways.

There have been broad interpretations of a university's role as a 'professional' training for 'society'. Universities, said Lord Hailsham, were both an induction into human society *and* a form of vocational training (for the church, state, business or technology).[92] The universities, considered a Nuffield College Group in 1948, needed to resist *narrow* pressures for professional training, but to base forms of specialization on the universities' own values and choices.[93] One of the primary purposes of the university in the past, it has also been suggested, has been to reproduce itself – that is, to act as a school of professional training for university teachers.[94] A pre-war view of the universities was that they were a form of professional or vocational training for the ruling class.[95] The debate about professional training and vocational relevance was basic to the creation of nineteenth-century colleges such as Mason's College, Birmingham, with the founder proposing to establish a centre to promote 'practical scientific knowledge' and T.H. Huxley persuading him to include a 'literary side' and to allow for later revisions of the curriculum.[96] The debate was widespread and continuous,[97] and surrounded the creation of Keele[98] and the new universities of the 1960s.[99]

The response of higher education to pressures for any increase in professional or vocational involvements was of course highlighted particularly by the expansion of higher education, and government and political expectations of the increasingly articulated higher education 'system' had to measure its responsiveness to them. The fear was not so much of state or political interference, though the nature and meaning particularly of the universities' relationship to government was a mounting preoccupation in the 1960s and 1970s.[100] Resistance and doubt were expressed rather in terms of standards and the damage – as we have already seen – that technological and similar studies might do to the essential purposes of the university. Opposition to an increased vocational orientation was expressed therefore in such forms as that of a professor of moral philosophy at Edinburgh University, when he spoke in 1948 of the 'spread of the technological obsession within the University', which was 'insidious' and unfitted the university for 'its primary cultural function'. The main feature of a university was that it represented the unity of knowledge, and everything needed to be taught in relation to 'knowledge as a whole' – otherwise it became 'merely a training in technical pedantry'.[101] In an attack on 'The Threat of the Practical' in 1961, Kingsley Amis and colleagues at University College, Swansea, attacked the pursuit of 'practicality' as the *greatest* threat to education, saw in it a loss of faith in the academic, and asserted that education 'is not *for* living. It is an initiation into inquiry.'[102] The university was being rapidly dragged down by narrow engineering and technological courses 'to the level of a technical college',[103] and the view was being expressed that it was not the job of the university 'to prostitute learning to modern requirements'.[104] A confused discussion began to emerge of the nature of excellence, which, said one vice-chancellor, was the only thing the universities had to sell. Excellence, he insisted, meant none the less knowing how to change.[105]. What emerged as part of this discussion was that excellence had something to do with effectiveness also, as the increasing preoccupation with teaching methods began to show.[106] If, as two researchers pointed out in 1976, 'excellence' was for staff a *raison d'être*, even an 'ideal, extra-personal, fixed standard of attainment to which students should aspire and by which they are measured', for students, once embarked on a course, what mattered was 'the quality of teaching . . . excellence in teaching'.[107]

It is not easy to disentangle the various meanings ascribed by participants in these debates to notions of the 'professional', the 'vocational' and the 'relevant', and it is not easy to determine the balance of opinion within higher education or the precise motives for institutional change. It has been suggested that university teachers have been happier in retrospect about expansion than they were at the time, and that at the end of the 1970s – whilst they saw the polytechnics as inferior institutions – 'the idea that the university sector should confine itself to traditional subjects, leaving the newer and more vocational subjects to the polytechnics, is opposed by over two-thirds of university teachers'.[108] In the midst of the earlier preoccupation with expansion there was much argument and little systematic analysis of the meanings of the categories and definitions in use. A Gulbenkian discussion of 'excellence' in 1969 seemed to produce five different interpretations of 'relevance': the demand that courses should relate to contemporary, social and political issues; training for the job; relevance to expertise in the subject; relevance to moral problems; social mobility and manpower relevance. As the director of North East London Polytechnic indicated in the discussion, interpretation was everything: 'the reason that colleges like mine have something to contribute is that they are oriented to a quite different concept of excellence to the academic one'.[109] One critic of the universities pointed out in 1968 that: 'the demands of academic education are becoming as difficult to reconcile with those of vocational education as with those of liberal education – academic demands are becoming narrower whilst vocational demands are becoming broader'.[110] F. R. Jevons suggested similarly in 1972 that vocational courses were in fact broader than single-discipline academic courses.[111] Two professional associations in technical education expressed the belief in 1951 not only that the technical college did not offer a narrow training in industrial and commercial techniques, but also that the functions of the technical college and the university were converging.[112] Given the complex structures of higher education, the seriousness and ambiguity of the pressures on them, and the varying meanings of the expressed demands and responses, it is not surprising that the main debates of the 1960s and 1970s were either about numbers, finance, projections and degree structure, or about vague anxieties over standards and purposes. Discussions about how to reconcile the *demands* of society, the *needs* of society, and the *responsibilities* of higher education[113] did not make significant headway within the traditions and constraints of British higher education.

One important theme does, however, emerge from a cluster of research analyses conducted mainly in the 1970s into student perceptions of the relationship between higher education and occupation or vocation. The first, published in 1967, was an account of Australian university students' motivation in entering one of the universities, the conclusion being that

the students entering the university have quite definite occupational expectations. Very few, less than 10 per cent of each intake, admit to being uncertain or undecided about the occupation which they expect to enter. They appear to have made their vocational decision and assume that their university course will provide entry and the necessary skills for a specific occupation.[114]

In a further report the following year the researchers described student motivation and expectations in terms of a consensus around four main items, which constituted important objectives expressing 'generalised aspects of personal growth and development and generalised vocational preparation'. The crucial point was that this student support for 'generalised vocational preparation' did not extend to support for more specific forms of vocational preparation: 'the degree of importance attached to objectives and consensus amongst the respondents decreases as the objective expressed becomes more specific or defines a specific aspect of the relatively undifferentiated objective which the respondents rate as highly important.' These findings were not significantly different for students in different disciplines, though the students questioned in the faculties of rural science, agricultural economics and economics showed a general tendency 'to rate vocational preparation more importantly' than did those entering the faculties of arts and science.[115]

An American project, the findings of which were published in 1970, but the student samples (at the University of Hawaii) for which were in 1960-3, found that the majority of students were 'degree-bound, security-minded, and achievement-motivated'. Higher education was for them a means to an economic end – although a significant minority was interested in 'the satisfaction to be derived from the academic enterprise'.[116] A British investigation, of four Yorkshire grammar schools, the findings of which were published in 1970, came to some similar conclusions. Whether these sixth formers were aspirants for a university or college education, they considered the 'definite vocational purpose' of a university education as important (university aspirants 71 per cent; college aspirants 87 per cent): 'Expectations were strong that learning at university and college should above all else be "applicable", seven out of ten pupils seeing the university's task as preparing the student for a definite vocation or occupation'.[117] A survey of applied science and engineering students at Portsmouth Polytechnic published in 1972 indicated that these students in general attached great importance to education which would 'provide vocational training' and which would enable a student 'to apply fundamental knowledge to new

198 Education as history

problems in practical situations'. Taken with other responses these indicated, so far as it was possible to generalize from this, and the Australian and American evidence, that 'both intellectual and vocational goals are highly important to students'.[118]

In 1972 a study of Swansea university students by Richard Startup similarly concluded that '90 per cent of the students indicated that considerations to do with future occupations did contribute to their attempts to gain entrance to the university'. Some three-quarters of the students were attracted to the university because it would give access to an occupation or position which involves 'doing more interesting work', and about half the students thought it important that the university would give access to a better-paid occupation and provide a wider choice of occupations. A small majority of students did not even mention the study of an academic subject for itself as being among their reasons for entering the university (occupational, intellectual, social, personal and others); 42 per cent of the men gave occupation as their first reason (with 20 per cent giving personal and 18 per cent intellectual), and of the women 25 per cent gave occupation (as against 34 per cent personal and 18 per cent intellectual). Approaching a half of pure and applied science students ranked occupational reasons first (and substantially) above the other categories, and of arts and social studies students occupational reasons were ranked third and second respectively. The clearest finding of the research was the low priority generally attached to 'intellectual' reasons for coming to university.[119] One commentator on this research, however, expressed reservations about the 'vague' nature of the occupational pressures postulated in the examination of students' vocational interests.[120] A study commissioned by the University of Wales and published in 1974 also found that sixth formers and undergraduates considered that the most important function of universities was preparation for life and qualification for a career, rather than membership of a scholarly community or the pursuit of truth.[121]

A study published in 1973 found that polytechnic students believed their education to be more 'relevant' to the needs of society than that provided by universities,[122] and studies of sixteen to nineteen year-olds published in 1975–7 suggested that subsequent economic advantage was an important element in attitudes towards higher education. The majority of the sixth-form respondents 'had a particular career in mind – 52 per cent definitely and 28 per cent probably. Girls were more likely than boys to have a firm idea of what they wanted to do: 56 per cent claimed to have definitely made up their minds compared with 48 per cent of boys.'[123] When asked 'why they chose particular institutions or courses, two-thirds of the eighteen year olds intending to enter higher education rated the usefulness of the course for a job and the reputation of the department or institution as important or very important'.[124] A related analysis suggested that 40 per cent of students applying for university did so because it would help them to obtain the job they wanted.[125]

The evidence points to a strong 'vocational' expectation of higher education by the students entering it. There are reservations to be expressed and questions to be asked about the *way* in which students perceive the link between studies and subsequent careers, and the nature of their 'generalized' and 'specific' expectations. There are differences to be established between pre-entry and post-entry expectations, and perceptions at different points of the extent and form of vocational preparation. Nevertheless, it is clear that there are, as Cohen and Startup particularly underline, grounds for conflict between staff and students, especially in universities, if the staff are in general committed to the 'intellectual' purposes of the institution, and the students enter it with high expectations of its 'occupational' functions.[126] It is important to note, however, that an analysis of staff and student values at a technological university in 1968 – a survey not primarily concerned with occupational choices – concluded that there was close correspondence between the values of the students and those of the institution: student values 'broadly coincided with those of the academic staff'.[127]

There are wide open ends in much of this kind of research. Expectations of higher education and careers by secondary school leavers, for example, have to be seen in relation to the pattern of changed expectations which is produced by early experience in higher education. Brennan and Percy, for instance, underline that student goals may be formed as a result of entry, rather than explain it.[128] Expectations and intentions also change significantly with changing employment availability, changing social values with regard to production and service employment, and changing climates of student and public opinion with regard to the image, status and desirability of certain kinds of career. A research project on the aims and expectations of university students in Federal Germany offers an example. The evidence on 'the outcomes of university education', published in 1979, indicated that the majority of the population stressed the professional, income and social advancement goals of university attendance. Graduates, on the other hand, stressed the personality development outcomes, playing down the privileges attached to a university education, and emphasizing the critical-intellectual role of higher education, rather than the moral qualities stressed by legislators and university representatives.[129] It is doubtful whether all of these emphases would have been the same in a parallel survey conducted ten years earlier.

All of this research indicates that the intellectual/occupational distinction may not be as clear as was sometimes suspected.[130] It also tends to examine students in fairly broad categories, and it is therefore important to consider one piece of research which explores the perceptions or 'wants' of students in a variety of disciplines. Brennan and Percy in 1976 analysed the goals and aspirations of British students and the efficacy of higher education in satisfying them. They did so in terms of a typology of student goals along two axes: curricular/extra-curricular and intrinsic/instrumental. Students of English generally thought the instrumental/curricular goals of self-development most important, found it difficult to separate curricular from extra-curricular goals, saw their subject as non-vocational and were happy about it. Physics students tended not to enter the university with curricular/intrinsic goals, and had a mixture of pragmatic motives. Most of them saw physics as a 'pure' subject, and if they started out with vocational goals tended to replace them by curricular/intrinsic and curricular/instrumental goals of self-development. Since sociology students had not studied the subject at school, their choices at entry were often negative (deciding what they did *not* want to do) or accidental. Their most common goals were curricular/instrumental, dividing equally between vocationalism and self-development, their satisfaction being expressed mainly in terms of the latter. They tended to reinterpret their goals over the three years. Students of mechanical engineering had predominantly vocational reasons for entry, their occupational choices having already been made and their course being seen as a necessary step towards the chosen career. They tended to have low satisfaction with course content, because its relevance to their future career was 'perceived only dimly': they were critical of both content and presentation, and were 'sceptical about its relevance to their future careers'. Business studies students in general 'appeared to "suffer" their courses for the occupational benefits which they hoped would accrue', but they turned to extra-curricular activities for more general and immediate satisfactions. Students on specifically vocational courses were investigated in two polytechnic departments – librarianship and landscape architecture. The students perceived the vocational relevance of their work and this enabled them to 'take a resigned attitude to "some things" ' – and were content even when they did not necessarily see the relevance.

The authors of this study felt that most students would accept almost all the goals in their typology. They concluded that it seemed obvious 'to urge lecturers in academic disciplines to design their courses to meet goals other than (or in addition to) that of the production of other academic specialists'. They were struck by the 'distinctiveness which participants on some vocational courses ascribed to their courses' and they argued that 'there is a sense in which vocational goals are relevant to all students in higher education'.[131]

A general point to which it is important to return is that of the widely expressed expectation of 'relevance' and the extreme difficulty of detecting any consensus as to its meaning. In the discussions so far – and as it will be continued in the next section on expectations of curricula and forms of education and training – the focus has been mainly on interpretation of the practical and the technical. It is crucially important to emphasize the range of values associated with the vocational or 'relevant' elements in higher education. At one end of a spectrum are the occupational aspirations on which we have concentrated. The University Grants Committee (UGC) lent support to recognition of such aspirations in 1958: 'Most students take up a subject in order to acquire a body of specialised knowledge which they intend to apply in earning a livelihood and it would be unrealistic to deny the importance of this utilitarian purpose.'[132] Even in 1948 the UGC was suggesting that universities would fail in their purpose if they did not combine vocational functions with the provision of a 'broad humanistic culture and a suitably tough intellectual discipline'.[133] The Brennan and Percy research two decades later translates such messages into precise recommendations to university teachers. Further along the spectrum, the need for stronger links between the universities and the professions has been emphasized. In 1968 Lord Butler thought these links should be expanded along the lines of the traditional relationship between the universities and medicine.[134] Two years earlier Sir Edward Boyle had talked about education needing to become more vocational, in order to respond to the needs of the world outside – 'part of the justification for greatly increased expenditure on universities must be their success in strengthening the professional infrastructure of our society'.[135] Butler also saw education as an 'investment in the future', and thought it inevitable and desirable that the universities would change, although he saw a risk of making 'a fetish of technology at the expense of liberal arts courses and the social sciences'.[136]

At the other end of the spectrum, different interpretations of relevance have been frequently stressed and have been previously alluded to here. In general terms 'relevance to the community' is often underlined. An Australian study of *The University and Its Community* in 1964 underlined (as was apparent also with many American and other universities during the campus troubles of the 1960s) the tensions between loyalty to academic subjects and to the outside community, to instrumental values. The authors concluded, in a noteworthy phrase, that the universities needed to be seen by the community to be relevant to 'the life which the community has decided to lead'.[137] In a House of Lords debate on higher education before the Robbins Committee was set up, Lord Beveridge offered a different version of such an argument, proposing that the purpose of a university in the modern world was 'to make youth fit and eager to render professional service to their fellow citizens, not simply to sharpen wits'.[138]

The various searches for relevance indicate the depth of the problems it raises for the providers, the patrons and the customers. The problems remain salient in two major ways. The first is the attempt to direct discussion into channels other than that of vocational/non-vocational distinctions. A recent expression of long-standing dissatisfaction with this neat but elusive categorization (and its embodiment in national and local government structures) is that of George Tolley, director of Sheffield Polytechnic: 'It would remove a good deal of the snobbery from higher education . . . if only those of us in education would remove ourselves from the empty battlefields of the nineteenth century . . . it would be helpful to eschew an over-simple categorisation of courses into vocational and non-vocational.'[139] The second continuing anxiety relates to the danger of narrowness, a possible preoccupation with skills and techniques, rather than (or in addition to) principles and critical understandings. A forthright and interesting expression of this continuing dilemma was made in 1976 by a Member of Parliament with a major interest in higher education:

No one would object to higher education being 'relevant', in the sense that it prepares people for some line of work – a wholly desirable outcome. But when vocational objectives become too narrowly focused, as they are in danger of being in the mind of the Prime

Minister, then it seems to me that they have lost much of their claim to be educational.

The fact that this comment was made by Keith Hampson, a Conservative MP, of James Callaghan, a Labour Prime Minister, engaged in the processes of the 'Great Debate', is what makes the concern expressed most interesting.[140] The concern may be equally acute in the minds of Labour Members of Parliament under a Conservative administration. Neither major political party holds a monopoly of the problem or of possible answers. How difficult it is in the whole of this area of discussion to establish a consensus of approach or of meaning can also be seen, to take a final example, in the report of the Fulton Committee on the civil service in 1968. A majority of the Committee established a 'preference for relevance' in the matching of disciplines to future occupation in the service. A minority of the Committee, however, did not 'place the same emphasis on the relevance of studies taken before entry', and in fact thought that the notion of relevant study could be 'overrated'.[141] The professional, the practical and the relevant remain categories which are easily used, only apparently understood, and the focus of intense and continual controversy.

SPECIFIC OR BROAD, OR LEARNING TO LEARN?

In 1956 Sir Harry Pilkington advised the universities to place technology and specialization in a wider context. Which was worse, he asked, that a technologist should be brought up like an American guided missile, 'to think in a closed circuit', or that he should break out, not knowing why, and completely unguided?[142] While there have in past decades been the demands we have discussed for a more vocational emphasis in higher education, anxieties have been continually expressed – at one extreme – about the effects of narrowness, thinking 'in a closed circuit', and – at the other extreme – of breadth without adequate signposts and career outlets. The point to be emphasized here is concern like Pilkington's about the closed circuit, the strong – and continuing – sense among many employers and others that in responding to the apparent needs of the outside world, higher education should not be too narrow, too specific, too enclosed. If the most acceptable formula has been that of a 'balanced education', it should also be stressed that the way to implement the formula has been endlessly pondered and often ferociously fought over.

The discussion has frequently been concerned with fairly generalized goals and expectations of higher education. For example, an officer of the British Aircraft Corporation, speaking as a representative of the CBI in 1978, discussed the problem in some detail, and it is worth presenting his argument. He began by discussing the view that had long been expressed that university curricula should be broadened in response to new jobs, wider scope and increased responsibilities:

> We agree ... that it would be of value to the economy if more graduates entering industrial and commercial employment emerged from the universities better equipped to deal with the outside world. But this could be achieved by a broadening of mental attitudes rather than by teaching more subjects in the first degree. It is difficult to forecast the numbers of graduates in particular disciplines who will be needed. It is even more difficult to forecast how many of these need to know particular languages. Even if they learn the subject, they may not have the right personality. We take the view that the universities and the polytechnics are teaching their graduates how to continue learning. The ability to be creative and flexible is needed by every graduate wherever he or she is employed.
>
> We know that an employer will ask if there is a good graduate, available now, with such-and-such knowledge. The provision of courses cannot be built upon such requests ... People probably do not realise how much training takes place after graduation ... We think, therefore, that the knowledge required for a particular task should be given to the individual at the right time, after graduation. This gives the universities the bigger problem, that of stimulating individuals to learn whatever may be required.[143]

The 'broadening of mental attitudes', 'how to continue learning', 'creative and flexible', specific training at the 'right time after graduation' – these are concepts and themes which recur in discussions in recent decades.

The questions relating to 'breadth' are of central importance in considering what employers (including private and nationalized industries, national and local government) have expected of the universities in producing suitably trained and qualified graduates. Throughout the period since the Second World War many have stressed the need for future graduate employees, in industry and commerce especially, to develop much wider understandings than those directly related to their technical, scientific, or other specialist studies. In 1956 Sir Willis Jackson stresses the need for technologists to appreciate 'the over-riding importance of human relations'.[144] The FBI tells the Robbins Committee of the greater complexity of industrial society, and of the need for vocational elements to be set in a broader understanding of the 'political and economic forces determining the future form of our society'. It stresses the importance of 'breadth of outlook' and the 'necessary background to appreciate both socially and morally the impact of technological innovation in the local, national and international fields'.[145] With a parallel but somewhat different argument and emphasis, the TUC stresses to the Committee that higher education should foster personal development and democratic citizenship as well as vocational interests. It deplores over-specialization and emphasizes 'wider social and cultural interests'. Courses in higher education should require 'all students to attain an acceptable standard of truly general education', and the TUC therefore welcomes a trend it sees towards broader courses of undergraduate education.[146] In 1963 Lord Nelson, of English Electric, urges the encouragement of general education, so that students can learn to understand the civilization in which they live.[147] In 1967 Monty Finniston emphasizes how much the 'single-culture education of scientists' has been debated, and how they need 'to appreciate not just the technical content of a situation but its relationship to the broader aspects of company practice and policies'.[148] Nelson, Finniston and many others stress the need for future industrial employees to have some knowledge of management, planning, trade unionism . . . and in doing so reflect a pressure for undergraduate management education, one which is discussed by and with the Robbins Committee, but which the Committee rejects.

The pressures for breadth also take other forms, reflected with great clarity in the post-war reports of the UGC. The first such report, for example, presents the case for broader programmes of study, a case strengthened, it suggests, by advances in learning on borderlines of two or more subjects. In the same period, it is clear from Sir James Mountford's account of the foundation and early years of Keele, the UGC was one of the sources of pressure for a widening of the originally conceived curriculum.[149] There is widespread comment from the 1950s about overloaded university courses,[150] and about over-specialization (though often at the same time resisting the idea of additive liberal studies courses).[151] There are many doubts expressed about the wisdom of continuing to produce what a Science Policy Studies report in 1968 calls 'superfluous' specialization, increasingly so since a high degree of specialization makes graduate engineers and scientists extremely vulnerable in a period of rapid technological change.[152] It is often pointed out that graduates are increasingly rarely doing the job they were officially trained for,[153] and in 1972 a university careers officer argues against the expansion of the vocational sector of higher education, citing as one reason the fact that more specialist chemists were taking 'non-relevant' jobs.[154] The Dainton Committee on the flow of science and technology candidates into higher education extends the argument for breadth and against premature decision-making back into the schools, providing one of the strongest post-war pleas for a 'broad span of studies in the sixth-forms' and for the infusion of 'breadth, humanity and up-to-dateness into the science curriculum and its teaching'.[155] The very pressure for expansion, as we have seen, produces proposals for breadth in various froms, to meet the perceived different needs of new constituencies of students. In a memorably cynical response, Brian Chapman writes in *Nature* in 1964 that broader courses mean a 'smattering of several subjects', and it is not clear whether universities should respond specially to more and weaker students – which would result in more intensive teaching and the civilizing force of 'offering sherry around'.[156]

It is inevitable in this situation that there should be disparate and conflicting views, ambiguity and uncertainty. British Rail, in 1972, sees two routes that would be followed by those 'young men and women of high potential whose intelligence and personality have already been developed by their experience at university or polytechnic, and who are capable of further development'. Some would be taught 'knowledge and skills, such as engineering or computer science' and others would 'obtain their degrees in more general subjects which would strengthen their powers of reasoning and teach them to apply their minds to any problem, without teaching them any technique which is directly relevant to our business'. There are obviously problems attached to this categorization, but the important point is that British Rail goes on to say that it is satisfied that 'the universities should continue to produce both types of graduates', accepting the Robbins view that there is 'no single objective of higher education'.[157] This and previous examples illustrate how far industry has been from having a clear or unanimous view of the value of highly specialized training for all – and in some cases of any – of its future recruits.

The crucial point that emerges from this discussion is the strong emphasis that has been placed in many sections of industry, especially the larger firms, on higher education as a base on which industry – and other employers – can themselves build the necessary specialism (or which can be built at post-graduate level in higher education). The chairman of Shell Transport and Trading and of Shell International reflected in 1971 on 'what industry expects from graduates', suggesting that they needed to be 'of higher all-round ability than formerly'. He outlined a number of qualities and characteristics, and added: 'Tomorrow's executives will have to be competent in a much wider field than at present, and in Shell we are applying more scientific methods in order to find them in good time and then equip them for their future responsibilities.'[158] The word 'then' in the last sentence is the crux, carrying the same weight as 'the right time, after graduation' in our earlier quotation from the spokesman from the British Aircraft Corporation and the CBI. A conference of the former FBI had twenty years earlier heard pleas for the universities to concentrate on 'fundamentals' (for example, by Sir Arthur Fleming) and on personality, leadership qualities and good English (from Sir Humphrey Gale). It heard a report from a working party which indicated that a questionnaire to a sample of industrialists had revealed that the 'qualities and characteristics' most sought were knowledge of fundamentals and personality, leadership, breadth of outlook and logic. Given these, emphasized Sir Arthur Fleming, industry can afterwards supplement the fundamentals with practical education, and can do it better than the universities or technical colleges.[159] This kind of view continued to be expressed firmly through the 1960s and 1970s. The Fulton Committee on the civil service, while welcoming certain kinds of studies which combined specialisms with a grounding, for example, in economics and business studies, thought that at least for the time being 'it must be the task of the Service to equip its specialists with the additional administrative, managerial and other skills they need'.[160] Many industrial and other enterprises were, at the same time, instituting their own programmes of post-graduate, in-house training of graduate recruits, release for in-service training or higher degrees, or collaborative schemes with higher education institutions. Differences in approach to the graduate and to specialist training have obviously varied according to size and type of firm, and to the kind of skills and knowledge which is either capable of being put to immediate use or which appears to be 'superfluous'. It has even been suggested that companies *prefer* to retain specialist training at the post-graduate level and in their own hands, so as to keep control over the industrial secrets on which their success depends.[161] Whether it be a director of a university department of physics in 1949 comparing engineers to doctors, in need of a broadly based fundamental education to which specific knowledge can later be added,[162] or the Swann Committee on the employment of scientists, engineers and technologists in 1968 decrying specialization and calling for 'the production of science-based generalists',[163] important voices amongst the employers and inside higher education have resisted the too-early (including undergraduate) specialization that has been a feature of much of British higher education.

From starting-points such as these various anxieties and hesitations there have been frequent attempts to indicate what qualities it is that a higher education can and should encourage, in order that graduates can have the potential to learn and re-learn and adapt once in employment. A strong emphasis has therefore been placed on the uselessness of specialist knowledge if students do not, at the same time – in the words of the UGC in 1953 – 'learn to think'. The UGC continued to be emphatic in the 1950s that among the characteristics of the educated persons the universities aimed to produce 'first and foremost we would place a capacity to think'. It was the role of the universities to teach students how to think, including by the mutual interaction of students themselves. The UGC also saw this as one source of student dissatisfaction, given their expectations on entry: 'We believe that a number of arts students find their honours courses an unsatisfying experience. They embark on them with somewhat vague expectations that they will receive great intellectual stimulus and encounter profound thinking, and they are disappointed.'[164] *Nature* thought this emphasis by the UGC important enough to quote it and to emphasize that students needed, among other things, 'a general appreciation of the art of learning'.[165] A Fabian Society author, in 1959, expressed the view that the feature which distinguished a university from other institutions was that they were, or should be, concerned 'with ways of thinking about things rather than with techniques for doing things'[166] – a distinction that has been explored with one degree or another of acceptance or rejection in discussions of higher education internationally throughout the nineteenth and twentieth centuries.[167] Many have rejected the dichotomy, proposing like Lord Eustace Percy that 'the aim of all education is to teach men to think, and the method of all higher education is, while encouraging the student's mind to work in all sorts of spheres and on all sorts of subjects, to exercise it intensively on some

particular body of knowledge'.[168] Percy's double emphasis on *all* has
gained increased relevance in the second half of the twentieth century
with the proliferation of types of higher and further education institutions. It is clear that in relation to university education specifically there
has been a continuing demand inside and outside the institutions that
students should learn to learn. A professor of history at a new university
in the early 1960s expressed his ideal as 'an independent student,
helped to discover not only new knowledge but himself, becoming
increasingly self-reliant (and self-critical) as he becomes more
knowledgeable'.[169] Against the background of recent expansion of
higher education such an emphasis has been consistent and strong. A
working party of the Association of University Teachers on *Universities
in the 1970s* underlined that even when university education was
vocational, it was concerned with principles, with creativeness,
criticism and flexibility.[170] A professor of social policy described the
purpose of higher education as being 'to induct our students into the
practice of sound argument within a discipline'.[171] GKN added 'self-
learning as a continual process' to the Robbins objectives for higher
education.[172] Research into higher education took on a new dimension
in the 1960s and 1970s, including student differences, learning, and
aims and intentions. Reflecting on his research into student experience
of higher education, Peter Marris offered the view that higher
education 'aims to teach students how to abstract, from a particular
context, principles by which they can organize the perception of their
universe of thought'. It 'sets out to meet the need of those who want to
develop their power of understanding as an unbounded skill: and by
this aim it asserts the value of this skill, both to its students and the
society which supports it'.[173]

The attempt to define, from the employer's and everyone else's
viewpoint, the desirable balance between specific and general preparation for occupations, for service, for leadership, for whatever, is
obviously central to definitions of higher education and of its component parts. The distinction between what is vocational and what is
academic is, as we have seen in a number of ways, difficult to make and
to sustain.[174] Within the expressed expectations of higher education,
and within its responses, there is, however, a clear indication of
resistance to the over-specific, interest in the process of learning how to
continue to learn, and a search for the right kind of breadth. As the
Joint Advisory Committee on Engineering Education put it to the
Robbins Committee – 'a liberal education which produces a balance of

outlook and interests' was what it considered to be a requirement for a career in engineering.[175] All of these attempts to define content and aim are ultimately part of a centuries-old debate about the nature of a 'liberal' (or 'broad' or 'general') education.[176] The Swann Committee's insistence on the need for 'science-based generalists', or employers' stress on 'all-round ability' or 'character' or other pre-requisites, have to be viewed against this background. Statements such as one by the FBI in 1961 that it supported an expansion of university entrance so as to permit more students 'a more prolonged period of broadly based education',[177] continue a tradition, seek to adapt it and continue to present familiar and difficult questions of definition. In an effort to solve such problems there have in recent decades, in addition to the promotion of 'liberal studies' courses for some science and technology students, been attempts to promote new structures in higher education, based on varied conceptions of general education – a prominent one being the Pippard proposal for a two-year basic and general higher education rooted in the 'mainstream' subject'. There have also been strategies for approaching technology as a liberal study.[178] Controversy around these and similar approaches and issues has aroused passion on all sides.[179] It has related to specific questions of, for example, work experience and student choice. It underlies the view of the Institution of Production Engineers expressed to the Robbins Committee that engineering education should both be broad and identify students with the engineering profession and practice from the outset.[180] It underlies, similarly, the recommendations of the Finniston Report on the engineering profession some two decades later, when the committee – finding that 'most current first-degree courses are not generally well-matched to the requirements of industry' – stated: 'our firm view is that formal engineering teaching should be closely oriented to practice and applications'. It should therefore provide work experience from the early stages, and attempt to provide an integrated mix of theory, application and experience, where possible through collaborative schemes with employers.[181] More broadly, Lord Butler thought students whilst at university should come into 'closer contact with professional life'.[182]

In relation to choice, the paramount question has, of course, been that of delayed specialization, reflected in various ways in our previous discussions. Butler talks about the university needing to 'organise specialization, to come at a later date'.[183] The Engineering Employers Federation rejected the Finniston Committee's proposed restructuring of engineering education partly on the grounds that the identification of leadership potential is notoriously difficult, especially in isolation. Consequently there are grave doubts about the ability of academic institutions to select after only a year, and at the age of nineteen, individuals who are likely to become the managers and leaders in the industry.[184]

Alongside the voices raised to accomplish such delayed specialization in higher education have been those in favour of such delays at the school level, producing the debates of the 1960s and 1970s about the nature of examinations at age sixteen and eighteen, and related questions of curricula – especially those of the sixth form, and of direct interest to the universities. Again, in this context, the strongest message came from the Dainton Committee on science and technology at the end of the 1960s – opposing premature decisions against science and technology, and calling for 'broad courses of study' for sixth formers.[185] All of these discussions have also led directly into those about institutional structures and differences.

INSTITUTIONAL DIFFERENCES

Nineteenth- and twentieth-century discussions of higher education have included strong and confused threads of debate about the existence or whereabouts of frontiers between a general or liberal education and a vocational or professional education. These debates have therefore been about the expectations of higher education of different groups in society – the established church and nonconformity, the liberal professions and industrial, commercial and public employers, students and the institutions of higher education themselves – their own interpretations of their curriculum and roles, and the interpretations of those who have attempted to speak for them. Around technology and the applied sciences, around an increasing range of 'utilitarian' subjects pressing for entry into the higher education definition, there have been prolonged controversies – focusing in particular on what it is proper for institutions to teach. In England the debates of the nineteenth century encompassed both what was appropriate within the ancient universities and what was appropriate to the newly created university colleges and universities. The debates extended to the nature of a proper form of higher education for the provincial captains of industry and commerce, and to the acceptability of models developed in Scotland or continental Europe or the United States.

An analysis of what the various constituencies have expected of higher education, especially in the late nineteenth and twentieth centuries, shows the extent to which these various discussions have been bound up with conflicting perceptions of the need for and nature of different kinds of institutions. Expectations of higher education have increasingly become expectations of sectors of higher education as the system has expanded – especially with the designation of the second generation of 'polytechnics' in the late 1960s and of colleges and institutes of higher education in the late 1970s. These developments have raised important further questions of definition, including the nature of what is on offer in the different sectors and institutions and sectors of the more and more complex 'higher education'. The controversies about vocational and non-vocational, liberal and professional education, narrowness and breadth, and all the other issues surrounding the shape and content of higher education, are reflected in the comment of a university vice-chancellor in 1969 – after the designation of the polytechnics: what worried him about the new institutions was 'that they are a good deal too "technic" and not enough "poly" '.[186] Such an anxiety is, in modern dress, part of two centuries of difficulty in England in locating a proper position and status in higher education for the disciplines born of or evolving with the pressures of the changing world. An 1860s version of it was John Stuart Mill's view that education for the professions was not the job of universities, that schools of medicine or industrial arts should be separate from (if adjacent to) the universities, and that such schools were not 'education properly so called'.[187]

Discussion of institutional differences, therefore, relates not only to the changing shape and status of knowledge and skills, but also to the changing scale and pattern of recruitment to a wider range of institutions attempting to meet the demands of a developing and more open society. In Britain, as in other countries, wider access to higher education, and the creation of new institutions and sectors to fill out a pattern of expanded higher education, have transformed the discussion of 'expectations' of higher education, and the definition of higher education itself. Different expectations of new institutions have developed on the part of different publics, as well as uncertainties and confusions about the nature and purposes of different types and versions of institutions. The history of diversification in English higher education relates to the establishment of London as a new kind of university, the subsequent development of the range of new university colleges and then universities. It relates to the emergence and upward 'drift'[188] of the late nineteenth-century polytechnics, to the colleges of advanced technology of the 1950s and their absorption into the university system, and the creation of polytechnics in the 1960s, and most recently the colleges and institutes of higher education. The intentions of the founders of the earlier additions to the system were often ambiguous, or resulted in compromises between utilitarian and 'general' interpretations of the needs of the new student populations of Manchester or Birmingham or Leeds. The establishment of universities at centres such as these altered the pattern of expectations of higher or technical education or professional training. The 'binary' decisions of the 1960s have likewise affected expectations of higher education or of sections of it.

The binary distinction between universities and 'public sector' institutions, from the issue of the Labour government's White Paper on the subject in 1966, was intended to produce visible distinctions of control of financing and of courses. The ostensible commitment of Anthony Crosland and his advisers and successors was to a higher education sector more responsive to national or public needs, more geared to the productive and service sectors of the economy, and on a footing of something like parity with the universities. The Robbins Committee had been urged, for example by the Association of Education Committees, to remove status differences between 'academic' courses and those of a comparable level which were denied 'the same status in the public mind',[189] and the Committee itself called for the removal of status differences between institutions performing 'similar functions':

> We wish to see the removal of any designations or limitations that cause differentiation between institutions that are performing similar functions. Distinctions based on adventitious grounds, whether historical or social, are wholly alien to the spirit that should inform higher education.[190]

The creation of the binary system seemed to many people, including Robbins, not to be in the spirit of these demands, and Sir Edward Boyle emphasized in 1966, quoting Robbins, that the binary system did not mean 'eternal separation'.[191] One critic of the proposed new structure in 1967 quoted Crosland as preferring a binary system to a 'ladder' hierarchy, but felt that Crosland's arguments were based on an outmoded view of the universities as conservative and high-level institutions, and that the necessity of a new sector was not proven. Equally important, he thought the new proposals only nominally changed anything for the polytechnics, in reality represented a cutting back of plans for higher education, and had led Crosland himself by 1967 to begin to withdraw from the binary concept.[192] The two sectors, emphasised the AUT in 1971, were not providing distinct forms of education, and the binary assumptions about their respective definitions were untenable: 'What manner of sense is this?'[193]

The statements about the new polytechnics by Crosland and Patrick Gordon Walker, in the White Paper itself, and the discussions surrounding it and the establishment of the polytechnics from 1968, contain profound ambiguities about the distinctive nature of the new institutions, and about the range and levels of their work. Commentators on the political right and left and in all reaches of the educational system have since stressed how nebulous or non-existent were the terms of reference of the polytechnics at their creation. The polytechnics, suggested John Pratt and Tyrrell Burgess, were designated without explicit objectives, their intended role as comprehensive academic communities was left unexplained, and they were allowed to take part in the 'historical process of aspiration' which they termed 'academic drift'[194] – and in so commenting they implied that the polytechnics were and ought to be at a level below the university one towards which they 'drifted' upwards. A Conservative Research Department author wrote in 1978 that:

> Polytechnics were not established with any clear directive that they should concentrate on technical and scientific education . . . While it was expected that polytechnics would be more industry-based and would concentrate on vocational, practical, scientific and technical education, the 1966 White Paper did not make this clear . . . They have grown to be very similar to universities and face broadly the same problems.[195]

A parliamentary select committee on science and technology expressed the view in 1976 that the polytechnics had, like the earlier colleges of advanced technology, been allowed to drift and had an 'ambivalent and ill-defined role'. It regretted that no effort had been made to establish a parallel system of technical institutions and colleges which would have been excellent in their own right and would have represented a new concept in higher education.[196] The Secretaries of State for Education and Science and Industry, replying to the select committee report, denied that the role of the polytechnics had been 'ambivalent or misunderstood'.[197]

The ambiguities surrounding the future institutions can be located in discussions about their intended student body, degree and pre-degree levels of work and research, and along a number of other axes. One of these, regarding the level or quality of students, is one to which we shall return, but one important area of public confusion to underline has been the question of 'lower level' work at the polytechnics, with extensive ignorance being constantly revealed about the nature and level of work being conducted there (and in the colleges of higher education). Nowhere have these misconceptions been greater than amongst university staffs and political activists. The extent of the confusion has been visible in a whole range of public discussions about the binary system, the polytechnics, the colleges and institutes of education, and the 'distinguishing features' of these institutions and the universities. In response, the polytechnics had to fight to clarify their role in the 1970s and were clearly pulled in different directions. The Committee of Directors of Polytechnics (CDP), in particular, has increasingly emphasized a 'strong' definition of the institutions and their differences from universities. The CDP announced in 1974 that the polytechnics wished not to be given but to earn 'parity of esteem' with the universities, that they had been given by government the 'innovative task of developing higher education along polytechnic lines', and that the development of higher education in colleges 'under the aegis of local authorities' had been 'one of the relatively unacclaimed achievements in education in this country, and the emergence of the polytechnics is the culmination of a development which has gone on for more than a hundred years'. The word polytechnic meant 'many arts, many skills', and polytechnic education covered a wide span of studies, including the technologies, the arts and humanities, studies in professions such as law and accountancy, in the social services for social workers, health visitors, probation officers, and courses for teachers, architects, librarians, planners, designers and so on.[198]

The assertion of the 'polytechnic' and 'comprehensive' quality of the new institutions, however, did not easily demarcate them from the universities, or from the new colleges and institutes of higher education which were created in the late 1970s out of some of the remaining colleges of education and other colleges engaged in advanced further education. The polytechnic directors' strong self-definition was affirmed more clearly, and at the same time with new anxieties, to a House of Commons select committee early in 1980. A memorandum from the CDP states:

The polytechnics are committed to a vocational emphasis in all their courses; the universities (broadly) are committed to the progressive validation of basic academic disciplines through research. There is a proper overlap of courses in the two types of institutions with different approaches to teaching. In this sense, the polytechnics and universities have a role definition. What is not clear is the distinctiveness and role of the other colleges. Role definition is important and so what is done and how it is done flows from this. The clearer the role definitions, the more distinctive is the ethos and objectives of the institutions. When the objectives are clear, the performance of the institution can be measured with more clarity and indicators of performance can be developed.[199]

The CDP here reaffirms distinctions which have been common in discussions of higher education since the creation and development of new institutions in the second half of the nineteenth century, and it suggests clarities about commitment and role that have in fact been controversial throughout that period. The extent of the uncertainty that underlies the claim of distinctiveness can be seen in the difficulty of defining what constitutes different 'approaches to teaching' and the curriculum comparison which, it has frequently been pointed out, is more than an 'overlap'. One of the polytechnic directors himself spelled out in detail why it is not possible to portray the polytechnics and universities as largely distinct but overlapping in their curriculum range. The argument is simple:

English, French, German, Spanish, Classics, Law, Sociology, Applied Sociology, Business, Management, Mathematics, Computing, Physics, Chemistry, Biology, Geology, Electronic Engineering, Polymer Science and Technology, Geography, Librarianship, Teaching Studies, Architecture and Environmental studies, Accounting and Applied Economics, Institutional Management . . . Is this a university or a polytechnic? Answer – the Polytechnic of North London. Consider the following subjects – accountancy, building, ceramics, commercial food science, fuel technology, glass technology, brewing, mining, oil technology, pharmacy, surveying, textiles – found in universities or polytechnics? Answer – in British universities.[200]

And in similar vein a Liberal Party spokesman on education talked of the 'fallacy that there is a difference of role between universities and polytechnics, the one providing the highest quality of research-oriented academic education, and the other learning the more prosaic duty of training people to do particular jobs'. Universities, he pointed out, produce - among others - doctors, dentists, speech therapists, town planners and naval architects.[201]

It is important, in considering expectations of higher education, to be aware that statements of clear role differences amongst institutions, and the various ways in which it is attempted to define and categorize these roles, are in fact surrounded by uncertainty and ambiguity. They form part of long traditions of British and international debate about the aims of higher education and of education in general. The assumptions, definitions and classifications involved have become important areas of debate in many countries. Students, employers, parents, tax-payers, constituencies of all kinds - including the institutions themselves - are concerned with the basis of claims about the distinctiveness and purposes of the different institutions, and with their relationship to hoped-for solutions to salient social problems.

There remains, as a central factor in this discussion, the long-standing awareness that differences amongst institutions include differences of status - hierarchies - and that expectations of higher education and of future position and rewards are conditioned by them. Whether it be Lord Hailsham in 1961[202] or the Committee of Vice-Chancellors and Principals (CVCP) in 1970, there has been a concern for the distinctive university commitment to research - and by implication a strong assumption that research is either non-existent, weak or inappropriate in other institutions. The CVCP statement of 1970 is clear in this respect, describing the distinctive character of the polytechnics as 'comprehensive', in that they have not only first degree but also non-degree courses, reflecting their involvement with vocational training. Undergraduate teaching in universities, on the other hand

> is centred almost exclusively on degree level courses, and is undertaken over a much broader subject range and in the context of a deep involvement of the teaching staff in research, thus permitting the ready development of many areas of cross-disciplinary study as well as a high degree of specialisation in single-subject honours courses. The special character of university courses lies in the fact that they reflect the direct link between teaching and research and scholarship up to the boundaries of existing knowledge.[203]

Some of this ('broader subject range' for example) again raises questions of overlap of definition with the polytechnics, but the important point is the strong insistence on the assumed exclusiveness – or at least 'special character' – of university research-based activity, with all the implications this has for the status of the institution, and the character of its clientele.

There is a widely perceived university–polytechnic hierarchy, whatever the distinguishing characteristics to which appeal is made. Lord Hailsham, as we have seen, was aware in the early 1960s of the university/technical institution snobbery based on 'heresies' about what it is more or less 'gentlemanly' to study. University staffs in the 1970s saw the polytechnic system as

> different and inferior to their own . . . The polytechnics, at least so far, have not become a serious alternative form of higher education in the minds of university dons. They impinge very little on the consciousness of those who have been brought up and now hold posts in universities. They are thought of vaguely as a tier below the universities in the ramifications of post-secondary education. The typical view is that the universities do and should be equipped and paid to do advanced teaching and research at a higher level.[204]

Universities, as we have also seen, are expected by many to be the homes of pure science, as against the technical institutions which are the producers of the lower ranks, assistants, craftsmen.[205]

To a greater or lesser extent, therefore, the existence of non-university higher education is often explicitly justified in terms of the protection of the universities and their 'proper' functions from functions more appropriately located elsewhere.[206] The expansion of higher education in a binary structure has been explained and was seen by its designers as protective of the universities from the intrusion of levels or kinds of work not appropriate to them.[207] Becher and Kogan point out that the UGC welcomed the binary proposals, because they would enable the universities to become 'more national than local in their recruitment, more free to determine their own field of academic activity and standards' (though they also suggest that the polytechnics have not recruited the distinctive clientele intended for them, and that their catchment has also become national rather than local).[208]

There have been other ways of approaching institutional differences, leading perhaps to other expectations of the work and purposes of universities on the one hand, and the new institutions on the other hand. One familiar approach has been to suggest that the differences are not hierarchical, but what the UGC in *A Note on Technology in Universities* in 1950 described (referring to universities and technical colleges) as a difference 'not in status or grade, but in kind'.[209] The aims of the technical college, suggested Lord Eustace Percy, were essentially the same as – and the constraints similar to – those of the university:

> If it be asked whether the specialised courses at technical colleges are in fact calculated to teach a man to think, the answer is that the same doubts may well be entertained about them as we have already suggested about the specialised degree courses of universities.[210]

In their different ways both of these suggest a common-but-different approach to categories of institutions, and on such a basis the emphasis has been on specific 'functional' differences. One author pleads that technical courses should be left to technical colleges, 'which are better fitted to teach the mechanics of business'.[211] Differences, as we have seen, have been expressed in terms of the 'teaching' commitments and other features of the polytechnics, and most of these relate to the vocational/non-vocational issues we have discussed, and have raised fundamental difficulties of various kinds.[212]

A version of the argument in relation to the binary system and the polytechnics has related to the 'functions' of the polytechnics in providing 'all-through' routes, from sub-degree to post-graduate. The existence of sub-degree courses in the polytechnics can be seen both as a means of preserving the essential purity of the all-degree university,[213] and as a positive feature of institutions which are at all levels offering 'second chance' or alternative routes through the higher education system. This argument relates also to the large polytechnic commitment to part-time courses. A university director of extra-mural studies summarized the identity of polytechnics in 1973 as follows:

> The distinguishing characteristics of a polytechnic are that it is primarily technologically based, serves a particular neighbourhood, is devoted primarily to teaching rather than research, is open to part time students, is dependent on the services of part time teachers, and is notably less autonomous than a university.[214]

Both aspects of the part-time tradition are important to this definition. Two research studies of polytechnics have emphasized the distinctive view of the role of polytechnics held by their staffs and the conflicting views within that overall perception – with older-established staff being described in 1975 as stressing the needs of industry and increased links with employers, and newer staff emphasizing the provision of higher education not available elsewhere and becoming more like universities.[215]

Perceptions of the different roles of different institutions have clearly had to be tested against the rhetoric and the realities of the binary structure since the late 1960s. There are those who have seen the crystallizing binary structure as incurring the danger of a permanent division of 'utilitarian' and 'non-utilitarian' education.[216] There are those who have seen it as a preliminary – perhaps a necessary one – to diversification, the provision of new dimensions of 'mass' higher education, and as the best way to achieve collaboration across existing divides. Within the universities themselves the policy has been met with divided and confused reactions.[217] The accusation of upward academic drift on the part of the polytechnics has continued to be made. The polytechnics, suggests Guy Neave, have emulated the universities, because no distinct objectives were set for them, and they have therefore – like the universities – based their programmes not on defined need but on student demand.[218] Jack Embling has described the failure of the polytechnics to establish a new and different role, and their attempt to achieve a difficult balance towards and away from the university model.[219] Keith Hampson, presenting a Conservative view of higher education, has appealed for an end to the academic drift.[220]

It is important but difficult, against this background of uncertainty and controversy, to see the extent to which students' and employers' expectations of higher education have been influenced by the binary division.

So far as students are concerned, the evidence relates mainly to attitude and to choice. Donaldson in 1970 investigated entrants to degree courses at Enfield College of Technology and reported some largely inconclusive data: 67 per cent of respondents saw the polytechnic sector 'as offering an education which was more relevant to the needs of society, with only 2 per cent of respondents giving this honour to the universities', though 51 per cent of them had previously applied to a university. Students' perceptions of differences between the two types of institution focused overwhelmingly on this issue of social relevance, with much more ambiguous response to suggestions of differences based, for example, on access to careers and benefit from contact with research.[221] A study carried out in 1976 of factors affecting student choice of and admission to a university, a college of education and a polytechnic in Coventry, started from the assumption that institutions on either side of the binary line were intended to fulfil different functions. In all three institutions, however, it was found that students allocated priority motives for entering higher education similarly, with the highest importance being attached by students in all of the institutions to the motive 'to obtain access to more interesting jobs'. The conclusion reached by the investigators is expressed as follows:

> the three institutions have a markedly different image in their own eyes and, it was thought, in the eyes of the public. From a national point of view they were divided both by the binary line and by what in America would be termed their different 'missions'. Yet their candidates for admission seemed to have almost precisely similar motives for entering higher education and very similar reasons for accepting places at each of the three institutions.[222]

It is not clear that the questions asked in these two instances make it possible to comment confidently on the nature of student attitudes and perceptions. What is more clear is that different choices *are* made on the basis of some form of differential image or motive. Two research projects have made it clear that however students may define their motives, they do in fact form separate constituencies.

In the Lancaster University investigation of fifth and sixth formers to school, work and higher education, carried out in 1975, the conclusion reached was that students separated out into different constituencies. The students who give a university as their first choice of higher education institution for the most part also gave universities as their second and third choices. Only 8 per cent of those who gave a university as their first choice 'seriously considered another type of institution a desirable second choice' (for three-quarters of them it was a polytechnic); a further 1 per cent had considered another type of institution as their third choice. The investigators found that those whose first choice was a polytechnic were 'slightly less exclusive in their tastes' (a quarter had a second choice of another type of institution, and another 20 per cent gave another type as their third choice). College of education students were 'closely wedded to that type of institution'. The final verdict was that 'it does appear from this evidence that each category of institution has a fairly well defined clientele of its own'.[223]

By the time this project was being reported on the colleges of education and some other institutions were forming colleges and institutes of higher education, and entrants to three of these colleges were studied between 1976 and 1979. A conclusion reached was that 'about two-fifths of B.A. students would have preferred to have gone to university but very few students would have preferred a polytechnic'. Of BEd students in these three colleges, in fact, only 3 per cent would have preferred a place at a polytechnic (13 per cent would have preferred a university). Of BA students overall only 4 per cent would have preferred a polytechnic (45 per cent would have preferred a university).[224]

The background discussed above has obviously had a sustained impact on generations of students' thinking about what to expect of a university education (as well as of an education at different categories of university) on the one hand, and of an education at a technical college, late nineteenth-century polytechnic, college of advanced technology, 1970s polytechnic, or college or institute of higher education, on the other hand. The images of the institutions have been composite ones formed from a variety of historical elements, and influencing not only prospective students, but also those who surround them – schoolteachers, advisers, parents and potential employers. A group of researchers at University College, Swansea, in the late 1970s, explored both students' attitudes to employment, and employers' opinions of university and polytechnic graduates. The former study confirmed earlier ones which showed that students in higher education had strong vocational motivation for entering it. The interesting finding was that in this case it was the university students who had the stronger vocational reasons for attending their institutions ('university gives a more interesting job'). The conclusion was that a high proportion of polytechnic students had tried and failed to gain admission to a university, and that polytechnics were therefore

> chosen by students not so much because of positive reasons of career orientation, but as a second best university education . . . It is difficult to see how polytechnics can be regarded as different but equal to universities when their intake of students is clearly inferior to that of universities . . . Whatever the intention, amongst students and careers advisers, polytechnics are considered not just as different, but inferior to universities.[225]

The parallel study of employers' opinions produced the clear view that employers considered that there was a difference of academic quality between university and polytechnic graduates (71 per cent perceived a difference and 29 per cent did not). Of the ones who perceived a difference, 83 per cent thought that 'universities produce better students academically and intellectually'. Reasons given included the lower standard of polytechnic courses, the poor attitude of polytechnic students and the practical orientation of the polytechnics. Employers of university and polytechnic graduates sought almost identical qualities, but mentioned leadership potential significantly more often in the case of university students. University students were more frequently seen as 'potential higher management, whereas polytechnic students were seen as filling posts at a lower level'. The researchers felt that the most surprising and worrying finding was the 'lack of importance given to vocational training by employers'. The crux of the analysis in both of these pieces of research is as follows:

> there is agreement between employers and both university and polytechnic students that vocational training was not a factor which was important when a firm was looking for graduates . . . The many differences between employers' perception of university and polytechnic graduates suggest that the polytechnics have a distinctive character. However, it appears that polytechnics are viewed as producing second-rate graduates both intellectually and socially.[226]

There has been little unanimity amongst students, employers, the institutions of higher education, and the public at large, as to the identity and purposes of institutions on either side of the binary line.

As throughout the history of higher education in Britain over the past two centuries, new institutions have produced diversity, but have not disposed of hierarchy. Expectations of higher education, whether those of students and their advisers, of their prospective employers, or of those who plan and provide the institutions and what they offer, incorporate that awareness of the present, as well as flourishing legacies of the past. The arguments and concepts enshrined in the most familiar literature look less stable and serviceable when set amongst the expectations and opinions of those whom the spokesmen were perhaps only dimly aware of as audiences.

IMPLICATIONS

We have taken a number of elements necessary to an historical study of expectations in the nineteenth and twentieth centuries, and we have explored mainly the more recent ones with an eye to available evidence of the attitudes of the various constituencies involved. We have not systematically analysed discrete groups, and we have had to omit, for example, art, commercial and teacher education. Our analysis and discussion have indicated the ambiguous and controversial nature of the concepts concerned in discussions of higher education in recent decades. They have demonstrated how open are questions about the 'vocational', 'relevant', 'professional' or other – including opposite – expectations of what higher education can offer or produce. The discussions have been situated in a long-standing historical debate about dichotomies and polarities. A version of this discussion occurs in an American commentary on 'Value Patterns and Power Conflict in American Higher Education' in 1969, in which John D. Millett, chancellor of the Ohio Board of Regents, discussed the two cultural goals of American higher education – 'humane learning' and 'professional education'. He suggested that value patterns amongst scholars prevented them from acknowledging 'that the major objective of American higher education is professional education, is the preparation of talent for meaningful and productive participation in the professional pursuits of American society'. Whilst reluctant to admit that purpose,

> we are nonetheless vigorous in our pursuit of it. At the same time . . .
> we are almost all of us loud in our declaration of loyalty to the concept
> of liberal education or humane learning, but exceedingly inept in any
> endeavor to give such purpose real meaning or process.[227]

This reluctance, conflict and confusion expresses the complex problems of values involved in the history of autonomous and mass education, universities and polytechnics, functions and institutions. It reasserts the difficulty of defining the frontier between the liberal and the vocational, and of acting on the basis of the definition. Burton R. Clark, in American but internationally recognizable terms, talked in the early 1960s of the tension between 'the opening door' to higher education through which new and expanded groups of students were passing, and 'the closing door' of many public and private colleges applying more rigorous criteria of selection. The nature of work was changing, living standards were rising, expansion was running in parallel with the arrival of students of lower social class origins, with the need for more experts of all kinds:

> the strain between the open door and selectivity may be seen in large
> measure as a clash between the ideal of the specialist and the older
> ideal of the cultured man. Max Weber maintained forty years ago that
> this clash of ideals was at the root of nearly all educational problems
> and debates in modern society.[228]

In Britain, as in the United States and elsewhere, the 'clash' has resolved itself into the search for alternative curricula or new institutions, the emergence of new ways of tracking and routing students, and agonies over the degree of responsiveness and accountability of institutions to outside forces and agencies. The demands for accountability have, especially in the 1970s and 1980s, grown to unprecedented levels. In the United States the mounting fear has been of higher education 'becoming more governmental',[229] being subjected to increasing state and federal regulation and pressure. In Britain, as we have seen, there have been protracted disagreements about the definition of different sectors of higher education – and therefore about the different nature and extent of their accountability and its channels. Economic vagaries, manpower needs, and considerations of national defence, technological viability and future standards of living and social stability, have all affected the attitudes of the constituencies we have considered, and have brought 'pragmatic considerations' into play: 'the society pays for education because it is thought to be to the advantage of those who get it'.[230]

Against these trends, it has often become unpopular or difficult to assert 'traditional' values of 'humane learning' or 'liberal education', or even – as in the 1920s and 1930s – to suggest where they can or should coincide. It has not always been impossible, however, to assert these values within the context of the technological, industrial and economic pressures themselves. An example from the political world was offered by Michael Stewart in 1957, arguing the need for a royal commission on higher education. It was the duty of universities, he told the House of Commons, to meet society's vocational needs, but also to hand on to the next generation 'standards of values and beliefs on which our civilization rests'. In planning the distribution of resources, he argued, the whole structure of technology and technical education was 'ultimately determined by our idea of the place and purpose of a university ... No sound relation between university and technical education can be established without clear ideas as to the function of a university'. He indicated also that industrialists and scientists like Sir Alexander Fleck, A. D. Bonham Carter and Sir John Cockroft, had made it clear that industry was asking of the universities a supply of graduates 'who can think and act for themselves, capable of choosing between truth and falsehood, wisdom and folly, beauty and ugliness; nor can it be suggested that the State, the public corporations, local government and commerce need men and women less qualified in these respects'.

Stewart coupled these emphases on liberal values with the declaration that it was 'not right to suggest that the universities of Great Britain are indifferent to the problems of fitting students to life in the modern world'.[231] Historically, it is important to see what patterns of popular opinion are reflected or challenged by statements of this kind.

A history of expectations obviously implies an analysis not only of this balance, but also – as we have seen particularly in the case of students' expectations – of the tension between what people have *wished* to happen or *hoped* would happen in and as a result of higher education, and on the other hand what they have expected *would* happen. Furthermore, concepts like 'expectations' and 'constituencies' have to be broken down historically into meaningful components (categories of student, scale and nature of company, and so on). The concepts have to be seen as historically fluid, especially in the conditions of the second half of the twentieth century. Certain kinds of expectation can be seen to have been more central, differently defined, in some economic situations, climates of opinion, hopes of employment rewards or satisfaction, than in others.

Ultimately, the question explored here in relatively recent terms is one of the meaning and use of the past. The nature of the analysis informs judgements about how we capitalize on the past, erode it, adapt it or reject it. The picture presented here is one in which traditions, familiar values, rights, choices, have remained as part of the present pattern of higher education provision, difficulties and decision-making needs. What the history demonstrates most in this case is the insecurity of the categories and concepts used in the organization of debate across the decades, the lack of clear permanent distinctions. That debate has failed, as in the case of schooling, to profit from the explorations of the early decades of this century, when men like J.J. Findlay and A.N. Whitehead rejected the 'sharp antithesis' that had been discovered 'between liberal and technical education', because they saw an intimate 'alliance between the two; the ends both of vocation and of leisure need to be pursued in unison, if not always in conjunction'.[232] The history of the decisions, institutions, concepts, involved is more complex but more revealing when the attitudes and expectations of others than the decision-makers, providers and institutional spokesmen are moved into the centre of the historical analysis.

Notes

1 Board of Education *Report of the Consultative Committee on the Education of the Adolescent* (London, 1926), pp. 115–16.
2 Anon., *Metropolitan University. Remarks on the Ministerial Plan of a Central University Examining Board* (London, 1836), pp. 3–4.
3 See, for example, Joseph Ben-David, 'Science and the University System', *International Review of Education*, vol. 18, no. 1, 1972, pp. 44–5.
4 University Grants Committee, *University Development from 1935 to 1947* (London, 1948), p. 60.
5 Michael Sanderson, *The Universities and British Industry 1850–1970* (London, 1972), pp. 6–8.
6 David Redwood, 'The Philosophy of University Education in England from the Reforms at Oxford and Cambridge (1877), to 1914', University of Manchester PhD thesis, 1951, ch. III.
7 Stephen Cotgrove, 'Education and Occupation', *British Journal of Sociology*, vol. XIII, no. 1, 1962, p. 34.
8 D.S.L. Cardwell, *The Organisation of Science in England: A Retrospect* (London, 1957), p. 185.
9 Eric Ashby, *Technology and the Academics: An Essay on Universities and the Scientific Revolution* (London, 1963), p. 48.
10 Joan N. Burstyn, *Victorian Education and the Ideal of Womanhood* (London, 1980), pp. 41, 52.
11 W.M. MacQueen, 'The Current Over-Emphasis on Technological Universities', *The Vocational Aspect of Education*, no. 8, 1956, p. 3.
12 W.H.G. Armytage, *Civic Universities: Aspects of a British Tradition* (London, 1955), pp. 221–5.
13 Sanderson, *The Universities and British Industry*, pp. 2–3.
14 Michael Sanderson, *The Universities in the Nineteenth Century* (London, 1975), pp. 131–2.
15 Federation of British Industries, *Report of the Conference on Industry and the Universities* (London, 1950), p. 79.
16 W.H. Brock and A.J. Meadows, 'Physics, Chemistry and Higher Education in the U.K.', *Studies in Higher Education*, vol. 2, no. 2, pp. 115–17. See also Brian Simon, *A Student's View of the Universities* (London, 1943), pp. 28–9.
17 Quoted in Sir Walter Moberly, *The Crisis in the University* (London 1949), p. 243.
18 Sheldon Rothblatt, 'The Past and Future Freedom of the British University' (review of Sanderson, *The Universities in the Nineteenth Century*), *Minerva*, vol. XIV, no. 2, 1976, pp. 253–4.
19 A.H. Halsey, 'The Changing Functions of Universities in Advanced Industrial Societies', *Harvard Educational Review*, vol. 30, no. 2, 1960, p. 127.
20 Abraham Flexner, *Universities: American, English, German* (New York, 1920), pp. 255–7.
21 A.B. Robertson, 'Sir Joshua Girling Fitch, 1824–1903: A Study in the

Formation of English Educational Opinion', Newcastle University PhD thesis, 1980, pp. 174–5.

22 Sanderson, *The Universities and British Industry*, p. 391.

23 Quoted in *The Times Review of Industry and Technology*, 'Industry and the University: Need for a Mutual Change of Outlook', vol. 3, no. 29 (new series), 1949, p. 6.

24 Quoted in *Nature*, 'Education and Industry', vol. 187, 1960, p. 470.

25 *The Times Review of Industry and Technology*, 'Industry–University Debate', vol. 4, no. 8, 1966, p. 75.

26 Committee of Inquiry into the Engineering Profession, *Engineering Our Future* (Finniston Report) (London, 1980), pp. 80–1.

27 H.M. Finniston, 'University Science and Industry', *Political Quarterly*, vol. 38, no. 1, 1967, p. 29.

28 Engineering Employers' Federation, Submission to the Secretary of State for Industry on the Finniston Report of the Committee of Inquiry into the Engineering Profession, mimeo, April 1980, p. 1.

29 Flexner, *Universities: American, English, German*, p. 5.

30 Kenneth R. Minogue, *The Concept of a University* (London, 1973), p. 51. See also Colin Crouch and Stephen Mennell, *The Universities: Pressures and Prospects* (London, 1972), pp. 1–3; J.F. Maitland-Jones, 'What Do Students Expect from the University?', in John H. MacCallum Scott (ed.), *University Independence: The Main Questions* (London, 1971), p. 116.

31 S.P. Chambers, *Education and Industry. The Chuter Ede Lecture* (London, 1964), pp. 3–4. For the university response see Eric E. Robinson, *The New Polytechnics* (London, 1968), p. 80.

32 Anthea Collins, *Non-Specialist Graduates in Industry* (Birmingham, 1955), p. 7.

33 Lord Butler, *The Responsibilities of Education: The Inaugural P.D. Leake Lecture* (London, 1968), p. 21.

34 Collins, *Non-Specialist Graduates in Industry*, pp. 4–5.

35 Committee on Higher Education, *Higher Education*. Evidence – Part One, vol. F (Memorandum submitted by the Ministry of Education) (London, 1973), p. 1891.

36 For a discussion of this theme see Harold Silver, Introduction to *Equal Opportunity in Education* (London, 1973), pp. xxvii–xxviii.

37 A.G. Watts, 'Higher Education and Employment', *Universities Quarterly*, vol. 29, no. 1, 1974, p. 97.

38 Brian Chapman, 'Education as a Political Exercise', *Nature*, vol. 20, no. 4924, 1964, p. 1069.

39 P.H. Calderbank, 'The Balance between Engineering Science and Practical Experience', in R.E. Bell and A.J. Youngson (eds), *Present and Future in Higher Education* (London, 1973), p. 55.

40 David Barran, 'Industrial Requirements from the Universities', in MacCallum, *University Independence*, pp. 123–4.

41 D. Chapman, *Industry and the Role of the Universities – Collision or Co-operation* (Sheffield, 1968), pp. 10–11.

42 Richard Lynn, *The Universities and the Business Community* (London, n.d. [1969]), pp. 11–13.

43 House of Commons, *Reports from the Expenditure Committee, together with the minutes of the evidence taken before the education and arts sub-committee in session 1971–72 . . . Session 1972–3: Further and Higher Education*, vol. II, Evidence (London, 1972), p. 278.

44 E.G. Barber, *Further Education for a Changing Industry* (London, 1977). pp. 7–8.

45 D.T.L. Jones, *The Education of Scientists for Industry: Report of a Survey of the Views of Professional Scientists* (London, 1969), p. 35.

46 House of Commons, *Report from the Expenditure Committee* (1972), pp. 278–9.

47 Dennis Child et al., 'Parents' Expectations of a University', *Universities Quarterly*, vol. 25, no. 4, 1971, pp. 486–9.

48 Louis Moss, 'Education and the People: A Study of Public Attitudes towards Education and the Education Act', *The Social Survey*, new series 46/1, mimeo, 1945, p. 11.

49 Peter Scott and W.V. Wallace, in Association of University Teachers and *The Times Higher Education Supplement*, papers presented to a one-day conference organised on 23 February 1978, pp. 44, 12.

50 Simon, *A Student's View of the Universities*, p. 29.

51 Chapman, *Industry and the Role of the Universities*, pp. 8–9.

52 Sanderson, *The Universities and British Industry*, p. 363.

53 R.F. Lambert, 'Is a Degree Really Necessary?', *The Times Review of Industry and Technology*, vol. 4, no. 10, 1966, p. 91.

54 *Nature*, 'The University Graduate and Industry', vol. 174, pp. 115–16.

55 Sir Raymond Priestley, *The English Civic Universities. A Paper Read to Teaching Officers of Overseas Universities at Cambridge in August 1949*, pp. 5–6.

56 Crouch and Mennell, *The Universities: Pressures and Prospects*, p. 47.

57 See, for example, Richard C. Griffiths, *The Prospect for Universities: From Robbins to 1984. A Page Fund lecture* (Swansea, 1974), p. 3.

58 For Leicester see Jack Simmons, *New University* (Leicester, 1959), especially pp. 70–1; for Keele see R.A. Lowe, 'Determinants of a University's Curriculum', *British Journal of Educational Studies*, vol. XVII, no. 1, 1969, pp. 41–53.

59 Trades Union Congress, *Higher Education* (London, 1956), p. 12.

60 G. Templeman, 'Research and Education in a New University', *Nature*, vol. 202, 1964, p. 636.

61 Tony Mansell and Harold Silver, 'Themes in Higher Education: Britain, America and Germany', in W.E. Marsden (ed.), *Post-War Curriculum Development: An Historical Appraisal* (Leicester, 1979), pp. 64–5; Minogue, *The Concept of a University*, pp. 3–6; Rothblatt, 'The Past and Future Freedom of the British University', pp. 255–6.

62 T.W. Bamford, *The University of Hull: The First Fifty Years* (Oxford, 1978), pp. 25–43.

63 Quoted in Crouch and Mennell, *The Universities: Pressures and Prospects*, p. 5.

64 Committee on Higher Education, *Higher Education*, Evidence – Part One, vol. A (Memorandum submitted by the National Union of Students), pp.

230 *Education as history*

219-20, 231.
65 See, for example, Graeme C. Moodie, *The Universities: A Royal Commission?* (London, 1959), p. 4.
66 Sanderson, *The Universities and British Industry*, p. 17.
67 Association of Universities of the British Commonwealth, *Conference of the Home Universities* (London, 1950), pp. 10-11, 20-5.
68 Jack Butterworth *et al.*, 'Towards Excellence', *Universities Quarterly*, vol. 23, no. 3, 1969, pp. 259-60.
69 Chapman, *Industry and the Role of the Universities*, p. 13.
70 Engineering Employers' Federation, *Graduates in Engineering* (London, 1977), pp. 12-13.
71 Lord Hailsham, 'New and Larger Universities', *Universities Quarterly*, vol. 15, no. 2, 1961, p. 125.
72 In David Daiches (ed.), *The Idea of a New University. An Experiment in Sussex* (London, 1964), p. 182.
73 Sir W.L. Bragg, 'The Place of Technological Education in University Studies', in Association of Universities of the British Commonwealth, *Conference of the Home Universities 1949* (London, 1949), pp. 73-6.
74 For reactions to Bragg's analysis see *Conference of the Home Universities 1949* (contributions by Dr P. Dunsheath, Prof. A.F. Burstall, Sir Roderic Hill, Sir John Hobhouse and Prof. J.F. Baker).
75 Michael W. Perrin *et al.*, *The Case for the Technical University*, reprinted from *The Times Educational Supplement* (London, 1950).
76 Butler, *The Responsibilities of Education*, pp. 16-17.
77 See, for instance, Maurice Broady, 'Down with Academic Standards', *New Universities Quarterly*, vol. 33, no. 1, 1978, p. 3.
78 Malcolm Cross and R.G. Jobling, 'The English New Universities - A Preliminary Enquiry', *Universities Quarterly*, vol. 23, no. 2, 1969, pp. 172-3.
79 University Grants Committee, *University Development 1957-1962* (London, 1963), pp. 85, 94.
80 Priestley, *The English Civic Universities*, pp. 5-6.
81 For a discussion of 'mere survival' see Eric Ashby, *Technology and the Academics* (London, 1958), edition of 1963, pp. 67-8, and for a reaction see Mansell and Silver, 'Themes in Higher Education', pp. 64-5.
82 University Grants Committee, *A Note on Technology in Universities* (London, 1950), p. 4.
83 Redwood, 'The Philosophy of University Education in England', *passim*, but especially vol. I, pp. 97-8.
84 M.L. Oliphant, 'University or Institute of Technology?', *Universities Quarterly*, vol. 4, no. 1, 1949, pp. 20-2.
85 Robert Peers and P.J. Madgwick, 'Problems and Attitudes in Higher Technological Education', *The Vocational Aspect of Education*, vol. 15, 1963, pp. 88-90.
86 Ministry of Education, *Higher Technological Education: Report of a Special Committee Appointed in April 1944* (Percy Committee) (London, 1945), pp. 5-6, 10-12. See also Association of Technical Institutions and Associations of Principals of Technical Institutions, *Future Development of Higher*

Technological Education (London, 1951), pp. 1-5.
87 Donald Hutchings, 'Sixth Form Scientists in Search of an Image', *Universities Quarterly*, vol. 17, no. 3, 1963, pp. 254-9; Donald Hutchings, *The Science Undergraduate: A Study of Science Students at Five English Universities* (Oxford, 1967), p. 9. For the quality of recruits to engineering and technology in the 1970s see E.G. Barber, *Further Education for a Changing Industry* (London, 1977), especially pp. 6-8.
88 Richard Startup and Ranbir Singh Birk, 'The Academic Careers of Science Students', *Universities Quarterly*, vol. 29, no. 2, 1975, pp. 220-1.
89 Committee appointed by the Lord President of the Council (Barlow Committee), *Scientific Man-Power* (London, 1946), p. 6.
90 Association of University Teachers and *The Times Higher Education Supplement, The Universities and Britain's Future* (London, 1978), p. 31.
91 Flexner, *Universities: American, English, German*, pp. 29-30, 162-5.
92 Lord Hailsham, 'Functions of Universities', *The Engineer*, vol. 212, 1961, p. 735. See also Richard Hoggart, *Higher Education and Cultural Change: A Teacher's View* (Newcastle upon Tyne, 1965), p. 12.
93 Nuffield College, Education Sub-Committee, *The Problem Facing British Universities* (London, 1948), pp. 88-9.
94 Chapman, *Industry and the Role of the Universities*, p. 11. See also J.T. Allanson, 'The Modern University', *Conference*, vol. 5, no. 3, 1968, pp. 17-18.
95 Simon, *A Student's View of the Universities*, p. 109.
96 M.T. Gammage, 'Newspaper Opinion and Education: A Study of the Influence of the Birmingham Provincial Press on Developments in Education, 1870-1902', University of Leicester MEd thesis, 1972, p. 254.
97 Redwood, 'The Philosophy of University Education in England', especially pp. 49-63.
98 Lowe, 'Determinants of a University's Curriculum', pp. 43-9.
99 For example, the University of Sussex. See the contributions by W.G. Stone and Lord Salisbury to Daiches, *The Idea of a New University*.
100 See Hailsham, 'Functions of Universities', p. 736; Minogue, *The Concept of a University*, especially Part III; Lord Eustace Percy, *Education at the Crossroads* (London, n.d.), pp. 4-5; Lord Simmon of Wythenshawe, 'University Crisis? A Consumer's View', *Universities Quarterly*, vol. 4, no. 1, 1949, pp. 74-5; House of Commons, *Report from the Expenditure Committee*, 1972 (Memorandum submitted by the Committee of Vice-Chancellors and Principals), pp. 596-9.
101 Professor John MacMurray, in Association of Universities of the British Commonwealth, *Report of Proceedings of the Sixth Congress of the Universities of the British Commonwealth 1948* (London, 1951), p. 104.
102 Kingsley Amis et al., 'The Threat of the Practical', *The Observer*, 26 February 1961, p. 21.
103 Oliphant, 'University or Institute of Technology?', pp. 20-1.
104 See Stephen Cotgrove, 'Education and Occupation', *British Journal of Sociology*, vol. XIII, no. 1, 1962, pp. 37-8.
105 Butterworth et al., 'Towards Excellence', pp. 259-60.
106 The main expression of this preoccupation was the University Grants

232   *Education as history*

Committee's *Report of the Committee on University Teaching Methods* (Hale Committee) (London, 1964).
107 K.A. Percy and F.W. Salter, 'Student and Staff Perceptions and "The Pursuit of Excellence" in British Higher Education', *Higher Education*, vol. 5, no. 4, 1976, pp. 459–68.
108 A.H. Halsey, 'Are British Universities Capable of Change?', *New Universities Quarterly*, vol. 33, no. 4, 1979, pp. 408, 411–12.
109 G.S. Brosan, in Butterworth *et al.*, 'Towards Excellence', pp. 265–7.
110 Eric E. Robinson, *The New Polytechnics* (London, 1968), pp. 74–5.
111 In F.R. Jevons and H.D. Turner (eds), *What Kinds of Graduates Do We Need?* (London, 1972), pp. 13–14.
112 Association of Technical Institutions and Association of Principals of Technical Institutions, *Statement of Policy on the Future Development of Higher Technological Education* (1951), pp. 1–3.
113 Jean Floud, 'The Demands of Society', in Marjorie Reeves (ed.), *Eighteen Plus: Unity and Diversity in Higher Education* (London, 1965), p. 19.
114 F.M. Katz and Cecily N. Katz, 'Occupational Aspirations of University Students', *Australian Journal of Higher Education*, vol. 3, no. 1, 1967, pp. 8–11. An earlier Australian study by Hugh D. Philip *et al.*, *The University and Its Community* (Sydney, 1964), had concluded that 70 per cent of students entered the university for vocational reasons (p. 44). A 1950s American study had reached more ambiguous conclusions about vocational and academic goals – see Rose K. Goldsen *et al.*, *What College Students Think* (Princeton, NJ, 1960), pp. 7, 10, 21–2, 209.
115 F.M. Katz and Cecily N. Katz, 'Students' Definition of the Objectives of a University Education', *Australian Journal of Higher Education*, vol. 3, no. 2, 1968, pp. 111–18.
116 A.A. Dole, 'Stability of Reasons for Going to College', *Journal of Educational Research*, vol. 63, no. 8, 1970, pp. 375–7. An American project which produced somewhat different results was Burton R. Clark *et al.*, *Students and Colleges: Interaction and Change* (Berkeley, 1972). The students questioned gave priority to general over vocational education in three of the eight colleges studied – three selective, non-denominational, high-status colleges – Antioch, Reed and Swarthmore. The reverse was true of the state universities studied (see especially pp. 127–32).
117 Louis Cohen, 'Sixth-Form Pupils and Their Views of Higher Education', *Journal of Curriculum Studies*, vol. 2, no. 1, 1970, pp. 68–72.
118 Robert Oxtoby, 'Educational and Vocational Objectives of Polytechnic Students', *Universities Quarterly*, vol. 26, no. 1, 1971, pp. 87–8.
119 Richard Startup, 'Why Go to the University?', *Universities Quarterly*, vol. 26, no. 3, 1972, pp. 319–30.
120 Watts, 'Higher Education and Employment', pp. 97–8.
121 Clive Williams, *Determinants of University/College Choice in Wales: Summary Report of a Survey Commissioned by the University of Wales* (Cardiff, 1974), pp. 69–71.
122 Lex Donaldson, 'Students' Perceptions of the Binary Policy', *Higher Education Review*, vol. v, no. 2, 1973, p. 53.
123 Alan Gordon and Gareth Williams, *Attitudes of Fifth and Sixth Formers to*

School, Work and Higher Education (report submitted to the Department of Education and Science) (Lancaster, 1977), p. 179. For further related discussions see Clem Adelman and Ian Gibbs, *A Study of Student Choice in the Context of Institutional Change: Final Report* (a research project funded by the DES) (Reading, 1979), part III; C.L. Jones and A.F. McPherson, 'Why Don't Those Girls Go to University?', 'Do They Choose or Are They Pushed?', 'College Has Been a Second-Best', *Times Educational Supplement*, 2, 9 and 16 June 1972.

124 Gareth Williams and Alan Gordon, '16 and 19 Year Olds: Attitudes to Education', *Higher Education Bulletin*, vol. 4, no. 1, 1975, p. 30.

125 Frank Brian Fidler, 'Sixth Formers' Choice of Higher Education Institution', University of Lancaster MA dissertation, 1979, pp. 43-4.

126 Cohen, 'Sixth-Form Pupils and Their Views of Higher Education', pp. 71-2; Startup, 'Why Go to the University?', pp. 328-30.

127 F. Musgrove, 'Educational Values in a Technological University', *Durham Research Review*, vol. 5, no. 20, pp. 230, 237.

128 J.L. Brennan and K.A. Percy, 'What Do Students Want? An Analysis of Staff and Student Perceptions in British Higher Education', in A. Bonboir (ed.), *Proceedings of 2nd Congress of E.A.R.D.H.E.* (Louvain-la-Neuve, 1976), vol. 1, p. 126.

129 Johann-Ulrich Sandburger and Georg Lind, 'The Outcomes of University Education: Some Empirical Findings on Aims and Expectations in the Federal Republic of Germany', *Higher Education*, no. 8, 1979, pp. 182-3, 200.

130 For other discussions of the intellectual goals of higher education, see Allanson, 'The Modern University', pp. 17-18; Donald A. Biggs, 'Recent Research on British Students: A Brief Analysis', *Research in Education*, no. 15, 1976, p. 83; Daiches, *The Idea of a New University* (especially contributions by W.G. Stone and Granville Hawkins); University of London Institute of Education, *Conference on Objectives in Higher Education* (London, 1969), p. 3 (quoting Richard Hoggart); Bryan Wilson, 'The Needs of Students', in Reeves, *Eighteen Plus*, pp. 53-60.

131 Brennan and Percy, 'What Do Students Want', pp. 125-50.

132 University Grants Committee, *University Development 1952-1957* (London, 1958), pp. 37-8.

133 University Grants Committee, *University Development from 1935 to 1947* (London, 1948), p. 60.

134 Butler, *The Responsibilities of Education*, pp. 21-2.

135 Edward Boyle, 'Parliament and University Policy', *Minerva*, vol. 5, no. 1, 1966, p. 17.

136 Butler, *The Responsibilities of Education*, pp. 36.

137 Philip et al., *The University and its Community*, p. 16. Relevant to this discussion is Martin Trow's distinction between the 'mass' or 'popular' functions of higher education on the one hand, and the 'élite' or 'autonomous' functions on the other. See, for example, Martin Trow, 'Elite and Popular Functions in American Higher Education', in Roy Niblett (ed.), *Higher Education: Demand and Response* (London, 1968).

138 Quoted in *Nature*, 'University Education in Britain', vol. 187, no. 4739,

1960, p. 720.
139 George Tolley, 'Access, Community and Curriculum', in Norman Evans (ed.), *Education Beyond School: Higher Education for a Changing Context* (London, 1980), p. 80.
140 Keith Hampson, 'Conservatives and Higher Education: We Must Regain Our Sense of Vision', *The Times Higher Education Supplement*, 12 December 1976, p. 13.
141 Committee on the Civil Service, *Report of the Committee, 1966–68* (Fulton Report), vol. 1 (London, 1968), pp. 80–1.
142 Association of Universities of the British Commonwealth, *Home Universities Conference 1956* (London, 1956), p. 74.
143 T.E. Dean, in AUT and *The Times Higher Education Supplement*, one-day conference, 1978, p. 21.
144 *Home Universities Conference 1956*, p. 76.
145 Committee on Higher Education, *Higher Education*, Evidence – Part One, vol. B (Memorandum submitted by the Federation of British Industries), pp. 573–4.
146 Committee on Higher Education, *Higher Education*, Evidence – Part One, vol. E (Memorandum submitted by the Trades Union Congress), pp. 1441–2.
147 In *The Times Review of Industry and Technology*, 'Robbins: The Great Debate', vol. 1, no. 8, 1963, p. 73.
148 H.M. Finniston, 'University Science and Industry', *Political Quarterly*, vol. 38, no. 1, 1967, pp. 32–3.
149 Sir James Mountford, *Keele: An Historical Critique* (London, 1972), ch. 4.
150 See, for example, UGC, *University Development from 1947 to 1952*, p. 45.
151 F.H. Perkins, ICI, in *The Times Review of Industry and Technology*, 'Robbins: The Great Debate', p. 74.
152 M.C. McCarthy, *The Employment of Highly Specialised Graduates: A Comparative study in the United Kingdom and the United States of America* (Science Policy Studies No. 3) (London, 1968), pp. 1–3.
153 *Nature*, 'Education and Industry', vol. 187, no. 4736, 1960, p. 471.
154 B.J. Holloway, in Jevons and Turner, *What Kinds of Graduates Do We Need?*, pp. 29–31.
155 Council for Scientific Policy, *Enquiry into the Flow of Candidates in Science and Technology into Higher Education* (Dainton Report) (London, 1968), pp. 87, 90.
156 B. Chapman, 'Education as a Political Exercise', p. 1069.
157 House of Commons, *Report from the Expenditure Committee* (1972) (Memorandum by the British Railways Board), pp. 284–5.
158 Barran, 'Industrial Requirements from the Universities', in Scott, *University Independence*, pp. 120–2.
159 FBI, *Report of the Conference on Industry and the Universities* (1950), pp. 36–8, 51–2, 80–2.
160 Committee on the Civil Service, *Report*, p. 78.
161 Alain Touraine, 'Decline or Transformation of the Universities?' *Prospects*, vol. X, no. 2, 1980, p. 192.
162 Oliphant, 'University or Institute of Technology?', pp. 20–2.

163 Committee on Manpower Resources for Science and Technology, *The Flow into Employment of Scientists, Engineers and Technologists: Report of the Working Group on Manpower for Scientific Growth* (Swann Report) (London, 1968), pp. 74-7.
164 UGC, *University Development: Report on the Years 1947 to 1952*, p. 46; *University Development 1952-1957*, pp. 39-41.
165 *Nature*, 'The Function of Universities', vol. 182, 1958, p. 1625.
166 Moodie, *The Universities: A Royal Commission?*, p. 8.
167 The tradition in which this approach would be located would include Cardinal Newman, Thorstein Veblen and Robert M. Hutchins.
168 Lord Eustace Percy, *Education at the Crossroads* (London, n.d.), p. 63.
169 Asa Briggs, quoted in Daiches, *The Idea of a New University*, p. 200.
170 Association of University Teachers, *Universities in the 1970s* (London, n.d.), paragraphs 11-14.
171 Broady, 'Down with Academic Standards', p. 17.
172 House of Commons, *Report from the Expenditure Committee* (1972) (GKN Group Submission), p. 278.
173 Peter Marris, *The Experience of Higher Education* (London, 1964), pp. 175-6.
174 The point is made strongly by Guy Neave, in 'Academic Drift: Some Views from Europe', *Studies in Higher Education*, vol. 4, no. 2, 1979, p. 148.
175 Committee on Higher Education, *Higher Education*, Evidence - Part One, vol. D (Memorandum submitted by the Joint Advisory Committee on Engineering Education), p. 1220.
176 For the fullest analysis of this debate see Sheldon Rothblatt, *Tradition and Change in English Liberal Education: An Essay in History and Culture* (London, 1976).
177 Quoted in Sanderson, *The Universities and British Industry*, p. 363.
178 A.B. Pippard, 'The Structure of a Morally Committed University' in John Lawlor (ed.), *Higher Education: Patterns of Change in the 1970s* (London, 1972), pp. 69-87; J.L. Montrose, 'Technology and the Universities', *The Universities Review*, vol. 29, no. 1, 1956, pp. 25-6. For attitudes to liberal studies see J. Heywood, 'Technological Education', in H.J. Butcher (ed.), *Educational Research in Britain* (London, 1968), pp. 305-7.
179 For student attitudes see Eric Ashby and Mary Anderson, *The Rise of the Student Estate in Britain* (London, 1970), pp. 100-2; Startup and Birk, 'The Academic Careers of Science Students', p. 221.
180 Committee on Higher Education, *Higher Education*, Evidence - Part One, vol. B (Memorandum submitted by the Institution of Production Engineers), p. 406.
181 Committee of Inquiry into the Engineering Profession, *Engineering Our Future* (Finniston Report) (London, 1980), pp. 83-7, 91-2.
182 Lord Butler, *The Responsibilities of Education*, p. 39.
183 Ibid.
184 Engineering Employers' Federation, *Submission to the Secretary of State for Industry on the Finniston Report of the Committee of Inquiry into the Engineering Profession* (London, 1980, mimeo), pp. 2-3.

236   *Education as history*

185   Council for Scientific Policy, *Enquiry into the Flow of Candidates in Science and Technology into Higher Education*, pp. 84-5.
186   Charles Carter, 'A Programme for 1969-1989', *Universities Quarterly*, vol. 23, no. 3, 1969, p. 309.
187   John Stuart Mill, *Inaugural Address Delivered to the University of St Andrews* (London, 1867), p. 4.
188   See John Pratt and Tyrrell Burgess, *Polytechnics: A Report* (London, 1974) for the elaboration of the theory of upward institutional 'drift' (especially pp. 23-30).
189   Committee on Higher Education, *Higher Education*, Evidence - Part One, vol. C (Memorandum submitted by the Association of Education Committees), p. 760.
190   Committee on Higher Education, *Higher Education*, p. 8.
191   Boyle, 'Parliament and University Policy', p. 9.
192   J.R. Lukes, 'The Binary Policy: A Critical Study', *Universities Quarterly*, vol. 22, no. 1, 1967, pp. 6-39. Martin Trow, in 'Binary Dilemmas - An American view', *Higher Education Review*, vol. I, no. 3, 1969, discusses Robbins's view that the binary system was based on misconceptions about the nature of a university (p. 6).
193   House of Commons, *Report from the Expenditure Committee* (1972) (Memorandum submitted by the Association of University Teachers), pp. 550-1.
194   Pratt and Burgess, *Polytechnics: A Report*, pp. 23-30, 174-5.
195   John Ranelagh, *Science, Education and Industry* (Old Queen St Papers, *Politics Today*, no. 2, London, 1978), p. 32.
196   House of Commons, Select Committee on Science and Technology, *Third Report: University-Industry Relations* (London, 1976), pp. 26, 29-31.
197   Secretary of State for Education and Science and Secretary of State for Industry, *University-Industry Relations: The Government's Reply to the Third Report of the Select Committee on Science and Technology* (London, 1977), p. 10.
198   Committee of Directors of Polytechnics, *Many Arts, Many Skills: the Polytechnic Policy, and Requirements for its Fulfilment* (London, 1974), pp. 4-10.
199   House of Commons, *Minutes of Evidence Taken before the Select Committee on Education, Science and Arts, February 1980* (Memorandum submitted by Committee of Directors of Polytechnics: 'The Planning and Control of Higher Education') (London, 1980), pp. 116-22.
200   Terence Miller, quoted by the AUT in the House of Commons, *Report from the Expenditure Committee* (1972), p. 551.
201   Alan Beith, 'Liberals and Higher Education: Wanted, Flexibility and Single Funding', *The Times Higher Education Supplement*, 17 December 1976, p. 13.
202   Hailsham, 'Functions of Universities', p. 735.
203   Committee of Vice-Chancellors and Principals of the Universities of the United Kingdom, *University Development in the 1970s: A Statement of Views by the Committee* (London, 1970), p. 6.
204   A.H. Halsey, 'Are the British Universities Capable of Change?', *New*

Universities Quarterly, vol. 33, no. 4, 1979, pp. 411-16.

205 See, for example, the Barlow and Percy Reports, and discussions by Cotgrove in 'Education and Occupation', and Lord Hailsham in 'New and Larger Universities'. The question of hierarchies in higher education is discussed in Harold Silver, 'Enforced Conformity or Hierarchical Diversity?', in Evans, *Education Beyond School*.

206 This theme became prominent in the United States in the 1960s and 1970s. See, for example, Burton R. Clark, 'The Coming Shape of Higher Education in the United States', *International Journal of Comparative Sociology*, vol. II, no. 2, 1961, pp. 203-11; Martin Trow, ' "Elite Higher Education": an endangered species?', *Minerva*, vol. XIV, no. 3, 1976, pp. 355-60.

207 See Peter Scott, 'The Prophet Who Had His Way' (interview with Sir Toby Weaver), *The Times Higher Education Supplement*, 10 February 1978, p. 9. Also Scott's discussion of 'The Failure of the Binary Policy' in *What Future for Higher Education?* (London, 1979), pp. 6-10. See the discussion of Crosland in Lukes, 'The Binary Policy: A Critical Study'.

208 Tony Becher and Maurice Kogan, *Progress and Structure in Higher Education* (London, 1980), pp. 36, 124.

209 UGC, *A Note on Technology in Universities*, p. 4.

210 Percy, *Education at the Crossroads*, pp. 61-4.

211 Collins, *Non-Specialist Graduates in Industry*, pp. 14-15.

212 The issues arising from these defined differences of commitment or function in Britain and the United States are discussed in Harold Silver, *Education and the Social Condition* (London, 1980), ch. 8, 'Higher Educations'.

213 See, for example, Griffiths, *The Prospect for Universities: From Robbins to 1984*, p. 8.

214 John Lowe, 'The Other Side of the Binary System', in Bell and Youngson, *Present and Future in Higher Education*, p. 119.

215 Caroline Cox, Maurice Mealing and Julia Whitburn, 'Polytechnics: A Better Tomorrow?', in Colin Flood Page and Mary Yates (eds), *Prospects for Higher Education* (London, 1975), especially pp. 54 and 65-6; Julia Whitburn, Maurice Mealing and Caroline Cox, *People in Polytechnics: A Survey of Polytechnic Staff and Students 1972-3* (Guildford, 1976), especially pp. 38-9.

216 W.R. Niblett *et al.*, *Some Policy Issues in Higher Education: A Group Report* (London, 1974), p. 8.

217 Peter Scott, 'British Universities 1968-1978', *Paedagogica Europaea*, vol. 13, no. 2, 1978, pp. 30-1.

218 Neave, 'Academic Drift: Some Views from Europe', p. 147.

219 Jack Embling, *A Fresh Look at Higher Education: European Implications of the Carnegie Commission Reports* (Amsterdam, 1974), pp. 28-31.

220 Hampson, 'Conservatives and Higher Education', p. 13.

221 Donaldson, 'Students' Perceptions of the Binary Policy', pp. 52-62; Lex Donaldson, *Policy and the Polytechnics: Pluralistic Drift in Higher Education* (Farnborough, 1975), pp. 54-63. See also A.J. Massey, 'Rating of Some Characteristics of Polytechnics and Universities by GCE A-level Students',

Bulletin of Educational Research, vol. 7, 1974, pp. 5-11.
222 P.A. Walker *et al.*, 'Factors Influencing Entry at a University, a Polytechnic and a College of Education', *Higher Education Review*, vol. 11, no. 3, 1979, pp. 36-45.
223 Gordon and Williams, *Attitudes of Fifth and Sixth Formers to School, Work and Higher Education*, especially pp. 175-9.
224 Adelman and Gibbs, *A Study of Student Choice in the Context of Institutional Change, Synoptic Report*, p. 12.
225 C. Bacon, M.M. Gruneberg and D. Benton, 'Polytechnic and University Students' Attitudes to Employment', *The Vocational Aspect of Education*, vol. XXXI, no. 78, 1979, pp. 31-6; See also Fidler, 'Sixth Formers' Choice of Higher Education', pp. 71-2.
226 C. Bacon, D. Benton and M.M. Gruneberg, 'Employers' Opinions of University and Polytechnic Graduates', *The Vocational Aspect of Education*, vol. XXXI, no. 80, 1979, pp. 95-102.
227 John D. Millett, 'Value Patterns and Power Conflict in American Higher Education', in W. John Minter and Patricia O. Snyder (eds), *Value Change and Power Conflict in Higher Education* (Berkeley, 1969), pp. 11-12.
228 Clark, 'The Coming Shape of Higher Education in the United States', p. 210.
229 Burton R. Clark, 'The Insulated American: Five Lessons from Abroad', reprinted from *Change* (1978) in Philip G. Altbach and Robert O. Berdahl (eds), *Higher Education in American Society* (Buffalo, 1981), p. 300.
230 Daniel P. Moynihan, 'On Universal Higher Education', in *Coping: On the Practice of Government* (New York, 1974), pp. 293-5.
231 Michael Stewart, quoted in *Nature*, 'Education for Modern Needs', vol. 180, 1957, pp. 1149-52.
232 Findlay, *The School*, p. 150.

9 Policy as history and as theory

Educational policy and its roots in political and social processes have not been a favourite concern of British historians - except, as we have seen in a number of connections, in a preoccupation with legislation, enactment and the public aspects of political controversy. Policy studies in general have a more established place in the United States, and their relationship to history has attracted scholarly attention on a much wider basis. *Unpopular Education*, published from the Centre for Contemporary Cultural Studies at Birmingham University in 1981, afforded an important opportunity to move in the direction of re-examining and reappraising educational policy and experience in recent decades, given its subtitle: 'Schooling and Social Democracy in England since 1944'.[1] The book pointed towards discussions of the definition of education, of its relationship to dominant political ideologies and formations, and of a history-theory interface rarely approached in the history of education. It suggested, for example, that a way out of inhibiting, functionalist approaches to education was to reject its 'drastic simplification of history' and to 'write and think more "historically"'. The passage is crucial to the book, and to judgements we might make about Marxist and other approaches to themes like 'schooling and social democracy', to the relationship between experienced processes and organising abstractions:

> By historically, we do not merely mean in a way that is concerned with the past, though this longer historical reach is important. We refer to two main features of the best historical work: first, a concern with close and detailed description and analysis, firmly set in time and place, and second, a preoccupation with continuity and especially

with change, with crisis and with transformations. There is, in our view, a close association between historical understanding in *this* sense and a hopeful, progressive, politics.[2]

This passage announced an approach to policy and to theory with a firm and precise commitment to 'close and detailed' historical description and analysis, and it served also as a reminder of the lack of serious and sustained attention to the processes of education in Britain since the Second World War, in spite of the large amount of sociological, political and even historical analysis of particular educational events, processes and types of institution. There has been little such analysis in other countries, the handful of American examples including Joel Spring's *The Sorting Machine* and Bowles and Gintis's analysis of *Schooling in Capitalist America. Unpopular Education* offered a moment of reflection and synthesis not unlike that attempted in the previous decade by the latter.

Education since 1944, like any social process or institution in any period, raises difficult questions of description, and therefore of selection and emphasis. Whether historians remain committed to description and selection, or move explicitly into interpretation, their work is influenced or informed or governed by some kind of theory – from the least explicit, 'common sense' kind, to the most explict and overtly ideological. Historical selection is not random, and is conducted within the terms of the historian's understandings of social, economic, political, cultural or otherwise defined processes. The very conceptions of 'social', 'economic', 'political', 'cultural' and other categories involve commonly understood and accepted definitions and models – some of which we have previously seen emerging clearly only in the late nineteenth or early twentieth centuries. Historical description and analysis are often conducted as or amount to case studies in the relevant theory – whether or not it is explicit. As generations of historians have learned and relearned, to try to identify the history–theory relationship is to be involved in cross-frontier debates and disputes with sociologists, philosophers, and political and economic theorists. It also means involvement in profound controversies amongst historians themselves, and amongst variants of the same historical or theoretical standpoint.

The process of establishing historical understandings, especially of the recent past, therefore involves an ability to portray and evaluate experience, a willingness to recognize the presence of theoretical pressures in such evaluations, and a readiness to conduct sensitive dialogue between the experience and the theory. The determination of historical themes and periods – case studies of historical practice – needs to be that kind of sensitive dialogue, and helps us to make judgements and to take next steps ('hopeful, progressive, politics', in the words of *Unpopular Education*). Since the Second World War we have seldom been without a basis on which to analyse the relationship between education and society, to make short- and long-term judgements about possibilities and potential and policies, and to act. We have never, of course, been without the dangers of idealism and error, or of excessive confidence or over-simplification. In the context of post-war reconstruction and expansion, of welfare state planning and the analysis of welfare state limitations and social and political tensions, we have always, however, had a range of educational choices which have seemed to point towards some recognizable goal and better futures. Right or wrong, the possibilities gave rise to some form of policy formulation and to action How and why those forms of confidence, that sense of choice, the apparent possibility of action, were diminished in the 1970s are widespread international questions to which we shall return in the next chapter. They have involved loss of direction, the same kind of uncertainty and confusion in the United States or Denmark, Australia or Britain. A sensitive dialogue between the historical evaluation of experience, and the intrusive nature of theory, has never been more necessary. Without it, the dangers are now either those of unproductive frustration, or the denial or romanticization of past, limited gains, and the abandonment of policy to the rhetoricians. The signs of such dialogue have in recent years been meagre and mainly unhelpful.

If we are concerned with 'schooling', with the experience of education in schools and more widely with the formation and impact of policy, and with the relationship of these to political or social categories of various kinds, it is important to establish a sense of the main issues identified by those involved. It is possible to cluster the main such issues under a number of headings, and although historians do not have to agree with the participants about the priorities to be attached to such categories, they would be unwise to ignore them. Contemporary perceptions of reality are part of the reality. Historians have privileged information, but it does not replace what people in day-to-day action fought over to understand, to define, to protect or to change. In the three decades since the 1944 Education Act, without allocating any order of priority, the issues at stake in Britain could be summarized in ten rough-and-ready categories.

1. *Structure, provision and scale.* This had to do with the length of
   school life and the raising of the school leaving age, the financing
   and level of provision in all sections of the educational system, the
   structure of organization and control – including teacher education,
   the provision of nursery education, and the reorganization of
   secondary education – and particularly the issue of the comprehensive school. Involved in many of these questions were others which
   had to do not only with organizational, administrative and financial
   issues, but also with technology and manpower and the ability of
   Britain, or British capitalism, to continue to compete successfully
   amidst mounting problems of international competition. They
   related also to notions of equality and opportunity, and the kind of
   social structures to which educational development and access
   seemed to point.

2. *Curriculum.* This resolved itself at different times into widely
   different issues to do with the subject matter of teaching, factors
   affecting the position of subjects in the curriculum and student
   choice of – outstandingly – science and mathematics as career-
   oriented studies, the nature of the curriculum in a period of the
   democratization of secondary education, the modernization of
   subject content, the in-service education and updating of teachers,
   and behind them all the structure of, and access to, knowledge.

3. *Method.* This involved the scrutiny of and research into teaching
   styles, the development of new teaching techniques – team
   teaching, the language laboratory and other teaching technologies,
   including programmed learning and the use of micro-teaching in
   teacher education. In the early part of this period the British
   interest in the 'open classroom' and informal infant teaching, the
   development of 'integrated' and 'open' teaching methods –
   especially in the primary school, became the focus of international
   interest.

4. *The social determinants of education and of pupil achievement.*
   Although of international concern, especially in the 1960s and
   1970s, these issues related in Britain in particular explicitly to
   questions of social class, of correlations between class and level of
   school achievement, and of the linguistic and other factors involved
   in the failure of working-class children to achieve the higher levels
   of secondary and tertiary education. In the late 1950s and the
   following decades, sociologists of education turned this into a major
   set of educational issues, related to all the policy issues subsumed
   under other headings.

5. *The social functions of education.* The issues concerned here were related to some of those above, but ranged through questions of the social mobility and welfare aspects of education to the curative and socially useful functions of schools with regard to salient social problems – promiscuity and venereal disease, drug abuse, traffic accidents, the seduction of the media and advertising, juvenile delinquency, 'the generation gap'. Debates, often fiercely fought debates, about these issues, raised questions of the relationships between educational institutions and the wider society – and increasingly between schools, universities, polytechnics and colleges on the one hand, and industry and employment (or unemployment) on the other hand.

6. *Learning and cognitive development.* Parents were often vociferously worried about the basic skills, learning readiness and the willing-ness or unwillingness of the infant school to teach children formally to read. Teachers and teacher educators were increasingly involved in questions of the stages of children's cognitive development. Behind the curricular and methods issues lay disputes about how children learn, about motivation, about learning skills across the whole range of human development.

7. *The 'special' child.* Increased attention to old issues, and pressures to recognize new ones, led to changing perceptions and policies regarding the 'special' child. The educationally subnormal became the backward or slow, or the child with special needs. Those special needs were extended from the physically and mentally handicapped to the emotionally disturbed and the gifted. Long-standing commit-ments to special provision gave way to policies of integration in the normal environment.

8. *Examinations, hurdles, certification, qualifications.* More than in any other country, Britain was preoccupied with the apparatus of public, nation-wide structures and standards of testing and examining. Most controversial, and most long-running as a contro-versy, was that of public examinations at age sixteen, once the minimum school leaving age had been raised to that level. The General Certificate of Education and the Certificate of Secondary Education, their control, content, variety, monitoring, and existence, were crucial issues to public bodies, and to generations of children, parents and employers. Examinations at eighteen, entrance to higher education, the BEd for an all-graduate teaching profession, the length of specialist higher education training for

engineering and other professions – and the qualifications to be awarded, were issues pervasive to the period.

9. *Purpose and values.* If sociology, psychology and economics had their central places in many of the above debates, philosophy and 'common sense' interest in educational ideas and outcomes were much in evidence. Discussions of accountability implied notions of purpose. Discussions of skills and basics and creativity and discipline implied notions of a 'good' education for the 'right' purposes. Involved in debates about school governors and government, the rights and roles of parents, the 'community' school, part-time higher education, adult education, and a host of other issues were notions of the ends of education. In discussions of the expansion of the universities or the reorganization of secondary schools were contests about the aims of educational institutions and of education itself. Books by philosophers and others about authority, about a liberal versus a vocational education, about schools and social change, about the roles and purposes of the various constituent elements and partners in the educational enterprise, very often came from and fed back to specialist audiences, but reflected concerns which were voiced with different intonations and intentions across the spectrum of society. The fact that, for example, religion or the public schools rarely surfaced in this period as major or prolonged public issues did not mean that previous levels of interest in and controversy around educational topics had subsided. The purposes and values under discussion were embodied in new forms of argument around a wider range of institutions and processes.

10. *Politics, government and policy.* The issues at stake here are in some respects more tenuous. Who decides? What is the right balance between the central and local arms of government? Who has rights and how far can defiance be taken (against an order to reorganize secondary schools, against an instruction to cut expenditure, against the intention to close a school)? Debates have obviously been less about how policy is formed or implemented than about specific policies, their origins, the interests they represent or undermine or ignore, their likely outcomes. Immigration from the late 1950s and early 1960s, and its impact on the schools – first in connection with the English language, later in connection with cultural pluralism or inequalities – was obviously one area in which concerns about decision-making, community involvement, political stances came to the surface in education. More than any other

category, this general one brings us close to questions about the 'real' agenda of the educational system and its controllers. Who decides, how, and to what end, are questions which bring us directly to those of ideology, of concepts which analysts bring into history from the political and social sciences, and from politics – capitalism, industrialism, social control, reformism, hegemony . . . and social democracy.

Whatever else a discussion of schooling in modern capitalism, or schooling and social democracy, needs to do, it must do what the authors of *Unpopular Education* recommended – be concerned with a 'close and detailed description and analysis, firmly set in time and place', and with continuity, change, crisis and transformation. Schooling is both experience and policy, and the concerns of the schooled and the policy-makers are both part of the scenario. Educational policy, social democracy, capitalism, are questions of theory, and 'theory' has no more of a hold on reality than has 'history'. They are all, equally, questions of history, which has no more of a hold on reality than has theory. Without the historical test, theory may be beautiful but may be beyond validation and understanding. Without the theoretical test, history may be busy but blind. The history of education has to examine its own organizing concepts (including, for example, that of 'education'), and at some point engage both with the broad reaches of policy, and with the close and detailed description and analysis of the processes of education, and of people's experience and perceptions of them. The most dangerous moments are when theory *claims* to be history, and when policy *claims* to be experience.

In 1977, Finn, Grant and Johnson published a paper that gained some currency entitled 'Social Democracy, Education and the Crisis',[3] which was the ancestor of *Unpopular Education*. It was a case study in the application of a certain kind of historical workmanship within a set of theoretical, Marxist explanations. The theory and the critique, however, tended to be shorthand and assertive, and the history of post-war Labour revisionism, sociology of education, teacher profession-alism, and the like, carried heavy but unexplored messages of social democratic ideology and of the capitalist state. The conceptual machinery was robust and repetitive if not always clear. The paper talked of the 'history of hegemony', the 'master category "hegemony"', a series of educational, incomplete and other hegemonies, the hegemony of sociological assumptions, 'the hegemony of the Labour Party', and a newly emerging 'political discourse' within which a 'new hegemony' was being forged on the basis of corporate capitalism. The paper was an exercise in a new kind of assertiveness, and as with all such single-minded positions the most difficult part of the exercise was to establish an acceptable – indeed any – dialogue between the theory (or in many cases the rudimentary vocabulary of theory) and the history (or in many cases the rudimentary guesswork of history). The result was a series of interesting and often useful messages, which were clearly intended to cohere into something more than that – the 'hopeful, progressive, politics' of the later formulation. In presenting its under-lying assumptions about the workings of society, and of capitalist society specifically, the paper rejected what it saw as functionalist approaches and social democratic policy. It set out to present an alter-native analysis of society and events based not on tangible, analysable conflicts and choices, but on theoretical positions to do overwhelmingly with power, intention and will. That the assumptions were focused on ruling class and 'hegemonic' power, intention and will, made the argument no less abstract, even idealistic, and the history no less subservient to, merely illustrative of, the organizing theory. There was no close-up sense of history, no engagement with the kinds of processes or experience of education and its tensions suggested above, only a preoccupation with illustrating the crisis and its social democratic roots, without history, and with some surfaces of education.

If the 1977 paper was weak as an integrated case study of the pro-cesses and perspectives it appeared to set out to present, it was also – like much British and American radical literature of the decade – disappointing in offering an analysis which in fact pointed nowhere, left little or no hope for outcomes or action. It performed a set of ritual and circular logics – capitalism exploits, education under capitalism is part of the exploitation, social democracy fails to recognize and confront the class nature of capitalism, social democratic education policy is constrained and defeated by capitalism, capitalism exploits. The very subtitles of the 1977 paper pointed towards *inevitable* defeat for social democratic policy, whatever form it might take: 'The Elements Are Contradictory', 'The Objectives Cannot Be Realised', 'The Policies Must Fail'. The argument was tentative, conjectural and assertive in turn. It even ended with a bewildering admission that it did not 'supply an adequate explanation in fully Marxist terms of the post-war expan-sion of the educational system' – an omission it promised to remedy in further work. The object of the paper was 'primarily the study of educational ideologies, not the educational expansion as such'.[4] This was a fundamental admission, since the paper had been structured as a piece of history, and the nature of post-war educational expansion has to be central to any form of analysis of the period. That somehow the ideology can be separated from the processes to which it relates is a suggestion indicative of the kind of disembodied Marxism that became fashionable in Europe in the 1970s. In Britain, as in America and across the world, expansion was at the centre of all educational discussion and thinking in the late 1940s and subsequent decades. Its forms and meanings are critical to the history of the period, and to attempt to detach 'ideology' from the realities of economics, demography and social pressures in the period is an evasion. The evasion suggests that it is possible to write a history, even a Marxist history, of the ideologies without reference to their social roots and the success or failure of their outcomes – or at least to subordinate the world of action to a form of intellectual history. The bulk of the paper discussed the changing ideological condition of the Labour Party, the role of R.H. Tawney, post-1944 socialist revisionism, the sociologists, teacher professionalism and the expansive framework of the 1960s. The final admission and the tenor of the paper in general, therefore, gave the impression that social movements, conflict and debate over policy, social democracy and social democrats were merely puppets or counters in the argument. The 'crisis' was a crisis of theory, not of people caught in the difficulties of action. The paper pinned massive blame on the Labour Party's persistent failure 'to educate the popular classes from within' – it had instead sought access to the state 'to educate from there'.[5] The implication that in some way the trade union, radical, labour and socialist movements of the late nineteenth centuries should have acted as if in the conditions of the early nineteenth century was the kind of argument that made the paper romantically unhistorical, and Marxist only in the loosest sense.

These limitations of the earlier paper are important to emphasize, because *Unpopular Education*, four years later, attempted to move on from them. It took a more extended look at its own theory, expanded and deepened the historical structure of the earlier work, and directly confronted the past problems and ambiguities of a Marxist theory of education in a capitalist state. The strengths of the book were considerable in this respect, including its sense of the magnitude of the problems facing this kind of analysis. It presented perceptively the difficulties of the radical approach to education, and was anxious, in seeking a 'complex Marxism', that what it offered should be seen as 'a practical demonstration that Marxist forms of analysis, drawing also on a whole range of 1970s' insights, need not slip into a historical abstraction and mechanical "functionalism" balanced only by a hopeful rhetoric'.[6] It therefore set out to explore the period since 1944 in ways which avoided 'functionalist' and therefore over-simplified history, but which also avoided the pitfalls of some theoretical writing – ones which resulted from 'too swift a move from simple description, theory, or abstraction to the full account of complex, concrete historical events and determinations'.[7] It sought a form of enquiry which allowed for major structural change, and did not leave education standing still, waiting for other fundamental transformations. It rejected as 'hopelessly crude' those models of cultural struggle and reproduction which 'assume a system of perfect communication or transmission'.[8] It criticized the work that had been unhistorical, and it offered a 'more historical perspective' than the 'stronger versions' of Marxism prevalent in the 1970s.[9] The book was therefore unquestionably more aware than the paper had been of the dilemmas of and need for analysis which can contribute to understanding and action. It set out to be less historically speculative than some of the familiar texts of the 1970s, including *Schooling in Capitalist America*. The mission was explicit, and needed.

Such intentions, and the messages in which they were conveyed, were all the more important since existing attempts at historical portrayal and analysis of the period since 1944 have been surprisingly sporadic and piecemeal. Historians have not attempted studies of the complex interrelationships of the kinds of category and process suggested at the beginning of this chapter. Sociologists have attempted partial retrospects, and policy analysts out of a largely political science tradition have mapped, for example, moments of decision, the comprehensive school controversies, pre-schooling and the politics of curriculum change.[10] There have been histories of the system and parts of the system, of county and local machinery, and historical excursions into debates about education and culture, equality and – especially – social class. *Unpopular Education* entered a ground where the historical skirmishes have in Britain been around attempts to situate education in relation to aspects of social change and only to a limited extent to grapple with the conceptual machineries of such analyses. The main – though sometimes distant – echoes of controversy heard in the book, therefore, were those which come from tensions within the sociology of education between the political arithmetic tradition and the Marxists and neo-Marxists. Echoes came, secondly, from the ground on which Edward Thompson had set out to reassert a Marxist historiography, and on which it had been criticized by 1970s' forms of structuralism.[11] A problem in approaching this kind of history in Britain, as we have previously indicated, is the paucity of the attempts at the history of policy. Since the late nineteenth century and such work as that of Michael Sadler and Henry Craik's *The State and Its Relation to Education*,[12] there has been a tradition of historical analysis of education and government, parliament, legislation and the growth of a system and an administrative machinery. The first half of the twentieth century produced an array of descriptive work on government decision-making and policy implementation, both in general and in relation to specific processes – as for example in the case of John Graves's *Policy and Progress in Secondary Education* in 1943. In more recent years there have been basically two kinds of extension of this tradition. The first is the more sustained analysis of political processes in relation to education – including Maurice Kogan's work on policy-making and the politics of education and its various agencies and component parts, Rodney Barker's and other work on the Labour Party, and Brian Simon's collaborative work on the comprehensive school. These, and Brian Simon's *The Politics of Educational Reform 1920–1940* represent efforts to map and to understand the political processes underlying the growing attention to education by the state and society in the twentieth century.[13] The second kind of development is also rooted in the workings of political parties, pressures and processes, though this time at the local level, and exploring a different kind and content of policy formulation and implementation. Much of the unpublished thesis and dissertation material discussed in an earlier chapter is concerned with local structures and policy implementation in the nineteenth century and the early part of the twentieth century. Much of it is concerned with local school boards and local authorities, the local representation of national policy decisions and emergent structures. Taken collectively, much of this literature does not sustain Norman Morris's views that these are merely local *reflections* of national patterns,[14] since the divergences of structure, policy and emphasis are often greater than at first suspected, but it is true that from the point of view of the history of educational policy it does not often offer a serious approach to the local elements of policy formulation and decision-making. It is about *implementation* in a narrow sense. More recent efforts at local policy history – not directly out of history-of-education traditions – suggest more complex approaches to these issues. Peschek and Brand's 1966 study, *Policies and Politics in Secondary Education: Case Studies in West Ham and Reading*, and the 1970 study of differences in decision-making in Gateshead and Darlington, in Batley, O'Brien and Parris's *Going Comprehensive*, indicate other elements in an emergent British interest in the history of educational policy.[15]

The literature of this historical work, however, is small, and only a fraction of it deals with issues of the recent past. Much of it is descriptive map-making and engages only marginally, if at all, with the theoretical problems of analysing policy formulation. Little of it approaches policy as history in contexts of experienced conflict and choice. The history of educational policy since the Second World War has not been subjected to the comprehensive treatment of late nineteenth-century government, bureaucratic and party processes undertaken by Gillian Sutherland's *Policy-Making in Elementary Education 1870–1895*.[16] The historical literature of education in the period since the Second World War has been for the most part uncritical of its own conceptions of policy, of the state, of legislation, of the nature of political processes. Assumptions about the nature of power, of knowledge, of dominant social values, of the processes of learning and attaining and failing, have been allowed to remain unquestioned or relatively unexplored in the historical literature, at the same time as they have been the focus of intense controversy in other fields of educational discussion. Insights into the purpose, nature and outcome of educational policies in recent decades have been mainly by-products of the work of political scientists and sociologists having to grapple with historical issues, rather than of historians who have seen the recent past as an important area of analysis.

When the Marxist historian or educationist enters this arena, therefore, there is available a canon of work of which he is suspicious, a set of theoretical issues for elucidation, and a stock of 'common sense' Marxist assumptions about class and power and the relationship of education to the economic processes of capitalist society. It is understandable, then, that a book such as *Unpopular Education* should in present circumstances be tempted to be more concerned with its own theory than with an existing corpus of knowledge about the period under discussion, or with the homework needing to be done. Without doing that homework and engaging with the educational content of the history it purports to write, however, it has to lean heavily – as did Bowles and Gintis in another situation – not on the problems of making history, but on those of refining theory and making deductions. The central weakness of *Unpopular Education*, in fact, was apparent in its struggle to escape from an inhibiting and frustrating theory, but its ultimate willingness – and perhaps need – to remain within that theory, and to use the history like the captions on archaeological exhibits – produced as shorthand guides to an already established collection.

As a result, dominant social forces were presented as influencing government policy, shaping the forms and contents of schooling, governing the calculations of educational agents – pupils, teachers and parents alike: 'Public policy is structurally weighted, in other words, towards capitalist solutions.'[17] However helpful the book's disentangling of, for example, different conceptions of social class, the massive, shaping presence of the capitalist state remained over-whelming in the argument – making the promised 'close and detailed description and analysis' superfluous. The dominant impression, as in Bowles and Gintis, was that *whatever* is done in the name of any liberal radical pressure is and must be wrong. Choice becomes illusory. The book – like the 1977 paper – found itself presenting the state, elevated to a theory of 'statism', as the central, organizing theme of the argument, and – as with the 1977 paper – the outcome was to present reform as marginal to or a strengthening of the capitalist state. Education under capitalism remained capitalist education, outstandingly because the Labour Party had led socialism into the wilderness of the search for educational solutions through the capitalist state, failing to recognize that it is not neutral and consensual. The analysis from the starting-points of the state and statism therefore presented the authors with the same problems as were encountered in 1977, and in spite of their protestations they remained held fast in the same trap. Assertions to the contrary, and an awareness of the dilemma, did not prevent the analysis from massively using a model which ruled out any tangible negotiation or conflict that could change the position. The argument could only lead back into a position familar in the 1970s – the coupling of analysis with an unrelated radical rhetoric – a position which the book explicitly attempted to avoid. It presented instead a romantic, anti-statist version of the kind of discontinuous nineteenth- and twentieth-century socialist traditions after which the 1977 paper and *Unpopular Education* both go in pursuit, and which the latter saw re-emerging even in the conditions of the early 1980s. The version was romantic simply because it offered no insight into how these 'pre-statist' or 'anti-statist' elements could be made accessible in the conditions and relationships of the late twentieth century – and the implication therefore became a radical utopianism from which the book also sought to escape. It appealed again and again to the need to 'challenge social democratic orthodoxies', to establish the conditions 'for a new popular politics of education', a 'more adequate socialist politics of education', a 'more developed socialist politics', for educators to become 'serious socialists and feminists', and for analysis and politics that would be 'both socialist and feminist'.[18] This is not just an anthology of phrases from different points of the book, it is a thread, a theme, a consistent appeal which drowned and prevented the very historical exercise the book appeared to wish to conduct. The book became a reminder to the 1980s that historical intention, when coupled with strong theory, remains an elusive ambition. It became a case study in theory attempting to use, or to be, history, and in the ease with which history, theory and radical rhetoric can coexist without communicating.

One key explanation of the failure to implement the book's intentions was the fact that the history was, paradoxically, approached 'from the top'. It matched the need to illuminate the captialist state, not the need to produce an historically understood vocabulary of socialism, feminism and popular politics. The history was of rival views of policy, or what was wrong with the views of John Vaizey or A. H. Halsey or whomever, without any sense of what such social scientists were responding to, of popular emphases or priorities in the processes we have previously discussed, or the lives and concerns of people across recent decades. There was, again, a rhetoric of the popular presence, of 'the living, active force of the vast majority of historical populations',[19] but the reality of the text was different. People were presented as experiencing oppression, as having their expectations 'demobilized', as being disadvantaged at school, and being ignored and imposed upon in a variety of ways.[20] All of that may, of course, be true, but it is part of the truth, seen from the starting post of theory, and without the need to think about the experience of education in changing historical circumstances. 'Popular constituencies' were presented as having 'educational dilemmas', but these did not become recognizable in the book as anything other than preconceived theoretical positions. Those purporting to speak for these constituencies – notably the Labour Party and the 'old' educational sociology – were presented as jousting for control, forming alliances, reaching settlements, narrowing down demands, defining problems in limited terms of access, and indulging in administrative reforms – without consulting or involving those constituencies.[21] Yet there are no people in *Unpopular Education*. The alternative spokesmen seem to have been hard to locate (the 1930s and 1940s are represented by one communist president of the NUT, who is simply proclaimed as being 'typical' of English leftism in the period)[22] and the educational concerns of the majority of the people merely evaporate. Popular understandings of the comprehensive school, of the examination system, of technical education, of nursery education or lack of it, of the experience of the primary school, of 'opportunity', of the relationship between school and work – in other words of education other than as a figment of theoretical consciousness, did not appear in the argument. The points at which 'close and detailed' concern with the preoccupations of the period after 1944 became most needed in the book, it was most lacking. It was as if local battles over grammar and comprehensive schools never took place. It was as if teachers had sat around for decades merely awaiting or debating professionalization. It was as if 'schooling and social democracy since 1944' had been fashioned exclusively by rival interpretations of the state. Even Labour Party history was approached 'from the top', as if local Labour Parties and local organizations of many other kinds had not been involved in the processes, with different outlooks and energies.

A book with the historical claims of *Unpopular Education* is important to our historiographic and educational concerns because it points explicitly to important needs, and demonstrates crucial dangers. While it is easy on the small scale to forget the larger issues and frameworks, it is perhaps *more* dangerous when, on the larger scale, history is misrepresented as being about depopulated events and processes, about people as digits. If anything, *Unpopular Education* moved not towards a more 'historically' thought-out analysis, but further away from historical exploration of experienced processes towards adjustments of theoretical models. The nature and meanings of British, American and other attempts to *evaluate* the policies of the 1950–70s, their implementation and successes and failures, remain crucially important to any interpretation of the period, and cannot in a work that claims to be a serious history of the period be relegated to the flimsy and superficial place they were allotted in *Unpopular Education*. In the peremptory discussion of compensatory education programmes, for example, the extensive, controversial and often contradictory British and American literature was almost totally ignored.[23] In 1970 a group of Fabian authors, looking ahead at educational planning over the following decade, talked about the educational system as being perhaps 'the most important means of distributing life chances'. Social equality,

they underlined, had 'improved relatively little in the past 40 years' and
it was necessary therefore 'to ensure that state education gives particular
support to those whose educational needs are greatest'.[24] The
underlying views expressed here were familiar emphases of the late
1960s and early 1970s in Britain and elsewhere, and were central
features of educational debate and policy discussion. The imperative,
thinking historically about the decade, should have been to examine
that intention in the light of the accumulation of evidence in the 1970s
about the outcomes of the policies designed to improve social equality,
and particularly the policies directed towards 'those whose educational
needs are greatest'. Although the book looked, from the top, at the most
obvious policies (including Educational Priority Areas) concerned, it
made no attempt to see these in practice, to examine evidence, to
interpret historically.

The book's other weaknesses were mainly of the same order, and
pointed to similar historical difficulties and dangers. It argued, for
example, against historical hindsight and arrogance – 'modern
Olympianism', it called them[25] – and yet in its recurrent references to
feminism it indulged precisely that tendency. It talked of Tawney in the
1920s neglecting gender in his analysis of class, and of the Plowden
Report in 1967 as having a 'strongly conservative attitude towards
female dependence and vulnerability'.[26] Any non-Olympian historical
account of the two respective periods would have gone on to note the
absence or weakness of alternative, available forms of consciousness,
and would have shown that 'more socialist' or 'more radical' sources or
whatever attracted the book's authors were no less neglectful or conservative. As Elizabeth Wilson suggests of the whole post-war record of the
Labour Party in relation to women, it 'was not . . . a glorious one', but,
she rightly adds, 'the left was no better'.[27] In this kind of argument and
judgement *Unpopular Education* stood a long way from historical
thought and analysis. In its constant stress on struggle, seldom on
action, it similarly made a retreat from history. Its focus on the
purposive, goal-oriented nature of struggle made it impossible to
remedy the principal weakness of the 1977 paper, of Bowles and Gintis,
of much British and American radical literature of the previous decade
– the failure to describe and evaluate the possibility and nature of action
as undertaken by people. Tapper and Salter have suggested that
'hegemony' is an example 'of those high level generalisations which
have been devised to avoid, rather than answer, difficult questions',[28]
and it was in fact in such conceptual anchorage that *Unpopular*

Education encountered its main difficulty in understanding action, experience and policy, and reconciling them with its approach to both history and theory.

As a work of restless Marxist theory, with important successes as such, it raised central questions about education since the Second World War, and about historiography, and left them unanswered. What was worse, it appeared satisfied that it had answered them.

Notes

1 Steve Barron *et al.*, *Unpopular Education: Schooling and Social Democracy in England since 1944* (London, 1981).
2 Ibid., p. 20.
3 Dan Finn *et al.*, 'Social Democracy, Education and the Crisis', *On Ideology: Working Papers in Cultural Studies 10* (Birmingham, 1977).
4 Ibid., p. 196.
5 Ibid., p. 189.
6 Barron *et al.*, *Unpopular Education*, pp. 21, 246.
7 Ibid., p. 20.
8 Ibid., pp. 23, 29.
9 Ibid., pp. 18, 247.
10 Examples would include much of A.H. Halsey's work, including *Educational Priority*, vol. 1: *EPA Problems and Policies* (London, 1972) and A.H. Halsey, A.F. Heath and J.M. Ridge, *Origins and Destinations* (Oxford, 1980); work by Maurice Kogan, including Tony Becher and Maurice Kogan, *Process and Structure in Higher Education* (London, 1980); Brian Salter and Ted Tapper, *Education, Politics and the State* (London, 1981).
11 E.P. Thompson, *The Poverty of Theory and Other Essays* (London, 1978); Richard Johnson, 'Edward Thompson, Eugene Genovese and Socialist-Humanist History', *History Workshop*, no. 6, 1978.
12 Sadler's contributions include two papers with J.W. Edwards in *Special Reports on Educational Subjects*: 'Public Elementary Education in England and Wales, 1870–1895' (vol. 1), and 'Statistics, &c., of Elementary Education in England and Wales, 1833–1870' (vol. 2). Henry Craik, *The State in Its Relation to Education* (London, 1896).
13 Maurice Kogan, *The Politics of Education* (Harmondsworth, 1971), *The Politics of Educational Change* (Glasgow, 1978); Rodney Barker, *Education and Politics 1900–1951* (Oxford, 1972); David Rubinstein and Brian Simon, *The Evolution of the Comprehensive School, 1926–1966* (London, 1969); Caroline Benn and Brian Simon, *Half Way There: Report on the British Comprehensive School Reform* (London, 1970); Brian Simon, *The Politics of Educational Reform 1920–1940* (London, 1974).

14 Morris, 'The Contribution of Local Investigations to Historical Knowledge', in History of Education Society, *Local Students and the History of Education* (London, 1972).

15 David Peschek and J. Brand, *Policies and Politics in Secondary Education: Case Studies in West Ham and Reading* (London, 1966); Richard Batley *et al.*, *Going Comprehensive: Educational Policy-Making in Two County Boroughs* (London, 1970).

16 Gillian Sutherland, *Policy-Making in Elementary Education 1870–1895* (London, 1973).

17 Barron, *Unpopular Education*, pp. 142–3. For the historical explanation of the 'statist' route, and the negation of statist agitation and 'victories' by the state and the class structure, see especially pp. 37, 40, 43.

18 Ibid., pp. 7–9, 13, 86, 162, 249.

19 Ibid., p. 14.

20 Ibid., pp. 138, 47, 38.

21 Ibid., pp. 107, 65, 38, 44, 60.

22 Ibid., p. 69.

23 The superficiality is most obvious in the discussion of compensatory programmes on pp. 177–9, where the extensive, controversial and often contradictory British and American literature is almost totally ignored.

24 Fabian Society, *Planning for Education in 1980* (Fabian Research Series 282), (London, 1970), p. 3.

25 Barron, *Unpopular Education*, p. 104.

26 Ibid., pp. 42, 121.

27 Elizabeth Wilson, *Only Halfway to Paradise: Women in Postwar Britain 1945–1968* (London, 1980), p. 175.

28 Ted Tapper and Brian Salter, *Education and the Political Order: Changing Patterns of Class Control* (London, 1978), p. 60.

10 Education against poverty: interpreting British and American policies in the 1960s and 1970s

It is obviously a major difficulty for the historian if he has been implicated in recent events which he attempts to analyse. It is common for historians to claim distance as a prerequisite. Contemporary or recent or oral history has established itself precariously against resistance and suspicion derived from this lack of distance. The politicization of the intellectual, including the historian, has in some countries strengthened suspicion of a historical entanglement with the recent past. Distance, it is argued, lends objectivity and perspective: proximity means partisan. Historians could not and should not, therefore, look too close behind.

The misapprehension is with regard not to the recent, but to the remote. It is not that historians cannot distance themselves from the near, but that they cannot distance themselves from the far. Involvement in recent opinion or action may require a historian to tread even more carefully as he retraces step, but the problems of rediscovery and interpretation are the same wherever he fixes attention. He is as beset by the history-theory dilemmas, and as enmeshed in the various layers of ideology and opinion, when approaching education and social science in the 1860s as when approaching the sociology of education in the 1960s or the educational politics of yesterday. Deliberately to stand aside from the immediate past is not historical prudence, but historical cowardice. Historians need to be as engaged in the battle for perspective on the last decade as in that for the last or any other century. Not to do so is to leave the recent past not just to social and political science, but to ahistorical social and political science, not just to political rhetoric but to fiction and romance. The historian's contribution to such perspective is not privileged, but it is necessary. If, in the present, hope and utopia are not enough, historians have a role in exposing the sources of past and renewed action.

Discussions of education in the 1960s and 1970s were internationally related to wider questions of social policy. Education after the Second World War, in many European countries, was related not only to aspects of reconstruction, but also to fairness and justice and equality. The reorganization of secondary education was in many countries the main item on that agenda. For a decade or more after the war there was widely and strongly held belief, however, that social and educational policy could produce reorganization and redistribution in the continuing framework of economic expansion. However hard some of the battles over new secondary structures, or other educational issues, the consensus pointed towards greater equality as an outcrop of economic growth. From the late 1950s and early 1960s that assumption became increasingly subject to doubt. In America and Europe, poverty was rediscovered. Social tensions did not diminish. The inadequacies of welfare provision were underlined. Politics returned to the realities of inequality, unfulfilled hopes and promises, discrimination, injustice, poverty. The return was visible in the creation of a new left, demonstration, disturbances in school and university, new dimensions of protest and campaign. Educational expansion was not going to bring social solution. The new patterns of the 1960s included new, optimistic policies and visions for education.

The 1970s were characterized by a decline in the confidence in educational policies which had aroused high expectations in the previous decade. The 1980s began with what appeared to be fundamental changes of direction away from redistributive, socially instrumental roles for education. This was increasingly true of the United States as it had been of Britain since the late 1970s, and the changes in both countries – and not only there – were being carried out partly in the name of revised educational attitudes, but more profoundly in the name of economics and public economies. In the 1960s especially, in the United States and Britain, as well as in many European and other countries, education had been elevated to a central role in social and economic policy-making and planning, in pursuit of the ideals of the welfare state or the war on poverty or the Great Society or simply social

change and the solution of major social problems. In the 1970s education stood in uncertain light just off centre stage. The 1980s began with
the scene dominated by a traditionalist or conservative dramatis
personae, and education somewhere in the shadows.

What are the problems in looking at the education–poverty relationship? If Berger and Luckmann and the new sociology, Michael F. D.
Young and the new sociology of education, taught educationists and
historians anything in the 1970s, it was the importance and the difficulty of defining the problem – the need to investigate how knowledge
and problems are constructed, who controls them, what structures of
power lie behind the question mark. Whoever might claim theoretical
responsibility for defining the problem – and although we are all in the
business of deciding what is a theoretical, a sociological, a political, or
any other kind of question – the problem of knowledge and definition is
a profoundly historical one. Building a clear narrative of the 1960s and
1970s means perceiving the zigzags of competing pressures and choices,
and debating interpretations.

A poverty–education connection is a nineteenth- as well as a
twentieth-century phenomenon. At various stages of the past two
centuries that relationship has been defined with a variety of emphases.
It has been interpreted as an ethical relationship, with education being
called to social rescue, to induce right behaviour, to help the victims of
social change to accept old or modified values. It has been an economic
relationship, expressed in terms of the contribution of education to
manpower provision, or to the containment of public expenditure (for
example in the form of the cheapness of schools as compared with the
public bill for crime and prisons). The relationship has been expressed
in political terms, with education being asked to reinforce social
stability as new electorates have entered the country or won political
suffrage. The relationship has been expressed in both radical and
conservative terms, and the ensuing educational and social policies have
been defined and interpreted in terms of both – often barely separable.
The distance between the conservative hope that education protects an
old order, and the radical hope of educational contributions to social
improvement and reorganization, in fact has not always been easy to
establish.

In the past two centuries the education–poverty relationship has been
underlined at points which can be plotted along different kinds of axis –
demographic, economic, industrial, etc. – and none of the graphs of the
timing and the rhythm of the connection have yet proved entirely satis-

factory – though recent work in the United States by Carl Kaestle and Maris Vinovskis, and by David Tyack and his colleagues, have been revealing and helpful.[1] What is clear is that the connection, real or intended, has been associated with the rhythm at which poverty has been discovered and rediscovered in both countries in the past two centuries. The awareness of the extent and concentration of poverty in Britain in the industrializing period of the late eighteenth and early nineteenth centuries, the heightened awareness of poverty and its implications resulting in the mid-nineteenth century from the writings of Henry Mayhew, at the end of the nineteenth century from the researches of Booth and Rowntree, and the rediscovery of chronic poverty by British sociologists such as Titmuss, Audrey Harvey and Willmott and Young in the 1950s and 1960s, relate to the re-emergence of education as a central policy instrument in various forms. They directed attention both towards poverty and towards its apparent effects.

In a variety of ways also education has been linked with poverty over the past two centuries at times of heightened public consciousness of the need to protect the social order by reasserting ideal social and national types. This has been true of periods of immigration and social tension, and – as with the 1960s – at periods of what appear to be potentially difficult or sensitive social changes. All of those linkages between education and poverty are incomplete and even misleading as explanations, since at the same time education has become an autonomous demand, an ideal, a right, a claim as a cultural or economic asset. The relationship is therefore too complex and fluid to subordinate to some simple social control theory. If the nineteenth century established education as a central social mechanism, it also witnessed its emergence as a constantly changing battlefield. There is no one simple and straightforward explanation of the confidence of a Horace Mann or a Lyndon Johnson, of a Robert Owen or an Anthony Crosland, in education as a basic strategy for eradicating poverty.

What, if anything, was new and different about the emphases and strategies and definitions of the 1960s? It is useful to begin with the United States, and to look at the context in which the rediscovery of the education–poverty relationship in post-war America took place. The central thrusts of the rediscovery were to be expressed in terms of a new and more effective federal politics of education, new forms of intervention through education, a new scale of funding and newly defined target populations, a new concentration of interest in disadvantage, and a conjoint interest in community action and compensatory strategies. The context out of which the range of policies emerged, especially from 1964, included the growing federal interest in educational policy-making in conditions of the cold war and technological change – symbolized by the space race which began with sputnik in 1957 – and the passing of the National Defence Education Act the following year. The context included perhaps most of all the civil rights movement of the late 1950s, and the new militancies, public action and orchestration of demands and policies that accompanied and grew out of it. It is against that background that poverty began to be rediscovered, con-ceptualized, translated into political terms by President Kennedy and his close associates in the period 1962–4. Up to this point there had been a widespread belief in both the United States and Europe that poverty as a major social problem and defined as such, had been cured, or had gone away. As a significant issue, and expressed in that vocabulary and form, poverty surfaced as a political issue only in 1964.[2] Sundquist commented in 1969:

> Lyndon Johnson had added the word 'poverty' for the first time to the lexicon of recognized public problems when he proclaimed, 'This administration today, here and now, declares unconditional war on poverty in America'. Until 1964, the word 'poverty' did not appear as a heading in the index of either the *Congressional Record* or *The Public Papers of the President*.[3]

For the previous two years the Kennedy administration had been seeking its new frontiers, and Kennedy's experience of Appalachian poverty had contributed to a heightened sense of social policy involve-ment. The familiar story of John F. Kennedy's reading of Harrington's *The Other America* is neither apocryphal nor trivial, and there is clear evidence that that book, together with the seminal review of it by Dwight McDonald, captured a moment of awareness and urgency and made its dimensions politically accessible.[4] Harrington himself was to be invited to take part in the first poverty programme task force. By 1962–4 a number of factors were beginning to coincide, and to provide the basis on which Johnson was to act after the assassination.

One important element in interpreting the growing interest in poverty and education as related issues is the emphasis which many analysts have placed on the absence of any serious direct link between the poverty interest and major public pressures, including the civil rights movement itself. In the period preceding 1964 there were, it is true, no discernible pressures for anything that could be described as a poverty programme. The unemployment rate was low, the poor were unorganized, and were, in Murphy's words, making 'no demands for such legislation'.[5] Yarmolinsky, writing in 1969, described the 1964 task force which planned the Economic Opportunity Act as issuing a number of memoranda, one of which was entitled 'Why the Poverty Program is Not a Negro Program'. This was

> devoted primarily to the fact that the poverty problem in Appalachia and the Ozarks was almost entirely a white problem and the Deep South was a white as well as a Negro problem. The crisis of the northern ghetto was simply not foreseen in anything like its present critical character by the draftsmen of the program.[6]

In determining the roots of the 1960s and any other policies, of course, it has to be remembered that foresight does not have to be clear – vague messages, memories and fears can be translated into political action and social policy – as the history of inner-city issues, for example, often shows. In the absence of a clear relationship, however, between popular pressure and the Johnson declaration of war on poverty, some analysts have also looked to the debates of the late 1950s and early 1960s for other sources of ideas and energy and have found, for example, a major starting-point in the discussions of juvenile delinquency, with which Robert Kennedy was particularly associated.[7] Others have seen the 1964 programmes as coming at a 'pause' in the civil rights movement, and have emphasized its likely regrouping and renewal as part of the consciousness underlying the Great Society rhetoric. The poverty programme, claimed Earl Raab in 1965, was 'part and parcel of the Negro revolution, of the direct action demonstrations and anarchic ghetto restlessness'.[8]

What is clear is that the succession of education bills that had ended nowhere in previous sessions of Congress had not been linked directly to poverty. The 1963 National Education Improvement Bill, for example, when discussed in the House Committee on Education and Labor, raised – like so many previous bills – issues to do with federal aid to the states, vocational education, higher education opportunities and so on – but not directed towards a specific target population.[9] The language, concepts and linkages of 1964–5 are altogether different. They embody a number of factors which, coming together, rapidly announced the presence of a new consciousness, new emphases, and the launching of a new rhetoric. They contain elements of civil rights and desegregation, of the political objectives of Kennedy and Johnson and their close associates, and also of the newly and rapidly emerging ideas and research and experience of work being promoted by some of the foundations, notably the Ford Foundation – with people like Ylvisaker from the latter quickly contributing to the new movement. The result was 'an interacting sequence of theory, experiment, and demonstration that produced new strategic and tactical concepts for what became the War on Poverty'.[10] It was on that basis that the Economic Opportunity Act was passed in 1964, authorizing expenditures which produced Head Start in 1965 and Follow Through two years later. This was the basis of Title I of the Elementary and Secondary Education Act of 1965 (ESEA) – part of a wide-ranging attack on the 'root causes of poverty in the midst of plenty', and representing the widely held belief that poverty, having been discovered, would now soon be abolished.[11] 1964 was the beginning of a brief heroic period, in which ideas were debated, advice taken, task forces established, drafting done, policies defined and canvassed, and legislation enacted.[12] It was soon to become clear that the confident and specific strategies in many cases postponed or disguised old conflicts and confusions, and that expectations and expansionist educational aims had in many cases been dressed in extravagant stage costume. For Hubert Humphrey education had become 'the key to the door through which the poor can escape from poverty'.[13] For Johnson the problem was not one of income redistribution: the American people 'are going to learn their way out of poverty'.[14] In May 1964 Johnson told the students of the University of Michigan:

> in your time we have the opportunity to move not only toward the rich society and the powerful society, but upward to the Great Society. The Great Society . . . demands an end to poverty and racial injustice, to which we are totally committed in our time. But that is just the beginning. The Great Society is a place where every child can find knowledge to enrich his mind and to enlarge his talents . . . It is a place where the city of man serves not only the needs of the body and the demands of commerce, but the desire for beauty and the hunger for community.[15]

The New Republic liked that enough to reprint it in a book entitled *America Tomorrow: Creating the Great Society*. The dismissal of all or any of this as 'mere' rhetoric, or idealism gone sour, or political opportunism, or whatever, does not help. This was an important American moment that has to be understood, and the roles of the newly conceptualized poverty and educational war against it, its extent, its targets, and its limitations, have to be disentangled and evaluated as the decisions of real people responding to real imperatives and choices. The British narrative and its component parts begin quite differently. If there was a heroic period it has to be a much earlier one, surrounding the publication of the 1942 Beveridge Report on post-war social security, the drafting and publication of the 1944 Education Act, and the period immediately following the war, with the election of the Attlee Labour government, and the enactment of the series of legislative concerns with health, welfare and nationalization. The British moment was one which used a vocabulary of construction and planning, public ownership and control, not warfare. The goals were expressed in terms of the ending of a remembered, pre-war experience of widespread unemployment and poverty, and the legislation was in part a socialist commitment, in part a set of wartime promises redeemed. The problem of the 1960s in Britain was one of increasing realization that the post-war measures had been cloaked in a fair measure of idealism, and that serious underlying problems remained.

The rediscovery of poverty was an important feature of British social policy and social administration in the 1950s, and related directly to social class analysis, the influential interpretation of working-class culture conducted by Richard Hoggart, and the community-directed sociology that emanated outstandingly from the Institute of Community Studies. Poverty was rediscovered in a context quite different from the pressures and concerns of 1950s America. A second and crucial discovery in 1950s Britain was that education, as embodied in legislation and practice, had not made the expected inroads into the class structure. The implementation of the 1920s and 1930s slogan 'secondary education for all' under the 1944 Education Act, had not significantly affected the distribution of education and social opportunity – as perceived at the time in, for example, access to the grammar school, to academically oriented examinations, and to higher education. The sociologists mustered by David Glass in the early and mid-1950s, the crucially influential *Social Class and Educational Opportunity* by Floud, Halsey and Martin in 1956, and the increasing importance of the sociology of education, had by the 1960s altered the pattern of public discussion and redirected public attention. Whatever the later criticisms of their definitions and theoretical positions, the sociologists of the 1950s and 1960s profoundly altered the agenda of social policy discussion. They made social class, as a concept and a set of issues, as basic to the British debates of the 1960s as race had become for the United States.

The focus of educational discussion in the mid-1960s, especially after the election of Harold Wilson's Labour government in 1964, was the comprehensive school. The discussion did not point directly towards the concept of poverty, but it did so obliquely as a concern with social justice, fairness, equality of access, and educational efficiency and opportunity. By the late 1950s and early 1960s, however, other forms of social and political action and ideal had begun to shape discussion of all forms of social policy. The Campaign for Nuclear Disarmament and the New Left made their impact on a whole range of discussions which had for a long time been seen as outside the concerns of popular politics – and the issues of education and poverty were beneficiaries of newly released energies of this kind. In addition, by the end of the 1950s the profile of British social structure had begun to alter significantly. The newly defined problems of affluent youth and adolescence were obviously not far from any discussion of education. The main period of West Indian, Asian and African immigration came from the late 1950s. By the 1960s sharper awareness was beginning to be expressed of the stresses of the inner city, of concentrations of poverty, of social problems, of crime, of the anxieties of an increasingly pluralist society. The policies which were sought and adopted did not necessarily coincide – as was also true of the United States – with moments of great economic or political pressures, but they certainly related to a sense of potential, and major, causes for concern. As in the United States also, although to a lesser degree, the new policies were formulated in expansionist and confident terms, though British politicians and government commissions express themselves more guardedly than their US counterparts!

A 1963 Advisory Council report on pupils 'of average and less than average ability' contained a chapter on 'Education in the Slums'.[16] The Robbins Committee on higher education, in the same year, drew heavily on the work of the sociologists to demonstrate that working-class children were not being recruited adequately to advanced secondary and higher education.[17] The Plowden Committee of 1963–7 on *Children and Their Primary Schools* soon followed, with its emphasis on positive discrimination and Educational Priority Areas (EPAs), and on forms of educational and social action not unlike those of mid-1960s America.[18] By the second half of the 1960s a remarkable convergence of definitions, vocabulary, research and policy formulation had taken place between Britain and the United States, even if the scale of implementation was vastly dissimilar. The contexts, starting-points, national structures and public issues were incredibly different, and historically they cannot be dismissed as merely different expressions of underlying dilemmas of varieties of capitalist society. American liberalism is not the same as British social democracy, and neither of them is homogeneous. It is not helpful, historically, to attempt to write off the two sets of transatlantic actors as puppets manipulated by the same demon or underlying force.

It is not possible here to itemize in detail the British and American policies which emerged within such a short space of time in the middle and late 1960s, but it is important to underline the general pattern. In the United States from 1964 the Economic Opportunity Act authorized federal expenditure for a variety of purposes connected explicitly with poverty, and launched the processes that quickly resulted in community action programmes and Head Start. With doubts about the gains being made by Head Start children being sustained in the elementary school, Johnson authorized Follow Through in 1967, a project poised uncertainly between a service model to supplement Head Start, and an experimental, developmental model to improve early schooling.[19] From 1965, Title I of ESEA, operated through the States, but on the basis of federal funding and guidelines as to target populations and expenditure, and federal monitoring of action by the states, brought poverty and educational policy centrally into a new profile of federal action. Job Corps, Vista, Upward Bound and an enormous number of related federal, state and local projects which followed the Economic Opportunity Act of 1964, publicly and privately funded, rapidly made new strategies and vocabularies familiar, with the concept of compensatory education at the centre of the exercise. In Britain, from 1964 to the end of the decade, the move towards comprehensive reorganization centred on government circular 10/65 which put pressure on local authorities to submit reorganization plans so as to end selection at the age of eleven and establish the comprehensive secondary school. This was the period of the peak of research and publication regarding the relationship between social class and the family on the one hand, and the school on the other.[20] The Plowden Report proposed its policy of positive discrimination in favour of children in poor environments, and its recommendation for the designation of EPAs was acted upon. EPA action research projects were funded, and were to produce, in 1972 and 1974/5 the most notable reports on British compensatory (or complementary, as the project organizers preferred) educational schemes on anything like a scale that can be compared with the American experience.[21] The use of Urban Aid money for pre-school purposes from 1969 and the establishment of a National Community Development Project in 1970 diversified a picture which at many points resembles the American one.

While Washington in the 1960s was busy with academics and specialists of many kinds advising the federal government and its agencies on the whole range of educational concerns, London was - though to a much more limited extent - bringing together the British equivalents to advise the parties - in this context mostly the Labour Party - and to talk to publishers. In Britain this was the great age of the literature of education and disadvantage and deprivation, of the comprehensive school, of education and social change, of education and social class, of sociolinguistics, education and streaming, testing and selecting.

There are immediate points about all of this to underline. *First*, the American experience, especially from 1964, began to attract attention and enquiring visitors from the United Kingdom. A.H. Halsey, with J. Floud and C.A. Anderson, made some of the early American literature widely known in Britain.[22] The Ford Foundation and OECD arranged a conference in the United States in January 1969 at which European participants could explore the issues with some of their American counterparts;[23] and Marris and Rein published a well-known account of poverty and community action in the United States.[24] Members of the Plowden Committee visited the United States to see and discuss some of the American developments. The Plowden Report makes only rare reference to the American projects, but the report is extensively constructed in ways which suggest what was learned from across the Atlantic. Halsey's 1972 report on the EPA projects contains a chapter on 'Poverty and American Compensatory Education'. The fortunes of Head Start and its evaluations became familiar to British educationists.

Two aspects of British experience transmitted important messages in the reverse direction. First, the British infant school, the 'open classroom', 'progressive education', attracted incredible post-war American interest, and were as important to the transatlantic airlines as the American programmes were. The infant classroom was widely, if not always realistically, reported in the United States, and its apparent 'informal' methodology was incorporated into some of the 'planned variation' models available to Head Start and Follow Through children.[25] Second, the British sociology of education and social class had important echoes in the United States, both in the 1960s and then in the radical review it encountered at the beginning of the 1970s, most notably in the volume on *Knowledge and Control* edited by Michael F.D. Young.[26] The outstanding contribution to the American developments was that of Basil Bernstein, whose early work on working-class and middle-class language 'codes' was widely used by influential early childhood and education specialists in the mid-1960s. Deutsch, for example, used Bernstein's work in 1964 to explain 'the communication gap which can exist between the middle-class teacher and the lower-class child', and Deutsch's and others' vocabularies of class analysis were influenced by and in turn influenced Bernstein.[27] Bereiter and Engelmann used Bernstein in support of their approach to *Teaching Disadvantaged Children in the Preschool*, in 1966, and in developing the idea of an 'academically oriented pre-school for culturally deprived children'.[28]

The various kinds of interchange contributed, of course, to the shared confidence and the shared sense of a major shift in public attitudes to social issues and their educational implications. The vocabulary of 'disadvantage' and 'compensatory education' and 'cultural deprivation' was shared initially with confidence, increasingly with uncertainty as attacks were mounted on the concepts – outstandingly of 'cultural deprivation' and 'compensatory education' on both sides of the Atlantic.[29] Shared confidence inevitably meant shared disappointments, shared debate, shared confusion. What, after all, *was* poverty? What did the concepts and the policies actually mean when stripped of their expansionist economic assumptions? Was it possible to discuss the education–poverty relationship without imposing 'middle-class values'? What, in Atlanta or Liverpool, did 'maximum feasible participation of the poor', or similar phraseology, really mean?[30] What implications for policy were there in the Westinghouse evaluation of Head Start, or in the Coleman Report, or in Jencks's *Inequality*? Alongside all of this kind of sharing, we have to remember other elements of it. Britain was sharing with other West European countries, including Germany, France and Sweden, attempts to restructure secondary education under pressures for democratization. The American and British issues were discussed in European forums, and underpinned the interests of the OECD. Australia has been discovering poverty, and the British and American experience.

The questions of interpretation which arise from all of this are obviously extremely difficult. The most contentious of the interpretations has related to outcomes, and the problems can be expressed in three ways.

First, they have to do with the difficulties of evaluation. It is clear, for example, that between 1965 and 1974 the available evaluations of ESEA Title I were of little or no value, since the lack of proper guidelines, experience and standardization meant that the data produced were virtually unusable. The result was the mandate in 1974 to the National Institute of Education to conduct its Compensatory Education Study, and the contract with System Development Corporation to conduct the still ongoing Sustaining Effects Study. Neither of these has had the notoriety of earlier evaluations of, for example, Head Start and Follow Through, since their results have been more positive and encouraging. The difficulties encountered by evaluators in interpreting some of the data, especially in the late 1960s and early 1970s, will make it difficult for historians to see much of the evaluation produced as helpful in making serious interpretations of the projects and their outcomes.

Second, and directly related to the former, are measurement difficulties. Since the 1966 Coleman Report it has been difficult to understand what kind of measures are appropriate as well as really indicative. Measurement techniques have been used which are not only controversial within the scholarly community, but also based on criteria which have too often been taken for granted. The comment has been endlessly made that cognitive measures are neither as reliable as often claimed, nor indicative of more than a fraction of the outcomes, intended and unintended, with which educational processes are concerned. In relation to Follow Through, for example, one of the sponsors has pointed out that major areas such as motivation and parent involvement are ignored by the measures and the intentions of those designing and using them.[31] One local Follow Through project organizer has commented that the project has had to make a constant effort to try to persuade people to understand 'that everything we do is not measurable by standardised tests, that things that you do with the child for positive self-concept – you can't measure that on a standardised test'.[32] The measurement obsessions of the 1960s and 1970s may be judged by historians to have been a feature of the sophisticated arrogance of a primitive science. Jack Tizard and his colleagues in Britain stressed in *All Our Children* that nursery education had to do with happiness, well-being and the development of children and their families, with relatively immediate goals, not with hoped-for and measurable long-term effects.[33] The formulation is understandable, given the previous history of attempts to measure and evaluate, but given also the search for new targets and instruments, the formulation is also unsatisfactory.

Third, the difficulties can be described in terms of the concern with overall impact. If education is to be used to combat poverty, then clearly some sort of assessment of effectiveness or otherwise is necessary, and social class, social mobility, intra- and intergenerational studies are important. But modesty and caution have been sadly lacking. An example is a sentence from Jencks's *Inequality* which suggests that the 'egalitarian trend in education has not made the distribution of income or status appreciably more equal over the past 25 years'.[34] Given the resources and the methodology available, and even if there are grounds on which to make judgements about social mobility, status distribution and income trends over such a period, to make them with a confidence which suggests the impossibility of change is inappropriate to that kind of exercise. That is the prerogative of politician, political theorist, and hunch. We should have been more hesitant about all of this, as some people have tried to be more recently in Britain about, for example, Bennett's or the Oracle Project work on teaching styles and pupil performance, or Rutter's *15,000 Hours*. But too many people on the right and on the left were only too eager in the late 1960s and 1970s to use the evidence of an immature science to support bold interpretations. Bowles and Gintis, for example, used it to proclaim gleefully that 'the liberal school-reform bubble has burst . . . The disappointing results of the War on Poverty . . . have decisively discredited liberal social policy.' They quoted approvingly a judgement from the Rand Corporation that 'virtually without exception all of the large surveys of the large national compensatory educational programs have shown no beneficial results on the average'.[35]

There is now a different picture that could be drawn of the effects of the educational programmes against poverty – not in order to suggest that it is *the* true picture as against *the* false picture presented by the negative evaluations – but in order to suggest that many, like Bowles and Gintis, leaped too enthusiastically into accepting initial evaluations as gospel. By the beginning of the 1980s there were at least ten sources for an alternative picture of the outcomes of the projects conceived in the 1960s and 1970s. In the United States there has been, for example, the NIE Compensatory Education Study which indicated the redistributive effects of Title I, together with positive data relating to student gains in first and third grades, and to the fact that students making such gains on compensatory programmes did not then slip back. The Executive Summary of the evaluation is a crucial set of positive statements to set against the earlier and more publicized negative evaluations.[36] The same is true of the reports produced by the Sustaining Effects Study from the second half of the 1970s. Barbara Heyns, one of Jencks's collaborators on the *Inequality* study has in *Summer Learning and the Effects of Schooling* (1978), offered a more optimistic view of the effects of public education than previous literature in the same investigative mould. She concludes:

> schooling has a substantial independent effect on the achievement of children and ... the outcomes resulting from schooling are far more equal than those that would be expected based on the social class and racial origins of sample children ... Although achievement differences persist, and schools cannot be regarded as equalizing in an absolute sense, the pattern of outcomes clearly implies that the achievement gap between children of diverse backgrounds are attenuated by education.[37]

In his foreword to Heyns's book, and in his own more recent work, Jencks takes a less assertive position than previously on the possible effects of education.[38] Also in the United States the consortium of fourteen infant and pre-school experiments re-analysed from 1975 the pre-school programmes which had been the subject of much previous analysis and debate. The outcomes of the work of the consortium teams pointed to the effectiveness of some pre-school programmes on a number of significant criteria: 'The most important finding is that low income children who received early education are better able to meet the minimal requirements of their schools as shown in a reduced rate of assignment to special education and in-grade retention.'[39] Some recent analyses of the Follow Through programmes have come to quite different conclusions about their effectiveness than did earlier analyses.[40]

In Britain, the first EPA report by A.H. Halsey in 1972 suggested some more positive conclusions than the American literature had done about the possibility of sustained gains by pre-school children on compensatory programmes. Although the evidence from the London EPA published three years later was less optimistic, other evidence from the project, especially from the West Riding, suggested cautiously optimistic outcomes.[41] A recent book by Halsey, Heath and Ridge on

Origins and Destinations concludes that the record of educational policy-making does not point to easy optimism, but also indicates that it does not endorse defeatism either.[42] The *15,000 Hours* study by Rutter and his colleagues suggests that differences in student performance can be attributed to certain kinds of difference in the schools.[43] Although in relation to this, as to other items in this list, there are methodological and other reservations to be expressed, the cumulative effect of all of these American and British studies is to leave wide open questions which earlier evaluations considered to be closed. Whether it is yet possible to share the confidence of the title of Halsey's 1980 article – 'Education Can Compensate' – is not clear, but it reflects some of the changed emphases that have emerged since Basil Bernstein wrote his 1972 article in the same journal under the title 'Education Cannot Compensate for Society'.[44]

Are there any conclusions about these anti-poverty policies and programmes, given the present state of our knowledge and analysis? The existing literature which attempts to look back over the 1960s and 1970s experience seems to fall into three rough and ready categories in both Britain and the United States. The first is the description and analysis which comes from what the contributors might consider some kind of 'objective centre', handling the actors on more or less their own terms, probing their meanings, exposing the interactions of the players. Some of it is autobiographical, or accounts from witnesses at the centre or the periphery of the events. Some of it emanates from the evaluative tradition built up in the 1960s and 1970s, and much of it is more in the tradition of portraiture and landscape painting than sustained analysis. A great deal of it is invaluable as source material, as perceptions which check and balance once another, and is of major importance to the historian, without itself being history.

The second category is profoundly judgemental, often of the very attempt to bring education into a political and social arena, and embraces a politically right-wing perspective. This has until recently been less articulate, less raucous and less influential in the United States than in Britain, because this position has been less easy to occupy in the face of major public issues in the United States – especially those connected with race. It has been visible, nevertheless, and was most clearly and directly embodied in the Heritage Foundation's 1980 report to President Elect Reagan, proposing, for example, that programmes should not be funded 'which foster hostility to traditional values, or which unquestioningly accept moral relativism as an ethical theory'.

The emphasis in the report was on federal aid, but also on the withdrawal of federal control and, for example, on the ending of affirmative action. It proposed that all federal agencies should be staffed by individuals who 'oppose any further Federal support for "humanistic" or psycho-social education, activities, projects or programs'.[45] This was an American equivalent of the British *Black Papers* which from 1969 sought to expunge the record of the previous decade, and were less concerned with appraising that experience than with asserting the need to return to older, traditional, understood, tried and tested academic and cultural values.

Thirdly, on the political left there have been often equally assertive and declamatory positions, Marxist, anarchist, radical. The best-known British version of the 1970s, as we saw in the last chapter, was Finn, Grant and Johnson's paper on 'Social Democracy, Education and the Crisis', describing 'an educational system under siege', and the growth of a ruling class-dominated educational ideology and structure. There, and in the 1980s follow-up, *Unpopular Education*, the role of social democracy in filtering through the ideology and promoting the structures, was central to the argument. The key text in Britain and the United States, however, was Bowles and Gintis's *Schooling in Capitalist America*, with its underlying message of an almost inescapable trap for educators and reformers in capitalist society. Reforms have in the main, in their argument, been manipulative, reactive, compromising. The open classroom, they suggest, was 'perceived by liberal educators as a means of accommodating and circumscribing the growing antiauthoritarianism of young people and keeping things from getting out of hand'. The history of twentieth-century education 'is the history not of Progressivism but of the imposition upon the schools of "business values"'. Education has historically played the role not of a complement to economic reform, but as a substitute for it. Education 'plays a major role in hiding or justifying the exploitative nature of the US economy'.[46] Whatever grains of truth might lie in any of this, these are political assertions masquerading as history. Bowles and Gintis *needed* the 1960s reforms, like any other reforms to be seen to have failed, and rushed into accepting evaluations and judgements and data from sources, such as Rand, which for other purposes and in other circumstances they would have resisted and rejected. Their argument ends in the same trap as does that of Martin Carnoy, for example, in 1976, when he insists that 'fundamental changes in schooling . . . will require fundamental changes in the basic structures of the society',[47] apparently inviting educators to maximum apathy and inaction, since as long as our present 'basic structures' remain intact there is no point whatever in trying to alter anything. Henry Levin, looking at European secondary school reform, in 1978 saw the tensions arising from these reforms producing frustrated expectations which would result in postponing the tensions to the higher education stage. As a result

It is likely that these frustrations and feelings of dissatisfaction with both the educational system and the labor market will lead to increasing manifestations of class conflict and struggle. Individual incidents of sabotage by frustrated and underemployed workers, rising political activism by the unemployed, and other forms of disruption such as strikes (both on and off campus) are likely to increase as it becomes evident that appropriate jobs will not be forthcoming, even in the distant furture.

Levin goes on to underline his conclusions from the European experience of school reorganization in previous decades:

Political demands for worker control of enterprises and nationalization of industry as well as increased public employment are likely to besiege both firms and governments. Coalitions of radicalized workers and students will contribute to the rising instabilities of the liberal, capitalist, Western European countries by pushing for egalitarian changes.[48]

This is assertion, without roots in historical analysis (not even Levin's own) of the experience apparently under discussion. In its approach to the kind of phenomena with which we are dealing in the 1960s and 1970s it ultimately produces nothing more than an alternative, inhibiting rhetoric.

To historians all of this is a familiar problem, only this time expressed in terms of relatively recent events. In relation to historical processes in general historians frequently have to face the dilemma of contemporaneous and post-facto judgement. They can accept and record the actors' own accounts of their actions and the events in which they were participants or witnesses, acknowledging that such accounts are likely to have recognizable partialities, prejudices and limitations. Or they can introduce into their accounts and analyses the consciousness of 'underlying forces' which were not perceived by, were unknown to, were not accessible to, the actors themselves. The difficulty in this case is that ultimately history may be left behind altogether in favour of speculative

theory. Whatever Bowles and Gintis, Carnoy and Levin, Finn, Grant
and Johnson are doing in their discussions of and assertions about
liberalism, capitalism and social democracy, it is not history. If what
they are doing is theory, it points to the need all the more strongly for
more sustained and sensitive ways of conducting a dialogue between
theory and history, and this cannot be done on the basis of rhetorical,
assertive theory from the left or the right, especially if it purports to be
history or to be grounded in historical analysis.

It is obviously no easier to find solutions and conduct acceptable
historical analyses in terms of the 1960s than it has been to interpret
policy and reform in the late nineteenth and early twentieth centuries.
Historians of the recent, as of the distant, past have to look hard at the
complex motivation behind developments, at the diverse meanings on
both sides of relationships such as the poverty–education one, at the
ways in which people have evaluated and judged, at the real choices
available, at the possibilities and purposes of action. It is all the more
important to think in these terms and to deal with the significant recent
past in such ways, since our capacity for renewed and effective action
may depend on them. It is important, similarly, to see beyond our
limited national experience and to be aware of the utility and difficulties
of approaching the converging and diverging elements in other versions
of similar issues. Having shared in many ways the experience of the
1960s and 1970s, there are enormous virtues in continuing to share the
experience of the later hazards which have features so internationally
recognizable.

Notes

1 Carl F. Kaestle and Maris A. Vinovskis, *Education and Social Change in
   Nineteenth-Century Massachusetts* (Cambridge, Mass., 1980); John W.
   Meyer *et al.*, 'Public Education as Nation-Building in America: Enrolments
   and Bureaucratization in the American States, 1870–1930', *American
   Journal of Sociology*, vol. 85, no. 3, 1979.
2 Byron G. Lander, 'Group Theory and Individuals: The Origin of Poverty
   as a Political Issue in 1964', *The Western Political Quarterly*, vol. 24, no. 3,
   1971, p. 154; Theodore R. Sizer, 'Low-Income Families and the Schools for
   Their Children', *Public Administration Review*, vol. 30, no. 4, 1970, p. 340.
3 James L. Sundquist, 'Origins of the War on Poverty', in James L.
   Sundquist (ed.), *On Fighting Poverty: Perspectives from Experience* (New
   York, 1969), p. 6.

4 Lander, 'Group Theory and Individuals', pp. 519-20; Adam Yarmolinsky, 'The Beginnings of O.E.O.', in Sundquist, *On Fighting Poverty*, p. 38; Sundquist, 'Origins of the War on Poverty', p. 7.
5 Jerome T. Murphy, 'Title I of ESEA: The Politics of Implementing Federal Education Reform, *Harvard Educational Review*, vol. 41, no. 1, 1977, pp. 37-8. For a detailed discussion of this theme see Lawrence M. Friedman, 'The Social and Political Context of the War on Poverty: An Overview', in Robert H. Haveman (ed.), *A Decade of Federal Antipoverty Programs: Achievements, Failures and Lessons*, (New York, 1977). See also Sundquist, 'Origins of the War on Poverty' for a similar account which does not tackle the issue explicitly, and also Lander, 'Group Theory and Individuals', pp. 514-17.
6 Yarmolinsky, 'The Beginnings of OEO', p. 42.
7 Sundquist 'Origins of the War on Poverty', p. 11; Lander, 'Group Theory and Individuals', pp. 512-13.
8 Earl Raab, 'What War and Which Poverty?', *The Public Interest*, no. 1, 1965, pp. 46, 56.
9 National Education Improvement Act. Hearings before the Committee on Education and Labor, House of Representatives ... on HR3000, Washington DC, 1963.
10 Sundquist, 'Origins of the War on Poverty', pp. 9, 19.
11 Murphy, 'Title I of E.S.E.A.', p. 37.
12 Thomas E. Cronin, 'The Presidency and Education', *Phi Delta Kappan*, vol. 49, no. 6, 1968, pp. 295-6.
13 Hubert H. Humphrey, *War on Poverty* (New York, 1964), p. 141.
14 Quoted by Charles I. Norris, Introduction to Nelson F. Ashline *et al.* (eds), *Education, Inequality and National Policy* (Lexington, Mass., 1976), p. xvii.
15 *America Tomorrow: Creating the Great Society, The New Republic* (New York, 1965), p. 41.
16 Ministry of Education, *Half Our Future*, a report of the Central Advisory Council for Education (London, 1963).
17 Committee on Higher Education, *Higher Education: Report* (London, 1963).
18 Department of Education and Science, *Children and Their Primary Schools*, a report of the Central Advisory Council for Education (London, 1967).
19 The literature on Follow Through and other compensatory projects is enormous. See, for example, John S. Bissell, 'Planned Variation in Head Start and Follow Through', in Julian C. Stanley (ed.), *Compensatory Education for Children, Ages 2 to 8: Recent Studies of Educational Intervention* (Baltimore, 1973).
20 The best known example of this literature in Britain was J.W.B. Douglas, *The Home and the School: A Study of Ability and Attainment in the Primary Schools* (London, 1964).
21 Department of Education and Science, *Educational Priority*, report of a research project sponsored by the Department of Education and Science and the Social Science Research Council, 5 vols (London, 1972-5).
22 A.H. Halsey, Jean Floud, and C. Arnold Anderson (eds), *Education, Economy and Society: A Reader in the Sociology of Education* (New York, 1961).

23 Alan Little and George Smith, *Strategies of Compensation: A Review of Educational Projects for the Disadvantaged in the United States*. The British participants were A.H. Halsey, and the two authors of this review, the latter of whom was also an EPA research officer. See also Schools Council Working Paper 27, *'Cross'd with Adversity'* (London, 1970) for similar evidence of awareness of the American experience.

24 Peter Marris and Martin Rein, *Dilemmas of Social Reform: Poverty and Community Action in the United States* (London, 1967).

25 See Bissell, 'Planned Variation in Head Start and Follow Through'.

26 Michael F.D. Young (ed.), *Knowledge and Control: New Directions for the Sociology of Education* (London, 1971). See also Richard Brown (ed.), *Knowledge, Education, and Cultural Change: Papers in the Sociology of Education* (London, 1973).

27 See Fred M. Hechinger (ed.), *Pre-School Education Today* (New York, 1966), pp. 88, 13.

28 C. Bereiter and S. Engelmann, *Teaching Disadvantaged Children in the Preschool* (Englewood Cliffs, New Jersey, 1966), pp. 32-3, 37. See also Hechinger, *Pre-School Education Today*, pp. 112-3.

29 The seminal article in Britain was Basil Bernstein's 'Education Cannot Compensate for Society', *New Society*, 26 February 1970. An important book was Nell Keddie (ed.), *Tinker, Tailor ... The Myth of Cultural Deprivation* (Harmondsworth, 1973; the subtitle was used as the title in the American Penguin edition of the same year). A strong, direct attack was mounted by William Ryan in 1971, *Blaming the Victim* (ch. 2, 'Savage Discovery in the Schools: The Folklore of Cultural Deprivation').

30 Daniel P. Moynihan, *Maximum Feasible Misunderstanding: Community Action in the War on Poverty* (New York, 1969). The participatory nature of the community school in the Liverpool EPA project is probably the nearest British educational equivalent to the American intentions after 1964 - see Eric Midwinter, *Priority Education: An Account of the Liverpool Project* (Harmondsworth, 1972), Ch. 1, 'The Solution: The Community School'.

31 Walter Hodges, 'The Worth of the Follow Through Experience', *Harvard Educational Review*, vol. 48, no. 2, 1978.

32 Interview with Mrs Fay Ross, Atlantic schools Follow Through Project, Atlanta, Georgia, April 1981.

33 Jack Tizard *et al.*, *All Our Children: Pre-School Services in a Changing Society* (London, 1976), p. 184.

34 Christopher Jencks *et al.*, *Inequality: A Reassessment of the Effect of Family and Schooling in America* (New York, 1972, edition of 1973), p. 261.

35 Samuel Bowles and Herbert Gintis, *Schooling in Capitalist America: Educational Reform and the Contradictions of Economic Life* (London, Routledge & Kegan Paul, 1976), pp. 5-6, 18.

36 For a summary of the findings, published between 1976 and 1978, see the Executive Summary, *The Compensatory Education Study*, July 1978, National Institute of Education, Washington DC, 1978.

37 Barbara Heyns, *Summer Learning and the Effects of Schooling* (New York, 1978), pp. 9-10.

38 Christopher Jencks, Foreword to Heyns, *Summer Learning*, and *Who Gets*

278 *Education as history*

Ahead? The Determinants of Economic Success in America (New York, 1979).
39 Irving Lazar *et al.*, *The Persistence of Preschool Effects: A Long-Term Follow-Up of Fourteen Infant and Preschool Experiments*, final report, US Department of Health, Education and Welfare, September 1977.
40 Hodges, 'The Worth of the Follow Through Experience'.
41 *Educational Priority*, vol. 1. *EPA Problems and Policies*, vol. 3: *Curriculum Innovation in London's EPA's*, and vol. 4: *The West Riding Project*.
42 Halsey *et al.*, *Origins and Destinations*, p. 216.
43 Michael Rutter *et al.*, *Fifteen Thousand Hours: Secondary Schools and Their Effects on Children* (London, 1979).
44 A.H. Halsey, 'Education Can Compensate', *New Society*, 24 January 1980; Bernstein, 'Education Cannot Compensate for Society', *New Society*, 26 February 1970.
45 The Heritage Foundation, report of the Mandate for Leadership Project, Washington DC mimeo, 10 November 1980, pp. 13, 30, 71.
46 Bowles and Gintis, *Schooling in Capitalist America*, pp. 5, 13–14, 44, 240.
47 Martin Carnoy, 'Is Compensatory Education Possible?', in Martin Carnoy and Henry Levin (eds), *The Limits of Educational Reform* (New York, 1976), p. 216.
48 Henry M. Levin, 'The Dilemma of Comprehensive Secondary School Reforms in Western Europe', *Comparative Education Review*, October 1978, p. 450.

Part Three

Research and the history
of education

11 Comparative and cross-cultural history of education

What we have attempted to discuss and illustrate is the complexity of the levels at which the history of education needs to be written. If it is about pioneers and their reputations, it is also about ideas and movements. If it is about ideologies, it is also about the interactive nature of popular expectations and attitudes. If it is about policy on the grand scale, it is also about experience. If it is about theories, it is also about the historian's own methods of interpretation, understanding of the meaning of 'education', and theories. In using mainly English and American touchstones, we have identified important ways in which national experience and histories can touch and clarify, or can diverge and complicate. Against that background it is worth asking the question – to what extent is it possible or valuable to attempt to write the history of education across frontiers? If history very easily disappears into theory, is there a serious possibility of writing 'comparative' history which does not become simply a cumulative set of illustrations to grand theory? American history of education provides a useful starting-point in approaching such a question, precisely because it is the national historical endeavour which in recent decades has been most explicitly concerned with its own methodology and theory.

Most educational history is parochial, and that written by American historians is no exception. There *are* benefits to being parochial, and American history of education *is* profoundly parochial. There are ways of suggesting that this latter judgement is not true, but none of them is convincing.

It can be pointed out, for example, that from the beginnings of a serioᵤs interest in the history of education in the United States there was an awareness of the European roots of American institutions; that C.F. Thwing, for instance, from his earliest contributions to the history of American universities – written in the 1900s – was concerned with the French, German, English, Scottish, influences. Through to the recent past, in the work of Jurgen Herbst and Carl Diehl this can be shown to have been the case. It can be argued that in the increasing concern of American historians of education with the history of the family and childhood, they have responded to the appeals of Bernard Bailyn and Lawrence Cremin to understand the wider social structures inherited and adapted by early colonial America. It can be pointed out also that in recent decades notable American historians of education have written about historical phenomena elsewhere – perhaps notably British, including Michael B. Katz on official British education reports from the late nineteenth century to the 1960s,[1] and Carl Kaestle in a comparative examination of élite attitudes towards schooling in early industrial England and America.[2] Lawrence Stone has written about European literacy and schooling. Sheldon Rothblatt has relentlessly disentangled strands in English university education, and Robert Berdahl has explored the history of its administration.[3] *History of Education Quarterly* has made determined and distinguished efforts to be international in scope.

American history of education profoundly influenced the early development of comparative education, though the basis of comparative education in historical studies of national systems virtually ground to a halt in the 1960s. In various ways and with different emphases and intentions, Robert Ulich, R. Freeman Butts, Henry Perkinson and Fritz Ringer have written about the West, about civilization, about Europe.

None of this, though convincing, answers the charge. Much of it relates to the world before the United States, or to the origins and roots of American institutions. Some of it is concerned with the world outside, but is in a sense also parochial – concerned with discrete events and situations, and suggesting little or no relevance to the historiography of education in the United States. If nineteenth- or twentieth-century Canada or Europe creep into the American picture, hardly any of the resultant American writing is concerned with how historians outside the United States view their own or the American past, or with how such concerns might illuminate the history of education in the United States. Occasional articles in *History of Education Quarterly*, and occasional sessions at conferences of the History of Education Society, the American Educational Research Association (AERA) or elsewhere, do not basically alter the picture of the insularity of American history of education, and particularly of its historiography. There are sporadic exceptions, when historians discover, say, an Edward Thompson (and even then only his *Making of the English Working Class*), but generally speaking the literature of American history of American education does not draw on the historical problematics of the great elsewhere. That the United States may not be unique in this respect does not alter the argument.

There *are* benefits. The most important is undoubtedly that American historians of education have been able to tangle with political science, with sociology, with anthropology, with other kinds of history and focus, and to test theories and assumptions against the hard edge of American experience. In approaching the social and political sciences in the 1960s and 1970s, many historians, whether in established traditions, or in the expanded frameworks set by Bailyn and Cremin, or in more radical 'revisionist' or other moulds, found themselves continually forced back into *historical* activity. They had to look at the historical evidence regarding education (whatever its definition) in Chicago or St Louis, New England or the south, rural America or New York City. Historians found that they were still - despite, and conceivably even because of, entanglement with theory and ideology - trying to understand Philadelphia or the history of childhood, the historical relationship between ethnicity and class, the onward march of the public school. The weakness of parochialism is the narrow range of definition or conceptual machinery it encourages. The benefit of parochialism is that it makes it more difficult to lose sight of the pursuit of historical realities - especially the diversity of individual experience. The work of David Tyack and others in the late 1970s and early 1980s on truant officers, school superintendents, the 'take off' of public education in rural and urban America and the nature of 'leadership' in American public education, has emphasized the differences as much as the patterns. Kaestle and Vinovskis, in their study of nineteenth-century Massachusetts education, have done the same. The stress in the work of Grubb and Lazerson on the complexities of the history of vocationalism and of the youth-work relationship has been similar. Donald Warren's *History, Education, and Public Policy* is a collection which speaks to greater diversity of approach and intention than in many publications of the previous decade. The growing emphasis on the *experience* of education speaks to the same diversity – through the work of historians like Barbara Finkelstein, the search for biography and autobiography in the work of Geraldine Jonçich Clifford, and increased interest in the early American childhood experience of home and school. As in the work of Joseph Kett, the same is true of the experience of adolescence, school and religious conversion.

The benefits of all of this are obviously those of attention to trans-community, trans-cultural experience within the American nation at different stages of development, a process extended from the 1960s to the problems raised by the reinterpretation of the educational history of the American poor, black, minority, and female. It may appear eccentric or harsh to call this range of work 'parochial' when the United States is such a multi-cultural and multi-national nation. Nevertheless, in the overwhelming majority of the published work the frontiers of the research and of emphasis have been the frontiers of the United States. The contours of methodology have been overwhelmingly those of the United States – however radically those contours have changed since the early 1960s.

To what extent is the parochialism label an accusation, or merely a recognition of the inevitable? In what ways might a cross-national, cross-cultural or comparative educational history prove more attractive or feasible? Can sporadic or systematic concern with the history of other people's education, with their interpretation of their own 'history' and 'education', have implications for educational historiography generally? Does cross-cultural history not inevitably become some kind of sociology or theory, concerned only with models and paradigms? Is the real implication of the accusation of national parochialism not a recognition that historians must concern themselves exclusively or mainly with that level of unit or conceptual analysis which their methodology can cope with – the city, the cultural group, the state, the nation? Is the role of historians beyond that perhaps to help, to service the comparative, sociological and other enterprises where their contribution is useful and acceptable – and occasionally to synthesize as best they can? What future is there for a 'comparative social history of education'?

The past relationship with comparative education colours the question and the discussion. Comparativists have on occasion seen themselves as the inheritors of the historical exercise, continuing – as Kandel put it – 'the study of history of education and bringing that history down to the present'.[4] They have grappled with problems of cause and influence and borrowing across nations, and with problems of 'juxtaposition' and analysis – what Bereday described as 'the preliminary matching of data from different countries to prepare them for comparison'.[5] Such juxtaposition and comparison have been pursued historically as well as with regard to contemporary analysis of systems. Historically, the comparative exercise has been one of determining, portraying and analysing national educational 'character' or characteristics. A range of American and European comparativists in the early twentieth century scrutinized national structures, legislation and institutions, in pursuit of concepts that would permit cross-national comparisons – devising or adopting a conceptual machinery which included 'national psychology', centralized and decentralized systems, totalitarian and democratic states. From Michael Sadler to Vernon Mallinson in Britain the search for national character suggested patterns of characteristic behaviour. Mallinson, one of the last spokesmen of the tradition, described the components of national character as those 'forces of cultural continuity which determine the social behaviour of a nation as a whole'.[6] In his search for the fundamental, for the foundations of educational systems, Kandel in the United States pursued 'those forces that determine the character of an educational system'.[7]

From the 1960s the nature of comparative educational scholarship changed, amidst widespread expressions of relief and congratulation. Brian Holmes in Britain talked of the 'transfer of attention from descriptive studies of national systems to analyses of problems', with the 'methodological objective of replacing the names of systems and countries by the names of concepts and variables'.[8] Harold Noah in the United States graphically described how R.V. Winkle, Professor of Comparative Education, asleep from 1959, awoke in 1970 to a new style of work which had ousted the dominant forces of Kandel, Hans and Lauwerys.[9] We are not concerned here with the nature and problems of comparative education, but with the importance that this change represents, as a movement away from a certain kind of history, 'from "country characteristics" to "problems", from problems to the specification of relationships and formulation and testing of theories', away from the comparison of data towards a social science attempt to explain and predict rather than simply to identify and describe.[10] Comparative education, whatever fresh difficulties and confusions it was to face in defining problems and producing explanations, had abandoned its commitment to a history of national psychologies.

The new comparative education broke with a historical past at exactly the moment when American history of education plunged into its successive phases of historical revision. The new versions of history of education also discarded various cumulative traditions and conceptual frameworks. It is understandable, given the motivations to revise and to reassess, that American historians were preoccupied with the American, and with Europe as largely pre-American. Some slight attention was paid to the nature of US–Canadian educational relationships. At points where history has come closest to ideological debate, non-America has been largely used as supporting historical evidence – for example, the parallel roles of European pioneers of intelligence testing or the similarities of European education in relation to social stratification or corporate capitalism. It is true, as we have suggested, that *History of Education Quarterly*, the History of Education Society, the AERA and other bodies, have presented historical concerns with education in other countries. American scholars – including research students – have in recent years probed aspects of Latin American, African, European and other educational pasts in new ways, but the emphasis has been most often on detailed investigation which has been little concerned with its own historiography, or with implications for American historiographical discussion.

It can, of course, be argued that historians of education in other countries, listening to the American debates of the 1960s and 1970s, were aware of a tradition and a profession that had approached new frontiers, that were at the cutting edge of historical controversy. Historiographically, therefore, the rest of the world has in a sense had more to learn from American historians of education than Americans from others. European and other historians, listening to the signals from Bailyn and Cremin, from Michael Katz's first books, from *Roots of Crisis*, from *Schooling in Capitalist America*, from Diane Ravitch's critique of the revisionists, from David Tyack's *The One Best System*, have been listening to historiographical reappraisal as well as focusing on American historical content. Historians of education in other countries may be none the less parochial for that, and may have assumed perhaps that critical historiography was a short-lived American aberration, more to do with American politics than history of education. In Europe, a cross-cultural, comparative history of education has been no less sparse than in the United States, although Europe-wide and international encounters amongst historians of education have taken place. Whatever purposes European seminars or international conferences may have, the production of cross-national or cross-cultural history may not be one of them. The directions of American history of education cannot, however, be determined by the weaknesses of other people's condition.

What is it that American historians of education may be said to have evaded outside the United States? The answer cannot be located in lists of 'relevant' historical moments or texts elsewhere, as any such list may be belied by the scholar who has in fact taken or is taking an interest in some piece of Japanese or French or Islamic or British colonial or other history. It is, of course, valuable for American scholars to be engaged in such historical tasks, but this does not necessarily point to any work that is in any sense 'cross-cultural'. The argument here is not for a new, even a more advanced, form of juxtaposition. Nor is it merely a suggestion that Americans should be more familiar with specific, recent developments in history of education elsewhere – such as recent European work on the history of literacy or particular types of educational institution or impact or enterprise.

The notion of 'cross-cultural history' or a 'comparative social history of education' raises questions about what historians have to say to one another about education, about their definitions of the territory, about the strengths and weaknesses of their traditions, about their methodologies. Without such a starting-point, cross-national history of any kind in this field must remain imprisoned in two basic difficulties – the reduction of the exercise to a persistently cumulative, non-analytic level; or the temptation to analyse on the basis of concepts which have little or no foundation in historical analysis and debate. American and other historians in the 1960s and 1970s discovered how intractable their vocabularies were, how elusive was the machinery with which they attempted to order their perceptions of rediscovered and re-evaluated past realities. They went through a multitude of interpretations based on such concepts as modernization and industrialization, bureaucracy, social control and centralization, only to find that the concepts proved troublesome and would not stay still. One of the most instructive and attractive features of American history of education in the past two decades has in fact been the very explicitness of its concerns. Some of those concerns may have seemed less relevant or acute to historians in some other countries with older or better-established radical or Marxist traditions and reactions to and debates about them, but the American debates have provoked fresh reflection on what 'history' of 'education' is *about*. In the United States and elsewhere historians have developed a need to hold and an interest in holding dialogue with social and political scientists grappling with the same conceptual difficulties. At the same time, the historian's difficulties and enterprise return something to social science debate. A prerequisite of cross-cultural history across frontiers therefore has to be sustained dialogue amongst historians, not only about the cross-cultural meanings and possibilities, but also about cross-disciplinary experience.

A second prerequisite is to identify useful focuses of historical attention within this framework, and to understand the processes of historical interpretation involved. At one level this is concerned with the changing meanings of concepts. For example, 'cultural transmission' was a concept used in the United States by Monroe in the 1930s and Kandel in the 1950s, within their historical-comparative framework.[11] The same concept has also been central to the work of Pierre Bourdieu and European sociologists since the 1960s. The concept, the traditions, the intellectual basis of the analysis, is an important frontier of historical research in education, whether it be a concept borrowed from social science literature or one which – like industrialization – has become a stock feature of 'common sense' historical vocabulary. An example of this conceptual basis of comparative historical analysis would be that of 'accountability'. The history of accountability in United States education has to do, for example, with relations between school and community, with the testing movement, with changes in the direction from which political pressures come – including increasingly the federal involvement with education since the early 1960s. The English version of such a history might include variants, although enormously different ones, of all of those, but it would relate directly to the existence of channels of public accountability which do not exist in the United States – including the emergence of a nation-wide public examination system from the mid-nineteenth century, the roles of Her Majesty's Inspectorate over nearly a century and a half, and the relationship between local government and school governing bodies – including those of church schools. At this level of conceptualization, historians in a cross-cultural field would find themselves exploring not just parallel and juxtaposed traditions or data, but also different perceptions of educational and political relationships. The exercise would in this case be not the comparativist's interest in elucidating problems and issues, but a historical interest in describing and analysing how processes converge conceptually and diverge in the social complexities of apparently common phenomena. The pursuit would be not national character and structures but historical processes, as perceived by participants, as negotiated into historical statements. Another example would be that of the different national experiences of institutions or processes which have common historical origins. The British and American social science movements of the second half of the nineteenth century both derive from an initiative taken in London in 1857, and for several decades had organizational and ideological affinities and relationships. In this case the cross-cultural interest to historians lies in the processes of transmission, interpretation and adaptation, the meaning of the relationship, as well as the divergent or parallel characteristics of the two national movements. The creation of sociological associations in the United States and in Britain, both in the mid-1900s, and after the earlier social science movement had lost its momentum and identity, suggests similar questions – with the added interest of seeing how the two movements domesticated third-party inputs, such as that of Durkheim. Since the nineteenth- and twentieth-century developments, in both countries, were concerned with the definition of social institutions (including education) and with directly educational activities and concerns, it is historically helpful to disentangle their relationships to quite different emergent patterns of educational provision and control.

These prerequisites of cross-cultural history across frontiers must, therefore, suggest an extremely self-conscious historiography. An area such as the history of adolescence would indicate how self-conscious the rudiments of this history already are: Selwyn Troen's analysis of the American definition of adolescence in the first two decades of this century is explicitly described as an 'economic' interpretation. The work of Joseph Kett and of John Gillis indicate how widely the historical net has to be cast in order to produce explanations of the emergence of a socially accepted category – including the conception of when childhood ends, what society wants from or owes to the child at that point, the changing nature of religious experience and authority, the emergence and nature of youth movements, changes in schooling, employment, the onset of puberty, the family, attitudes towards vocational elements in curricula.[12] These and many other elements in such a history point both towards major social and cultural differences and towards profoundly controversial ground on which historians of many kinds have done battle. Cross-cultural analysis therefore becomes concerned in this way with the details of small-scale relationships, not just the larger patterns of past approaches.

Examples such as this indicate ways of attempting not just cross-national, comparative history, but the cross-*cultural* elements in such history. The emphasis could bring history of education closer to anthropological definitions suggested by Bailyn in *Education in the Forming of American Society*. Cross-cultural interests obviously go beyond institutional patterns into related areas of experience and explanation. Such interests include the social construction and acceptance of symbols, or what Margaret Mead discusses in terms of 'images'. Her educational images include different types ('expectations' might be a suitable word) of teacher in different eras and settings.[13] The teacher, the schoolhouse, the student, however, are for historians more than types or images – they also represent varieties of expectation or experience shaped and conditioned in different ways. Numbers, argued E.H. Carr, count in history – citing a million discontented peasants as being historically important, where a single one is not.[14] Cultural history, however, cannot be dominated by the composite, by the known outcomes of scale. It is not concerned solely with images, socio-economically defined groups, patterns of class relationships, the statistics of mobility. It is concerned with varieties as well as uniformities of experience, with teachers as well as the image of the teacher, the biographical reconstruction of schooling as well as its relationship to the social order. This sense of variety and individuality is difficult to hold in view when history of education is pulled towards the grand scale – the cross-national explanation of capitalism, the role of the school, the mechanisms of control. A historical approach to cultures and sub-cultures is pulled in both directions – towards patterns and theories, and towards the individual biography in specific settings. A cross-cultural history which leans on individual perceptions of the educational condition, as well as on cross-frontier resonances of larger dimensions, has yet to begin to be constructed. Here again, it is necessary to underline the critical historiography that would have to initiate such an exercise. If the purpose is to do more than anthologize, historians will have to debate the cultural complexities they wish and could be able to investigate.

The kind of concept which suggests all of these levels at which comparative historical analysis might take place would be that of 'reform'. Reform points historically towards patterns of national policy-making, legislative and institutional change, and at that level is already strongly represented in the literature. It points secondly towards communities and experience, the declared and undeclared motivations of reformers, and the processes and agencies of change and resistance to change. At this level there are patchy and often fumbling attempts at description and analysis, often without clear targets and merits beyond superficial biography and local or institutional history. It points, thirdly, to the most recent and difficult of the levels of historiography – that of ideology and of the conflicting bases of interpretation. At this level the attempt has often been to demythologize, to dispel accepted assumptions, to suggest the socio-historical construction of categories and issues and purposes – whether elevating the actors to manipulative, conspiratorial positions, or relegating them to the role of puppets of underlying, larger forces. The history of reform motivation is perhaps the most complex and difficult kind of educational history, and for that very reason could perhaps benefit most from a new comparative historical approach – supplementing and challenging untested and often untestable macro-theory and macro-diagnosis. The nature, elements and boundaries of educational reform are the kind of research territory which could prove most profitable, if subjected to rigorous cross-national scholarship and confronting the methodological and ideological problems it must inevitably raise.

Extensions of and debates about social and cultural history have only recently begun to intrude upon the history of education. The 'cross-cultural' and 'comparative social' dimensions of historical research will need to benefit from those intrusions if they are to become serious fields of analysis and research. A historical extension of this kind begins, therefore, with glances back at an older historical, comparative education, at anthropological and other social science debates, at national uniformities and diversities, and at the historiographic issues the very intention provokes.

Notes

1 Michael B. Katz, 'From Bryce to Newsom: Assumptions of British Educational Reports 1895–1963', *International Review of Education*, vol. 11, 1965.
2 Carl F. Kaestle, 'Between the Scylla of Brutal Ignorance and the Charybdis of a Literary Education: Elite Attitudes towards Mass Schooling in Early Industrial England and America', in Lawrence Stone (ed.), *Schooling and Society: Studies in the History of Education* (Baltimore, 1976).

3 Lawrence Stone, 'Literacy and Education in England 1640-1900', *Past and Present*, vol. 42, 1969; Sheldon Rothblatt, *The Revolution of the Dons: Cambridge and Society in Victorian England* (London, 1968); Sheldon Rothblatt, *Tradition and Change in English Liberal Education: An Essay in History and Culture* (London, 1976); Robert O. Berdahl, *British Universities and the State* (Berkeley, 1959).

4 I.L. Kandel, *The New Era in Education* (London, 1954), p. 46.

5 George Z.F. Bereday, 'Reflections on Comparative Methodology in Education 1964-1966', in Max A. Eckstein and Harold J. Noah (eds), *Scientific Investigations in Comparative Education* (London, 1967), pp. 5-8.

6 Vernon Mallinson, *An Introduction to the Study of Comparative Education* (London, 1957, edition of 1975), p. 263.

7 Kandel, *New Era*, p. 45.

8 Brian Holmes, 'General Introduction', in Reginald Edwards *et al.*, *Relevant Methods in Comparative Education* (Hamburg, 1973), pp. 8, 15.

9 Harold J. Noah, 'Defining Comparative Education', in Edwards, *Relevant Methods in Comparative Education*, p. 109.

10 Ibid., pp. 109-12.

11 Paul Monroe, *A Text-Book in the History of Education* (New York, 1935), p. 758; Kendel, *The New Era in Education*, p. 22.

12 Selwyn K. Troen, 'The Discovery of the Adolescent by American Educational Reformers, 1900-1920: An Economic Perspective', in Stone, *Schooling and Society*; Joseph F. Kett, *Rites of Passage: Adolescence in America 1790 to the Present* (New York, 1977); John R. Gillis, *Youth and History: Tradition and Change in European Age Relations 1770-Present* (New York, 1974).

13 Margaret Mead, *The School in American Culture* (Cambridge, Mass., 1962).

14 E.H. Carr, *What Is History?* (London, 1961, edition of 1964), p. 50.

12 Case study and historical research

In educational and social science research the concept of case study reflects a concern to approach questions of social action and consciousness in ways which are not subject to the methodological constraints and problems of the large scale. In this sense, much of the previous discussion in this book – for example, of a reputation, of a movement, of a moment of policy change – might be described as efforts at historical case study. Field researchers using case study approaches have attempted the difficult and elusive task of circumscribing a complex area of reality and engaging with it sufficiently to portray and to elucidate some central process. The case study in its formulations and theories has in recent years become one attempt to confront the difficulties previously raised for the social sciences by controversy over their conceptual and methodological bases. In educational and social sicence research, therefore, case study approaches raise critical questions of definition, aim, theory and method – and they reflect underlying methodological disputes in the fields to which they contribute. They present major problems concerning the nature of the 'case', that is, of how a specimen of social interaction can be taken as representative, or typical, or illustrative, of some constituency of similar interactions. In educational research particularly the nature and value of the 'case' have become a focus of stringent analysis. Historians have always been involved with problems of the specific and the general, the unique and the pattern, the datum and data. Surprisingly, whilst accepting the vocabulary of the representative and typical (for example, 'institutions', 'the family' or 'bureaucracy') they are rarely concerned about the nature of the relationship between 'cases' and the generic.

Nevertheless, historians – and none more than historians of education

– use the term 'case study' frequently, indiscriminately, and with a variety of weaker meanings than one would expect to find in the literature of field-based educational research. Its use may signal less an attempt to grapple with problems of generalization or typicality in social processes than an evasion or an admission of impotence: the history of an educational institution presented as a case study may indicate only the haziest notion of the regularities and irregularities of that *type* of institution, or of that *kind* of process of social change or stabilization. It may merely indicate that the historian is aware of the existence of accepted categories or nomenclatures, and realizes that his description or narrative account bears some undefined relationship to those generalities. More often than not in the writing of an historical thesis an author will claim case study status for an account of a particular institution or group of institutions (school, school board, mechanics' institute, pressure group, etc.) in order to suggest a relevance wider than that immediately implied by the account – at the same time as setting it in an introductory historical sweep which is assumed to be required ritual in higher studies. What is true of a particular institution or place *may* somehow be seen to be true or in some way relevant elsewhere. A particular analysis or story may strengthen or weaken the held orthodoxies about the picture in the sector or nationally. In spite of the contemporary status of local history, researchers may find the concept of case study valuable in trying to ward off accusations of parochialism.

The more critical the account presented is of common assumptions or orthodoxies, the less in fact it is likely to be offered as a case study – and appears to be an 'anti-case study', or perhaps an unwitting, hesitant case study of a *possible* alternative strategy or interpretation. A doctoral student, exploring the Liverpool labour movement in the late nineteenth century, finds his analysis in conflict with accepted accounts of national labour movement attitudes to education, and the result appears therefore neither a case study of what is commonly accepted, nor – by its very nature – generalizable to other cities.[1] Another doctoral student finds his study of Sunday schools in conflict with the most authoritative existing picture of the Sunday schools – that contained in Tom Laqueur's *Religion and Respectability* – and his account and his findings – in particular or in general – may seem too new in an insecurely understood field to be presented as a 'case'.[2] The problem of definition and strategy has to be seen against the commonly, frequently accepted practice of offering as historical case study only that which appears to reinforce some generalization or assumption already held or partly held by some constituency of scholars or readers. Historical case study has most often been a form of weak, descriptive illustration.

It is arguable, of course, that the concept of case study is inappropriate in historical work. It might be suggested, for example, that *all* historical writing is case study, in the sense that all historical narrative, description and analysis concerns single and particular cases, events, instances – but indicative always of that small number of dichotomies which are the permanent concern of historians – tradition and change, stability and instability, continuity and discontinuity. If *all* historical work is part of such an endless tapestry, then the concept of case study loses any real meaning. Alternatively, it might be suggested that history *never* produces 'cases' because of the ultimate uniqueness of all historical events. Although these may be cumulative, they do not produce any sense of historical pattern. In such a view, the only history is detailed narrative and biography – indicating the unpredictability of human action, and the inapplicable, unrepeatable nature of the historical event. Whilst both of these arguments may caricature what historians actually do, they indicate real obstacles to bringing together meaningfully the work of historians of education and those forms of educational research which have attempted to use and to elucidate the case study approach.

The obstacles arise principally from misleading, 'common sense' approaches to historical uniqueness. I have argued elsewhere that historical description and analysis are inescapably engaged with the conceptual machinery which historians either invent or, more commonly, simply take over on trust from the social sciences, in order to organize their data and arguments.[3] In terms of recent historiography – especially American – outstanding examples include bureaucratization and centralization, professionalization and urbanization. These and others – including industrialization and social control – have had a serious presence internationally in the organization of historical scholarship in recent decades. Some of the concepts that have been central to historical writing, or to specific sectors of it, have been subjected to long and rancorous dispute over questions of definition and viability. These have included vocabularies which suggest periodization or structure – such as feudalism, capitalism and imperialism, and those which suggest widely recognizable processes, such as secularization or modernization – all of which concepts bring historians into territory shared with social and political scientists.

There are other levels of generalization and conceptualization which permanently interrelate with the historian's concern with the 'unique', for example in the historian's constant and necessary reference to institutions and processes which he must use in accepted or taken-for-granted forms – the regiment, the clergy, the working class, the universities, maidservants, the cabinet, the party, administrators, or education. However hard historians try to localize such vocabulary, they are constantly a prey to the generalized image. All history exists, of course, only via a process of reconstitution which relies on forms of imaginative generalization at several levels removed from the lived experience – what Paul Rock describes as 'an organization of ideas which (the historian) has synthesized out of others' syntheses. He regroups and reformulates typifications of typifications, unable to obtain any immediate access to the settings which he explores.'[4] The question mark over case study which results from a historical concern with uniqueness has to be removed by a discussion which is rooted in a view of history as a permanent dialogue between the instance and various levels of generalization and conceptualization. From such a starting-point it is possible to approach case study strategy with more than a simple, illustrative model in mind. Educational researchers have developed an interest in case study not only as an analysis of multiple realities but also as a methodology which permits of the incorporation of the widest range of angles of vision of the participants – an approach which has some echoes in educational historiography.[5] A view of history which is both interpretative and self-consciously resistant to unilinear explanations offers the best possible approximation to the past experience under scrutiny. It shares with case study field research a number of important characteristics, of which the literature seems to underline several central ones. The case study, it is emphasized, is not representative, but exemplary. It is concerned with 'the portrayal of a single instance locked in time and circumstance'.[6] It is 'the examination of an instance in action'.[7] It is an 'umbrella term for a family of research methods having in common the decision to focus an enquiry around an instance'.[8] Dissatisfied with research methods based on 'statistical-experimental' paradigms and sampling, it deliberately accepts the challenge of tangling with the acknowledged uniqueness of the individual case.[9]

Case study research is concerned, in its approach to the instance, to explore the possibilities of cumulation and categorization different from those inherent in the statistical tradition. It therefore confronts questions to do with the selectivity of data, the reliability of findings, the judgement of the researcher, and a range of related methodological problems. We cannot here consider these in detail, but it is obvious that such problems are not unrelated to historical method, and that the issues of case study verification and application can also be discussed in relation to historical analysis. Categorization in history is an issue to which I have already referred. Selectivity, judgement and reliability are questions central to historiography. Before we can consider, however, the points at which the two sets of methodological problems meet, we must first approach the questions of verification and application more specifically from within a historical frame of reference.

Verification is concerned not just with evidence, but with the acceptability and legitimacy of evidence. Lawrence Stenhouse draws attention to the fact that historians characteristically appeal to 'publicly available evidence'. He suggests that 'history is in one of its aspects the public discussion of accessible evidence aimed at drawing the boundaries of the range of reasonable interpretation'. Elsewhere he underlines the importance of the historian's invention of the footnote in the nineteenth century, and he suggests a possible recourse for case study researchers to historical method: 'Any generalization from case studies must appeal to the same criterion for its validity, and since this cannot be replicability it would be well to adopt the historian's appeal to the concurrence of trained judgement of publicly accessible sources.'[10] It is crucially important, as Stenhouse indicates, that 'evidence' cannot be separated from 'the concurrence of trained judgement'. The historian relates to data within what Paul Rock calls 'the limits of manageable comprehension',[11] limits within which some kind of 'concurrence' as to the possible range of meanings and interpretations is constantly having to be renegotiated. The professional boundaries within which trained historical judgement can operate may have constricting and even stultifying effects, but they provide a working area and sets of conventions within which 'concurrence', 'manageable comprehension' and the renegotiation of interpretations are possible.

Case study researchers in education are constantly aware of the related problems of verification and audience: social scientists report primarily to their peers, whereas in case study research the audience may include the objects of and participants in the research.[12] The historical footnote, reference, bibliography, are appeals to fellow members of a community who share respect for the same scholarly conventions, and who are able to have resort to the same 'publicly accessible sources' and explicit methodologies. Subsequent scholars can in this way check on a historian's accuracy and reliability, follow his steps through the data and the interpretation, and make judgements about his 'scholarship' and findings. The approach to evidence therefore relates also to the 'professionalism' of the constituency, and indeed much historical research has its origins in the attempt to measure up to and go beyond the 'work' – that is, the data, the methodology and the analysis – of previous scholars.

There is danger in this argument, however, of treating data and evidence as inert. There is no need here to rehearse the long and complex attempts to define historical 'facts', but in relation to the problem of verification there is one critical point to underline, as E.H. Carr does in *What Is History?* The discussion of the nature of historical facts, he points out, is *not* about accuracy. That is merely a precondition: however you come at the problem of historical method and the work of the historian, it has to be assumed from the outset that historians try to get their facts 'right'. For a historian to get his names and dates and events correct is merely the base-line from which historical problems begin – just as an architect must assume that the bricks for his building will be of the right quality and dimensions.[13] Historical evidence must obviously be 'reliable' in that sense. It is only from that point onwards that the dispute begins about the historian's *relationship* to his facts, his selectivity, his ideology. There is a sense, of course, in which the data of educational history are no more 'inert' or 'reliable' than those which derive from case study research in educational field settings. The field researcher is used to balancing perceptions in situations of 'critical intersubjectivity', which – rather than 'objectivity' – is what Stenhouse considers the researcher is seeking.[14] It is clear that some oral historians are operating in a similar frame of reference, and make a similar appeal to subjectivity – 'that area of symbolic activity which includes cognitive, cultural and psychological aspects'.[15] Such an operation in oral history brings the historian into relationships which are not dissimilar from those of the researcher in the school, and raise similar questions of 'intersubjective' dialogue. But what of the historian who is dealing with the more distant past, with documents, with data already covered over with layers of selection and interpretation, and whose authors are not available for interlocution? What dialogue is possible with the dead?

I would argue that the supreme test of the historian is, in fact, his ability to conduct such a dialogue. If all history is imaginative reconstruction, then the historian must constantly re-invent the answer-back. This does not mean to ventriloquize – quite the opposite. It means that the historian needs to listen to the resonance of his own and others' attempted descriptions and explanations, and must allow historical sources to respond and disturb and upset them. It means a constant effort to lower the historian's own voice and the stridency of his own time. It means a constant diminution of his sense of knowing the outcome, of the arrogance of his own judgement after the event. However unsatisfactory the conversation, it has to take place – in order to treat evidence as elusive and unreliable and the opposite of the inert – within the controlling, changing and growing imagination of the historian. If this process is not the same as that in which social scientists and field researchers are engaged, it is one which has recognizable implications for them, and which has a great deal to learn from their experience. An appeal to the historical method of submitting to 'the concurrence of trained judgement of publicly accessible sources' carries the danger of not recognizing that the historian, his judgement, his publicly declared sources, are in some ways as insecure as those of case study research. Nevertheless, the historical appeal to some kind of verification is a necessary and valuable process, once it is recognized that the historian has to conduct the same constant struggle to understand the nature of his own selectivity, the validity of his categorizations, the limitations of his form of 'immersions' in the experience he attempts to recreate.[16]

Historical data and 'case studies' are, like other forms of case study, cumulative and applicable in only a limited sense. Take, for example, the discussion in the earlier chapter on Robert Owen's reputation as an educationist. In it I set out to show that Owen's reputation had been increasingly lost from view after the 1830s, and had begun to be re-established towards the end of the nineteenth century – to be made secure only in the late twentieth century. I tried to explain the changing fortunes of that reputation and found myself also suggesting that there were other reputations which had fared similarly, notably that of George Combe, phrenologist and educationist, who had shared a considerable prestige and from the middle of the nineteenth century more or less vanished from historical recognition. My explanations lay in the changing emphasis on institutional (I could have argued state-supported or state-legitimized) success and survival, and the manipulation – conscious or not – of the record in order to exclude the inconvenient, the institutionally unremembered, or the embarrassing. Owen and Combe, however prominent in their day and way, became all of these, while Brougham, Kay-Shuttleworth and Lowe, for example, secured their historical places through legislation, administrative innovation, the library of texts catalogued under aspects of both, or their contributions to what came to be seen as a system and an integral part of the modern consciousness of the state.[17] The analysis I attempted of Robert Owen was a case study – whether I intended it to be or not – of the way history and historians remember and forget. It was generalizable, in my view, to Combe and to a number of other nineteenth-century figures I had in mind (radicals, social science proponents and others, such as James Simpson, William Ellis and William Ballantyne Hodgson). In its content and its methodology the study might suggest some meanings and generalizations beyond the particularities of Owen's recognition and loss of it. It is possible that such a historical exercise might be informed and enhanced by a consideration of, for example, sociological discussion of the processes of legitimation. J.F.C. Harrison raises this sort of question in his analysis of late eighteenth- and early nineteenth-century millenarian belief. His book is concerned with specific examples and he relates them to particular contexts in the hope of attaining 'historical understanding'. Millenarianism can be studied, however, 'from many different angles by anthropologists, psychiatrists, sociologists, political scientists, and theologians; and the historian is not in such a strong position that he can afford to ignore the benefits of interdisciplinary study'. In considering millenarianism

> as a type of salvationism we may gain from the sociologists some useful hints on typology ... By the use of theoretical models we may be able to sort out some of the divergent and confusing positions of those who are loosely grouped together as millenarians.

Harrison's is a modest and tentative appeal beyond the specifics of his narrative, and my own appeal beyond Owen is not – and certainly was not at the time – any stronger than that.[18]

As a second example take the study which I co-authored of a National School in Kennington, London, under the title *The Education of the Poor*. The original suggestion for the title of the book – one which the publishers rejected – was *The Instruction of the Infant Poor*, a quotation from one of the early nineteenth-century documents we were using, and a common form of expression of the time. In doing the research and writing the book we were aware from the bginning that the work was unique – in that the records we had found enabled us to write the first reasonably substantial history of an elementary school. On the other hand, we treated the story of the transition from the education of the 'infant poor' to what the late twentieth-century school documents called the education of 'each child', as being in some way a 'representative' case or example. Our subtitle, *The History of a National School*, for all its specificity hints that it is in some way indicative of the story of National *schools*. We did not call it a case study, but we might well have done, given what we considered it to be at the time. I have indicated above in Chapter 1 that any representative claim for the account was based at crucial points on little or no evidence.[19] The book seemed to suggest that St Mark's, Kennington, as an early monitorial school, was more efficient and humane than we had expected, and that existing accounts of monitorial practice were thereby made suspect. What I realized was that I had made unwarranted assumptions about the state of our knowledge of the institutions at large against which we were setting the Kennington story. I had not previously realized that no existing textbook account of monitorial education had been based on any attempt to research that practice, as distinct from researching what the theorists of the system had proposed for the schools. We had not allowed for any historical answer-back. It was from that starting-point that I was led to some other unexplored assumptions and other 'aspects of neglect' in key areas of the history of education – many of which came as a complete surprise to me, even after having also contributed the nineteenth-century chapters to *A Social History of Education in England*.[20] The lesson was one which I might have learned more easily with a greater understanding of how far the social sciences are concerned with revealing and exploring what appears to be familiar.

A final example, related to the last, is the work also discussed in an earlier chapter on British and American social science in the late nineteenth century, and especially its educational content and impact. This has been a major area of neglect, since historians of education in both countries have not been concerned at all with the social science movement in the second half of the nineteenth century, and the historians of social science in both countries have had no interest whatever in its educational dimensions and implications. Increasingly, however, in pursuing the work I found myself involved with the historiography of reform – the historical literature relating to the development of the characteristic institutions of the nineteenth century – for example, penitentiaries, reformatories, welfare organizations and institutions - as well as with the organization of reform and the motivation of reformers. There was no way of approaching the specifics of the educational work of the NAPSS or the ASSA, without taking account of ideological controversies around the work of liberal reformers, around the nature of liberalism, and around the 'concealed' motives of humanitarian and progressive reform. Any paper on the educational work of the social science movements would become a 'case study' of Victorian reform and would be situated in those debates. It would be taken as some kind of example, if only of how I would approach reform movements in general. No matter how specific my account and analysis, it would have 'case' implications, and it would need to confront the wider implications of my work in relation to the various kinds of literature which had attempted to portray reform movements as seeking increased social control, ways of 'blaming the victim', and new patterns of social order and legitimation of the *status quo*.[21]

There is nothing particularly new or revealing about any of these examples. Historians come upon the unexpected, find extensions and implications beyond the points from which they begin, discover their own ignorance, re-examine their assumptions, realize that other people have things to say about their problems, and discover that even what appears most straightforward and taken-for-granted may become the focus of differing interpretations and profound controversy. The point I would make from these examples, however, relates to the form of 'application' of historical case studies. They indicate, first of all, that historical case study is not necessarily a 'method' on which a historian embarks - it may unexpectedly *become* a strategy and a direction - and it may (as with field researchers) lead him to go back and revise his original intentions, and certainly his assumptions. A study of historical detail, of an instance, of a unique event, may point towards wider generalizations, the need for sustained revision, a search for applications. A 'case' may become the necessary starting-point for other 'cases', for a process of fresh historical debate and understanding. In that sense, the validity of the methodology becomes of central importance: a historical case study becomes above all an example of 'how to do it', of how to conduct the argument. As with field researchers, though with quite different outcomes, what the case study comes to be about relates intimately to how it has been and may be done. Historical analysis of periods and processes may be carried forward, therefore, by the application of what is learned from particular studies about tactics, about emphases, about limitations and about possibilities.

Analytical history benefits from the tension between the case study and what is previously known or assumed also in terms of the ability of historians not merely to pile narrative on narrative, data on data, but to contribute to decisions about what it is important to understand and how to shape the process of understanding. Attempts to find research strategies in education which are alternative or supplementary to those based on quantification and replication, place the researcher and his judgement in centre-stage as a deliberate act, and not as often happens in the latter case by an apparent flaw of stage-management. The case study researcher knows that his 'case' is not replicable, and Stenhouse's important appeal to history is part of a search for ways not only of redefining verification but also of understanding how what is apparently and self-consciously unique can have wider applicability. The historian's products must be derived, he stresses, as independently of present concerns as is possible, but those products are nevertheless useful in the present precisely because of their influence on the historian's judgement –

> the utilization of history in present and future works through the refinement of judgement, not the refinement of prediction. In the face of an unfolding experience which is largely unpredictable history attempts to equip us to understand the unpredicted by being able to fit it very rapidly into a systematically ordered and interpreted grasp of experience so far.[22]

Historical case study may attempt to equip the historian and his constituency with a larger talent for encountering the 'instance in action', and especially its unexpected elements, and for making more complex and satisfying the process of explanation. My examples above illustrate the need to see how attention to historical detail may foreshadow and require a transition to the status of the 'case', and how the application of historical case study may – as with field-based research – need to be defined in non-traditional ways in which important messages are carried across disciplines Neither historical nor any other kind of case study becomes applicable by virtue of pseudo-replicability. The historian stands at the intersection of the generalized images which result from past experience, and the revised images which result from fresh 'cases', and from reflection on them and reaction to (or against) them. Forms of application can be sought only in the knowledge of that complexity.

In the history of education one 'inadvertent' case study may trigger revised understandings at many levels. The 'case' of the Liverpool labour movement may reopen deep assumptions about national policy and action. The 'case' of schooling in a pre-industrial rural area may lead to challenges to assumptions about the role of urbanization in the growth of school systems – and to the validity of the concept of 'social control' in historical explanation. The case may, of course, lead to misplaced confidence in what the case indicates. Michael Katz's exploratory and crucially important case studies of nineteenth-century Massachusetts were used by Martin Carnoy to 'prove' wide-ranging and hysterical demolitions of educational progressivism and reform in *Education as Cultural Imperialism*[23] reminding us only how closely intertwined are evidence and ideology, case study and theory, and that today's case study may become tomorrow's theoretical orthodoxy. Case study research in education, including its history, has to be wary of developing over-simplified versions to replace those forms of research or description or analysis which it attempts to replace. If, as MacDonald and Walker suggest, the case study researcher is like the artist in portraying, through a single instance, 'enduring truths about the human condition', then the methodology employed, in history as elsewhere, will reflect the complexities and uncertainties of that condition, and of the range of human activities designed to capture and represent its truth.[24] In the history of education, which is concerned – as we have suggested throughout – with regularity and diversity in human experience, a case study in always more than illustration. It is part of a constant and difficult exercise of reinterpretation.

Notes

1 Geoffrey C. Fidler, 'Aspects of the History of the Labour Movement in Liverpool in Relation to Education, *c*. 1870–1920', McGill University PhD thesis, 1979. See also his 'The Liverpool Trades Council and Technical Education in the Era of the Technical Instruction Committee', *History of Education*, vol. VI, 1977; 'The Liverpool Labour Movement and the School Board: An Aspect of Education and the Working Class', *History of Education*, vol. IX, 1980; 'The Work of Joseph and Eleanor Edwards, Two Liverpool Enthusiasts', *International Review of Social History*, vol. XXIV, part 3, 1979.

2 Malcolm Dick, 'English Conservatives and Schools for the Poor *c*. 1780–1833: A Study of the Sunday School, School of Industry and the Philanthropic Society's School for Vagrant and Criminal Children',

University of Leicester PhD thesis, 1979. See also his 'The Myth of the Working-Class Sunday School', *History of Education*, vol. IX, 1980.

3 See Harold Silver, *Education and the Social Condition* (London, 1980), pp. 71-84.

4 Paul Rock, 'Some Problems of Interpretative Historiography', *British Journal of Sociology*, vol. XXVII, 1976, p. 355.

5 See David B. Tyack, 'Ways of Seeing: An Essay on the History of Compulsory Schooling', *Harvard Educational Review*, vol. XLVI, 1976.

6 Barry MacDonald and Rob Walker, 'Case-Study and the Social Philosophy of Education Research', in David Hamilton *et al.* (eds), *Beyond the Numbers Game: A Reader in Educational Evaluation*, (London, 1977), p. 182.

7 Rob Walker, 'The Conduct of Educational Case Studies: Ethics, Theory and Procedures', in W.B. Dockrell and David Hamilton (eds), *Rethinking Educational Research* (London, 1980), p. 33.

8 Clem Adelman, David Jenkins and Stephen Kemmis, 'Re-thinking Case Study: Notes from the Second Cambridge Conference', *Cambridge Journal of Education*, vol. 6, 1976, p. 140.

9 Lawrence Stenhouse, 'Case Study and Case Records: Towards a Contemporary History of Education', mimeo, Centre for Applied Research in Education, University of East Anglia, n.d, pp. 1, 7.

10 Lawrence Stenhouse, 'Case Records as an Archival Resource for Educational Research: An Inter-Institutional Programme', mimeo, Centre for Applied Research in Education, University of East Anglia, n.d., pp. 5-6.

11 Rock, 'Some Problems of Interpretative Historiography', p. 365.

12 See, for example, Walker, 'The Conduct of Educational Case Studies', p. 35.

13 E.H. Carr, *What Is History?* (London, 1961), *passim*. See especially ch. I, 'The Historian and His Facts'.

14 Stenhouse, 'Case Study and Case Records', p. 27.

15 Luisa Passerini, 'Work Ideology and Consensus under Italian Fascism', *History Workshop*, no. 8, 1979, p. 85.

16 For a discussion of 'immersion', see Walker, 'The Conduct of Educational Case Studies', p. 30.

17 See ch. 3 above.

18 J.F.C. Harrison, *The Second Coming: Popular Millenarianism 1780-1850* (London, 1979), p. 8.

19 Pamela and Harold Silver, *The Education of the Poor: The History of a National School 1824-1974* (London, 1974). See also ch. 1.

20 John Lawson and Harold Silver, *A Social History of Education in England* (London, 1973).

21 William Ryan, *Blaming the Victim* (New York, 1971). For a discussion of the historical 'social control' literature see Harold Silver, *Education and the Social Condition* (London, 1980), pp. 78-80.

22 Stenhouse, 'Case Study and Case Records', p. 3.

23 Martin Carnoy, *Education as Cultural Imperialism* (New York, 1974), ch. 5, uses Katz's *The Irony of Early School Reform* (Boston, 1968), and *Class, Bureaucracy, and Schools* (New York, 1971), extensively.

24 MacDonald and Walker, 'Case-Study and the Social Philosophy of Educational Research', p. 182.

Index

Abrams, Philip, 104, 135
'academic drift', 214, 220
accountability, 225, 288
Adams, Francis, 87, 89
Adamson, J.W., 18, 75
Addams, Jane, 121
adolescence, 289
Alcott, A. Bronson, 121
All Our Children, 269
American Academy of Political and Social Science, 119-20
American Association for the Promotion of Social Science, *see* American Social Science Association
American Economic Association, 118, 139
American educational historiography, 23-4
American Educational Research Association (AERA), 283, 286
American Historical Association, 118, 139
American history of education, 282-4, 286
American poverty-education relationship, 260-4
American Social Science Association (ASSA): and consensus, 112; death of, 119; and education, 112, 114, 115-17; formation of, 102-3, 110; lack of research into, 122; motives of, 123-5; and NAPSS, 111, 112-13, 117-18, 120-1, 125; and science of reform, 114-15; and specialization, 137; and women, 121-2
American sociology, 144-5
American universities, 142, 188
American vocational education, 165-6
Amis, Kingsley, 195
Anderson, C.A., 267

apprenticeships, 154, 158-9
Armytage, W.H.G., 85
Arnold, Matthew, 66, 84, 86, 91, 151
Association of Education Committees, 213
Association of University Teachers, 185, 209
'Athenian' view of society, 90
Atkinson, W.P., 114
Aydelotte, Frank, 166

Bailyn, Bernard, 23, 24, 282, 290
Baines, Edward, 106
Baker, Robert, 39, 42, 45, 47, 49, 50
Balfour, Graham, 81, 82
Barker, Rodney, 249
Barlow Committee, 193
Barnard, Henry, 101
Barron, Steve, *et al.*, 239, 240, 247-8, 251-5, 254, 273
Bartley, George, 67
Batley, Richard, 250
Becher, Tony, 218
Beer, Max, 74
Bell, A., 27, 66, 67
Bell's Weekly Messenger, 82
Bentham, Jeremy, 103, 134
Berdahl, Robert, 282
Bereday, George Z.F., 285
Bereiter, C., 268
Bernard, L.L. and Jessie, 122
Bernstein, Basil, 268, 272
Besant, Annie, 72
Bestor, A.E., 139
Beveridge, Lord, 202
Beveridge Report, 264